Dr Paul Tempora

D1586577

Corporate Charisma

How to achieve
world-class recognition
by maximising your
company's image,
brands and culture

PIATKUS

To my daughter Maria, for bringing so much
love and happiness into my life

First published in 1998 by
Judy Piatkus (Publishers) Ltd
5 Windmill Street
London W1P 1HF

This paperback edition first published in 1999

The moral right of the authors has been asserted

*A catalogue record of this book is
available from the British Library*

ISBN 0-7499-1825-X

Data manipulation by
Professional Data Bureau, London SW17
Printed and bound in Great Britain by
The Bath Press, Bath

CONTENTS

Foreword by The Hon Sir Rocco Forte

The world is a much more competitive place than it was even five years ago. Businesses have to work harder and present themselves more effectively if they are to retain their customer base let alone attract new customers. In *Corporate Charisma* Dr Paul Temporal and Dr Harry Alder have, for the first time, shown how to stay ahead of the competition by creating a corporate personality.

The need for companies and their products to have more appeal and to distinguish themselves from the competition has become paramount. The sophistication required is greater and the marketing techniques used more developed. The active cultivation of a personality through an organised and well considered approach is completely new. The ensuing chapters of this book examine in great detail the issues and techniques involved in developing a successful corporate personality. This personality, or charisma, of a company cannot be changed too often as it then becomes self-defeating. Dr Temporal and Dr Alder have carefully thought through all aspects of the identity, taking account of the longer term development of the business.

By following the excellent guidelines contained here, your business will be clearly defined, the Board will be in touch with the product and the customers' reaction to it, and all levels of staff will understand the personality and the direction the company is taking. So much so that it becomes part of their every day lives and actions. A consistency develops which the customer understands and is drawn to. The strength that develops from this process is that when something goes wrong it is seen as abnormal by the customer and therefore excused.

Corporate Charisma is essential for any business looking at the longer term. It will help you to carefully consider, develop and nurture your business, to stay a step ahead of your competitors and return a loyal and loving customer base.

CHAPTER ONE

THE POWER OF A WINNING PERSONALITY

Organisations are inhuman!
Why don't they treat us as people?
Why don't they behave like we do?
What do people think of our company when it behaves like this? It's embarrassing!
Why do we have to try and explain U-turns all the time? Can't they be consistent?
This is not my kind of company!
Organisations are impersonal!
I just don't feel comfortable here!
I saw their new ad. What does it mean? Is it a joke?
Why do they waste money on this advertising?
Whatever they promise, they'll never deliver!
How can they say these things and not do them?
Promises, promises!
We've no credibility any more!
I could do better myself!
How can I trust that company any more?
They treat us like this because things are going well — they wouldn't dare do these things if times were hard!
We don't get value for money any more!
I'm a long-serving customer, and they still don't listen!
We've complained many times but they just don't seem to care!

Every day you can hear these commonly heard complaints from employees and customers alike. The chances are your own company is not exempt from such remarks. Such frustration and disappointment, inwardly felt even if not always voiced, if ignored, soon translates into lost customers and inevitable failure.

Companies that take an interest in their customers, that know how their customers think and feel, look from the outside in. They judge the feelings of people, care about them, hold to good values, and build long-term relationships and friendships. They treat people as people want to be treated. Unfortunately, these companies are rare. Most companies are self-oriented. But even those who deny any such selfishness, who boast worthy mission statements and customer service training, have to admit that the perceptions of their customers often tell a different story. In any event it is what your customers *think* — rather than a mission statement framed in the corridor — that will determine your company's success.

This book is written somewhat out of frustration. Many years of experience with companies covering all industries in many countries of the world have witnessed too much lip service to visions, values, customer promises and employee dreams. Many companies have forfeited the profits that their excellent products and services could have commanded if they had only put the customer first. Some have paid the ultimate price and more responsive, attractive, caring competitors have taken their place. Our frustration comes from the fact that this need not be so. The solution, as evidenced in the companies that are doing it right, although neither easy nor quick, involves, as usual, just common sense and a bit of know-how. That is what this book provides.

Whatever our frustration, this book is not a damning indictment of the guilty companies which turn out to be far from excellent. On the contrary, it is written with hope and faith in the common sense of those who will lead companies well into the next millennium. It is a practical guide to help you and your company colleagues to:

- create value-driven visions and missions
- develop a lasting corporate identity
- establish a road map for future strategic direction
- create a sustainable competitive advantage
- create and manage a powerful brand
- reverse declining customer loyalty
- boost employee morale and commitment
- attract new customers
- dramatically improve internal and external customer service
- provide focus and direction for advertising and public relations
- escape the product life cycle trap
- achieve corporate immortality

That's a lot of benefits from a single book. The common sense secret is not in being super-excellent in every facet of your business, but in getting the central ingredient right — the part of your business that most affects all the above customer-related achievements. But before even introducing this central ingredient we have to say that there is no 'quick fix' formula. Nor will any lasting solution mean anything other than a lot of hard work over a long period of time and substantial investment. But such aims are not optional extras. Your success and, in some cases, very survival, may well depend on all or some of them. The good news is that there is a practical, proven way to corporate success and world class status. The central ingredient is personality; corporate personality — *corporate charisma*.

Charisma and corporate personality

Your personality embraces everything about you — what you are and want to be, your values, dreams and unique characteristics. It is what makes you you. We often refer to a person as having *charisma* when there is something special and attractive about them. Their personality seems to go beyond any of the more visible talents and resources they might possess. Whatever their other characteristics, charismatic people attract others to them. A company's personality is what makes it different to its competitors. And, just as with individuals, there are companies that have that special charisma, and others, even large conglomerates, seem nondescript by comparison. A distinctive corporate personality is what enables the customer to single you out, what makes them remember you, and what creates loyalty. It is what gives a company, organisation or institution *life* — human qualities in the mind of its customers that they can relate to. It is what can make an otherwise soulless legal entity seem dependable, caring, loveable, professional or cute and cuddly. A company, depending on your own personality, you *like* to do business with.

A company's personality often reflects how its customers see themselves, or how they would like to be seen. On the other hand, if a company is perceived as aggressive, sinister, two-faced or untrustworthy (never mind their product quality), people will not deal with it, just as they will not associate personally with those who do not reflect their own values and characteristics. We tend to like people who are like us. And that 'likeness' is perceived in terms of human characteristics that go to form personality.

Of course it isn't vital to be charismatic to succeed. We all know people who we would not describe as having charisma yet we admire and respect them for who they are and their own, unique personality. And the same applies to companies. Some world class businesses that attract millions of loyal customers may be dependable, sensitive, caring, mature, trendy, or classy — in fact they have a distinctive personality that appeals to a certain market segment. And that genuine, consistent personality is the key to their long term success. In this book we describe a strategic process for creating or changing your corporate personality, whether you want to be charismatic or conservative. The term *corporate personality* embraces the ideal of charisma that many companies aspire to, but does not exclude other characteristics that might appeal to your customers.

Charisma, or any personality trait, is in the eye of the beholder, of course, and a successful personality strategy will depend on perception and positioning in the minds of your customers. But this book is not just about image. In the long run people will be attracted to you for who you really are — your true identity, not an image or facade. So the strategic process we describe allows you to identify your true personality, and if need be to change it to align with your mission, vision, values, culture, branding and positioning strategy, and of course your customers. In this way you can project a unique personality that will attract and keep customers and be your foundation for world class recognition.

Who should read this book?

This book is addressed to CEOs, marketing executives, brand managers, consultants, agency staff and anyone who is responsible for corporate growth. It is for people concerned with change in organisations. Personality and charisma are as much to do with who or what you want to be, as what you are now — it is about what you see yourself becoming, what you aspire to be. Our personal vision of the future usually dictates how we act today. Similarly, values, although they may be ideals a little loftier than our actual behaviour, nevertheless influence everything we say and do. In the same way many organisations are not satisfied with where they now are, especially in terms of their current customers, potential customers and their image in the market-place. You personally may be concerned with changing things in terms of the quality of your product, your internal culture and values, your service to the public, or how they see you.

We shall see how a company's vision, mission, values, culture and day-to-day operations all go to form its unique personality, and how every member of the staff is part of this personality package. So whether you are managing major corporate change or are involved at a job-specific level, you can be part of creating and maintaining a successful corporate personality. What you will read has an impact also on every function at every level:

human resources management
production and quality control
customer service
marketing corporate strategy and leadership

There is nothing more central than corporate charisma and there is nothing that affects every member of the staff in quite the same way.

At the same time there are many outside agencies and consultants who are involved in organisational change and marketing. Just as change will affect your culture, management and operations, so will your personality permeate your PR and advertising. So a whole range of outside specialists, including those concerned with promoting brands and image, as well as those supporting internal changes, can benefit from this book.

How this book will help you

Companies that single-mindedly set about creating and managing their corporate personality will be the survivors and winners in the next century. This book shows you how to create a personality for your company that will add a unique dimension to your strategies and enable you to compete — whatever your size — at a world-class level. Successful corporate personalities don't happen by accident. There are some fundamental things you have to do — and do right. What you need is the understanding and ability to put several key strategies in place. This book is your complete guide to establishing and managing a corporate personality. Use it as your personal specialist corporate personality consultant.

It not only explains the vital concepts that have to be understood, but shows you how to put them into practice. It starts from where you are now, allowing for your present customer relationships, culture and track record of successes and failures. There are no starting qualifications other than a willingness for major change, if needed, and the desire to be world class.

In search of what works for you

In this book we have not relied only on relevant examples to illustrate the range of organisations benefiting from a personality strategy. We have also identified principles, certain rules, some pitfalls and tips to enable you to make your own changes with a bit of common sense. Case studies are fine, perhaps, for illustrating management and other theories, but by their very nature they soon become dated in the present business climate of rapid change. But, if we have learnt anything from the 'In search of excellence' movement of the last decade, it is that studies of corporate excellence may not be transportable. What applied to IBM or Nike may not apply to your company. No seven-point model will ensure that you will position your company for growth through a unique personality. There are just too many variables and local circumstances. But common-sense principles and techniques *are* transportable, even though they have to be adapted to your needs. As we shall see, both customers and businesses around the world have extraordinarily common basic needs and wants. And every business, just like every customer, can have a unique personality of its own.

As well as simple principles, you will find here down-to-earth techniques, explanations, exercises and checklists that you can apply directly to your business, whatever sector you are in. So whatever the size of your company, you will have a blueprint for a successful personality strategy that will stand the test of time and competition.

Why 'personality'?

Let us now make it clear that corporate personality is not a discretionary extra, but, whatever your core product or service, the core attribute for your company to succeed competitively. Everything else from quality control to information technology can be copied, acquired or eventually home-grown. Personality is different. It is your unique identity.

In today's world there is fierce competition in every market. Survival, let alone profitable growth, is a struggle for most companies and good profits are often short-lived. Yet somehow some companies manage to just grow and achieve spectacular year-on-year profit increases. How do they do it? What is the secret to their success? And if they can do it, why can't others? The answer is that you need personality to differentiate yourself, to grow, and, in the long term, to survive.

People like people

Why do some products and companies seem to have a special power that draws people to them? The answer is that they have a personality. People like people — or at least people who are like themselves. They don't like dealing with machines any more than faceless bureaucracies. And they particularly like people who are like them. But relationships are a two-way process. So if a company can understand who its customers are and what they are like as people, then build a similar personality for them to identify with, they will create a *magnetic* attraction.

Personality is unique

Every human being is unique. And it is not only our physical looks that makes each of us different, it is also our personality. Consequently it is very difficult to copy someone else — to behave like them consistently. Not only are we unique, but we have an unerring tendency to act consistently over time. We tend to stay true to our personality. Wild swings in behaviour are regarded as abnormal; extreme swings, schizophrenic. And the same rules apply to a corporate personality. Inconsistency between what you say and what you do, or from one month to the next, will expose you as an impostor, a liar, a cheat.

There are two very important implications arising out of these facts:

- If a company can provide itself or each of its products with its own personality, then imitations will be difficult to create. In this way, personality is an invaluable intangible asset that cannot be copied or owned by competitors. Other companies can copy or acquire technology, processes, systems, structures and products, but not personality. If they try, not only will they will be seen as 'mimicking' someone else, but also it will be difficult for them to do that consistently.

- Companies must be consistent in their behaviour, otherwise they will be seen as wild, erratic or unreliable. This is one of the rules of personality.

Beating the competition

Personality then, because it is unique, provides a source of sustainable competitive advantage. And if customers or potential customers like what they see in this 'person' then there is every likelihood that they will develop a lasting relationship and they will become 'friends'.

Some of the world's greatest companies and products grow and prosper on the strength of their personality. An attempt to change the taste of Coke caused a reaction out of all proportion to the importance of a soft drink flavour. But this customer reaction came about not so much because of a technical change of ingredients (to which market research had already given the green light) but because a personality was being tampered with. Coke involved the deepest feelings and loyalties even at a national level. It was part of people's lives, memories and values in the USA — it was one of the family. That is the power of product and corporate personality: it can sustain competitive advantage.

The corollary of this situation is if a company or a product has no strong personality, then it will be extremely difficult to provide (in the eyes of the consumer) any clear sustainable differentiation. In addition to this, without a clear personality and the focus it gives, such companies are likely to act inconsistently and to be regarded with suspicion.

So corporate personality is not negotiable in the sense you can decide to do without it. You will in any case be *perceived* to have a personality, and by default the perception may not serve you well. By actively and strategically establishing or, if necessary, changing your personality you will start to take control of the key to long-term marketing success.

Personality accounts for the difference between world-class companies and products on the one hand; and also-rans and failures on the other. Whatever the cost and effort, the choice and opportunity is yours for the taking.

The family connection

To most people, the family stands for:

who we are
where we come from
what we stand for
what values we hold dear
what we believe in
what we won't let go
what we fight for
what we defend and protect
what we nurture
what we are proud of
what we work hard for, suffer for
what we will die for
what we want to show off
what we love, whatever happens
what can hurt us most, if things go wrong
who we like to be like
who we like to be with
what we want to live for

A company is like a family in all these respects. Some of the most successful companies — big and small — are those that have been true to their 'family values', projecting a consistent personality and a consistent image. Employee behaviour or corporate activities that are 'out of character' can result in a tarnished image, a loss of face, and even loss of company friends — customers.

Strong corporate personalities have much the same emotional bonding as families. Personality creates the bond, and the difference.

For companies, personality is the key differentiator — the one thing that cannot be owned by another company, but which can endure and attract more friends. It attracts the same sort of solidarity that families adopt in adverse circumstances. It reflects the sort of strong, common values that families inherit and display. It is big enough to recover from mistakes, just as a family makes allowances for errant behaviour. Personality may not be appreciated when things are going well, but in difficult times and in times of change it can be a corporate life-saver. With so much conformity in management practice and production methods it is the ideal differentiator.

Corporate personality is more than a name. As with a family, it is what is behind the name that counts. You will stand or fall by what your company name means to the outside world.

Personality and corporate success

Vision and mission

As we saw above, vision and mission statements are ways of expressing the aspirations of a company. Invariably, they include references to their philosophy of business and the values that underpin this. In other words, companies often start (sometimes unintentionally) to lay down the foundations for a corporate personality at this stage.

One well-devised and intentional vision statement comes from a bank which strives to be the 'heartbeat of the community' wherever it operates. Accompanying this vision is a whole set of strategies for exercising social responsibility, including dedicating a certain percentage of pre-tax profits for community wealth-creation projects. The bank's core values include being caring, friendly, responsible and resourceful. These have given rise to personality and positioning statements which differentiate the bank from any other. The concept is brought to life by skilful use of cartoon imagery created by the staff themselves, and involvement in national, regional and local community projects.

Brand building and corporate image

Some of the world's most successful companies have built their corporate and product brands, by adding personality. This can apply to intangible items which customers value and feel attracted to, over and above the basic products and services. People are attracted to personalities that are part of the brand proposition. So corporate personality can be the basis of a successful brand strategy.

Image is the pooled perceptions that consumers hold about a company. It is how people see you. The image that eventually appears in consumer minds is a product of a filtering process as they subconsciously sort out what they like and don't like about a company, its products and services. If the company develops a distinct personality and consumers identify with this, the image evoked is much more likely to be strong and favourable. Companies with strongly developed brand personalities usually have strong positive images. In some cases this image, or perception, may not fully reflect the true personality of the company, such as where the company, has changed its strategies and values, perhaps following a change of CEO or key staff. In this case the task will be to align the image with the true personality so that there is no mismatch between perception and reality.

Positioning and differentiation

Positioning is all about influencing the mind of the consumer to view the company (or its product or service) differently from competitors. How a company positions itself may not be the same for each target customer group. But even if alternative positioning strategies are employed, personality provides a consistent platform which can be seen across the whole market. Individual personalities who are well liked find it easier to interact with different people. So it is with companies — if a company is well liked by individuals, businesses and other market segments, success will be easier to achieve. But, as with image, positioning is the customers' perception rather than the company's intention. In this case it is what the customer sees *relative to another company*. (Positioning is discussed in depth in Chapter 7.)

Advertising and promotion

In order for companies to build strong brands and images, and encourage customer loyalty, there has to be a consistent platform upon which to base these. The key to successful advertising and promotion is to make your campaigns creative and different whilst making sure that they are both consistent and appropriate. Personality provides the foundation. Strong values and personality traits can be used in creative but appropriate ways to communicate consistent messages. The physical appearance of a company through sales outlets can be a turn-on or turn-off to customers. As with advertising and promotion, the company becomes more easily recognisable if colour, layout and materials, for instance, are kept consistent. People are largely consistent (even though seemingly unpredictable to market researchers) in their behaviour, and they like it when companies are too. The personality of the company can strengthen this perception if it is built into the physical interface with the customer. For example, Body Shop's caring personality and values are reinforced and incorporated in their green wooden shop façades, knowledgeable staff who share the attitudes of the company, products that reflect environmental values, and so on. The personality becomes reality and the customer becomes the company's friend. The design of every sales outlet should pass the corporate personality test.

Culture and employee attraction

Staff feel proud and exhibit loyalty to firms that portray the values important to them. Motivation is much higher than in companies that do not care about their values, and staff turnover is less of a problem. Recruitment becomes easier as the company's reputation as a value-driven organisation spreads. On top of this, inspired employees create profitable businesses, so values affect the bottom line. The impact of values on employees tends to be self-fulfilling. If staff see the company — and to them this usually means the CEO and senior managers — operating true to its personality, they will tend to behave in the same way. If the values are practised widely and continuously within the company, the value-driven culture and the personality become one. You cannot fake culture for long and inevitably people, particularly customers, notice.

The bottom line

Corporate personality and the personality values affect consumer and employee behaviour which combine to impact heavily on the bottom line — profit. Over time, large increases in sustainable profits and asset value are the rewards. The message is: personality pays.

Summary

1. What customers think and say is an indictment of most companies.
2. A company's personality is its true identity and what makes it unique. Corporate personality adds value to values. Because people like to relate to people, personality characteristics add life to an organisation.
3. A company's personality often takes on the characteristics of a family.
4. Creating a corporate personality will help your company to:

   - build brands
   - improve corporate image
   - create a unique position in the minds of customers
   - attract and retain customers
   - boost employee morale
   - sustain a competitive advantage.

CHAPTER TWO

VISION, MISSION AND VALUES

Personality comprises our values and beliefs as well as our desires, goals and aspirations. The danger in implementing corporate personality is to treat it as an add-on, like any other company change programme. A personality strategy means re-engineering your relationship with your customers for mutual understanding or perception.

So your corporate personality must be congruent with your vision, mission and culture, and in harmony with the overall direction of the company. On the other hand, embarking on a personality strategy is a good opportunity to revisit your vision and mission, as well as identifying once again your values. A person — or personality — is not a machine; a company needs a purpose. If you don't have vision and mission statements — where you want to be and how you intend to get there — then you will need to address this as part of any personality strategy.

Where you want to be

A vision statement is an expression of your company's aspirations and goals. It is a guide for the future; a destination that motivates all the staff, which profit alone does not. Profit is a historical indicator of relative success and a necessary economic measurement, but vision gives people a sense of destiny and unity. Having said that, a vision statement is more than a pipe dream, and should be accompanied by a succinct plan or route to competitive performance and long-term growth.

A corporate vision may stem from a weekend reverie on the part of the CEO or from a brainstorming session of top executives. Or it may be the result of a protracted company wide exercise perhaps also involving outside consultants and market researchers. It does not matter whether a company's vision is the result of analysis and structured thought or intuition and emotion. It is no less important for growth and success. And it needs to be written down — clear for all to see — as a vision statement.

Some do not go beyond general statements of intent. For example, Cadbury Schweppes's

> ... task is to build on our traditions of quality and value to provide brands, products, financial results and management performance that meet the interests of our shareholders, consumers, employees, customers, suppliers and the communities in which we operate.

Nevertheless the text has been carefully chosen. Logica, the computer software company, says:

> Our vision of the future is simple. The winners in our industry will be those who understand and respond to change — changing needs and changing means — and who continue to deliver what the customers want. We know our customers seek business understanding, flexibility, high-quality people and service, and value for money. We have unrivalled skills and experience amongst the talented individuals who are our staff, we have the strength and stability of our culture, and the determination to succeed.

Sometimes a slogan is incorporated into the vision. For

example, Birmingham Midshires Building Society says: 'At the heart of our strategy is our vision of being FIRST CHOICE for our customers.' And you will recall the memorable Avis car rental slogan ... 'We try harder' which powerfully positioned their personality in these three simple words.

How you aim to get there

If the vision statement is all about where your company wants to go and what it wants be, a mission statement, on the other hand, will show how you propose to get there. Although still at a 'high' level in comparison to the company's business plan, the mission statement will typically be more substantive and less open-ended than the vision statement. It introduces the 'how' into the what and where we want to be.

For Motorola the 'how' was its six-sigma quality programme that was established as a key initiative to achieve its overall objective in 1987. This meant tolerating only 3.4 manufacturing defects per million. By 1994 the figure had dropped from 6000 to 40 per million, and six-sigma has now become a reality for the company.

Hillsdown Holdings, the British conglomerate, says the group will:

Continue to invest in order to increase the added value proportion of its earnings. Reduce its exposure to the more highly cyclical areas of activity, promoting a greater degree of predictability in group performance. Place greater emphasis on cash generation.

So the style and content of both statements, which are sometimes merged into one, may differ widely. But the process is important, as it asks the important 'Who are we?' question, reflects the personality of the company and, at whatever level, starts on the 'how'. And your organisation will not have a distinctive personality unless you can clearly document:

- where you are going, and
- how you intend to get there.

This is part of your personality strategy.

But glossy documents or framed statements in the corporate corridors do not mean change and success. Many companies spend a great deal of time and money writing vision and mission statements and after a while begin to wonder why they are not having the desired effect of motivating and inspiring people to better performance. There can be several reasons why this happens and why expected things don't happen.

- The statements are too complicated to be understood
- They lack involvement of the staff in the process of formulating them — they are not 'owned'
- They are unrealistic and obviously unachievable
- They are too limited and do not inspire challenge and ambition
- They do not incorporate the key motivating element that transforms words into action — corporate values
- They are not in harmony with your organisation's personality

These statements can give a sense of purpose and strategic direction and be a source of motivation to staff. Or they can be a company joke. It depends on whether they reflect the shared values of the people who comprise the company and whether those values are reflected in the way customers are actually treated. Whatever the definitions and content of these key company documents, they must be congruent with the company's true identity — its values, beliefs, culture and behaviour. That is, they should reflect your corporate personality. Done well and honestly, creating and communicating a clear vision is an investment with very high returns.

Establishing a values strategy

Clear, uncomplicated, inspiring vision and mission statements will set out the direction and pace of the company. But these need to be supported by consistent values, which should in turn be aligned to the corporate personality — the true identity of the company.

Values are the things that are important to you — for example, honesty, integrity, dependability, loyalty. Beliefs — and companies espouse beliefs as part of their culture — are what you hold to be true. They are closely related to values, in that you may *believe* in being honest, loyal, and so on.

It is only in recent years that some companies have begun to make their beliefs and values explicit. Although they are not always articulated or defined, yet values are in evidence everywhere within the company and its culture, because they always translate into behaviour. And whether stated or unstated, it is these beliefs and values that can capture the hearts and minds of customers and staff alike. They are the essence of your corporate personality.

Defining values clearly is in one sense difficult and in another potentially dangerous. The *difficulty* comes in trying to objectively identify unwritten company attitudes and beliefs. Understanding a company's value systems and culture is very much like a psychologist trying to unravel a complex personality. Values get uncomfortably close to behaviour and because of this difficulty not so many companies have stated their values as they have their vision and mission.

The *danger* may be that people do not subscribe to certain carefully defined values or shy away from them. Values and beliefs are a sensitive part of any personality and may operate below the surface of conscious behaviour. We act as much intuitively as rationally. But that is what makes personality special — it includes heart as well as mind.

Overcoming these difficulties and dangers, however, is a necessary part of the process of creating a unique corporate identity that your customers can relate to.

Many companies who have gone through the process of

eliciting and defining core values have done so either out of desperation or during a period of corporate sickness that demanded radical turn-around action. Such was the case of Intel in the mid-1980s when heavy corporate losses led the incoming CEO to look for core values to give people something to work for and hold on to. Some companies have inherited values from their founders, while others have adopted values as a result of skilled or charismatic leadership. Sometimes values are changed following an acquisition, merger or demerger, or on embarking on a different kind of business or market.

But whatever the cause or the source, companies with well-defined values don't just talk about them, but act on them, constantly promote them, and reward the behaviour that demonstrates them. They tend to be the successful companies that stand out from the pack. It is the heart of the company that connects best to the heart of the customer. It is what loyalty and relationships are made from and a key feature of a strong corporate personality.

Values reveal what is most important in personal lives. Values in a business tell us what is important to that company and thus how they are likely to treat staff and customers. So, in considering your company's corporate personality, as well as revisiting your vision and mission statements, you may well have to establish and document your core values.

The characteristics of values

Although there are difficulties and dangers in identifying and publishing values, working out values, if approached in the right way, can be a very positive, enlightening and sometimes enjoyable experience.

1. *Values don't usually follow demographics*
   Value-based customer-type labels such as 'actualisers', 'achievers', or 'strivers' (see Chapter 10) might well include differing proportions of women, college-educated people, professionals, or people from a particular geographic location. Conversely, two households may have identical

demographics, but values which are worlds apart.

2. *Values do not predict all purchasing behaviour*
Typically, they work best on products and services that have plenty of meaning and symbolism: for example, large, complex purchases such as houses and cars, durable goods; or goods and services that are status-makers including food and clothing, holiday travel and books. They don't usually predict packaged goods and commodities purchasing.

3. *Values are context-specific*
For instance, the way a person buys a home may be different from the way the same person uses values to make a charitable donation. So you can't predict consumer behaviour with the usual multiple regression models.

4. *Values are slow-changing*
Opinions and attitudes will shift depending, for instance, on a change in the price of a product. In the case of computer-related products this can be frequent. But even so the *underlying* values tend to be slow changing.

The significance of these factors is that corporate values need to reflect the values of the customer rather than ideals that managers or consultants have formulated. This is because when it comes to attracting and keeping customers there needs to be a perceived *likeness*. This is a simple fact in creating rapport for good communication.

Translating values into competitive advantage

Many marketing executives are unhappy about dealing with anything below the level of visible behaviour, that which does not have a clear cause-and-effect relationship. Attitudes, beliefs and values may be considered irrelevant if simple facts (like prices and delivery terms) and features (like quality and functionality) can be translated into sales. In fact by seriously and strategically addressing values you can clock up very tangible benefits.

Values are qualitative rather than quantitative and it is more difficult to treat them as goals and targets than is the case with say, market share or return on investment. But they can nevertheless be instrumental in achieving success in many ways.

Changing corporate culture

Values and beliefs underpin the attitudes and behaviours inside a company. All these are reflected in corporate culture which is, in effect, 'How we do things round here'. It's the glue or mortar that keeps the bricks — the people — both together and apart. Creating or defining core values gives the company an opportunity to examine its culture and to change it.

Corporate culture is the expression of personality *inside* the company. It both reflects and affects the corporate personality. So changing corporate culture is sometimes essential to the process of building a new corporate personality or changing your present one. Even though corporate personalities differ widely, as indeed do cultures, in successful companies personality and culture will be in harmony. Moreover, each supports the other: 'accepted' behaviour reinforces personality, and a strong personality influences staff behaviour at every level.

Although essentially internal, culture spills into the outside world and in particular affects customers in their day-to-day dealings with the business. There are obvious benefits of a workplace in harmony: savings in recruitment, training and staff-related costs, as well as increased production and real marketing improvements. These are bound to result from a culture that supports the company's mission, believes in its products, empowers staff and puts the customer first — that embraces such *values*. Culture change is not the easiest corporate change to undertake, but it is one that generates a high and long-term return on the effort involved.

Research by Kotter and Heskett in their book *Corporate Culture and Performance* showed that 'performance-enhancing cultures' bring enormous bottom line benefits to companies. The research took four years and covered 200 companies in twenty countries. Companies with a strong corporate culture, based on a foundation of shared values, out-performed others by a huge margin, as the following shows:

	Average growth % with a performance-enhancing culture	Average growth % without a performance-enhancing culture
Revenue	682	166
Stock price	901	74
Profit	756	1

The message is simple: define your shared values and reinforce them with consistency and repetition.

Achieving superior quality and service

Articulating and reinforcing values can significantly change a company's performance in the form of better quality and service, or other customer benefits. Reliability, for instance, can be the benchmarking value that drives the company to achieving quality and service standards. This is a major area for competitive advantage as, with all the quality and service emphasis of recent years, the reality is still one of poorly perceived service.

Although values are not as visible as products and physical resources, they affect the business in a tangible way. Consistent product and service quality always boils down to staff attitudes and values, rather than public behaviour and special 'customer first' scripts. The Technical Assistance Research Programs Institute in Washington DC has published some alarming statistics that show just how significant customer service problems are:

- ... complaints about service have increased 400 per cent since 1983 ...
- 96 per cent of the customers with problems will never tell you they have a problem. They simply take their business elsewhere.

- For every customer with a problem a company knows about, there are twenty-six others that it doesn't know about. And six of these are serious
- The average customer with a problem talks to nine to ten other people about it
- 13 per cent of the customers with problems will tell as many as twenty other people
- For every customer with a problem there are 250 people who have directly or indirectly heard negative comments about the supplier
- One of the primary reasons customers switch loyalties is due to perceived neglect or indifference.

Conversely, according to the Strategic Planning Institute in Cambridge, Massachusetts, companies noted for outstanding quality and service:

- charge, on average, 9 per cent higher prices
- grow twice as fast as the average company
- experience yearly market share increases of 6 per cent, while the average company loses 2 per cent a year
- receive an average annual return of 12 per cent (the average during the research period was 1 to 2 per cent).

These statistics are no more than typical, and illustrate both the damage that can be inflicted when perceptions are negative, and the benefits when they are positive. A reputation for, say, reliability (a value) cannot be sustained for long unless the company is *actually* reliable. It is also true that perceptions may differ from reality if the right values have not been communicated. So a personality strategy involves projecting as well as owning and enacting values. Once the right perception exists, a loyal customer will make all sorts of allowances for the odd mistake if he or she believes in the company and empathises with its values. So you need to both communicate and live out your values — words *and* actions.

Many of the really great companies use closely defined values to avoid mistakes and satisfy customers. Disney

Corporation, for instance, has **safety** as one of its four core values. Every job has safety skills attached to it, because of the importance of the customer/entertainment interface and the complexity of the attractions (rides). Federal Express has **speed** as a core value to act as a key driver in meeting customer expectations. Intel has **quality** as one core value to help maintain its top level reputation in the computer industry. Motorola is famous for its six sigma **quality** code which many companies around the world try hard to emulate.

Through quality, service and better customer relationships values produce profitable sales. The message is that a value 'package' — a core ingredient of corporate personality — pays. Value is a long-term, slow-changing phenomenon, whether in a person or a company. But when values are clearly set and lived out they command premium prices, produce willing ambassadors, and command extraordinary customer loyalty.

Improving internal and external communications

Company values give people a talking point. If employees are involved in the value selection and definitions, vertical communication between managers and subordinates is made easier. Common values also lead to a shared understanding and better horizontal communications and co-operation between peer colleagues. All manner of communication problems are overcome when core values are shared.

This applies equally to external communications which are given focus and consistency since values provide the key messages. People like to know where they stand and at heart want to trust and be trusted. Values are the basis of such trust, and customers, suppliers, investors and other company stakeholders are attracted to people with values close to their own.

Establishing loyalty based on solid values is a sound investment. Several years ago Xerox established what it considered to be an ambitious goal. Within eighteen months it would move 90 per cent of its customers into a 'satisfied' category as reported in continuous customer surveys. But statistics proved that by shifting a customer one further rung from a 'satisfied' level to the 'very satisfied' level there was a 600 per cent greater likelihood that the client would return to Xerox as a repeat customer. The company quickly abandoned its 90 per cent 'satisfied' goal in favour of a 'very satisfied' level. The pay-off was too big to ignore.

Promoting specific behaviours

Values translate into specific behaviours as surely as night follows day. You can soon determine people's values, more by watching what they do than by listening to what they say. Culture is the corporate outworking of the organisation's values. As with an individual, the true corporate personality will always shine through. Behaviour is just the visible part of the iceberg that includes, below the surface and not always understood or even admitted, attitudes, feelings, values and beliefs. The more a company adopts and communicates these human characteristics, the better they will relate to the minds and hearts of their customers. And the process can be active as well as passive: companies that have values such as creativity and innovation, for example, can actively concentrate their efforts on making these happen. Successful behaviour inculcates beliefs just as beliefs and values are self-fulfilling in bringing about behaviour.

A group of Wal-Mart executives met with a sales team from a small supplier firm, Famous Fixtures, to review their relationship. The supplier sales team was a diverse group from every significant part of the company, including engineering, production and customer service. During the discussion a Wal-Mart executive happened to comment ruefully that the company was lacking a system for everyday distribution of a multitude of store displays among its various locations. Almost in jest, he said that if Famous Fixtures really wanted to help they should be tackling that particular problem. And the small company did just that. They brainstormed the problem on the plane on the way back and later proposed a display distribution system that was successfully tested in 250 stores. Famous Fixtures are now planning to sell the service to Wal-Mart and other retail customers.

What is unusual about this case is that the supplier company set out *deliberately* to build a long-term relationship and were quite prepared to solve their customer's problem as part of that strategy. In fact, this was part of their value system. The story says a lot for the personality of the supplier company.

Differentiating and positioning

Choosing one particular value and consistently supporting it, demonstrating it and promoting it can generate a leadership role for a company. A company can come to 'own' that value, and this differentiates it from the competition, allowing it to be seen as occupying a unique position in the eyes of consumers. In this way you can leverage a simple value into top-of-the-mind customer awareness.

Corporate personality is usually built by companies seeking to create a unique, differentiating identity that consumers will like and interact with. As with an individual, a corporate personality will comprise different traits or characteristics. There is no standard composition for these elements. Some companies use values, some use personality traits or characteristics and others combinations of both. Some companies even include business values and behaviours, as opposed to personality-type variables. So a personality value such as 'honesty' may be lined up alongside a personality trait such as 'self-confidence' and external and internal business values such as 'quality'. Some values, for example 'reliable', cross these borders. Intel, for instance, has six core values:

- risk-taking
- quality
- discipline
- customer-orientation

- results orientation
- 'great place to work'

The companies most successful in attracting customers invariably have core values at the heart of their personality. These values are normally the kind that employees and customers of the company can relate to and believe in, such as being trustworthy, caring, reliable and so on. By demonstrating values as well as other personality characteristics (see Chapter 4) a company will attract the emotional, beliefs-oriented side of its customers and staff, and bring warmth and friendship to any relationships. Even the largest company then becomes like a person, and, more than that, a likeable person. The task, then, is to position yourself to appeal to a segment of customers that you understand and emulate in your own personality, and, in doing so, creatively differentiate yourself from all the competition.

Perception and reality

In *The Marketing Imagination* Theodore Levitt wrote 'If marketing is seminally about anything, it is about achieving customer satisfaction by differentiating what you do and how you operate. All else is derivative of that and only that.' Differentiation is a key to effective marketing and, as we have seen, values are essential to achieving it. However, to satisfy the customer you have to be *perceived* as different. Values are not just subjective in the way they are defined and outlived, but also in the way they are interpreted or perceived by others.

World-class does not have to mean global, but it does mean having a personality that is known over and above your individual products and services. A clear, strong corporate personality will provide the platform for strategic marketing, for product and geographical expansion, and growth to any level. It is the heart and mind of your company which will win the hearts and minds of your customers. With ever-increasing competition and change, it is the foundation upon which your future depends. But changing a corporate personality is different to other forms of strategic management. Everything hinges, not so much on what you do, but on what you are perceived to do. Not so much on what you are, but what you are perceived to be.

Buying decisions are based, although this is rarely understood or articulated, on corporate personality. So the company has two major undertakings when it comes to establishing better relationships through a personality strategy:

First to establish the personality. This will probably mean change, not just in the personality message but in values, attitudes, culture and day-to-day behaviour.

Second, to project or communicate your personality so that your customers' perception — about the organisation, its products, people, culture, etc. is as close as possible to your own. When your respective perceptions are in alignment, there is mutual understanding and rapport. It is what happens in the mind that dictates buying decisions and customer loyalty. And it is what happens in the minds of company people, from the CEO to the lowest paid operative, who collectively form its personality, that will dictate a company's values, beliefs and behaviour.

Changing perceptions

Having said this, as a company, you will have to make some very real efforts to change perceptions. The goal is no less than *mutual* understanding — the equilibrium at which perceptions agree. You think you are youthful and dynamic and so do your customers. You think you are caring and thoughtful and so do your customers — or enough customers to form a profitable business segment. Sadly, in too many cases, a company is either surprised to learn what its customers think or simply refuses to believe it. In even more cases the company does not bother to find out in any objective way. That is why an active personality strategy is a good discipline. It gets to the grass roots of your values and those of your customers. It puts customers' qualitative perceptions higher in ranking than your own. They are the ones who, after all, pay the bills. It puts the responsibility for change on *you*.

However frustrating these personal perceptions might be to the marketeer, there are three factors you can turn to your advantage:

Perceptions tend to be long-term

People are slow to change their beliefs and any sort of mindset is a long time in the changing. This is because relationships are based more on values than the actualities of the moment. We stick resolutely to our beliefs and counter arguments are more likely to reinforce than change them. This means that you are likely to get a long-term return on investing in changing perceptions. Once changed, perceptions will be slow to change again, although they will have to be reinforced by consistent actual behaviour and a consistent personality message.

There are reasons for perceptions

However irrational on the surface, a reason can usually be found for perceptions. It could be a single encounter with a cashier or waiter that happened five years ago, or a dislike of the colour of the company's logo. However, what makes sense (a reason) to one person makes no sense to another person — 'I just don't understand how his mind works.' But customer perceptions are amenable to psychographic research; it may be as simple as asking what makes your customer happy.

Perceptions can be segmented

A personality strategy does not demand one-to-one marketing although it pays to adopt a one-to-one *approach* in finding out what your customers think. Customers' perceptions can be aggregated into customer types, which, however simplistic or exaggerated, allow segmentation just as much as demographic distinctions.

How can you change heavily entrenched perceptions? You

may need to be creative as well as persistent and patient. Bennigan's restaurants responded to complaints about slow service by putting a stop watch on every table and offering the meal free if it was not delivered in fifteen minutes. Bearing in mind that the food just had to be delivered from kitchen to table this was no great feat on the part of the staff, but its effect was dramatic. In the event, perceptions really were changed so that the worst complainers became ambassadors and loyal allies.

But you will have to think through your strategy as the human element is not always easy to predict. When Domino's Pizza tried a similar approach, delivering food to homes in a certain time, there were a spate of road accidents as enthusiastic deliverers raced to meet deadlines; this certainly did not do much for customers' or the wider public's perception of their methods. A simple enhancement that made the order worth waiting for, if late, would probably have fulfilled the same objective. Bringing some creativity to bear may be far more effective than launching into changes that may seem obvious and logical. There is room for intuition in marketing judgement.

As any quality or customer service professional will avow, it need not cost a lot to give top class service. A thank you or, when required, a simple genuine apology can work wonders. Just telling the truth, such as when you are running late or faced with staff shortage problems, can do more for positive perceptions than trying to bluff your way to 100 per cent service levels. In repeated surveys the lack of basic courtesy is cited as a chief complaint. And courtesy comes cost-free. Not surprisingly in these days, common courtesy gets talked about more than technical product specification; it is promotional gold-dust.

So customer perceptions can be changed, just as you can improve product reject rates or actual delivery times. Just be ready to abandon your own logic and get to know what and how your customer thinks. Use some heart as well as mind.

Summary

1. Personality characteristics are often closely linked to corporate values, and the vision and mission of the company. These should all be in harmony or they will clash with corporate culture.

2. A vision statement shows where you want to be. A mission statement shows how you aim to get there. Both are vital elements of your personality.

3. Corporate values are qualitative rather than quantitative, but they can be used to:

- express your vision and mission
- change corporate culture
- achieve superior quality and service
- improve internal and external communications
- promote specific behaviours
- create differentiation and positioning
- create bottom-line profits

4. To satisfy customers a company has to be perceived as being different. A clear, strong personality provides the platform for lasting differentiation. Perceptions of customers have to be changed by projecting the right image through your company message and actual behaviour.

CHAPTER THREE

THE PSYCHOLOGY OF CORPORATE CHARISMA

How do non-personal organisations like companies create charisma? We have just seen the importance of perception and the secret here is to get inside the minds of your consumers to create perceptions of personality. Personality creation is a mind-to-mind exercise. You have to do something yourself, inside the company, of course, but the big job is to do something in the minds of the people whose loyalty you want to foster. You need to appeal to those people in your chosen market, which means, as well as knowing where they live and what their typical income is, how they think and what makes them tick. Specifically, you have to identify which personality values and characteristics will trigger rapport, and how these are best communicated. Clearly you are operating at a psychological level. But you are not simply appealing to 'the mind'. You need to appeal at different levels and in different ways, because that's the way people think.

It is now necessary to establish the psychological basis on which to both create and communicate a winning personality. Although most companies are more than aware of the importance of the psychology of what they do, such as in advertising and person-to-person selling, this has rarely been given due attention at the corporate level. Carl Jung described four functions of the mind: thinking, sensation, feeling and intuition. Creating a successful personality depends upon how much a company can appeal to these four mind functions or combinations of them. Let us consider them one at a time as they might apply to corporate personality.

Thinking

Rational thinking appeals to a person's logic and good sense. Jung referred to this as the 'thinking function' and he was really referring to what we now know relates to the Left Brain with its capacity for analysis, logic and rationality. Some people tend to think in a logical rather than intuitive way, but the fact is that we all have a two-sided brain and we all think partly in a linear, logical way. The marketing mistake is to assume that a so-called logical thinker is logical all the time, and does not make impulse purchases based on intuition. In every case, although to different degrees, we all use both sides of our brain all the time — 'heart' as well as 'mind'. Our personality reflects this, and a corporate personality will similarly have to emulate a 'two-sided' mind — rational and emotional. As well as feeling right, people like to be able to give *reasons* for buying what they buy or being loyal to a certain company. **Ask yourself, does it make sense for people to buy from our company?**

Sensation

The sensation function of the mind likes to identify with the senses of smell, taste, sight, sound and touch. The visualisation representation system, or modality, as these senses are termed, is more closely related to the Right Brain. According to the neuro-linguistic programming (NLP) model, our thinking or perception mirrors these five senses. So understanding and changing perceptions means changing these inner sensations. Advertisers are well aware of what appeals to the senses, and of the power of multi-sensory media. **Ask yourself, do the brands and corporate image we project appeal to all the senses?**

34

Feelings

Feelings, in the emotional sense, are also associated with the Right Brain and, in some cases such as fear, with the older Mid-Brain. Building emotion into personality is a key ingredient for success as customers react with feelings of warmth, affection and belonging. Successful marketing appeals to emotions. **Ask yourself, does our company appeal to customers at this emotional level?**

Intuition

Intuition, another Right Brain process, is a major factor in all behaviour, including buying. It is, in effect, 'knowing without knowing how you know'. The intuitive feeling of 'I just knew it was the right thing to do' is the ultimate customer hot-button. Intuition seems to go deeper than the five senses and is harder to harness. But it should not be overlooked. Careful research can reveal lifestyle, and even unconscious attitudinal and aspirational motivations, behind consumer behaviour that reflects their intuitive character. All these can be built into corporate personality to create a rapport which, being based on unconscious feelings, transcends logic. Intuitive decisions can be a long way removed from rational decisions, but the fact is that a great many purchases are made intuitively.

Intuition applies a lot in people relationships. The intuitive reaction to a salesperson, for instance (stronger, it seems, in women than in men), might be a greater factor in the decision to purchase than a whole list of product features. Or the attitude of a hotel receptionist might make or break a customer's weekend, and thus the perception of the hotel group. Intuition also reflects underlying values even though these are not outwardly expressed. The intuition involved in first impressions of a person or company may be based on a 'reading' of values in which body language and nuances of action are interpreted. It is an example of the so-called sixth sense. **Do we know intuitively how our customers will respond to a particular message or image? Are they intuitively drawn to us as a company?**

This is the psychological basis upon which a personality relationship will be formed. How specifically do companies create the personality relationship? Let us first consider how people can relate to a corporate personality.

Needs and relationships

Personality characteristics can cover many things: age, socio-economic group, sex, beliefs and values, and other human traits. So, for example, Pepsi appears to be 'young', like Apple, whilst Dunhill and IBM are perceived as 'more mature'. Marlboro, on the other hand, is most definitely 'masculine', like Harley Davidson — whereas Body Shop and Revlon are 'feminine'. Mercedes is 'upper-class' whilst Audi is more 'conservative' and less 'well-off'. Hallmark believes in 'sincerity', Benetton in 'equality'.

People in all walks of life recognise these sorts of characteristics, in companies as well as in people. We are all, albeit sometimes subconsciously, drawn to people whose personality we relate to or who we simply like. And the reverse is equally true: we can be just as easily turned off with or without apparent reason. Even tangible products like computers or cars can enjoy our praise or suffer our wrath. Instinctively we personalise companies and products, even applying words such as 'good', 'faithful' or 'caring' to inanimate objects or invisible corporate entities. But this simply reflects deeper, universal human needs. Corporate personality adds another dimension of value to normal company-customer relationships by offering different ways for satisfying these basic personal needs. These include the needs for:

- friendship
- emotional release
- conversation
- links with the past
- self-expression
- partnership and sharing

- self-improvement
- belonging

Such needs can be both physical and psychological, simple and complex. But as with ordinary human relationships, the corporate personality can appeal to all these needs. To understand how to create a corporate personality it is worth considering these needs separately.

Friendship

Most people like to have friends. We all have people we like to be with, with whom we feel comfortable and look for a continuous, consistent and long-term relationship.

Friendship is characterised by thoughts or expressions such as:

- My friend understands me
- My friend cares for me
- I can depend on my friend
- My friend is always there
- We trust each other, my friend and I
- I like being with my friend
- I can't wait to see my friend again
- My friend and I have fun together — we really get along
- I love my friend

You might question whether such statements can apply to companies or products, but the fact is that they do, at least implicitly. Any product — be it an old shoe, breakfast cereal, car or cooker — can be a friend. So can a company, from your corner shop to a favourite airline or McDonald's. And some companies live up to just these sort of feelings and expressions. With values and characteristics such as being reliable, caring, friendly, trustworthy and tolerant, what are otherwise faceless corporate entities can establish consistent, friendly relationships with their customers.

We can get clues about creating a friendly corporate personality by considering human friendship. Human beings tend to look for friends who are like themselves, for example. If I like to travel I look for a travelling companion. If I'm adventurous, I look for someone who is more daring and outgoing and will share my outlook on life. If I enjoy keeping fit and sport, I choose friends who are athletic and health-conscious and share my enthusiasm for particular sports. I can choose to be with someone who matches my intelligence and sophistication, or someone who has the same old-fashioned traditional values that I like; someone who's tough and macho, or someone who's quiet and gentle. On this basis a company can create or change its personality to match its target market. McDonald's is more than just fast food to many families — it is a friend providing fun, enjoyment and happy times for the family. It is a home from home. In the same way, Disney's whole mission is to make people happy and friendliness is a key personality characteristic instilled into all staff. For them, it is a conscious personality strategy, and it works.

Emotional release

Human relationships are incomplete without emotion, and friendship and love affairs are strengthened by strong emotional bonding. Consumers of products and services can also develop close emotional ties with the products themselves and the companies who offer them.

Such emotions can give rise to feelings from disappointment to grief if the company's products are not available. Even a name can cause excitement, and there can be feelings of pride when choosing to stick to a company despite all the competition. We know from research that the emotional benefits associated with the feelings experienced when interacting with a company or product are very important. For instance, people might feel —

- healthy drinking Evian water
- safe in a Volvo car
- confident in an Armani suit
- free riding a Harley Davidson
- professional using an IBM computer

- distinguished staying at the Savoy
- relaxed flying Singapore Airlines
- trendy wearing a Swatch watch
- carefree eating Häagen-Dazs
- glamorous wearing Chanel

Experiencing the personality leads to feelings which provide emotional benefits which in turn enhance customer loyalty. Personality provides the emotional ladder to success.

Conversation

Life is very lonely without someone to talk to. As we have seen, people talk to products such as cars and computers and even have imaginary two-way conversations with them.

Researchers who have asked customers to describe what they think of particular companies by expressing imaginary comments about them have discovered interesting insights into customer's minds and the power of corporate personality:

You were always there but you never cared
You lied to me
I feel you're talking down to me
You didn't listen to me
I feel inadequate in your presence

Clearly a company's personality and behaviour can have a negative effect on our emotions, and a person can feel rejected and offended just as in a personal relationship. On the other hand a company can promote good, positive feelings:

You made me happy
I miss you when you're not there
No celebration is complete without you
You're a part of my life
You've always talked my language
You made me feel welcome
You made me laugh

How might a conversation go between a customer and

your company, or a competitor company? The answer will be a good check on whether you are communicating the desired personality.

Links with the past

Don't believe the graffiti when you read 'Nostalgia isn't what it used to be'! We like to think back on the good times, the people we used to know and be with, the places we grew up in. The sounds and smells of the past are vividly recalled, the things we have done in our lives replay in our minds, and emotions come flooding back. This amazing recall facility and tendency to resort to pleasant memories is a powerful customer hot-button. A company's personality can trigger such memories, and provide good feelings associated with them. That association becomes a round-the-clock salesperson for the company, resident in the customer's subconscious mind.

Self-expression

When a major world manufacturer of high-quality spirits and liqueurs decides it is in the fashion accessories business then you know there is a company that understands corporate personality and how consumers use its products to express themselves. A board-level discussion ended up with this outcome because they spent some time researching what types of consumers drank their products, where they drank them, on what occasions and with whom. The research revealed that customers tended to use the top-branded drinks to say something about themselves, very much in the way they would wear a top-branded watch or drive a prestige car. In fact, the videos and photographs of people drinking these brands even showed them holding the drinks in a way which clearly presented them as an extension of themselves. They were 'wearing' the drinks, as they would a Rolex watch or Mikimoto pearls or other designer accessories. The result of this customer-led business statement gave rise to some award-winning advertising and, of course, a much healthier bottom line.

When interviewed recently, a senior executive of the beer

brewer San Miguel Corporation said, 'There's a change in customer preferences ... people now want to express themselves by what they drink.' Self-expression is one of the most important influences in consumer purchasing decisions. In many countries every time the price of a Mercedes car goes up, the waiting list gets longer. The expression of status, prestige and other elements through a specific product or company purchase is much more satisfying (and has more impact on others) than carrying around a huge bag of money or pronouncing in company in a loud voice, 'I can buy anything I want'. People express themselves in their every action — the way they speak and dress, the lifestyles they lead, the hobbies they have, the friends they choose. But still they look for other opportunities to express any part of their personality in the world at large, and often choose a company personality as the vehicle. Canon uses the actual words 'express yourself' when advertising their EOS Rebel camera, employing Andre Agassi to humanise the personality. Similarly, people who want to associate themselves with leadership might support IBM, or if they've dreamt of winning an athletics gold medal, will respond to Nike. If they want to say 'I'm a tough guy and I love freedom and my country', Harley Davidson is one way to say it. As we saw earlier, we tend to like people like ourselves, and in the same way people relate to companies and products they feel are expressions of themselves.

Partnership and sharing

Having partners to share our lives with is a natural human inclination, and can be as important in business as in our personal and family lives. People like to be valued and appreciated by someone close, and to share events and experiences as well as hopes and fears.

Companies can satisfy some of this desire by instilling similar feelings in their customer relationships. Rolex have sponsored Wimbledon, for example, an event to be shared around the world. Similarly if companies build quality and reliability into their products and services customers feel appreciated and valued. They are then more likely to form a relationship with the supplier, as much as they would with the friendly corner shop. Citibank provide us with an example of how customer expectations can be surpassed and a relationship forged. Applications for home mortgages are guaranteed to be answered within 48 hours, but are usually dealt with within 24 hours. Speed is valued highly by anxious couples waiting to get their dream house before others have the chance to take it, and people quite happily pay extra for high quality, reliable service. They value it, feel valued as customers, and a bond is created. An important part of their lives has been shared. As with most relationships, the longer they last the more interdependent the partners become. They come to rely on each other and share mutual respect and loyalty. Such a relationship, in effect a bonding of personalities, is bound to be win-win, and hard for any competitor to undo.

Self-improvement

We all aspire to things that we have not yet got or cannot yet do. These aspirational desires can be built into corporate personality as in the case of Mercedes, Revlon, Pepsi, and Nike.

Nike epitomises everyone's dream of being a sports hero. Its 'Just do it' campaign symbolises the aspirational dream that there is nothing you cannot do if you really want to. Pepsi-Cola is embarking on a new and ambitious marketing campaign called 'Generation Next' with a single unified global voice and the slogan 'Pepsi Generation' appealing to the optimism of youth. Kent Horizon is also appealing to youthful aspirations and emotion with its advertisements showing young people doing 'way out' things with the tag line 'Make your own rules'. Revlon cosmetics is often quoted as being in the business of selling 'hope'; and who doesn't aspire to owning a BMW or Mercedes? Self-improvement is a powerful intangible benefit that can be built into your personality.

Sense of belonging

Everyone has a need to belong — to a club, family, country, cause or whatever. This may involve more than friendship and partnership though it may not imply personal relationships. It explains a sometimes obsessive preoccupation with wanting to know one's roots, as well as patriotism and professional, political or religious grouping. Corporate personality can offer this, as demonstrated so successfully by Benetton (World of Colours), Body Shop, Avon and others: Avon, famous for women's cosmetics over several decades, support women's causes and donate regularly to societies who help them, such as breast cancer; Body Shop attract the environmentalists and animal lovers; and Benetton seek to influence those who dislike racial inequality and the unfairness of life. So-called 'cause marketing' is now becoming a popular way for companies to address the personality issue while at the same time demonstrating social responsibility. A company personality can address all these needs and form the basis of a long-term company-customer relationship.

Projecting corporate personality

How can you project your corporate personality and capture the feelings of your customers?

People

You can use individual personalities. Most noticeably, this has been done with sports stars such as Agassi, Jordan, and Johnson, pop stars such as Michael Jackson, TV stars like Bill Cosby, Candice Bergen and CEOs themselves such as Bill Gates of Microsoft and Victor Kiam of Remington. And even if the personification of a product or company is fictional, as in the case of the Marlboro cowboy, it can still have the power of a real personality. The marketing adage 'think global and act local' also has its place in projecting corporate personality. In Asia, the Marlboro cowboy in TV commercials is sometimes played by an Asian actor, but the same personality message is communicated. Real success came to Singapore Airlines when they developed 'The Singapore Girl' with feminine, caring characteristics, and used their own staff to project the personality in advertisements. The dress, the smile, the look that you see, are all consistent. People, whether real or fictional, can powerfully project a corporate personality.

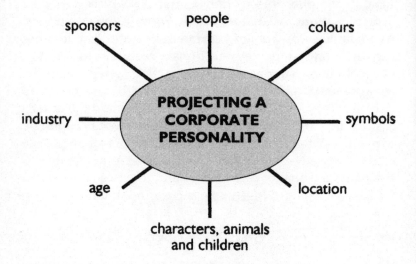

Figure 1 *Projecting a corporate personality*

Colours

Colour is another way of projecting values and personality characteristics, and it can be 'owned' by the company or product just as with a personality or slogan. Marlboro uses bold red-and-white packaging to symbolise their strength characteristics and no competitor can copy the trademark chevron. Body Shop outlets are all green outside to represent the environment issue with which the company strongly associates. Pepsi had to differentiate itself from Coca-Cola's red and white with a US$500 million 'Blue' campaign. Benetton bases its whole personality on colours to demonstrate its commitment to racial equality and fashion. The 'United Colours of Benetton' has become the trademark of the company. It symbolises everything the company stands for, with suggestions of united races, a united world and even the United States or a United Europe.

Colour is used to make social statements about topics such as war, AIDS, equality and the environment. For example, in 1989 Benetton's campaign for equality featured a black man and a white man handcuffed together, and a black mother nursing a white baby. In 1991 the company started publishing a magazine called *Colours*. The company also sponsors basketball, rugby, Formula One motor racing and volleyball, and sees sport as representing dynamism, loyalty, competition and colour, all of which Benetton wishes to reflect. The forceful execution of some of the advertising did, unfortunately, misjudge the feelings of the public and damaged the image of the company for a while. But it did create worldwide attention. Colours actually can have a physiological effect and can make people calm or angry, so it is no surprise that psychologically they are important in communicating a brand or corporate personality.

Symbols

Human beings are unique in the way that symbols, especially words and numbers, but also graphical symbols, have been central to their development. Symbols provide companies with an alternative outward representation of personality: the Rolls Royce flying silver angel — 'Eros' — symbolises grace, style, aspiration, power and status; McDonald's golden arches, Shell, the Intel Inside logo and the Perrier green bottle all trigger immediate thoughts about the personality of the company and its products.

So-called alpha-numeric brand names, incorporating both words or letters and numbers, have had a great deal of success. In this case the numeric symbols can have a rational significance such as a car's capacity or some other rating: for example BMW 730, Peugeot 306, Heinz 57 (57 varieties at the time), Fortune 500, Windows 95, Fifth Avenue. In other cases the numbers may have no explicit meaning, at least to the customer, other than to identify a unique product or company: for example, the Mazda RX-7, WD-40 oil, 7-Up, Lotus 1-2-3, DC-10.

Numbers can have important, profound meaning. Some research into the primary digits has shown, for example, that the smaller numbers were described as 'simple, complete, and weak'; large numbers (those over 3) were seen as 'smooth, powerful, complex and masculine'; even numbers were 'smooth and feminine'; and odd numbers were 'lucky and powerful'. In Asia the numbers 6, 8 and 9 are considered to be auspicious. The Chinese do not like number 4 because it sounds similar to 'death' in their language. Other research has shown that higher numbers, such as 100, 21 and 13 also have their own special meaning. What comes across is that alpha-numeric brand names evoke strong and consistent responses from customers, and that numbers have an emotive value of their own.

There are some three-quarters of a million trademarks registered with the US Patent and Trademark Office, and several million more unregistered but in use. So there is an increasing problem of finding a name that is not already in use. This gives some appeal to alpha-numeric brands. Another approach is to invent a name that does not exist in the language, that is, a 'fanciful' name such as Exxon, Kodak, or WD-40.

Of more interest is the message that is *perceived* by the customer through symbols, whether alphabetic characters, numbers, images, or any sort of representative icon. Even nonsense words may have their own special meaning. For example, the brand name Acura was developed by recognising that 'acu' was associated with words connoting precision in several languages.

So the power of symbols pervades all our language and culture. Whether to reflect a particular product and its attributes, or a deeper personality message at product or corporate level, it is part of the armoury of the marketeer. Corporate design is a growing field of business, and the design of logos and symbols is another route to projecting a strong corporate personality. The key throughout, however, is to maintain harmony between any message that symbols contain and the underlying personality you wish to convey. Even more so, your actions have to support the symbolic messages.

Location

The surroundings used to communicate corporate personality can also have great impact on consumer thoughts. Marlboro country represents freedom and independence, Kent Horizon beaches, fun and freedom. Dunhill's country and interior scenes give a sense of style and sophistication, and Nestlé's Milo sporting situations clearly demonstrate healthiness and winning moments. English Yorkshire village scenes can add to the powerful nostalgia of homemade bakery products and snow-clad mountains can lend purity, serenity or timelessness as an instant association to a product. Where would you expect to find a product or company? By a restful river, in a busy office, or out in the galaxies? Just as individuals are often associated with places (Where are you most likely to find John?), so a corporate personality can be associated with a place or kind of place, and this adds a realism to the personality that can be easily imagined.

Characters, animals and children

The old stage adage 'Never work with animals and children' does not always hold good. Met Life's use of Peanuts, Kellogg's Tony the Tiger, the Jolly Green Giant, the Slazenger Panther, the Dulux sheep dog and Esso's historic 'Put a tiger in your tank' have all been successful in creating a personality, and appealing to the emotions.

Age

Sometimes the age of the company can affect how people perceive the personality. IBM is seen as an older corporate personality, perhaps a little sedate, and, like older people, set in its ways. IBM is aware of this and is constantly trying to change this view. Conversely, a new insurance group proudly adds to its name 'Established 1997'. Some companies deliberately try to change people's perception of age as in the case of Met Life, an American insurance company which tried to explain the value of being older with their campaign which included an advertisement saying 'We're the old masters of financial security' featuring an oil painting.

Industry

The sector that the company is a part of can also affect how the personality is perceived. Having worked with several banks as clients, we know how difficult it is to break out of the expectations that consumers have. It is difficult to project a youthful, innovative, caring personality when the general public's experience has been that of meeting a somewhat snobbish, uncaring, serious, authority figure. But the banks' dilemma simply reinforces the point, that, rather than tinkering at the marketing edges, nothing less than a change in personality — in this case affecting the whole industry — is sometimes required. This is an opportunity for market leadership.

Sponsors

Carefully chosen sponsorship events can influence the personality as perceived by customers. Such sponsorship must be chosen with care and should always reinforce the corporate personality. The well-known story about Rolex is a good example. They were once asked to sponsor Wimbledon and for a couple of years rejected the request. Their top management felt it was not the right fit for such a distinguished brand personality. Eventually, Rolex visited Wimbledon, experienced for themselves the excitement of Centre Court, the film stars, royalty, strawberries and champagne and the general feeling of wealth and success. The Rolex executives had to conclude that 'This event is a Rolex'. The personality fit was good, and Rolex went on to sponsor Wimbledon. Rolex also now use successful world class personalities in different fields of achievement to endorse their corporate brand, and continues to support prestigious events.

One or more of these approaches can help you to project a strong, attractive corporate personality. Be sure to start with your visions, mission and values. And remember that whatever personality you decide upon has to be managed as a projection to the outside world, and actualised in the performance of every member of the staff.

From product to personality

When using outside agencies and spending large amounts of money on product advertising a certain amount of planning and thinking is necessary. But this is usually at a product level. Without applying the same rigours at a corporate level, in deciding upon and projecting a unique personality, many of the advantages at a product level will be lost. For instance, if different products portray different values, an advertising communication may be wasted or even counterproductive.

Similarly, if a product's value or personality perception differs from the perception of its parent company, the resulting mixed message may also be counterproductive, or certainly less than optimal. In the extreme, for example, if a racy sports car were promoted by a manufacturer known for refined, sedate understatement, not only would a lot of advertising budget be wasted — whether at the corporate or product end — but the confusion in the mind of the customer could actually reverse the message projected in the respective personalities.

The same principles and a similar range of factors apply whether applying personality at product or company level. In the case of products or services, however, the characteristics embodied will relate to a specific product, group of products, or service. A car, soft drink or toothpaste will thus have its own unique personality, distinct from but hopefully complementary with its parent company.

The role of personality can be illustrated by considering a typical product advertising process. When thinking about the objective for a product advertisement, for example, you will have to think about the product, your customer's perception, and the message you want to convey.

The product

Addressing first the product, you will have to describe what it does. As examples, let us choose three products:

Toothpaste plus mouthwash
A convenient diet product
Spicy fried chicken

These are **product features**, or attributes. But how do these translate into benefits for the customer, (which, presumably, is what you are selling and advertising)?

A cleaner breath?
An easy way to lose weight?
A unique exciting flavour?

These are the **direct benefits** you hope your customer will enjoy.

The customer

But as well as the more visible product benefits there may be other intrinsic benefits the consumer enjoys indirectly from using the product. For example, staying with the same examples:

A fresher breath and greater personal attractiveness
A smaller dress size (and greater personal attractiveness)
A more enjoyable meal, and the pleasure that brings

These might be called consumer benefits. And it may be more

important part of the message you want to communicate than product features and direct product benefits. Often it is an overriding factor in customers' perceptions, even though operating subconsciously and not always articulated. At this level you are addressing the values of your customers. This is about internal needs and self image, and what is important to them. These needs can be many and varied. For instance:

The part of us that nurtures
The part of us that wants to succeed
The part of us that wants to have a good time

The message

So when addressing the message you want to portray at a product level you will need to consider the consumer benefit that is most important for your product. In the case of our examples, these values may be:

For the mouthwash/toothpaste: a better self-image; greater personal attractiveness.
For the diet product: a better self-image; greater personal attractiveness.
For the spicy fried chicken: reinforcing self-image as a 'taste-leader'; a pioneer, pleasure-seeking.

The question to ask therefore is 'How does the benefit within the product manifest itself within *your* customer?' Where do values unite in the product-consumer relationship?

But world-class personality marketing will go further. Are the values portrayed consistent, both within the product, and as between the product and company? In the first case it would be inconsistent to portray a desire for personal attractiveness with simple hygiene and cleanliness, or a desire to be pioneering and daring with a value that portrayed the conservative comfort of grandmother's cooking. In the latter case it would be inconsistent to associate a risky, daring product with a conservative, solid bank-like corporation — or vice versa. Your message will also be diluted if your other products do not fit the corporate personality image.

Although we do have different parts to our personality, to try to model these in corporate or product personality would be far too complex, and the chances are that we would instead send mixed messages. It goes right back to corporate charisma. Decide on your personality, simplify it to a few key values or characteristics, then project it in every product you design and sell, and everything you say and do.

The personality process can be applied also to competitor products. In this way you will be considering USPs and vital differentiation but from a customer perspective. Try to think outside your own 'box', and focus on values and perceptions rather than measurable or visible features. In the same way you can view the process from the perspective of solving the customer's problems. In some ways this is a restatement of the customer's needs, wants and aspirations. The problem is that the need is presently unmet, the wants unfulfilled, and aspirations have not been achieved. Rather than just a semantic exercise this is an important reframing process in which you set out to solve your customer's problems rather than your own. The customer's perceptions take precedence. The customer is king. And this process makes much more sense when you address it from the point of view of personality.

Summary

1. Personality creation is mind to mind. It involves identifying which values and characteristics will appeal to the people you are trying to attract. It involves thinking, sensation, feelings and intuition.

2. People like people. This is the key to success behind corporate personality. Companies can gain what they want by building a personality that gives people what they need in terms of:

   • friendship
   • emotional release

- conversation
- links with the past
- self-expression
- partnership and sharing
- self-improvement
- belonging

3. In projecting personality, your company can use or be affected by:

- people
- colours
- symbols
- locations
- characters, animals and children
- age
- industry
- sponsors

4. A corporate personality has to be like a human being — consistent in its values and behaviour. It should therefore be consistently projected in everything your company says and does.

5. Charisma can be projected at a product or service level, but it should be consistent with your corporate identity.

CHAPTER FOUR

CREATING A CORPORATE PERSONALITY

In this chapter we describe the different stages you will need to go through to create a corporate personality, who to involve, what characteristics to choose, and some of the practical issues you will have to address.

Human personalities are extremely complex, comprising all our values and beliefs, thoughts, feelings and behaviour. Corporate personalities can never be as complex as those of humans but neither do we want them to be. The aim should be to project a strong but clear image that can be easily communicated to the minds of customers. They need to recognise who you are and what you stand for, identify with your personality, and be persuaded to enter into a long-term relationship. Although all too common in real life, people are not attracted to Jeckyll and Hyde, or deep, unreadable personalities. Keep your corporate or product personality simple and transparent, while maintaining your uniqueness.

Throughout this book we refer to what goes to make up corporate or product personality in terms of personality characteristics. They can be either values, beliefs or traits of thinking and behaviour, but for the sake of simplicity we will not categorise them. For instance, a belief might be 'honesty' and a behavioural trait 'outgoing'. It does not matter whether they are values or traits provided they indicate the type of personality you want your company to project.

Determining personality characteristics

The first step in creating a corporate personality is to identify the particular human characteristics which your company would like to be associated with.

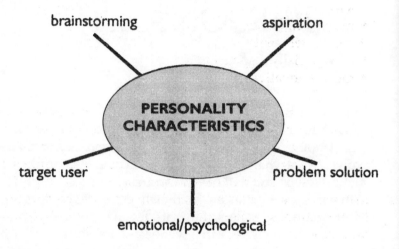

Figure 2 Five approaches to personality characteristics

Aspiration

The aspiration-driven approach concentrates on asking questions about what people want the company to be. This is related to values (see Chapter 2). It is about what the company thinks is important.

- What do we want to be seen as?
- What is our vision?

- What is our mission?
- What key behaviours do we need to concentrate on to get where we want to be?
- What do other companies do well that we could do better?

For example, we want to be seen as:

- a leader
- more fashionable
- more intelligent
- more socially responsible
- more innovative

Sometimes there is a difference between how people see themselves and how they would *like* to see themselves. Often true personality is more aligned to the latter — our aspirations, desires, hopes and dreams. The same applies to companies, so *where you are heading* may be more important than where you are. The Avis slogan 'We try harder' elicited all the natural sympathy for the underdog, and implied an aspiration to improve.

Problem solution

The 'problem solution' approach answers questions such as:

- What big problems do we currently have? What causes them?
- What do people think we are doing wrong?
- What are the most frequent mistakes that we make?
- What behavioural 'gaps' are there?
- What are people getting from other companies that they do not get from us?

We need to be, for example:

- faster, speedier
- more responsive
- more resourceful

- more creative
- more reliable

Typically a SWOT (strengths, weaknesses, opportunities, threats) analysis will throw up the problems that have to be addressed whether strategic (usually threats) or operational (usually weaknesses). This is the other side of the mission or MBO (Management by Objectives) coin; the *problem* is how to get from where we are to where we want to be, and — perhaps more important — how to be perceived by the customer as having got there. Personality — or the wrong personality —turns out to be part of the problem gap between where you are now and where you want to be. Identifying the key problem is usually the start of your road to success.

This approach will probably appeal to the 'thinking function'. The customer has a rational reason for coming to your company. It makes sense to go to someone who can solve your problems.

Emotional/psychological

We have already seen that emotion is one of the four 'thinking functions' as identified by Jung. We saw how the mind-to-mind or personality-to-personality relationship is very much a psychological dimension of marketing. Adopting the emotional/psychological approach we might ask questions such as:

- What should it be like to work here?
- How can we motivate our people?
- What will capture the hearts and minds of our customers?
- How can we build better relationships with clients?
- What will it take for people to think of us as a friend?

Perhaps we should be more:

- caring and nurturing
- friendly
- sincere

- patriotic
- honest and open
- environmentally concerned

This is a more creative approach since you do not start necessarily with a specific problem. You use your imagination, seeing mental scenarios, using your intuitive feelings rather than cold, logical analysis.

Target user

The 'target user' approach attempts to gain a better understanding of target customer groups.

- How do people see themselves?
- What values do our customer groups have?
- How do they live their lives?
- What are their attitudes, interests, opinions?
- What kind of people do they like to be with, or want to be like?

Typical answers to these questions are:

- adventurous
- home-loving
- strong
- rugged
- independent
- sophisticated
- carefree
- trendy

Based on the principle that we like people who are like us, this strategy identifies the characteristics of the target market so that its personality can be emulated in your company.

Brainstorming

Sometimes it is better to start the process with a more open-ended approach which involves three tasks for group work:

TASK 1	In a brainstorming session, think of as many personality characteristics as you can. This can often generate more than 200.
TASK 2	Choose the top six or perhaps eight characteristics by which you would most like to describe your company in the future.
TASK 3	From that shortlist then agree on the three to five characteristics that the whole group can subscribe to and to which they can make a commitment.

The importance of a brainstorming approach is to ensure that 'way out' ideas get consideration and no-one's ideas are suppressed.

Any of these approaches can be used to consider the kind of personality you want for your business. Different approaches might well lead to the same conclusions. It's a matter of choosing the most acceptable, appropriate and non-threatening intervention that will lead to a good consensus result.

Personality checklist

An extensive list of typical personality characteristics is given in figure 4 at the end of this chapter. To aid discussion, this list can be used to narrow down a handful of meaningful characteristics for discussion and subsequent agreement.

Measuring personality performance
Start off by choosing a shortlist of common traits and place them in the matrix according to the two criteria axes. These placements will be subjective, of course, but will enable you to quickly arrive at those that need to be addressed.

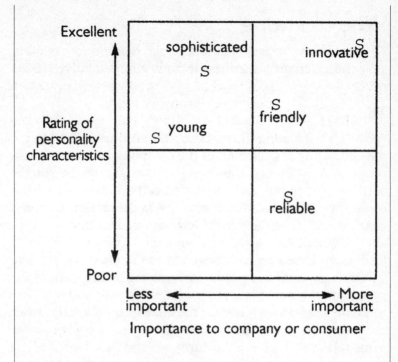

Figure 3 *Rating your corporate personality*

The matrix can also be used dynamically as a strategic planning tool. As well as plotting your current position, you can set goals for each trait and check over a period how you have succeeded in changing your perceived personality position. You can also use the technique to plot your main competitors' personality profile, and thus assess your own personality strengths and weaknesses relatively. The exercise can be part of your internal training when 'rolling out' the personality, and may be added to the specimen programme described in Chapter 6.

Who to involve

There are a few 'musts' for the selection of important personality characteristics, and these include who is involved in the process.

The CEO

At the risk of stating the obvious, it is absolutely vital to get the CEO and/or chairman of the company involved in this process. At the very least, their views should be sought because leadership style will shape the behaviour of the company and so affect its personality. In the case of powerful, charismatic CEOs, they might well impose their own personality, although this is not recommended as in the long term leadership is subject to change. At the other extreme some CEOs might not have particularly strong feelings about the personality characteristics themselves, but they will nonetheless have to nod their assent to the final list before any further work can take place. They will also have to commit resources to the relatively high expenditure involved. So whether or not the corporate personality reflects that of the incumbent leader, he or she will always be a main player upon which the success of any change will partly depend.

Senior Management

Having said this, it will have to be a team effort, involving, in particular, senior managers and directors. Although disagreements will inevitably arise, the end result will have to be gained through consensus and commitment. Involve all of the top management team, encouraging ownership. Whether you start with them or they become involved at a later stage, they must feel as though they have been part of the process, and their commitment to the outcome must be total. Those not convinced for one reason or another will act in a disruptive way and influence their key people, divisions or departments to work against the implementation process. That is human nature, and, however illogical, it is as well to take account of it.

The emphasis on the CEO and senior management is not to suggest that other staff are less important. Indeed, they have more actual contact with the customer. But it does reflect the fact that with their managerial leverage and control of resources they will have more chance of bringing about change.

Other staff

To get real staying power and common belief in the corporate personality, as many groups of people as possible should be included in the decision on characteristics. This can take time, money and a lot of effort but will be worth it. Alternative techniques include:

- questionnaires
- think-tanks
- workshops
- conferences
- task forces
- sampling employees' views by interview

Every employee will be an embodiment of the company's personality, whether actively or passively. The more interaction that staff have with customers, whether in person or on the telephone, the more critical they will be as links in the personality chain. Less visible staff will also contribute to the company's image by the quality of the products they produce, the standard of their work, and the culture their attitudes create.

Outside specialists

Outside agencies and consultants can also help in what can be a complex operation. It is particularly important to integrate outside advertising and brand specialists with the personality implementation strategy, preferably under the internal co-ordination of a very senior manager or the CEO. (Some specific guidance about using outside agencies is given in Chapter 6.)

How to achieve it

The process will be easier for a company that already communicates with and empowers its employees on strategic as well as minor operational matters. Otherwise expect cynicism and outright opposition. At worst, a planned programme that fully reflects your present culture will be needed. That is, start from where you are. It may be that you have to start communicating with staff before communicating with customers and the outside world. In any event, and this applies to the most progressive companies, do not underestimate the impact of a personality change strategy.

Avoid conflicting values

While going through the process, and certainly by the end of it, resolve any conflict between the new personality characteristics and old, existing values — whether explicit or implicit. Always check that the company vision or mission statements are in harmony with the new personality. If those statements, or any other communications that allude to values, are in conflict, the process must allow for debate and resolution of the issues. Usually the personality will add an important dimension to a vision statement already adopted.

Bring in the future

Make sure the characteristics reflect not only what people believe in but also what they envisage for the company in the future. Even if some of the characteristics are not yet evident, do not discourage this since it provides motivation for future improvement. However you proceed, there will always be a certain amount of political sensitivity, and this has got to be handled diplomatically. And everyone in the company must be made aware not only of what the personality is to be, and be committed to it, but also must be given the opportunity to translate this into what it means for them personally.

Client case studies

These real life case studies are ongoing and consequently the identities of the client companies have been withheld. These examples illustrate the scale of change often needed, the seriousness with which the strategy is treated, and the different approaches that personality strategy can take.

Company A

A relatively established Brand Management Unit was charged with establishing a strong 'platform' upon which all future corporate and product brand management activities could rest. Sessions were held over several weeks with around 100 senior managers to produce a list of sixteen to twenty proposed personality characteristics. The list was divided into 'probables' and 'possibles'; after debate, discussion and agreement, the 'probable' list eventually numbered seven.

On the basis of this list a corporate personality statement (and a positioning statement) was created and presented to the Management Committee for approval. Following this, over 100 product managers were briefed in two-day workshops to take them through the same process and introduce them to the new 'personality'. Currently, the company is in the process of doing the same for 3000 executives and 15,000 front-line staff. Plans are also outlined for a three to five-year programme of working through every department to apply these characteristics or values to work performance. This involves major investment and commitment, but is the key to the company's future.

Company B

A rapid sequence of takeovers of Stock Exchange listed companies by Company B gave rise to an urgent need to bring the new group together and present a unified image to various target audiences. These included government, regulating bodies, investors, shareholders, media, analysts and employees.

The short- and long-term solution was identified as a

personality issue. Core values were developed quickly with strategic planning personnel, and the management teams of the eleven subsidiary companies were quickly briefed and took part in discussions as to how these personality characteristics would now become part of a consistent Group Communications Strategy.

Company C
A large company with a somewhat tarnished image appointed a new CEO who, as well as moving swiftly in the first few months to redress the technical problems that caused the lack of consumer confidence, immediately understood the need to begin building a strategic corporate personality. He was involved right from the start and was present throughout the first session on the selection of characteristics with his twenty most senior executives.

Being a 'hands-on' type of leader, as well as being committed to success, he also attended subsequent sessions with over 100 senior managers, stressing that the selection of the desired personality characteristics was not final until everyone was agreed. Nor did he pre-empt the selection process by revealing what the senior group had come up with. As a result many views were accommodated before the eventual roll-out to every employee.

Company D
A financial services company new management team saw tremendous opportunities for business growth but recognised that the company had to be relaunched. The name was changed, as was the logo, and all the other corporate identity factors were put in place. But the company needed to be different not only in name but also in personality. Over a twelve-month period senior management created a new personality based on five core values, at the same time as the new vision of the company was finalised. A positioning statement was linked to a new mission, the company then having a completely new platform upon which to base all corporate communications. More and more managers were

involved over the twelve-month period, and many of the more junior levels of staff were asked for their contributions during a nationwide series of coaching skills sessions.

The eventual launch of the vision, mission, personality and positioning was a highly successful event to which all employees were invited, and the company is now embarking on a three-year programme of internal communications exercises:

- to show everyone how their job fits the personality
- to reinforce the vision and mission
- to extend communications to project the personality
- to create a new position in the nation's mind

The Avon turnaround

Any observer of the cosmetics company Avon will not fail to be impressed with the extent of their personality change in recent years. Throughout the 1980s they were under attack, not so profitable and out of touch with their customers. Avon had an old-fashioned, worn-out image, its products considered as 'yesterday's news', persisting with one-to-one sales calls made mainly on women at home. The fact that women were increasingly employed away from home hardly helped.

The world had moved on and the company's image did not mirror the contemporary woman they wanted to attract. Whilst it may well have had a sound corporate value-based culture, and large and competent human resources, it needed to rethink its direction, structure and personality. It had to change the perception of its customers and potential customers by repositioning.

It met the challenge head-on and set up strategies to restructure, removing regional HQs, decentralising decision-making, setting up franchises and providing top-class global support to every employee.

One of the things Avon learnt was that contemporary women wanted speed, convenience and flexibility. Multiple distribution channels were introduced and customers could order via fax or telephone, whether from home or office, with delivery to any destination. Customers also wanted more modern product lines, and global beauty brands were added along with clothing, gifts and costume jewellery. Joint ventures with major companies like Disney and Mattel gave Avon access to global brands, including the highly successful Barbie dolls.

All these changes increased Avon's competitiveness, and many new markets have been penetrated since. But the heart of all the changes was the question. 'Who are we?' The search for personality was all-important. Avon is clearly a 'woman's company' but their strategy has been to bring about a needed change of image. They now have a fuller personality:

- female
- friendly
- empathetic
- resourceful
- knowledgeable
- innovative
- contemporary
- 'on the move'
- a risk-taker
- confident
- slightly provocative

The first five of these were always Avon's strengths and they have clearly built on these while making the other changes. The final 'slightly provocative' trait is exemplified by the Avon USA advertising campaign which dares people to change their mind about Avon.

The result is a turnover approaching US $500 million. The success of their turnaround hinged on getting the personality identity and message right. In anything other than the very short term, competitive strength depended on such core changes.

The point here is that the vital image or perception change did not happen by accident. Major strategic changes had to be implemented and an ongoing management process installed. The extent of change will not always be so great, for in some cases tweaking of the personality message along with specific internal changes will do the trick. The important thing is to be aware of the importance of personality and the need to understand your customer.

How many characteristics?

Human beings are complex creatures, having differing values and exhibiting a wide range of personality traits. Some characteristics are even contradictory, and we all tend to change with circumstances, such as whether we are at home or at work, or even at different times of the day.

For corporate purposes such diversity is neither necessary nor possible. What is needed, rather, is a few key traits that can be clearly stated, understood and communicated. Some of the world's most powerful corporate and product personalities have just one or two, but focus heavily on them, such as Marlboro which consistently seems to project strength and independence. Just two or three personality characteristics have been enough for companies to build strong personalities in the past. Certainly, if you get into double figures you may have a problem communicating the personality with clarity and consistency.

In recent years, however, there has been a trend towards making corporate and product personalities a little closer to reality: richer, more complex, and to a great extent more intriguing. Levi 501s, for example, has seven items in its personality make-up:

- romance
- sexual attraction
- physical prowess
- rebellion
- resourcefulness
- independence
- being admired

As another example, Intel has six:

- risk-taking
- quality
- discipline
- customer-orientation
- results-orientation
- great place to work

Having several characteristics does give a company flexibility, in communicating with different target customer groups and adding variety to campaigns. For example, a personality might comprise:

1. reliable
2. caring
3. friendly
4. innovative
5. professional
6. ambitious

Depending on the business, marketing communications aimed at families might put emphasis on 1, 2 and 3, whilst those aimed at corporate and business customers might focus on 3, 4, 5 and 6. All six would be included for each audience but the stress should be placed where the expectations of the audience match the apposite characteristics.

The danger with multiple characteristics is seeming to be all things to all people. So the number and choice of personality characteristics may have to be a compromise between a simple, clear message and a reflection of a real, human personality.

Testing your understanding

Part of the implementation process is to test whether your corporate personality is clearly understood. This applies to employees, people outside the company, advertising agencies or whoever. One way of doing this is by playing the 'What if?' game. You can have some fun whilst seriously testing out people's views for consistency.

What if our company was:

- a car?
- a brand of clothing?
- an animal?
- a book?
- a film star?
- a tree?
- a place to live?
- a movie?
- a holiday destination?
- a type of food?

A place to live, for example, might be a thatched cottage or a lofty castle, a tree might be a wispy birch, weeping willow or an ancient, stately oak. These images can sometimes personify a company in a way that words cannot. There is no limit to the examples that can be used, and you can draw on nature, man-made artefacts, real or fictional characters as you wish. The point of the exercise is to test out consistency of thought by getting participants to match the personality to a different identity, and to understand their reasoning. (This is covered further in the training exercise at the end of Chapter 5.)

The group will have plenty of fun but the process will help to create the new company personality and suggest how it should be interpreted and communicated. The same process can also be applied to each of your close competitors, which adds an important dimension to competitive analysis.

The corporate personality statement

Once the characteristics have been chosen, most companies combine these in one or more sentences to describe the personality in a simple but coherent way. This provides a simple statement which can form the basis of a brief for advertising and PR agencies. It can also be the basis for any strategic change, such as acquisition or product diversification. As with the mission statement, although it is a long-term document, the company cannot be reminded of it too often.

Here are examples of personality statements.

1. ABC is a caring, friendly, and reliable person who prefers family life and old-fashioned values.
2. XYZ is a young, ambitious and contemporary person, who loves freedom and fun.
3. PQR is a visionary, innovative and intellectual person, who takes pride in being 'state-of-the-science' in his knowledge.

You will notice that the company is referred to as a person, and that there is no indication whatsoever of the kind of business it is in, what products and services it provides or what its aspirations are. This is to ensure that the personality is considered specifically and that each characteristic is stated clearly without any other messages interfering. Business-related characteristics are dealt with in the positioning statement (see Chapter 7) and are often covered in the company's vision and mission statements.

Differentiating personality

In many companies, the end result of the selection process might be four to six values or traits, and the question might be asked, 'How do these make us different? Many companies will probably choose the same.'

Just as people cherish similar values and display similar traits, so there might be many things in common between companies. But it is how these are combined that makes each company different.

The skill (and it is a skill) of projecting a unique corporate personality is to combine these characteristics into creative forms of persuasion positioned to different target audiences. The creativity lies in putting across the same values and traits in ways to appeal to sense and intuition as well as logic, using symbols, metaphors, stories and so on.

To differentiate yourself you will consistently embrace the same values but powerfully project your personality in what you say and do. Some companies start out with values then jump around in their advertising and PR. Not many companies have the discipline to stick to their values year in, year out. If you finish up with the same traits as a competitor, your competitive edge will be in how you *project* your personality, and how you support it in every aspect of your actual performance. Your personality communication will be differentiated by creative ways to reach your customers' minds, while your performance will be down to quality control and consistency.

There is also the importance of focus and degree. Certain values and traits might be highly visible and others more subtly introduced and communicated. It's what the public see that counts, and just as every person in the world is unique, in the same way there are unlimited opportunities for companies to apply and communicate their unique blend of personality traits. Think of how many tunes can be created by combining a relatively small number of notes. But, conversely, don't act out of character; don't play classical tunes today and next month, punk rock. The corporate world is awash with split personalities.

Multiple personalities and target audiences

The differentiation process is likely to raise important questions. Can we be all things to all people? Should we change our personality to suit different customer types? It can be argued that a personality should not be changed. Human personality tends not to change except due to trauma such as an accident or serious illness. It is otherwise remarkably resilient and consistent, and corporate personality should be equally so. Keep changing your personality and people will no longer view you as normal. Their trust and confidence will disappear. Multiple personalities are the corporate equivalent of schizophrenia. If you want customers to be friends, act consistently as a friend would.

On the other hand there is a case for presenting different personalities to different types of consumer. It can also be argued that people can be different in themselves, having many 'parts' to their make-up. For example a man who seems quite extrovert, energetic and aggressive at work, at home may be more introverted, calm and relaxed. Using this approach people will understand if you change a bit because they do too, and their personalities are multi-faceted. There are a few simple principles to remember when making personality decisions:

1. Consistency has been a characteristic of the personality for most of the world's top companies and brands.
2. Human personalities, when they do change, change only slowly, evolving over time so that any change goes unnoticed. In the same way, corporate personality should not be perceived to change. The essence of a strong personality is that your behaviour might change from time to time (hopefully for the better) but not in a way that is *out of character*.
3. People sometimes have aspects of their personality that need expression, and these are not always obvious. A corporate personality, therefore, might appeal to more than the obvious customer group. Even conservative, conformist people have a little of the 'rebel' inside them. You may not really be a bike rider, but when you see (and hear) someone riding a Harley Davidson you may feel you want to do it. We each have an inner world of dreams and aspirations in which emotions are easily stirred. We sometimes act out our dreams and fantasies. Personality can

appeal to these needs for personal expression.

4. What matters is whether or not the personality is strong enough — for whatever the reason — to attract people to buy.

5. A better understanding of potential market segments might allow the personality to be offered in different ways (this is an aspect of positioning, covered in Chapter 7). This might be achieved by psychographic analysis (understanding people's attitudes, interests, opinions, etc.) or alternatively by studying when and where they choose to get involved with the personality (lifestyles, behaviour patterns, etc.).

6. Different people might see the same personality but have a different attitude towards it, so be careful not to alienate them. The Visa (credit card) personality of the confident, higher income, educated, fashion conscious world traveller may appeal to many people who empathise with such an image. But more cautious, conservative, careful spenders from lower income groups may resent the personality and all it stands for. Mastercard's 'Smart Money' positioning appealed to a different customer attitude to Visa's 'We're everywhere you want to be'. Get to know what your customer thinks.

7. Presenting a non-contentious personality helps with a person's 'self-select' mechanism. Coca-Cola in recent times has used this approach by varying personality commercials so that a person can select the one that appeals most.

8. If in doubt about anything whatsoever, you can always fall back on the question 'Would you introduce this person to your sister?' Personalities have to be likeable.

Who needs a personality?

Corporate personality is usually illustrated by large, household-name corporations, or their global products. This can be misleading, for lesser-known and small businesses can also benefit from a strong identity. In fact, one of the few ways in which smaller or newer companies can stand out against market leaders is to acquire a unique, marketable personality.

A world-class company need not be global, nor need it be large. Being world class in quality, service, or innovation, you can become as well known as a corporate giant. Your USP is your special personality, present in every aspect of your strategy and operations.

Personality strategy and non-profit organisations

To counterbalance the household-name companies we have quoted, we will use the example of a non-profit organisation to illustrate not only how widely a personality strategy can apply, but also how amenable the process is to creative thinking. Based on a suggestion by Joe Marconi in his *Image Marketing*, here is what the armed forces might consider:

1. Show the best of what you do well. Recruiting officers like to promise career training so why not have testimonials and profiles of people who learned valuable skills which they have used to launch successful careers in private life? Or show what the military does well in times of disaster relief and other peacetime public services. Don't assume the world is aware of your strengths.
2. Dispel myths and misconceptions. How do you justify a large peacetime defence budget? Super-power deterrent? World policing/foreign policy? Anti-terrorist ability? What are the public's perceptions? If they are misconceptions or myths, communicate the reality, clearly and consistently.
3. Tell the public why it should be supportive. Show them the benefits. Let them know how their lives are affected. Again, don't assume support or respect without earning it.
4. Get a good spokesperson. Passing the buck or stonewalling will not endear your customers, whoever they are. Find a person who, as well as being

articulate and convincing, reflects the personality you want to get across. There are risks, of course, but a human being can be forgiven the odd mistake when a faceless institution would only antagonise.

Any of this advice could be adapted to your own company or organisation. It shows that you don't change perceptions just by throwing money at the problem. On the other hand you may have to spend moderately to maintain your image even when things are going well. Positive public perception is an invaluable asset that has to be painstakingly maintained. The process is more 'persistence' than 'quick fix', demanding a consistent unequivocal message and actions to support it — in short, good personality management.

Group exercise

Assessing personality characteristics

Take a look (below) at the list of companies and products and the personalities they may arguably appear to project. Check these against your own idea of the companies or products or of the general market awareness as you know it. This will test whether the *image* they are intending to project is communicated successfully. Secondly, and this will be possible if you have direct experience of dealing with them, does their image reflect their true personality based on your own experience or that of your colleagues? Does your perception conform to their message? Put another way, does their intended image reflect their true personality?

It may be that, on a continuum, a company fulfils its intended personality or, at the other extreme, fails completely to conform to it. Have a go at rating the companies on a scale of zero to five, where five means they fully succeed. On the other hand there may be one or more *elements* of the personality which fall short of your perception, such as 'friendliness' or 'sincerity'. You can also identify these, which will no doubt have influenced your earlier company rating. Identifying the problem elements will indicate where changes have to be made, such as in specific aspects of customer service or quality.

Federal Express	Fast mover, friendly, very reliable
General Electric	Self-confident, likes to keep things simple, a leader
Marlboro	Strength, independence
McDonald's	Friendly, fun-loving, dependable
Harley Davidson	Freedom, patriotism, heritage, macho, male
Nike	Athletic, outdoors, self-improvement, determined, ambitious
Kodak	Sincere, family person
Hallmark	Sincere, warm, friendly
Nestlé Milo	Healthy and energetic, a winner
Levi 501s	Romance, sexual attraction, physical prowess, resourceful, rebellious, independence, being admired
3M	Innovator
Intel	Risk-taker, disciplined, reliable
Disney	Polite, kind, friendly, helpful, likes fun, a 'be happy' person
Mars	Energy, enthusiasm, activity, excitement
Jaguar	Professional, stylish, ambitious
Marks & Spencer	Middle-class, family-oriented, careful planner of purchases, looks for value and quality
Rolls Royce	Successful, aloof, status-conscious, older person, always the best dressed
Tag Heuer	Adventurous, outdoors, sporty, brave, self-disciplined, achiever
Apple Computers	Non-conformist, friendly, creative
Absolut Vodka	Young, trendy, male, creative, professional
Volvo	Trustworthy, reliable, conservative, family-oriented

Swatch	Fun-loving, stylish, young, individualistic, contemporary
Häagen-Dazs	Sensual, affluent, sophisticated, self-indulgent, likes life's pleasures
Raffles Hotel, Singapore	Mature, artistic, aristocratic, rich
Savoy Hotel, London	Experienced, dignified, elegant, successful

By applying the same rigour to your own company's personality strategy you will gain insights into what has to be changed, whether in actual production or service standards or in the personality message you are trying to communicate.

Summary

1. There are six basic approaches to determining which personality characteristics are right for your company:

   - Aspiration
   - Problem solution
   - Emotional/psychological
   - Target user
   - Brainstorming
   - Checklist

2. When it comes to finalising the list of personality characteristics as many people as possible should be involved, including the CEO, senior management, unit heads and other levels of employees, and outside agencies.
3. To achieve a strong personality avoid conflicting values and reflect also future aspirations.
4. There is no right answer to the question 'How many characteristics should we have?' but seven or eight seems to be the limit. After that things get confused and the personality becomes hard to project.
5. The corporate personality statement will comprise few words, but will be of long-term value.
6. You can test your understanding of your present company's personality by asking metaphorical 'What if' questions.

7. You can differentiate your company by the mix of personality characteristics you choose and by the creative ways in which you project these into the minds of your customers.

8. Just as human personalities change slowly over time, once a company starts to project a personality, it should do so consistently. After consistency, *appropriate* is the key word. Nothing the company says or does should seem out of character.

9. Any organisation or group, profit-making or otherwise, can benefit from a corporate personality. It may be even more effective for a lesser known company.

Figure 4 Personality characteristics

Accomplished	Cuddly	Global	Obliging	Self confident
Able	Cunning	Gregarious	Observant	Seductive
Accurate	Cute	Good	Open	Selfish
Active	Daring	Gorgeous	Optimistic	Sensational
Adaptable	Decisive	Graceful	Orderly	Serious
Adventurous	Dedicated	Great	Patient	Sexy
Aggressive	Demanding	Groovy	Peaceful	Sharing
Amenable	Desirable	Happy	Perfectionist	Shy
Ambitious	Detailed	Hardworking	Persevering	Simple
Approachable	Determined	Healthy	Persistent	Sincere
Assertive	Diligent	High class	Playful	Smart
Attentive	Direct	High performer	Pleasant	Small
Attractive	Disciplined	High tech	Polished	Soft
Balanced	Discriminating	Honest	Polite	Solid
Beautiful	Dominant	Humble	Positive	Sophisticated
Believable	Dynamic	Humorous	Posh	Special
Benevolent	Eccentric	Ideal	Practical	Striking
Big	Efficient	Imaginative	Precise	Swanky
Bold	Elegant	Important	Proactive	Swift
Brave	Elite	In control	Productive	Superb
Bright	Entrepreneurial	Independent	Professional	Supportive
Brilliant	Emotional	Intellectual	Profitable	Sure
Calm	Emphatic	Intelligent	Prolific	Tactful
Capable	Endearing	Jolly	Pragmatic	Talkative
Captivating	Energetic	Just	Proud	Team spirited
Caring	Enquiring	Kind	Punctual	Thoughtful
Charismatic	Enthusiastic	Knowledgeable	Qualified	Thrifty
Charitable	Expert	Leading	Quality	Timid
Charming	Exploring	Lifetime	Quiet	Tough
Cheerful	Extraordinary	Light hearted	Racy	Traditional
Classy	Extrovert	Lively	Rational	Transparent
Clean	Fair	Loner	Reasonable	Trendy
Commendable	Fast	Lovely	Rebellious	Trustworthy
Communicative	Feminine	Lovable	Refined	Truthful
Competent	Focused	Loyal	Reflective	True
Concerned	Flamboyant	Macho	Regal	Understanding
Confident	Flashy	Magnificent	Reliable	Understating
Conservative	Flexible	Manly	Religious	Vigorous
Consistent	Fluent	Masculine	Resilient	Visionary
Constructive	Forward-looking	Mature	Responsible	Warm
Cool	Friendly	Modern	Responsive	Well mannered
Co-operative	Futuristic	Modest	Rich	Youthful
Courteous	Generous	Motherly	Raunchy	Young
Courageous	Gentle	Motivated	Romantic	Winning
Crazy	Gigantic	Nurturing	Rough	Wise
Creative	Glamorous	Objective	Safe	World class

CHAPTER FIVE

ROLLING OUT PERSONALITY

To create a corporate personality you will have to accomplish a number of things that will mean change at every level of the organisation. In particular, the culture of the company may need to change, and this is addressed in this chapter. You will need to translate your personality into real behaviour on the part of staff throughout the company, and initiate strategies for each personality characteristic you want to adapt and project. This chapter also covers these internal, practical aspects of rolling out the personality, including training and internal communication.

Corporate culture

Corporate culture has been a topic of interest and much discussion over the last twenty years or so. Culture can be likened to the mortar that keeps the bricks of a corporate structure, its systems and people, together. Culture, as we saw in Chapter 1, is 'How we do things round here'. Many companies now have elaborate training and awareness programmes that seek to shape or transform the existing culture of the organisation into one which hopefully will be more appropriate to the future. At the heart of this is the fact that a coherent culture helps to promote both efficiency and profitability.

Corporate culture is closely linked to corporate personality. It is so powerful that it can make it happen or prevent it from happening. The culture of a company is concerned with values, beliefs, attitudes and established behaviours. It will determine how the company is perceived from outside as well as inside, and be the very foundation of its personality.

Changing culture through personality

Conversely, creating and implementing a new corporate personality can be used as a vehicle for changing culture, one which culture intervention consultants do not appear to have paid much attention to. In fact, a new corporate personality is potentially a much easier and faster way of getting employees to buy in to the change process. It is seen as much less of a threat to individuals and jobs, more practical and less academic than trying to influence people by talking about change and culture concepts which are often misunderstood and feared by employees. Staff can see the commercial sense of the changes, and the company's personification in the form of advertising and promotion. The personality becomes visible, and relates to sales results as customers are attracted to it.

Personality is the identity of the company which hopefully translates into a corresponding image, which is what the customer sees or perceives. The culture is the way the company lives out *internally* its personality and attitudes in real behaviour. Although internal to the company, culture is far from invisible, and behaviour and attitudes spill over into every customer or other outside contact.

Rolling out the personality

Clarification and definition

Having established the personality characteristics, what comes next? Getting personality characteristics articulated is one thing, but getting them understood is another. It is important to clarify what they mean and this process must be carried out at two levels.

At an overall corporate level with generic descriptions of what the characteristics mean, so that managers and staff strive towards and become the desired personality. No less important, through a single corporate voice, advertising and public relations agencies can be thoroughly briefed for all their future activities.

At a job-specific level. Everyone in the company, sooner or later, has to know what each value or characteristic means for their particular job. How will it affect their behaviour? How should their attitudes change? For instance, a value of 'caring' will have vastly different implications for a front line sales person as compared to a backroom technical support person. Similarly 'product quality' or 'creativity' will translate into different actions on the part of different categories of staff. Job- and task-level objectives have to be set and performance measured and rewarded. This level of scope and detail is essential if the organisation is to behave consistently.

Defining the elements of corporate personality can give the company greater vision and focus. It can lead to rapid identification of real areas for improvement, whether strategic or operational. The characteristic of 'reliability', for example, can lead to a host of specific actions that will benefit consumers and build up the business. Like a rocket firework that explodes after launch into several stars, each characteristic breaks into other characteristics, and these tend to be increasingly behaviour-specific and practicable. Disney's personality characteristic of 'courtesy', for example, breaks down into 'polite', 'friendly', 'cheerful' and 'helpful'. At this level personality turns into performance. Sooner or later personality and actions have to be congruent if a long-term image is to be created.

Strategies for each personality item

Some companies spend a lot of time encouraging employees to do their best in their jobs to make the personality 'come alive' so that consumers will see the difference. Typically such programmes are addressed at lower-level staff, who are more likely to come into direct contact with customers. Whilst doing this it is all too easy for them to forget that the company at a strategic level has to plan how it is going to demonstrate commitment to each aspect of the personality.

The CEO and top and senior management will act as examples to their staff if they demonstrate that thought has led to genuine action at a corporate level. Top management must ensure that the right questions are asked:

What does this personality item mean for the company?
How do we start to make it happen?
What main strategy can be the means of delivery on this?
What specific actions are necessary for us to demonstrate company commitment to this item?

Starting from the CEO, managers have the responsibility to turn these questions into strategies then action in order to 'deliver' the desired personality items. 3M, for example, makes its characteristic of 'innovative' happen by ensuring at budget time that 25 per cent of next-year sales come from products introduced within the previous five years.

Corporate behaviour

It is important to turn personality characteristics into strategies and appropriate behaviour. Whatever we say or do affects other people's views of us. So it is with companies — consumers perceive them to be a certain type depending on what they see, hear, and experience. Quite simply, bad behaviour gives rise to a bad image and a poor relationship. The following list shows examples of corporate behaviour, and the possible personality that the customer perceives. It will remind you of the kinds of activity that can influence consumer perception and the strength of the relationship and loyalty between a company and its customers or potential customers.

Corporate behaviour	Possible perceived personality
Lots of promotions and discount campaigns	Unsophisticated, inferiority complex
Lots of advertising up-market	Extrovert, confident,
Glossy advertising	Snobbish, rich
Premium pricing	Classy, sophisticated, somewhat aloof
Consistency of logos, lettering, design, written communications, etc.	Reliable, trustworthy
Inconsistency of these	Changeable, shifty
Local sponsorships and community projects	Friendly, sensitive, caring
Mass, non-exclusive distribution	Roamer, 'Wherever I lay my hat . . .'
Exclusive, limited distribution	Concerned, principled
Promises not delivered	Cheat, untrustworthy
Good customer service	Caring
Poor customer service	Heartless

Don't forget that the personality you wish to project has to be supported by congruent behaviour. Whether or not you have a personality strategy you will always create some image in the minds of your customers. One way or another a personality will emerge. It is best to manage this as part of your overall strategy.

Internal and external customers

Both internal and external customers must be considered when defining personality characteristics. It is well known that service levels and relationships for and with external customers are unlikely to be any better that those that operate between departments and units within the company. This may involve structural changes, in which divisions and departments act in a quasi supplier-customer relationship. Systems and detailed job specifications will also have to support any changes. But at the heart of any personality changes will be attitudes, so communication initiatives and specialised attitudinal training will be critical. Equally important will be the example set by managers previously aligned to functions and departments. Professional and 'political' alliances will be challenged along with any obstacles that are not consistent with the desired personality. Major internal changes are usually needed when a single, unique personality strategy is pursued. For example, it may require better quality control procedures or customer service standards to achieve the desired values. Training programmes may be needed to achieve the staff calibre that the new personality characteristics demand. If staff are to be empowered to a far greater level, it will require both structural and systems changes. Typically, self-managing teams are established to achieve the new levels of quality and customer response.

Quality standards and other helpful data

If your company has gone through any significant programmes recently such as quality management or business process re-engineering, there may be a lot of helpful data available to help define which personality characteristics should apply to systems and individual staff practice. This is particularly important in the case of characteristics with operational implications, such as 'reliable', where data exist for delivery and installation times, customer service levels, etc.

The role of training

To create or change an individual personality through training is something most people would reject. This is not to suggest that our personalities never change, such as following major changes in circumstances, but that the process is not one which is amenable to training as we know it. 'We are what we are', referring to our unique characters, is a more common point of view. But the analogy is limited and the corporate process is more synthetic.

To start with, hundreds or perhaps thousands of people will need to reflect a single corporate personality. And not every individual will naturally embrace the chosen character-istics. For example, not every person is a natural innovator or would consider themselves conservative or daring in nature, characteristics which the company may well wish to espouse and communicate through its staff. However, people can change their *behaviour* and that is indeed amenable to train-ing.

At the overall corporate level short training courses brief all employees on the new corporate personality. These should instil why and how it has been developed, what it means for the company, and in general how each member of the staff can play their special part in bringing that personality to life. At the end of this chapter a specific training programme outline and explanation is given which has been used successfully with several companies.

At a more job-specific level, training workshops are usually the medium used for helping departments, units, and indi-viduals recognise what each personality characteristic means for their jobs and how they can be defined and implemented at these levels.

Companies that are serious about the personality creation process, and really believe in the characteristics they have identified, do not hesitate to spend large amounts of time and money to make sure that all their staff understand and 'live' the personality. Dupont, for instance, believes so strongly in the value of innovation that all 28,000 or so of its employees enjoy a training programme specifically on this issue. This supports their belief that everyone in the organisation — from cleaner to CEO — can and should be able to contribute ideas and make a culture of innovation happen. The training is not just a communication or appreciation programme, but involves training in specific, state-of-the-art techniques to stimulate creativity.

Personality is more than an add-on. It is central to the business and the company's future, and this should be reflected in both management commitment and training investment. Perhaps no company is as experienced and well known for instilling corporate values and personality characteristics into its employees as the Disney Corporation. Disney has a wonderfully short and clear mission — 'To make people happy' — and they really do. But this is no accident: all of their employees are trained from day one at Disney University on the Traditions 1 training programme as to what their individual roles are in living the Disney personality. They are not even called employees, but 'cast members', another reminder of the fact that even 'backstage', they have a role to play in the 'show'. With appropriate training, such obsessive personality devotion is bound to translate into results.

Nor are such examples confined to the West. In Asia, one of the telecommunications giants has established a new corporate personality with seven characteristics. It currently is mounting nearly 800 two-day training courses over nine months to ensure that 18,000 employees go through the process of personality creation and understand what the personality is, what it means, and how it will be implemented. Further programmes are already being planned at job-specific levels and a corporate personality video reinforces company commitment. Appropriate training is central to rolling out the personality.

Staff recognition for 'living' the personality

Few companies recognise people who, having been trained, deliver high-level performance *related to values and personality*. Recognition and reward systems are usually related to numbers and readily quantifiable performance rather than values and attitudes which are more difficult to monitor and evaluate.

'That's what we pay them for' and 'They will expect more'

are commonly heard excuses. 'Give the team something or they'll be upset' is another approach to recognition and reward. The best companies, however, know well that *recognition* generates pride in the individual and motivates others who witness it to achieve similar things. Your company can do simple things which mean a lot:

- 'Personality of the month' awards for good corporate personality behaviour
- certificates representing certain personality characteristics
- CEO Awards for overall excellent personality behaviour
- team and Departmental Awards if everyone in the group really deserves them
- publicity in corporate newsletters and magazines, and features in trade and professional journals
- special recognition when customers report outstanding service from an individual employee

Companies like Levi Strauss give both financial and 'psychic' recognition. To the people who receive these awards it is not the actual certificate or letter they receive that is important. Rather, it is the fact that they have been noticed and recognised that motivates them. Putting your people first will help you to put the customer first because the customers will inevitably get the benefit. Some companies, such as General Electric, tie values/personality performance into appraisal systems to prove they are serious about it. While values and attitude are more difficult to evaluate than number-based results, they are a far better long-term staff investment. Increasingly, personality characteristics are being translated into 'quality' behaviour that can have a remarkable effect on customers' perceptions of the company.

Summary

1. Corporate culture is closely linked to corporate personality.
2. Corporate culture reflects values, beliefs and attitudes that are deeply embedded in your organisation.

3. Implementing corporate personality might be difficult if the personality characteristics are very different to the cultural values. The existing culture will either help or hinder.
4. Creating and implementing corporate personality can be used to change a company's culture.
5. Personality values and characteristics must be clearly defined both at an overall corporate level, and at a job specific level. People have to be made aware of the characteristics and also be able to apply them to their jobs.
6. Strategies have to be developed for each personality characteristic.
7. Recognition systems are vital to the success of a corporate personality roll-out.
8. Constant reinforcement activities are necessary to maintain the personality, and to make sure that customers experience that personality in every encounter they have with the company.

Corporate personality training programme

This programme can be used in two ways:

1. To involve groups of people at various levels in eliciting the personality characteristics they desire in the company.
2. To brief employees about the 'new personality' of the company by taking them through the process that has been used to develop it.

In its basic format it is a one- or two-day programme. The format is, however, adaptable and is capable of expansion to become a five-day training-of-trainers type programme for those companies who wish to create an in-house capability for training/briefing large numbers of staff.

Introduction

The introduction should concentrate on explaining that world class companies always develop good corporate images. With a good corporate image, it becomes easier to not only retain your existing customers but acquire new ones too.

Developing a strong, attractive corporate image depends on two things:

1. Having a powerful, likeable *personality*
2. Establishing this in the minds of people you want to identify with it

As an ice-breaking exercise ask participants in groups to list those companies and products they think are famous all over the world, and words they would use to describe them. The results should be recorded to link to later exercises.

Session I

What is corporate personality? Why is it important?

Here the course leader will explain what 'personality' includes, emphasising:

- Values, e.g. honesty, dependability
- Behavioural traits, e.g. confidence, creativity

But we all have both and both are important. Values we don't often see, behavioural traits we do.

The company vision, mission, and current values can be brought in here. The course leader can refer to Chapter 1 for more input on the link between values, mission and vision. Also, material from Chapters 1 to 3 can be used to explain:

- why personality is important
- what the psychology behind it is

Session 2

Creating a corporate personality

The course leader should choose one approach to determine corporate personality from those given in Chapter 3. Choose whichever one is most appropriate to company needs at present if you are trying to create a personality. If you are briefing/training people in what has already been created as the corporate personality, use the same approach as was used in that process.

The exercise here is to give groups the opportunity to answer the questions of the relevant approach.

It is very important that you frame the exercise so that the respondents give their answers in terms of *personality characteristics* as shown in the Chapter 3 examples. Don't get side-tracked into discussing all the company's problems.

The outcome of this exercise, however you get to it, should be a firm consensus on no more than six to eight *personality characteristics*. Everyone should agree that these will form the basis of how they would like the company to be seen 'as a person' in the future. This stage is vital. Half-hearted agreements will not suffice.

If the personality has been decided already, and it has been done properly, there should not be much dissonance between what this group thinks and what others have suggested. If there is disagreement it has to be sorted out, particularly if the characteristics chosen now are greatly different from those of before. This is a test which must be passed. A re-think may be required, or alternatively culture and performance changes may be needed to match the chosen personality characteristics.

If no personality has yet been decided, assure participants that their views will be taken forward to the next stage where other groups will be matched with them, and a final consensus decision made. The aim is for all staff to 'own' the personality.

Session 3

Our corporate personality

This session is relevant to training/briefing sessions when there is no dissonance between the personality of the company and those characteristics selected by present participants. If there are no major differences, the new corporate personality should be revealed together with the thinking behind it. The session concludes by getting participants to write a corporate personality statement — one or two sentences incorporating all the characteristics in a meaningful way.

Session 4

What if . . .?

This is an enjoyable session in which groups answer the following questions:

What if our company (i.e. our corporate personality) were:

- an animal
- a car
- a place to live
- a holiday destination
- a film star/entertainer
- a type of food

The idea behind this is to test the consistency of thinking and understanding of what the corporate personality means.

Remind participants that they have to name actual things that most closely resemble the personality and as many of its characteristics as possible.

e.g.   If the company was a car what would it be? (Honda Accord? Mercedes 230? Volvo 850?)

e.g.   If an animal? (cheetah? rabbit? dog?)

They must justify their answers, and this should provoke valuable discussion about what customers think and how their perceptions can be changed.

The final explanation by the trainer will cover the fact that these are the kinds of questions we might ask when considering creative advertising. When TV commercials are produced, they may contain cars, locations, animals etc. The big question is — are these metaphors appropriate to the personality of the company?

Session 5

The next step — positioning

The course leader should explain here what positioning is, and why it is important. Chapter 7 gives various approaches and examples.

Session 6

Writing a positioning statement

Here you should get the participants in their groups to write a positioning statement for your company. The elements of a positioning statement are given in Chapter 7, and they should follow these rules. This is not an easy exercise and you will need to help them a lot. The outcome need not be a masterpiece, but should serve as a means to helping them to understand the corporate positioning statement. Even if they do not reach consensus the process is valuable and it may suggest the need for re-positioning or some change in the company's behaviour or the message you project.

Session 7

Our corporate positioning

Show them the positioning of the company and allow discussion.

Session 8

Examples of personality and positioning in media

advertisements

In this session participants are shown recordings of selected advertisements from television commercials and asked to answer the following questions in their groups:

- What is the target audience?
- Can you see any corporate values coming through in the ads?
- Is there a corporate or product personality evident?
- What are the key messages?
- What positioning strategy is being used?

Select four or five commercials containing at least one good example (where the answers are not difficult), one poor one (where there is confusion) and one in-between. Such a selection is not a problem in most countries of the world!

Session 9

Corporate advertising

This session is your opportunity either to tell them what you are going to do in terms of advertising/public relations to project the corporate personality and position it correctly or to show them what you have already created or executed. It is extremely important that whatever you show here clearly relates to the personality characteristics and positioning already chosen. If there are agencies already involved, this is the time to invite them into the programme to let them explain how they turned their Personality/Positioning brief into creative execution. Get them to explain what the results have been in terms of consumer perception or, if the advertisements are relatively new, how they intend to measure the reaction.

Session 10

The implications of corporate personality for our work

In this session, there needs to be an outline given of how the company is attempting to 'live' the personality. If possible, give participants examples of what the company is doing to create strategies for personality characteristics — how it is trying to deliver on the values and promises of the personality.

This is also a good time to get participants to consider what the new corporate personality means for their jobs and jobs of people who work under them. This session can last a whole day, particularly if you have reasonably senior people on the programme who are responsible for substantial employee groupings. However, even if the participants have less responsibility, you can still get them to focus on what the personality characteristics mean to their jobs and how they can do things differently to make their work more like that of the 'person'. It is particularly important that this exercise is developed with *all* staff who deal with customers, and all those who influence, in one way or another, customer relationships.

There may be a timing problem here in so far as it may be inappropriate to start advertising without the everyday behaviour living up to the promise of the personality. Emphasise the need to change behaviour immediately wherever necessary. Even without detailed job descriptions staff can usually 'integrate' a personality characteristic into their job. Individual discretion and initiative should be encouraged culturally if a strong personality is to be created. This is an opportunity to rectify a 'who to blame' culture.

Chapters 6 and 7 are of relevance here, and the session should end with group and/or individual action plans for personality implementation.

Conclusion

The programme will not close before answering any outstanding questions relevant to the subject matter, but it should also review the benefits of corporate personality. So address why personality is needed, and what benefits it will bring to everyone — customers, staff and suppliers alike.

Finally, the course leader should outline further activities or further follow-up sessions that the company is planning in order to make the personality come alive.

CHAPTER SIX

COMMUNICATING CHARISMA

A corporate personality strategy includes everything you need to do to create or change your identity, and how you communicate it internally, but it also includes how you will project your personality to the outside world. In the previous chapter we gave a blueprint for internal communication through training, briefing sessions, newsletters, competitions and the like. In this chapter we address the various ways in which you can project your corporate personality successfully to the outside world, how to choose an agent, and how to choose 'target publics'.

Personality affects the whole company and, by its very nature, is too important to be done at anything other than a corporate level. Personality strategy has got to be kept in the context of your overall marketing effort. Besides being championed from the top it has to have the support of the marketing people, being part of the marketing concept and drawing necessarily on extensive internal resources, whatever outside help is sought. A good discipline is to go back to your marketing plan and re-think it with your new focus on personality. A short synopsis of the elements of a marketing plan are given below as a checklist, and as a reminder to consider corporate personality at each phase or from each aspect.

It is equally important to align your image and true corporate identity. That is, this is not just an image-making exercise, but you are creating a real identity — a personality. The aim of a personality strategy is then to change your personality where necessary, for example in behaviour, performance standards and staff attitudes, and then to successfully project that new 'you' in the market place.

The marketing plan

To ensure that you stay in harmony with your total marketing effort, the marketing plan provides a good discipline and checklist, each point having an impact on your corporate personality and how you project it:

Situation analysis
What is your situation according to your knowledge and what your research tells you?
What are the market segment trends?
What market segments look attractive apart from those you are serving?
What are the needs and wants of customers in each segment?

Objective
What are your goals, desires and aspirations?
What does your research tell you you need to accomplish that may not be included in your own objectives statement?
Classify as qualitative (e.g. personality acceptance, image) and quantitative (e.g. market share).

Strategy
What strategy will best fulfil your objectives?

Tactics
What tactics need to be employed to implement your strategy?

Timescale
How long will it take? Is this realistic?

Budget
How much will it cost? Is this realistic to fund your strategy to meet your objectives within your timescale?

Image and identity

People might like what they see, but if they don't experience this as consumers, interacting physically with the company through actual products and services, they will soon become disillusioned. This means that you must align your company's image with your true personality, both by your internal culture and your behaviour to the customer. Moreover, you must continually test out consumer perceptions which may change with every product or services encounter.

External communications

A company has to project its personality and a lot of money can be wasted if this is not done well. There are several examples of brilliant communication campaigns but thousands of examples of poorly executed ones. To stress again the importance of personality, even though some had exceptional products, many of these companies are no longer in existence.

It is difficult to develop a highly effective communication programme that is perceived as different. It needs to effectively compete with all the other campaigns and programmes that are bombarding the consumer every day. There is no 'quick fix' answer to this, nor does it depend on the amount of money you throw at it. Your personality needs to stand out from the crowd through unique, creative strategies, through making all your communications activities consistent and appropriate.

In considering the various types of communication that will affect customers and others outside the company, communication is used here in its broadest sense. You can communicate values, for instance, by the quality of your products and dependability, as well as in the spoken and written messages you address to customers.

Whatever the medium of communication used, be it advertising, public relations, events, promotions, exhibitions, direct marketing, or personal selling, the message must be consistent in reflecting one personality. You have to speak with one voice. It is tempting to think of advertising as the main medium of getting the message across, but the fact is that your personality is communicated in many ways, whether actively or passively, intentionally or unintentionally. You cannot *not* communicate your personality — it will always be perceived in some way, however different to your own belief and intention.

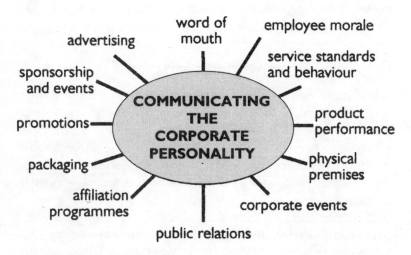

Figure 5 *Communicating the corporate personality*

Word of mouth

What every employee says to family, friends, customers or competitors will communicate the corporate personality. As first line ambassadors it is vital that staff reflect a good opinion of the 'person' they work for. Even if things are not perfect, if staff have been involved in the personality creation or change process they will 'own' the personality and seek to live it out. If they do not, a lot of damage can be done. Their inside knowledge of the company has credibility so they can strongly influence people for better or worse, intentionally or unintentionally. Training and briefings can help here, but the bottom line is that everyone really has to try to be that 'person' that the company is trying to promote. This is as much to do with attitude as actual behaviour, which is where training and briefings should be directed.

Employee morale

This is closely linked to 'word of mouth' above. If employee morale is low, the prevailing culture will work against the desired result. Standards of behaviour at work will also suffer, along with output and quality. So if you want to be young, different and friendly like Apple, flexitime and coming to work in casual dress may be important. A more professional IBM-like image will require different dress and different behaviour. Either way, the staff must do its part and live out the personality. All this should be built on a culture of genuine regard for staff and empowerment, rather than be imposed for the sake of a desired image. Staff will usually be proud to subscribe to a strong corporate personality and their morale will reflect this. In any event, you cannot fake morale, nor can you confine it to the company premises. As well as attracting customers, high morale means that each employee, without really trying, becomes an effective salesperson. Good people are attracted to the company so that the virtuous circle continues. A strong, unique personality — as was the case in the early days in IBM and Apple — is an extraordinary phenomenon for staff, suppliers and customers alike and a major factor in high growth.

Service standards and behaviours

Staff have to 'live' the personality. If the personality is 'reliable', the company and its people must be reliable. Service standards and behaviour must also deliver, just as the 'person' would. We soon become known for punctuality, faithfulness, integrity and so on, and establish a reputation. Thereafter, even if we fall short of our own standards people tend to make allowances for occasional faults. A well-established personality will support you in the long term, despite your present behaviour. But a reputation has to be earned in the first place by actual, repeated, consistent behaviour. In the case of a company, performance and the projection of the desired personality must run in parallel. You can be the best in the world but nobody knows it. On the other hand, if everybody knows about you they will soon find out whether you can live up to your reputation. The strategies are interdependent.

Product performance

It goes without saying that what the consumer experiences must be in line with the personality, and that includes the actual performance of the product or standard of service. Even though the value of a Rolex watch is symbolic rather than functional, it must never prove to be a worse timekeeper than other watches. A basic standard has to be met, and that applies to service, such as in a restaurant or bank, as well as to a tangible product. Day-in, day-out, product performance is a powerful communicator. Investing in product quality and after sales support will support your personality image.

Physical premises

If your company personality is fashionable and sophisticated your physical premises should be too. Body Shop's premises, for example, reflect its environmental values. The imposing entrance to an international bank will reflect not just its own personality but the personality of its corporate clients. Similar premises would not work with a financial institution aimed at the cut-price end of the market — it would indicate unnecessary waste at the customer's expense or even hypocrisy. If you really want to project personality and values such as 'heritage' and 'belonging', you can use physical premises to involve the consumer. Examples of this are Cadbury's Theme Park — Cadbury World — which receives more than half a million visitors each year, and the worldwide presence of Hard Rock Café.

Hard Rock Café is one of the great entertainment success stories of the last three decades. It is a great example of how companies can identify clear target markets and establish a relationship with them using emotional and aspirational appeal. As with all good strategic personality communications, consistency is the main feature. Wherever you go in most of the world's big cities there is a Hard Rock Café with its own distinctive decor. The external physical premises will differ due to location and local architecture, but once inside you step right back into the rock-'n'-roll era. Go into Hard Rock Café and you will find memorabilia of pop stars — musical instruments and clothing — which immediately brings back an atmosphere from when you grew up or reminds you of the person you idolised.

And as with any successful corporate strategy, others will follow and so we now have the film star/movie-based Planet Hollywood and supermodel-type ventures which carry their own themes but always with the consistency of physical décor, staff dress codes, etc.

Corporate events

Like all public relations activities, corporate events have to be managed to reflect the personality on *every* occasion. Remember the question we asked in Chapter 4: What would our company be if ...? Whatever metaphor is appropriate, each event will have to reflect it. The personality must be visible to everyone in every outside communication.

Event management can apply to the opening of a new facility, to celebrating a special occasion such as an anniversary, or receiving a representation award. Any of these can enhance the public's image of the company. Personality strategy should also apply to a sponsorship, public fund-raising event or the launch of a 'cause', but the event should align with the *present* rather than hoped-for customer image. If the present perception of customer service is poor, then winning an award, for instance, or opening a fancy new office will not remove that perception, and may indeed be counter-productive. The event should have its own plan and objectives for publicity and promotion. But integrating with an existing personality strategy will avoid 'mixed messages', strengthen the impact of the event, and at the same time support the long term personality message.

Note that event promotion has fast diminishing returns — it soon becomes history — and this should be another factor in deciding which form of communication to go for. On the face of it, short-term promotions would be of little use for a long-term personality message. As it happens, by supporting the personality message each event will have a cumulative long-term effect, whatever its specific objective short-term bottom line impact. And with proper co-ordination, there will also be little or no extra cost. Corporate advertising rarely makes an immediate impact, but its effect, if ongoing and well managed, can last for many years. Avoid publicity stunts unless you can maintain the integrity of the personality.

Public relations

PR can sometimes be a minefield of disasters, but if handled by a reputable agency can add tremendous value to the communications effort. Good PR agencies are experts at securing access and exposure into prestigious media which can project the corporate personality powerfully to the right people. They are particularly adept at handling crises and matters of political importance, and establishing good press relations. Once again, PR agencies will have to be well briefed on the personality characteristics.

Affiliation programmes

Customers need to *experience* the personality and different sorts of affiliation programmes can help. In particular they develop lasting loyalty. Swatch, for example, has launched a highly successful collector's club, and Harley Davidson's Owners Group keeps growing as more people buy into the personality so brilliantly created. People like to experience the personality, interact with it, and be friends with it. These affiliation programmes can reinforce loyalty that can extend to cult status on the part of existing customers. They can also help to spread the company image, and act as very effective word-of-mouth marketing arms of the company.

Packaging

Product packaging also reflects personality. If you are a serious, conservative person you don't wear a clown's costume. Dress is one way in which anyone can express their unique personality. In the same way product packaging should reinforce the product and corporate personality. And packaging can be as diverse as the products themselves. If a person buys an exclusive product, it requires the sort of physical package that denotes exclusivity. The packaging is part of the identity and the total 'offer'. Dress up your products and services in a way that displays your unique personality.

Promotions

Promotion is usually directed towards products, but companies also need to get involved in promotional activity that reflects the corporate personality. In any event, it is important that promotions do not devalue the personality. An affluent, sophisticated, professional, romantic person for instance, would be unlikely to respond to a 'buy one, get one free' offer. On the other hand, a competition offering a free trip to Spain to see how sherry is made might be quite appropriate to a discerning, wine-drinking clientele. The promotion should match the customer's personality as well as the company's. Different types of customer will be insulted or offended by promotions that others readily respond to. The key principle is *appropriateness*. Price-related promotions are a great temptation, but make sure they do not undermine the personality of your company or product.

Sponsorships

These can be high- or low-cost with high or low impact. Choose carefully, and think in terms of appropriateness again. Rolex might successfully sponsor Wimbledon, but an alcoholic drinks company sponsor might not be the right match for a sports- or health-based event, and vice versa. Sponsorship and events should always create positive associations and reinforce your corporate personality.

Advertising

Advertising has the power to shape the personality, and later in this chapter we give some thoughts on how to get the best out of advertising agencies, and how to achieve a consistent, appropriate approach to advertising the personality. Advertising is sometimes split into corporate or image on the one hand, and product on the other.

Corporate advertising, sometimes described as institutional or image advertising, aims at making your *name* better known. Rarely is a specific product mentioned. Its purpose is to raise awareness and recognition of the company or organisation — typically to the investment community rather than customers. The image of the firm's efficiency, management and financial performance is probably more important in this advertising than technical product quality. Such advertising seeks to position the company at the leading edge of the industry or the market in general. It tries to ensure that people *think of you*. Familiar corporate image tag lines are:

You can be sure of Westinghouse.
Toshiba: In touch with tomorrow
Nike: Just do it!
Motel 6: We'll leave the light on for you.
Eastman Kodak: For the times of your life.
Philips: Let's make things better
Ford: Quality is job one.

Product advertising is the least difficult to understand, yet just as difficult as any to produce successfully over the long term. These ads simply present the product, its qualities and benefits and why you should buy it. They comprise the great majority of advertising and what the general public think of as clutter, and invasive. They also have a fast response and at the same time rapid diminishing returns.

Each form of advertising can be more effective if it is part of an overall personality strategy. In this case the personality will be the 'top of the mind' awareness that is being aimed at. Each kind of advertising supports the others. Corporate image advertising helps to create long term awareness, while product advertising converts that awareness into next month's sales.

How to get the best out of agencies

We shall now offer some guidelines which will serve as reminders for anyone in a company who has the responsibility to choose agencies, monitor their work, brief them, or has to work with them in any way. This can apply to advertising and promotions, public relations, or specialist personality and image consultancy.

1. **Always give them a clear brief**
   Agencies are much happier and produce much better work if they have a clear brief to work to. For image and brand building the brief should include:

   a. The core values or personality characteristics of the company
   b. The personality statement
   c. The positioning statement

   These will give focus and direction, and should be discussed with agents fully. Take care to explain how they were derived and the thinking behind them.

2. **Always remain true to values and personality characteristics**
   Never act out of character. When your agency prepares media material, creative concept boards, commercials or whatever, always check that the personality comes through. Test them out on staff or family to see whether the key messages are communicated. In the case of a television

commercial, do some consumer testing before the final version is completed. You might see the character of the company because you are looking for it — but you need to know the effect on your customers.

3. Always try to promote the USP
As well as projecting your personality, ensure that all marketing communications indicate in one form or another why you are better than or different from other companies — your Unique Selling Proposition. Taglines such as in the advertising examples above are one way of reinforcing this.

4. Monitor the characteristics of campaigns and communications activities
If you run expensive commercials, make sure that research is conducted to track their effectiveness, in terms of your communications objectives, and consumer perceptions. This is essential both in terms of value for money and also to ensure that the right personality message is projected. It should be carried out by a reputable market research company separate from the agencies who have developed the materials and campaigns.

5. Be prepared to Invest
Building corporate personality, and positioning a company in a certain way can take a long time. It is a long-term investment and should be treated as such. Companies doing this seriously should be prepared to spend consistently over several years to develop the right result. People's perceptions evolve slowly and this requires long-term consistency in advertising and promotion to make a real difference.

6. Get heard — but know where to draw the line
In an attempt to get heard among all the advertising that blasts at people all day long, some companies allow agencies to lead them into shock tactics. This can be highly

effective in gaining attention, but it can also be a double-edged sword. Benetton and Calvin Klein have received both acclaim and negative publicity for such 'on the edge' advertising. Benetton actually lost a lot of customers during one campaign but has doggedly stuck with provocative advertising in order to put across its strongly held values.

Advertising has to have an impact and it is often tempting to go to extremes to make it memorable. Knowing when to draw the line is a matter of judgement, but advertising should never ever be out of character with the personality that you want your company to project. Advertising has the power to shape the personality but it can produce negative images too. Anything that appears on television, the Internet, radio, posters, billboards or wherever, must reflect the characteristics or values of the personality.

Selecting an agency

'Should our company use one or more than one agency?' The answer depends on the circumstances. A single agency helps to ensure a single, consistent, corporate personality message. Some of the bigger, global companies choose one big agency and use it around the world. Others use more than one agency to gain lots of different, creative ideas. Some agencies refuse to take on a job that involves their rivals. Most creative agency staff believe they are the best, are very proud of their ideas and will defend them strongly. So whether you have one agency or more, your company should be prepared to be forceful in keeping them in focus. If you find an agency you like and it contributes effectively, it is worth sticking with it, as the nuances of your corporate personality may take time to understand. If, on the other hand, you are more concerned to get plenty of creative options to choose from, you may need to involve more than one.

Checklist for agency selection

You can reduce the risks in implementing a personality programme by using a specialist agency. But you can eliminate all or most of the risks if you follow the following common-sense check list when choosing one:

Track Record
- In what industries has it been involved?
- What companies have been its clients?
- What awards has it won?
- Has it got a good track record in each of the key media?

Reputation/Operations
- Is it renowned for meeting or missing deadlines?
- Does it really give full attention to each client?
- What is its range of operations/disciplines?
- Does it employ high-calibre people?
- How does it rate against other agencies in creative ability?
- Does it structure itself to have dedicated staff for each client?
- How does it control the quality of any subcontracted work?
- Is it willing to be judged on results?
- Has it got financial stability for the long term?
- Does it mind working with other agencies?

Does it understand our company?
- Does it understand our vision, mission, values, personality?
- Does it understand our business direction?
- Does it understand our target market and proposed positioning?
- Can it translate these into a sound communication strategy?
- Does it listen to our ideas?

Target publics

When considering various communications strategies and media, select key messages and media appropriate to the intended recipient. These might include, *inter alia:*

- Government, regulating bodies
- Business partners

- Local and overseas investors
- Employees
- Other businesses
- The public at large
- Target segments of new consumers
- Existing customers
- Opinion influencers: media, financial analysts, trade associations

But whatever the target public and whatever the message, the message should:

- Reflect the corporate personality characteristics or values
- Be understandable to the audience
- Be relevant to them
- Be believable
- Be interesting
- Motivate them

Summary

1. Keep your personality communications in line with your overall marketing plan.
2. You can communicate your personality by:
   word of mouth
   employee morale
   service standards and behaviours
   product performance
   physical premises
   corporate events
   public relations
   affiliation programmes
   packaging
   promotions
   sponsorships
   advertising

3. Get the best out of advertising, promotions and PR by:
   giving a clear brief
   staying true to values and personality characteristics
   promoting your USP
   monitoring activities
   being prepared to invest
   getting heard but knowing where to draw the line.
4. When selecting an agency check:
   its track record
   its reputation and operations
   that it listens and understands you.
5. Direct all your personality activities to target audiences.

CHAPTER SEVEN

POSITIONING AND PERSONALITY

Understanding and influencing the minds of consumers is the key to business success. Positioning is now recognised as a fundamental part of strategy for market-driven companies. Positioning is strategic, and its main purpose is to differentiate the company from all its competitors in people's minds. It is sometimes referred to as the 'Battle for the Mind', because it involves *what people perceive* rather than *what you do*. And that is what makes positioning a difficult challenge for most companies: it seeks to create an association or set of associations in people's minds, to establish what the company or products mean to their lives.

Positioning strategies seek to influence people to think that there is something different or unique about this company. If people cannot see anything unique, then economic factors such as price come into play and govern the purchasing decision. The company's products or services are then little more than commodities, and no special value is perceived which can command higher margins.

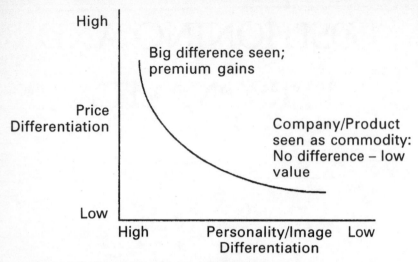

Figure 6 *Differentiating through personality*

The added value is created by the intangible benefits the customers perceive, and the personality characteristics that impact on their minds. Charisma cannot be copied. Companies can copy systems, technology, strategies, structures, products and just about everything else — except personality. Positioning gives the opportunity to present key personality messages to target customer groups.

The strategic positioning process

Positioning is the process of explaining to your target customer groups why you are different and better. If your company is looking to establish a new position, bear in mind the following steps:

1. Look at the target market — what it has and what it wants
2. Look at what the competition offers, and how they position themselves
3. Find the gap you can fill (look through the eyes of the customer)
4. Make it visible — make sure customers see it
5. Fill the gap, establish your position
6. Don't say things you can't deliver

The power of positioning

You can have the best personality in the world but unless you project it, it will not attract and keep customers. Positioning adds force to corporate personality because it relates the 'person' to the competitive advantage. It sets the company apart and gives the customer a reason to use it to the extent of long-term loyalty. It is the basis of the company-customer relationship so much in vogue, a relationship, in effect, between two personalities.

At the same time positioning is much more effective if it becomes more animated or personified. That is, if backed by a strong corporate personality. It can then reflect not just the tangible differentiation and competitive advantage — be it of the company, product, or service — but, if done well, corporate charisma as well. As well as life, personality means uniqueness or *difference* in the eyes of the customer. So positioning and personality are interdependent.

An example of how a world-class company achieves its position is Johnson and Johnson and their range of baby products. In the case of their Baby Shampoo, personality and positioning combine to create product charisma. The personality is female — motherly, caring, protective nurturing. The *summary* positioning is gentleness. The commercials clearly project the tender way in which the mother looks after the child, the loving way she washes the child's hair — the *gentleness* product positioning. Everything is in character and the personality message is strong and clear. The brand slogan 'no more tears' adds a further emotional appeal, as the last thing any mother wants is to see is a hurt, crying child. The basic product has been extended to other groups: to 'kids' in the form of a special brand with the tagline 'no more tangles', and to adults with a positioning line of 'baby your hair'. The caring personality and the 'gentleness' positioning have carried it successfully into different market segments.

Another example of powerful positioning is the battle between the credit card companies: Visa, with its impulsive spending, world travelling, adventurous confident personality; and Mastercard, with a more conservative, careful spending, family-oriented, less fashion-conscious personality. So Visa is 'we're everywhere you want to be' and Mastercard is 'smart money'. The positions both reflect and project the personalities, and the personalities add power to the positioning.

Alternative positioning strategies

Apart from price and quality which can be readily copied, there are various alternative strategies that can be used to position companies and products:

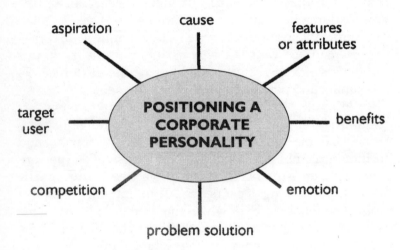

Figure 7 Positioning strategies

Features or attributes

This is an often-used strategy for specific products which focuses on the attributes, features or characteristics desired by consumers. Car, aircraft and some electronic consumer goods manufacturers employ this strategy to give people a reason to buy by promoting a USP (Unique Selling Proposition). Volvo with its 'safety' positioning and Lexus with 'big car luxury at a reasonable price' are typical examples.

The strategy works either by convincing customers that competitors do not have a particular attribute, or persuading them to choose an attribute that competitors are not claiming for their own. As a rule, it is better to focus on one special attribute or feature, as too many will blur the positioning and dilute your message. This is easier if, as is the case with Volvo, the corporate and product names are synonymous. If they are not, a company can focus on a personality characteristic and own that, such as 'innovation' with 3M. There is a danger, however, of concentrating too much on product features and not enough on human associations, and technology-led companies are particularly prone to this. As well as a feature being equalled by competitors, your company may become too tied to it.

In many ways, intangible characteristics can be more effective in influencing people. Factors such as healthiness, leadership and innovation have been used by major companies such as Sony who tend not to put product-specific associations in consumer minds. In any event, however, and depending on the type of product, features and tangible attributes may form part of the product positioning. This is not so important with corporate positioning.

Benefits

This is similar to the features strategy but takes it one step further, specifying the benefit that will accrue to the customer as a result of a particular feature, attribute or characteristic. For example, it makes sense to buy such-and-such toothpaste with fluoride (feature) because it prevents decay (benefit). The strategy can apply to companies in the same way: CNN with its worldwide network gives the benefit of 24-hour news in 210 countries — wherever you might be; Hong Kong Bank has developed personal banking products and services with the benefit of making things easy for the customer; 'Making things easy' is a positioning also used to great effect by Microsoft in their advertising campaigns.

Emotion

This strategy focuses more on the psychological benefits or feelings that the customer will experience. It can be applied at both corporate and product level. A person buying a Body Shop product, for example, might experience a great deal of satisfaction by *feeling* they have helped the environment and protected animals that may otherwise have been used in product testing. Emotional positioning is important in creating customer desire, touching the heart rather than the intellect.

Problem/Solution

Many people buy products and services not because they particularly want them but more for what they can do to help solve specific problems, so this too can be a rewarding positioning strategy. No one wakes up in the morning and gleefully shouts, 'What a great day for an overdraft!' More likely they wake up in the middle of the night worrying about how to solve a critical financial problem. So problem-solving positioning has a powerful appeal to customers. Companies can also position themselves at a corporate level as solution-providers, and this is a strategy used successfully by IBM in a global campaign.

Competition

Some companies position themselves directly against the competition, the best-known example being Avis in the car rental market. At one stage Avis decided to renounce its claim as No.1 in the USA, and promoted itself as No2 but with a 'We try harder' message. Customers associated this with honesty and hard work. Their historic advertising slogan also evoked the support that traditionally goes to the underdog. Avis is an example of *literal* (in this case second position) positioning that worked. Not only did it help relative to the No. 1 company, but it also made it difficult for the third place company to gain a position.

Car manufacturers frequently position models blatantly head-on against competitors' equivalent models. If you carry out this strategy well you can enjoy the reflected benefits of a competitor's brand leadership, and this is quite possible for lesser known companies with ever increasing technological advances. A single feature or benefit advantage, well communicated, can leap frog you into a leading position. If your chip outperforms Intel, for example, and you can get your message across, you can save yourself the millions of dollars that Intel's positioning has cost them and years of brand management. If your car runs more smoothly than a Rolls Royce and you can position it as such, you can steal a march on the very best.

Competition-driven strategy can be linked to features, attributes and characteristics such as quality, service, or safety, or benefits or solutions. So the strategies work happily in combination. But remember that positioning is in the eye of the customer or outsider. What you believe *as a company* is irrelevant even if you are right, and could be your downfall if you are wrong. You can be successful in making customers *believe* that you are better, whether or not this is fact. A world class positioning strategy sets out to be the best and be seen to be the best.

Target user

This positioning strategy targets specific customer groups or market segments as defined by whether they want or how they use the product or service. Nike and Reebok are good examples of this. Their sports shoes are basically a generic product adapted for use in different sports activities such as aerobics, jogging, long-distance running, sprinting, squash, tennis, basketball and so on. That is, different market segments or groups. If you happen to do everything, you can buy a cross-trainer! However slight the adaptation, each product is positioned to appeal to a distinct market segment. Consumers see the company as providing different products just for them.

A target user approach can also be successful in service industries. NatWest Bank developed a small business loan which was a generic product tailored to professional users such as doctors, dentists and lawyers. The product was packaged in their language using their businesses as examples, and was a great success, because the different professional groups saw it as a product designed specifically with them in mind. As with Nike shoes, minimal product differences translated into a major positioning differentiation, with obvious profitable consequences. The positioning trick is to change customers' perceptions.

Aspiration

Some companies use this strategy to appeal to the aspirations of their perspective customers: what they want to have, do or become. Pepsi did this quite successfully when they executed their 'Choice of a new generation' campaign. 'Weight watchers' from Heinz featured well-known personalities admitting to weight problems that have given the aspirational positioning double force — 'I not only want to lose weight but I want to be like her too.' It is closely linked to an emotional appeal, but relates to the future, and people's goals and dreams. Whenever possible people tend to live out their dreams, and this includes buying habits, so this is another positioning strategy that translates into sales results.

Cause

Somewhat of a cross between target-user and emotion-driven strategies, this positioning links companies to both customer groups and related causes. Avon for instance, specialises in products for women and strongly supports organisations that work on women's issues, such as breast cancer. Cause-related positioning has grown considerably in the last few years as companies around the world recognise marketing opportunities linked to socially responsible behaviour. There is a growing concern among international companies worldwide (enhanced in some countries by media pressure and even legislation) to be seen to be more socially responsible, and to give something back to the communities from whom they have profited.

Combining positioning strategies

As we have seen from some of the above examples, these strategies are not mutually exclusive. On the contrary, some of the most powerful corporate positioning comes from combinations of strategies. For example, Nike Corporation takes a target user approach, adds in aspiration in the form of sports superstar endorsements, and a dose of emotion in messages like 'Just do it' and scenes of success and achievement. There are no doubts about the bottom line results. The danger is only in diluting a clear, positive message by attempting to be all things to all people.

Positioning and self-concept

Another positioning approach is to match your corporate personality with the self-concept of consumers. This is sound marketing. Positioning and segmentation are inseparable. A company cannot position itself adequately unless it appeals to a particular market segment, and a market segment will not respond to a position it sees as being not relevant or likeable.

The best way for a company to position its personality is to try and match it with that of its target audience. It is a well known phenomenon that consumers attach symbolic associations to companies and products which will make them feel 'this company/product is right for me'. It is also well known that people buy things for what they are as well as what they do.

In bringing these together, best practice marketing attempts to match the corporate or product personality with the self concept of the target audience. People feel very strongly about their own self-image and will want to be associated with companies that present themselves as being consistent with this. Conversely they will tend not to be too attracted to companies that do not fit their self-concept. Companies that really understand the psychology of the customer come closest to understanding their needs and being a friend. Furthermore, if a company can position its personality so that consumers feel it matches but is *better* than their own self-concept (that is, it could improve their self-concept) they will make great efforts to associate themselves with it. This is an example of the 'aspiration' positioning strategy, cemented by a personal bonding.

In the relatively simple hypothetical case shown below, a chart shows how close the personality of the company perceived by a target customer group matches their own self-concept.

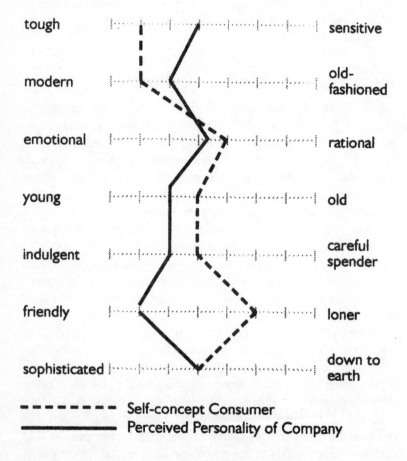

Figure 8 Perceived personality and self-concept

In this case the respective perceptions are reasonably well matched. But where perceptions differ a lot the company clearly has some repositioning to do.

The positioning statement

The positioning statement sets out how the company or product should be seen by consumers relative to the competition. The personality statement summarises the character of the company, whereas the positioning statement relates this to business considerations. Good positioning statements may well reflect personality characteristics but their purpose is to act as a guide as to how the company will communicate itself to chosen market segments.

A positioning statement should make reference to five things:

Target audience	It describes who are the main target audiences (or market segments)
Competitive set	It marks out the boundary of what the company is doing, such as telecommunications or multimedia
Benefits	It describes how people benefit by doing business with the company as related to their needs and wants
Differentiation	It describes why the company is better — what the main competitive advantage is
Personality	Key characteristics should be visible as far as possible, because some of these might represent competitive advantages, for instance 'innovation'

Together with the personality statement, the positioning statement is the other half of the platform upon which the company establishes its image in the marketplace. It reinforces personality while adding the business dimension. But the two are fundamentally different. The personality of the company should endure over time and the company should remain true to its elements or characteristics. The positioning of the company, on the other hand, might change from time to time to reflect changing conditions:

- The decline of existing and the rise of emerging new market segments
- Changes taking place in the industry
- Changing competitive advantages
- Changing customer perceptions of the company

In technology-based companies, where the rate of change of all these factors is rapid, companies might change their position every one or two years, or even more frequently.

Above all, the positioning statement must be:

Clearly targeted	Aimed precisely at certain market segments
Believable	Not saying things which the company cannot deliver
Easily communicable	Not confusing or complicated, understandable.
Motivating	Stimulating consumer interest from awareness and interest to desire and action

Preparing a positioning statement

Research

As with the corporate personality statement, consensus at the top of the company is vital. To begin to create a position in the minds of consumers, ideally it is useful to have some consumer research data. It is hard to create a position which is much at variance from the present public perception. An overt swing in positioning, especially if not supported by actual performance, is potentially dangerous as credibility would be lacking. So the groundwork is a combination of market and management perceptions, which normally involves both quantitative and qualitative research.

Positioning language

Here are some hints about the language to be used in positioning statements.

1. Although a positioning statement is primarily an internal working document, it should be expressed in language that consumers themselves would use. Good research material will help here.
2. Try to combine both the rational and emotional elements into your statement. Remember that people buy things for emotional or motivational reasons as well as for logical, rational reasons. If possible, appeal to the audience's aspirations as well. A positioning statement should provide a clear brief to advertising and public relations agencies as to key messages and the desired customer response.
3. Remember the characteristics of your corporate personality and build these in. Appeal to the personal values and behaviours that endear your customers.
4. Avoid vague terminology. This is an easy habit to slip into if you are not careful. Watch out for generalisations such as 'quality' and 'commitment', and phrases like 'meeting your needs' and 'customer satisfaction'. Try to be as specific as possible, with regard to target customer groups as well as the benefits.
5. As mentioned earlier, try to avoid feature-based positioning, remembering that any other company will be able to copy features very quickly. Unique Selling Propositions (USPs) don't last very long these days, unless of course, USP stands for Unique Selling *Personality*. Emphasise the intangible benefits rather than tangible features — they have more influence on customer thinking.
6. Keep it simple. In that way agencies will create messages that will not only be understood but also remembered. As a general rule try to keep the statement to just one or two sentences.

Writing a positioning statement is not an easy task, and you might have to make several attempts at it. When you are fairly certain you have got it right, you should test it out with customers and staff even though it is not meant for their consumption. This will give you the answer to whether or not the statement is believable, understandable and clearly targeted.

Competitive positioning

During the positioning process it is important to make a thorough analysis of your competitors. This analysis should consider:

- Which competitors do customers consider when making a purchase decision?
- Which competitors are associated with different target segments and usage situations?
- What positioning strategy are they using?
- Why they are using it?
- What key messages are they communicating?
- Which target customers are their priorities?
- What are their corporate personality characteristics?
- What is their competitive advantage?
- How effective are their marketing communications?
- How different are they claiming to be?
- Why do their customers buy from them?
- What do customers think about them?
- What essential differences do consumers see between our company and theirs?
- Who would people buy from if they didn't buy from us?

Global personality and positioning

Businesses which operate around the world have a choice of strategy: they can keep the same personality and positioning or they can change them in response to market situations.

Some companies, such as Coca-Cola, Gucci and McDonald's, are truly global in the sense of both standardised products and consistent personality and positioning. Others, such as Ford, have to respond to different market situations which demand different products, or changes to products, but not necessarily a change in personality and positioning.

The reverse of this situation is where market perception forces companies to change personality and positioning of the product. In Asia, Marks and Spencer is positioned as a well-off (higher income), sophisticated, and slightly snobbish personality. In Europe it has a 'value for money' and 'family caring person' positioning.

Some companies are almost fully adaptive in terms of product, personality and positioning. This is the case with Nestlé which adapts nearly all of its products and marketing activities, either partially or fully, to each local market.

Re-positioning

Sometimes it is necessary to re-position a company to change the existing perception of the company. Re-positioning usually takes place for the following reasons:

A poor image
If a company has a poor image, perhaps because of a media disaster, an unfortunate happening, or because customers' perceptions have seriously changed for the worse, re-positioning will be needed. Perrier, when it suffered an unfortunate pollution incident, recovered well in the eyes of consumers with excellent corporate communications to re-position and restore its image.

A new personality
A new company needs to quickly seek a position. When it creates a new personality it needs to inform people of why this has been done, reassure loyal customers that things are the same, and introduce the new 'person' to them.

Blurred/foggy perception
Some companies, after commissioning research, are surprised to find that their image is not clear, that customers do not really feel strongly about them one way or the other.

Given this important knowledge, re-positioning through advertising can help to create a more vivid perception.

A momentous event

Mergers, acquisitions, privatisation and other major corporate events may require significant re-positioning effort. The internal alignment of cultures must not happen without an alignment of customer bases, and clear messages to other interested parties, such as investors, stakeholders, and the media.

Changes in target customer groups

A company may change the priority of its target customer groups for strategic or profitability reasons. It might also switch targets. If Coca Cola, for instance, were to strategically decide to target the over-sixties age group, it would need to completely re-position itself in the minds of this segment, in order to convince them that Coke was no longer a younger person's drink. Johnson and Johnson, renowned for its baby products, had to actively re-position itself to appeal to adults who represented for them a hitherto untapped market.

A change in strategic direction

Entering new markets, or indeed industries, might require the establishment of a position or re-positioning if the company is already known to be migrating from its existing operations, or extending its breadth. Fujitsu, for example, has invested in expensive advertising to inform people it is now a diversified global telecommunications computer company.

Changes in competitor positioning

A company may consider changing its positioning in response to a competitor change. If it has a strong position in the minds of its target audience this may not be necessary. However, if its competitive advantage is likely to be weakened, re-positioning will be necessary. BMW had to re-position itself differently to Lexus in the USA. And another competitor scenario is where a company might wish to move *away* from the competition, as with Pepsi from Coke.

Re-positioning, for whatever reason, needs to be carefully implemented, and explained to consumers, so that the company is not seen to be inconsistent, or 'schizophrenic' in character. Having said that, while positioning can and should change from time to time for good reason, its personality should remain true.

Re-positioning — case studies

A company sees the need to position/re-position itself globally and clearly define its personality

A large Asian conglomerate has, over the last several years, enjoyed tremendous business growth and expansion through acquisitions and joint ventures. These initiatives have taken it into many new markets around the world, including Europe and the USA. In its own country, the organisation is a household name and in the region it is well known in limited markets. It is accessing new markets quickly and has set its sights on becoming a truly global player.

At a top management workshop held for CEOs of the major strategic business units, the subjects discussed were the personality and positioning of the group itself and some individual companies. The results of the group discussions were:

1. Participants' views of the values of the group were quite consistent across the business: the internal culture was strong.
2. However, the CEOs felt that these values were not perceived strongly by various target publics outside the group. The target publics usually considered by all large companies are:

- governments/regulators
- domestic investors
- overseas investors
- shareholders
- employers
- local media

- foreign media
- customers/public in general/different markets
- strategic alliance partners

In this case it appeared that to some of the target publics the image positioning was weak or unclear, and there was sometimes a mixture of positive and negative perceptions. Furthermore, there were always some negative or non-positive elements perceived, which was unacceptable.

3. The group personality had to be clearly defined and projected (this had never been done before) to provide a global unifying presence.

4. The group was to be re-positioned globally. This meant establishing a group-wide positioning with respect to several target audiences.

These activities are to provide a solid corporate framework which will support individual business and product positioning around the world.

A legendary example of strategic positioning

Prior to the appearance of Swatch watches, the market was basically split into two product groups which were positioned on *functionality* and *representationality*.

In the 'functionality' camp were a large range of low-cost, short-term purchase, down-market watches which kept time accurately, such as Casio and Timex. They did the job, looked OK, and appealed to customers with a disposable income that was not very high. In the 'representationality' camp was a small range of high-cost, more glamorous watches. These, such as Rolex and Piaget, represented status and prestige to their owners, and were often viewed as an investment and a long-term purchase. The gap between the two was very successfully exploited by Swatch, who founded a wide range of medium cost, limited production watches, which were fashionably different. Swatch combined functionality with fashion and attached representational value. Their success is legendary. The personality of Swatch (a fun-loving, innovative, outgoing, trendy, young and energetic *person*) is consistently projected through many campaigns to reinforce the position in people's minds.

Generic positioning

Generic positions are single or 'summary positions' that companies sometimes seek to occupy in the minds of consumers. A company may end up with a generic position whether it intends to or not, and the general public perception becomes the accepted position. They are quite general in nature, but can be used to summarise an overall personality and broad position. The following are examples of our perception, and you may be able to add some of your own.

Community	Ben and Jerry
Innovative	3M
Quality	Motorola
Expert	Microsoft
Professional	Shell, ICI
Friendly, family	McDonald's
Caring	Johnson and Johnson, Met Life
Global	Nestlé, Coca Cola
Fun	Disney, Club Med
Environmentally concerned	Body Shop
Heritage	A & W, Harley Davidson
Entrepreneur	Virgin
Service	FedEx, SIA, American Express
Relationship	Hallmark
Family	Kodak
Causes	Avon
Existential	Calvin Klein, Benetton
Ambitious	Nike
Performance	Intel, BMW
Stylish, contemporary	Versace
Status	Rolex

Any or all of the above corporate labels can be an overall focal point for the company, summarising vision, mission, values, personality and positioning. While summarising broad direction, however, it must be emphasised that these statements would not be sufficient alone for use with market communications agencies. Full positioning and personality statements would have to accompany them in the brief. Nevertheless, generic, or summary positions can be a useful type of shorthand to get employees to remember and buy into overall strategic direction and corporate personality.

Summary

1. Positioning is the battle for the mind of the customer. It is what the customer perceives, not necessarily what the company seeks to project.
2. Corporate personality needs to establish its own unique position in the minds of each target audience.
3. There are several strategies for positioning:

   - features or attributes
   - benefits
   - emotion
   - problem/solution
   - competition
   - target users
   - aspiration
   - causes

   Combinations of these can be particularly powerful.
4. Positioning should seek to reflect the self-concept of the target customer.
5. Positioning statements are needed to remind everyone of the desired consumer perception, and to focus advertising and public relations agencies on key messages needed to establish the position.
6. Companies need to consider how they will position themselves in different markets in different parts of the world.

Sometimes a single global positioning can be accomplished, but this is not always the case.

7. Re-positioning becomes necessary when, for whatever reasons, the desired perception of the company is not good enough. Consumer research will diagnose this.

CHAPTER EIGHT

PERSONALITY AND BRAND MANAGEMENT

Brands play a central part in any personality strategy. Corporate brands, such as IBM, Marks and Spencer, or Intel, reflect the identity of the whole company. Product brands, such as Porsche 911 or Yorkie Bar, need to be consistent with their parent company personality, as well as projecting a personality of their own. Having a sound personality strategy does not mean that you do not need good brand management. It means that, as a key element in communicating your personality, you cannot do without it.

Strong brands have shown themselves to be remarkably hardy. A Boston Consulting Group study compared the leading brands of 1925 with the leading brands of 1985. Amazingly, in nineteen of twenty-two categories the 1925 leader was still the leader in 1985! In the other three categories, the 1925 leader was either number two or number five in 1985.

In many industries today, the brand leaders are those of over sixty years ago, such as Kodak, Kellogg's, Coca Cola and Hoover. In some cases, their names became the generic description for all products in their field, as with Xerox. Each of them was able to fend off new competition for more than half a century because of their brand strength and corporate personality. To illustrate the power of such brand leadership, another study showed that consumers would pay over $400 more for an IBM PC than for a comparable Dell or Compaq, despite the identical chips that each used and almost identical performance.

The original purposes of branding were to identify the source of a product to customers and to protect that source against possible infringement and dilution. These reasons still remain, and the most successful brands have sophisticated policies and management for their protection, as well as positive promotion. But the power of brands to differentiate products and manufacturers is based more on an increasing knowledge of how to respond to customers' needs, wants and perceptions. A strong brand goes a long way to reflecting the personality of the customer, and projecting the personality of the supplier company, whether through its products or its own branded company identity. It is a major part of the marketeer's armoury, and, as the mysteries of the human mind continue to be opened up, has still not been fully exploited.

What is a brand ?

What is a brand and why are people prepared to pay more for branded products and services? Is it because of a logo, a trademark, a form of ownership or identity, a guarantee of quality or just a name for a product or service?

Brand identity and brand image

When used in connection with brands, the words *identity* and *image* have different meanings. Sometimes they are used interchangeably and this can not only cause confusion, but also result in wasted marketing expenditure and, at worst, misguided marketing strategies.

Brand identity is the total concept which the owner or sender is trying to communicate to certain target publics. It is not transitory, or superficial. On the contrary, it is strategic and constitutes the brand 'offer', involving depth, consistency, appropriateness, character and performance. The aim of providing a brand with an identity is to secure a desired place in people's minds. In other words, to *generate* an image, and therefore it should precede the brand image.

Brand image, on the other hand, is more to do with reputation. It is a receiver concept — the way in which people perceive or imagine a brand. It can be transitory, volatile, and changing if the identity is not strongly enough projected. It may or may not be the same as the true identity of the brand, because the identity messages need de-coding by consumers and even little things such as someone else's opinion may change their perception. Or the identity might be projected in a misleading way.

Some companies become too preoccupied with and even obsessed by image, tending to attach more importance to appearance than substance. 'Image campaigns' are all too familiar, and are often used to justify substantial marketing expenditure. But too much concentration on 'feel good' factors and having a 'nice image' can lead companies away from what really needs to be established and communicated in the long term. So it is vital to establish the brand identity — its core if you like — and then work hard to make sure that the perception or image is equal to it.

Corporate identity and design

Corporate identity can often be confused with brand identity, but corporate identity deals with descriptive recognition — names, logos, colours, signage and other design aspects. Brands also can have their own 'identity' in this sense, at a pure recognition level; often power brands started out with just a product and a name, but these and other recognition elements become part of the true identity. Names, and logos in particular, can be enormously influential, and must be selected with care. The famous tale of Chevrolet introducing a car into parts of Europe under the name 'Nova' (which literally translated means 'won't go') bears witness to this. Even the world's most powerful brand, Coca Cola, has in its time come under scrutiny and been subject to consumer pressure because of possible drug associations. Some brands take their names from founders, such as Disney, Charles Schwab, and Marks and Spencer.

When choosing names look for:

- availability
- protection
- something different
- something meaningful

And don't forget to test it out on consumers before you go ahead! Also, research suggests that short is better — 'easy to say, easy to remember, easy to show'. Avoid the tendency to use jargon that might mean a lot to you but little to the customer. Midland Bank launched an account called Vector, but what did it mean?

Logos can be equally important for brand recognition and are a valuable component of identity. Again, testing with consumers is essential to make sure there are no negative associations portrayed. Even colours can have a great impact on consumers, and improve recall.

Some companies even change their names to enhance their brand power, such as Federal Express with its switch to FedEx. It is worth thinking hard about names just as we would with our own children's. The Name Change Index of Publicly Traded Companies in USA is showing an increase in the number of companies changing names to better reflect their true identity, and The Schecter Group in its 1994 *Logo Value Study* showed that many well known logos actually detract from the brand image.

Brand differentiation

More than anything else a brand identifies you and differentiates you from the rest of the crowd. It sets you apart. Here is a typical sales encounter that most of us have experienced in one form or another:

What kind of business are you in?
We're in the training business.
What kind of training do you do?
Any kind.

Who do you do it for?
Anybody who'll buy it.

Answers like these will soon condemn you to oblivion. Unless you have a branded identity, you are into commodities — whether training or tractors — and are dependent on volume and economies of scale. Your market-place will be dictated by price and delivery and you will be vulnerable to competition, including price undercutting by a bigger or more cash-desperate competitor. Every new competitor will be a new headache. Apart from being counter to the longer-term customer relationship trend, prevalent in the 1990s, such a strategy does not make sense. Even a low cost strategy, at pain of re-engineering and corporate 'flattening', will mean low prices and low margins if you have nothing to differentiate your product. Brand identity is likely to be so important for growth and even survival that it has to be addressed strategically, and as a long-term investment rather than a special marketing project.

Brand focus may change in differentiating the supplier company that is willing and able to establish a long-term, perhaps one-to-one, customer relationship. Emphasis will inevitably move from the product to the customer or, specifically, to the customer's perception of the product. In relationship marketing, the corporate personality we have been discussing will take on special meaning. Respective brand messages, projecting *aspects* of the personality, may have to be aligned to individual customers. In any event, given the trend towards one-to-one marketing, a mission statement for the next century will probably mean having to build in such a strategy. Your customers will have to believe that your product is more valuable than the rest in your market and be willing to pay more for it. And that is the objective of brand identity.

Brand identity is what distinguishes one company from another, or one product from another. It is measured in the eye of the customer, not your marketeers or CEO, by the image it evokes. But even perceptions can change, and what was a surprising extra service a year ago is now part of the package, so you have to keep augmenting the perception of benefit. So not only do you need to create a brand identity, but you need to have a strategy for maintaining or managing it, just as you would manage any major investment.

Ask yourself what your customer receives that is special. 'On time' delivery is no good, as that is a promise of the 1980s. Nor is customer service — it is now expected. Once a major competitor — often from another part of the world — has raised customer expectations by consistent service standards, you cannot claim a USP by just matching them. Even quality, thanks initially to Japanese production methods, is now part of the no-surprise package. Since the introduction of sophisticated quality programmes, modern cars and consumer durables, for instance, have a level of reliability that was unheard-of a couple of decades ago. All these factors are the price of admission to the market, not of market dominance — that requires a unique brand identity that you can live up to. You can protect an invention with a patent. But the host of invisible benefits and customer perceptions that surround a modern product may have to be wrapped in a brand.

An example of brand identity — Häagen-Dazs

Häagen-Dazs is a brand which, when bought by Grand Met in 1989, rose from mediocrity to phenomenal success around the world. It broke into the ice-cream market which was already crowded with other brand names made famous by companies such as Mars, Nestlé, Unilever, and Movenpick, not to mention private labels. This in itself was difficult enough, and in Europe when it was launched in 1989, there was also a recession to contend with. On top of all this the Häagen-Dazs product range was put on the market at up to a forty per cent higher price than its nearest competitors. And still it succeeded, creating its own special charisma. The reason for this achievement was the creation of a strong brand identity. Targeted at

---

adults who had a higher income and were more sophisticated in their tastes, the identity it created was a premium, thicker, creamier and more expensive ice-cream. The advertising campaigns endorsed the identity with themes such as 'The Ultimate Experience in Personal Pleasure' and 'Dedicated to Pleasure'. Some of the print media advertisements were decidedly on the sensual side, but this also was consistent with the self-indulgent, pleasurable identity. Other aspects of the marketing image also ensured the 'appropriateness' of the brand. Only up-market ice-cream parlours and outlets in the better hotels and restaurants would go for Häagen-Dazs. Similarly, the brand was given prominence at carefully selected events such as opera, polo, tennis and sailing events. It took on a unique personality of its own through clever branding.

How do your brands rate?

Here is the sort of self-test you need to do on behalf of your company. You are succeeding if your customers:

- understand what makes your product or service special
- understand your product or service well enough to be able to describe it
- value your brand so much that they are willing to pay more for whatever it is they think makes it special
- feel so strongly about your brand that they will defend it when it comes under attack.

That is what you are faced with when considering creating or changing a brand identity. That is what branding is all about. It is a hard test to pass and there is a lot of work and investment on the way to achieving it. But the alternative is likely to be far more costly.

Why do people like brands ?

We are all familiar with different brands of products and services, and there are several reasons why we prefer to buy branded items rather than commodity-type products and services. Some of these mirror the characteristics and benefits of corporate personality we have already covered.

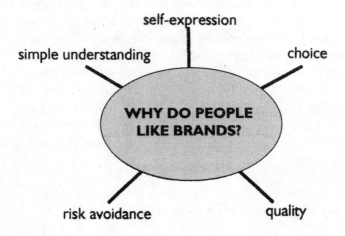

Figure 9 *Why do people like brands?*

Choice

One of the most important reasons why people prefer to buy branded goods and services is that they offer them a means of choice. We think, discriminate, and — whether rationally or irrationally — exercise our freedom of choice. The brand names themselves generate alternatives, so as well as choosing a branded rather than unbranded product, we can choose *between* brands. This exercise of choice through brands is certainly a feature of the rise in consumerism. A modern supermarket is an object lesson in consumer choice through branding. A large car manufacturer will typically offer a number of models or brands to give customers choice. Branding allows self-expression, responding to deeper customer desires. In effect it is like the choice we all have in choosing friends, an expression of our unique tastes and personality and how we perceive the personality of the other person.

Quality

When people buy a particular brand of product or service, they make judgements, whether consciously or unconsciously, about quality, benefits and value for money. If they are happy with the quality and value they receive, they will recall this feeling whenever they see that brand again. Even more importantly, they will trust that brand if they find, after more than one purchase, that the quality and value remain consistently good. Quality, of course, like value for money, is a perception. It will be enhanced by after-sales service policy, a customer helpline, and the trappings of a quality conscious company.

Risk avoidance

People in general do not like to take risks, especially when buying things. Buying a well-known or reputable brand reduces the risk factor, and stops people from worrying about whether or not it will live up to expectations. McDonald's may not be your first choice for a midday snack, but if you want consistency, speed and known value it may be the best compromise. The risk element is removed. And this applies to a lot of regular purchases where you don't want the hassle of upsets and the anxiety that goes with the unfamiliar. Once a buying habit is formed the strong brand product, weaknesses and all, becomes an old friend, dependable and faithful — values we rank highly. Brands can help to add some certainty in an uncertain life.

The choice of IBM as a computer supplier is often to avoid risk, not just in fast-changing technology but in terms of the ongoing support needed. This factor can easily override performance comparisons, and even product quality. It illustrates the high subjective value that a corporate personality can assume through branding. You are, in effect, buying the IBM personality.

There is an increasing trend of consumer pessimism and a move towards 'safe choices'. Consumers expect Disney, Sony, or Hallmark to provide consistent quality products and services with very low risk, and they are ready to pay for this. 'No questions asked, money-back guarantees' have become increasingly popular. The implication of this is that there will be even greater reliance on well-known brand names whenever there is uncertainty in the buying process. This is particularly the case when you cannot try out the product in advance. For example, how can you be sure that your life assurance cover is secure, or that your tour operator will not leave you stranded?

A strong brand does not need to spell out its features which are implicit in the brand name and parent company. You trust Liz, or whoever, because she is the 'sort of person' who will not let you down. That is her character or personality. And the same sort of reasoning accounts for loyalty to a product or company through branding.

Simple understanding

Another emerging trend is the desire to simplify choices. So-called 'brand blindness' afflicts customers when they are confronted with a multitude of brands and product features. Things are getting more complex, and technology influences every aspect of our lives. Brands can play a part in making things simple and giving reassurance. This is particularly evident in the computer industry. Apple notably disposed of all technical jargon, was consumer-friendly, and delivered a simple message of practicality to a massive new market of non-technical consumers. 'Making things simple', as well as being a feature of branding generally, can also be a powerful specific characteristic of your corporate personality, as Apple proved. Microsoft and Intel are also making things easy for people to understand and use their products.

Self-expression

Products such as platinum credit cards, Rolex watches and other prestige items help people to show that they are different, or have achieved something in life.

The automobile industry gives plenty of examples of strong brands commanding premium prices because of the owner's or driver's desire for self expression. Although Ford's Taurus is the best mid-sized car in America, hundreds of thousands of people buy the Mercury Sable which is almost the same car, made from the same moulds, using the same fittings, but which costs hundreds of dollars more. While the Ford brand has been synonymous with hard-working, middle class, middle-of-the-road motorists, the Mercury brand connotes more luxury, higher aspirations and greater disposable income. The Daimler badge on a Jaguar car, with precious few real additions to the already luxury specification, also commands thousands of pounds in price differential. In terms of self-expression, there can be room for brand positioning even in a narrow market segment. Clearly the customer's perception of strong brand personality is a major marketing factor.

The conclusion is clear: few buyers are unaware of the facts about a car's physical features, or, say, the probable actual cost of an expensive perfume; but the pedigree, the personality, relationship, dream or whatever you are buying — even more than a name on a badge — offers perceived value that customers will pay well for. Self-expression is a key personality characteristic that can be harnessed by customer-directed branding.

Levels of branding and personality

Branding can be applied in different ways or at different levels.

Corporate branding
This is where a company uses only the corporate name as the brand name. In other words, all of the products or services offered by the company are 'branded' with or carry only that name. They do not have names of their own. In this case the personality of the company is the strong influence in the branding of all products and services. They do not have a personality of their own and rely totally on the power of the corporate personality.

IBM is a good example of corporate branding, as in this case it branded its people before its product line: the blue suit, white shirt, red tie, neat hair, polished shoes. These people were well trained, competent and well presented, and customers at a loss with all the technicalities of buying computers were only to happy to put themselves in reliable hands. And the IBM look, the team, the presentation, the whole package, was what was being bought, at a premium price. The IBM corporate personality was the product bought.

Product branding
Here every product or service has its own brand name, and may have its own personality. Washing powders, soaps and detergents, for example, carry their own names and little use, if any, is made of the corporate name, which might be Proctor and Gamble, Unilever or whatever. In this case, in order to stand out and become world class, the product itself needs to be given a strong personality, as with Lux soap, the Lexus car or Michelin tyres.

House branding
Here we see a 'family' of products or services, each branded or named separately but with an endorsement from the company. This is also referred to as 'umbrella' or 'banner' branding. In such a case the product itself (as with the child of a family) gains support in the form of personality and overall brand image from the parent. Motor cars are good examples here, such as the Rolls Royce Silver Spirit. The endorsement of the company and its personality gives the consumer assurance of quality and heritage, on top of the product's own reputation. In some cases the corporate personality is dominant and the products merely get numbers and letters assigned to them, as with Mercedes Benz S320 or BMW 328i, even though they do signify certain technical features of the cars. In other cases, although having the advantage of a strong corporate parent brand, the product adds its own unique brand strength. Thus in its heyday the Austin Mini had its own unique brand identity which has

continued to enjoy cult status even after the demise of the manufacturer Austin-Morris. In the relatively few cases where there is harmony between a corporate and product brand identity, remarkably strong personality can result, as with McDonald's Big Mac, or Johnson's baby lotion. Examples of such brand synergy from the automotive world are the VW Beetle and Jensen Interceptor in their respective eras. Such personality-packed products uncannily take on personal characteristics in the eyes of their owners, taking pride of place even within a family hierarchy.

Combined with a product message, corporate and house branding provides companies with the opportunity to send a double message with every communication. As Akio Morita of Sony has been quoted as saying, 'The company name is the life of an enterprise. It carries responsibility and guarantees the quality of the product.' The exception in Sony's case is probably the Walkman which has carved its own unique product brand niche in marketing history, outshining even its prestigious parent.

Co-operative branding

Protecting a brand against dilution has become a complex task for brand managers. There is now widespread use of co-operatives, licensing, acquisitions, partnering, and extensions. Many manufacturers are endangering their own brands with practices that can obscure the source of a product and dilute a brand's association.

In the case of the growing practice of co-operative branding, customers obtain the benefits of multiple brands with a single product or service purchase. For example, you can eat a pizza in a Pizza Hut restaurant inside a Marriott's hotel. Or you can buy Baskin Robbins ice cream in a Dunkin Donuts restaurant and Thomas English muffins in a Burger King restaurant. Your well-branded car comes complete with a Pioneer CD and Michelin tyres. Inside your hi-fi is a Dolby system and inside your IBM PC is an Intel chip, a Seagate hard disk and Windows operating software.

Intel employs co-operative branding worldwide with most

computer manufacturers. They gain from Intel's quality reputation and Intel gets its brand name all over the world to compete with OEM and other manufacturers. Co-branding usually involves co-advertising which means that costs are shared.

An individual brand can risk weakening through brand association and the chances of brand asymmetry between manufacturers must be many-fold. The important thing is to adhere to and support your desired personality rather than go for short-term gains through co-operative associations. Remember that the customer — whether knowingly or otherwise — makes associations through brand exposure, so it pays to protect and manage your brand identity.

Types and applications of branding

Within these basic levels or combinations of brands there are also different types or applications, and this also has significance for corporate personality.

Brand extension

Manufacturers and service providers use any of the above levels and approaches to support their brands. In the ongoing attempt to dislodge competitors, markets are deliberately fragmented by brand *extensions*. The soft drinks market is an example: with colas and uncolas, regular and diet, caffeine and caffeine-free, multiple flavours, natural ingredients, clear colour, freshness dating, specialised containers, and so on. This of course is an obvious application of the product differentiation principle linked with market segmentation. The dangers are that speciality brands and private labels enter the fray and this can lead to so-called brand blindness.

From a corporate personality point of view, extensions need to support the corporate image message, contributing thus to long-term corporate success as well as short-term sales.

Brand families

A family can grow (as any family does) without the next offspring being any less a part of it. Consider the wide range of car models in the BMW brand stable ('3', '5' and '7' series), or a range of special models within a basic model type (turbo, estate, soft top, diesel), or differentiated soft drinks within a brand family. The number of products, or degree of brand extension, is not as important as the need to maintain the essential personality behind the brand. The addition of a diesel and estate version to the Porsche range would do nothing for its personality — whether at corporate or product (say 911) level. It would disproportionately *dilute* the existing brands. Ford or Peugeot would experience no such effects. So brand management involves what you extend and don't extend as well as management of an existing brand. Stick to your personality and, with a little creativity, you can project it a very long way.

Niche branding

One of the challenges of the big brands is to find strategies that will repel the proliferation of smaller brands and survive this fragmentation trend. The strategy of niche branding, one approach, is unlikely to be a viable one in the long term for most manufacturers. Either the niche will turn into a fully fledged brand category (*à la* diet soft drink, perhaps, or flavoured potato snacks) or otherwise will merge with other super categories. Retailers, of course, need not suffer from any of this as greater choice is offered to customers through the availability of speciality brands and this can encourage channel (i.e. the retail outlet), as distinct from brand loyalty. The personality of a food chain such as Tesco's or Sainsbury's in the UK might command greater loyalty than the many brands they stock, whatever brand warfare is being waged.

Who gets the credit?

There is an even more fundamental consideration in branding: who gets the credit? Because of the different ways and levels in which a brand reaches the customer it is not always possible to know what impels the buying decision or creates loyalty. A company can bask in the glory of one of its products or conversely a product can draw on the personality and standing of its corporate parent; or two independent brands can enjoy win-win benefits because of the synergy in customer perception, as may well apply, say, with IBM and Intel, Mercedes and Goodyear, or Nike and Velcro.

The 'two brand' rule

There is a useful rule that applies to brands: two different brands cannot occupy the same position in a consumer's mind at one time. For example, if Dove's (beauty soap) benefit claim that it 'doesn't dry your face' is usurped by a competitive brand, that brand will find it almost impossible to occupy that place without first demolishing Dove's USP. *Features* can be copied or even bettered, such as 'one quarter moisturising cream' or '0 to 60 in 7 seconds'. But *qualitative benefits* are different. For example, the Energiser bunny commercials (touting long-lasting batteries) increased Duracell's sales much more than those of Energiser because Duracell already owned the 'long-lasting' dimension in consumers' minds. Who got the credit? How many times have you remembered an advertisement but cannot recall the brand? The rule can easily be adapted to corporate personality: two companies cannot occupy the same personality 'territory'. Put the other way, two personalities cannot embody the same company — there can only be one IBM, one Federal Express, one Marks and Spencer. This is another reason for investing in long-term corporate personality. Charisma is *memorable*, and a charismatic company or product will tend to take centre stage in its customers' minds.

The 'first brand' rule

Credit, it seems, goes to the first brand encountered at the point of purchase, whereas blame typically goes to the second. According to this rule, a good experience in a Pizza Hut in a Marriott hotel (to stay with an earlier example) would leave most of the credit with the hotel if you chose Marriott first. A bad experience, on the other hand, would tend to blame Pizza Hut, even if not confined to the Pizza Hut meal. As another example, IBM would get credit for fault-free computing, and Intel (or any other recognisable associated brand that might be remotely at fault) would take the lion's share of the blame if the system crashes. Psychologically we tend to stick by (and indeed make excuses for) our decisions and actions (in responding to the 'first brand' appeal).

This does suggest that a lot of thought has to be given to any sort of co-operative branding, especially from a customer perception viewpoint. Inappropriate brand relationships can certainly mar a well-earned personality image. The 'first brand' rule also highlights the point that to maintain a good corporate personality you have to consistently 'produce the goods' as well as promoting an image.

Leap-frogging

One way to accrue corporate credit is to ride the success of a competitor, not by matching them but by beating them. In other words, by adding your own unique benefit. Several car manufacturers have challenged Volvo's brand position on 'safety' by introducing more specific benefits, from radar sensors to anti-lock braking and so on. They are offering 'active safety' rather than Volvo's 'passive safety' and that, it seems, is a meaningful enhancement in the mind of the customer. Leap-frogging becomes easier if the dominant brand is slow in introducing new technology or has weak promotional support for the brand. In the late 1970s Nike's innovative running shoes surpassed the then leading brand (Adidas) for those very reasons.

Product innovation and creative marketing can ensure that

yours is the brand that stays at the top of the customer's mind. It is no longer enough for a toothpaste to clean teeth and taste good. It has to prevent cavities, freshen breath, fight plaque, remove stains and guarantee you the partner of your dreams. Each is a distinct, brandable attribute. Each speaks to the customer with a personality of its own. The success of Arm and Hammer's baking soda toothpaste put brands such as Colgate ('cleans teeth') and Crest ('prevents cavities') on the defensive. Just as with 'active safety' in cars, a new dimension of competition was opened up. So the principle that two brands cannot occupy the same ground can work in your favour if you can relate to your customer's mind and personality with a distinct brand identity.

By leap-frogging you can gain competitive advantage by creating even a marginal perception of benefit — just enough to overtake your competitor. The real trick, however, is to have gained a perception (like Volvo's safety feature) that may have taken your competitor many years to earn. This also highlights the danger of investing your corporate personality with just one overriding characteristic, and a measurable feature rather than a qualitative benefit at that.

The 'halo effect'

Sometimes success begets success and the attraction of some entity is so strong that it benefits unrelated entities and people. If your product is featured in a blockbuster film, it can acquire overnight cult popularity. The 'halo effect' is well known to PR and marketing consultants, of course, and its power is reflected in the enormous figures that change hands so that companies and their products get media exposure. Most sports sponsorship is based on this principle. Who gets the credit? The fact is that a big enough 'personality', whether an individual celebrity or a company such as IBM or Microsoft, or a product like Coke or Big Mac, can produce lots of reflected customer perception. It's big business. Michael Jordan has earned a lot more in fees from Nike, McDonald's and Chevrolet than he ever earned playing basketball. The 'personality' does not even have to endorse the product. Michael Jackson appeared in three TV commercials for a reported fee of $10 million. But here is the power of the halo effect: he was not required to use, mention or even be seen in the same frame as the product or its name! Even the commercials themselves became top news. A lot of people can get a lot of credit through the halo effect.

Credits are balanced out by debits, of course. The macho John Wayne, decked in rugged western attire on horseback looked straight into the camera and spoke of his headache and why he chose Datril pain reliever. This was nothing less than embarrassing. The personality and product did not ring true — another case of marketing schizophrenia. To use another example, does the public really believe that Jack Nicklaus knows anything about cellular phones? So halo effects don't always shed light where you want it shed. If you are choosing a live personality to support your brand you should at least choose a personality that is close to the one you want to project.

Fallen angels

Things can be even worse. Pepsi had the unique fortune to do endorsement deals with entertainers Michael Jackson and Madonna and boxing champion Mike Tyson — quite a *coup* at that moment in time. Then the company had to fend off questions about the private lives of its expensive celebrities. All the free publicity was the worst kind to get. Mental images of child molestation soon shattered a long-cultivated 'Pepsi Generation' corporate image. Hertz Rent-a-Car went one better in their association with sport megastar O J Simpson who was charged with murder in the trial of the century. Hertz, in attempting to distance themselves from the association, just dug for themselves a deeper pit. You can't always get it right, but you can do a risk minimisation exercise that will sniff out likely notoriety. Add some caution to your creativity when projecting your own corporate personality. This argues for creating your own strong personality organically rather than resorting to the risky strategy of backing a winner.

Brand protection

Not surprisingly a lot of attention is being given to brand protection. From a narrow perspective this means legally policing your hard earned brand position, and big brands have built up an impressive track record. So much so that design infringement, as was alleged to be the case with Sainsbury's own-label Coke, will be sure to be an expensive and risky business. From a broader perspective, protection means ongoing management to prevent dilution, undeserved blame through association, and getting credit wherever it is due. There will inevitably be battles and own goals in the long life-cycle of a major brand. The soft drinks manufacturer Schweppes did an exemplary job in responding to product contamination. But their best insurance was probably an already dominant brand. As a rule, rather than reactive PR and slogans, a strong, consistent personality strategy is the proactive way to protect your brands.

How brands are built

Brands offer people benefits that are often intangible: image, security, status, dependability, prestige, success, quality of life. Products become strong brands when people see additional value in them over and above the basic product.

Added value can be achieved by introducing after-sales service, guarantees and warranties, easy payment terms and so on. The more of these that are added, or the greater the perceived value of the extras to the customer, the greater becomes the difference between this product or service and those of competitors. Moreover, it becomes harder for competitors to keep up, and they risk being seen as a follower. So the more value a company wraps around the basic brand, the greater the sustainable competitive advantage is likely to be. And this is an ongoing process as customer expectations rise and competitors respond.

Delivering the goods

The survival over many years of top brands offers its own lesson: in the final analysis products have to perform, and deliver the benefits and features promised. There is clearly a limit to the loyalty of even the most obsessive user of a product or service. And in terms of brand building the message has to be applied from both ends — on the one hand continuous improvement in product quality, and at the same time a realistic marketing message consistent with the product.

It's no good spending millions of pounds on the message 'We are the "listening bank"' if the experience of thousands of customers tells a very different story. In the revolution that most banks have had to undergo in the last ten or so years their problem was bigger than branding — or even marketing. There was a fundamental lack in culture, attitude and basic service quality. The same applied during the 1970s in the motor industry when some makes of car were chronically unreliable or rust-prone. A message inconsistent with the realities of the product is likely to be counterproductive since the customer is unnecessarily aggravated, insult being added to injury. A personality strategy may mean that you have to go back to basics.

On the other hand the marketeers need not down tools. Most companies and products have some positive features. For example, the VW Beetle, close to anachronistic after many years in production, and universally outperformed as a modern motor car, could still benefit from its smallness, economy and simply-engineered reliability. Advertising budgets would have been wasted on trying to directly counter the fact that it was noisy, smelly and of Second World War design standards. When you change the *perception* of the product, however, such as when the VW Golf GTi wins on the race circuits and captures the hearts of boy racers, you can change the marketing message. Even a limited track record of performance can be projected with confidence. Develop your strengths and embody them creatively in your personality message.

By rigorously reviewing your personality strategy and using good market research you will quickly become aware of deficiencies in product quality and service standards (which will have to be addressed at the same strategic level). In many cases this exercise is carried out under a quality or re-engineering banner without reference to outside perceptions of personality. This is a blinkered strategy, for although there are basic levels of quality that have to be achieved, reality *is* perception as far as the customer is concerned. In other words they are buying perceived quality just as they are buying perceived features and benefits. The customer may put up with the odd product breakdown, but may have zero tolerance for discourtesy or broken promises.

But even delivering the goods is a perception. Top-selling brands are by no means at the top of the objective quality ratings. But they are part of a marketing mix that works and they enjoy a personality loyalty that will forgive a few weaknesses, as we all would in the case of a close friend. Thus personality strategies should not only be pursued in parallel to production and quality strategies but they should be given equal status when the corporate investment pool is considered. The same harmony needs to apply when considering product and corporate branding. Deliver the goods and be perceived to deliver the goods. If you do anything well, don't rely on your competitors to tell the world about it. If any aspect of your corporate personality is marketable, start expressing it by a consistent message and consistent action. If any part of your corporate personality is lacking, be prepared to change it, at the same time projecting your strengths.

Brands that last

A clear message emerges from a study of brands over the ages. Good brands have a long life-span. Because success does not happen by accident, positive promotion management is needed, as well as actual product performance that stands the test of time. Differentiate brands along new dimensions that are relevant to your customers, such as in the earlier toothpaste or 'active safety' examples. Look out for creative 'breakthrough' goods and services for brand openings, and breakthrough benefits to strengthen existing brands. Create new and better distribution channels to benefit your customers and improve their perception of your product or service. And cultivate a positive corporate personality, which, although neither evaluated not accounted for in the balance sheet, is a priceless asset that will last for generations. At worst it can be a very high return investment and the best kind of insurance against the uncertainties of markets.

Appealing to customers

Brands are built by appealing to both the rational and emotional aspects of customers' minds.

Rational appeal

Some brands attract consumers by the rational, logical way in which they are presented, with emphasis on product features and economic benefits. For example, toothpaste with fluoride to give teeth greater protection; unit trusts which give a balanced investment portfolio; vitamins-enriched cereals for healthier diets.

Emotional appeal

On the other hand some brands appeal very much to people's emotions. Body Shop will not test its products on animals, Häagen-Dazs is dedicated to pleasure, BMW is the ultimate driving machine. Emotional branding can be very powerful if it is targeted at the right kind of consumer who feels deeply about particular subject areas. In this case qualitative product benefits tend to be emphasised in the brand message.

Rational and emotional

The most powerful brands combine the two. Life assurance (one of the more difficult products to sell) has for many years been offered on a rational decision-making basis — it is logical to have cover and a long-term investment for the future. Companies have added to this approach by appealing emotionally to would-be buyers: 'What will happen to your family if something happens to you?' and 'We offer you peace of mind' are examples of ways in which life assurance has been given an emotional edge. This is the appeal to heart as well as mind, or to both right and left brain. In consumer purchase decisions often the desire is there (emotion) but the rational mind wants a logical reason to buy now, particularly in the case of luxury goods and premium brands.

To brand or not to brand

The branding decision

The first stage in a successful branding process is to choose which products and services would best be enhanced by a brand identity, based on why people like brands and how they influence customers. Initially it will be wise to choose just one product or service so that you can learn from the process and fully evaluate the results. If your brand management resources are spread too thinly you will not get the best out of what could be an important asset.

The selection can be based on any number of criteria. Here are some examples:

- What product or service best solves a customer's problem?
- What product or service do I most want to distinguish from my competition?
- Will branding add either real or perceived value to this product or service?
- Will branding help us to advertise or promote this product or service more effectively?
- Will branding this product or service help our target audience make a more informed decision about it?
- Does branding this product or service help us to address the needs of our niche markets?
- Will this enhance our existing personality or help us to project a desired change?

In each case we have included services as well as products.

This is not just to embrace service providers such as banks or hotels, but to remind us of the fact that there is a service or intangible aspect to every product. This intangible aspect is more amenable than the generic or commodity aspect of the product to unique selling features and personality.

'Green field' branding

In contrast to making changes to and managing an existing brand, in a 'green field' situation there is more opportunity to apply all these principles. For example, your brand identity could be based on a chosen market segment. Cadillac and Mercedes Benz are examples of market branding. They reflect a well-defined 'personality' already out there. In this case you would look at your own client list and ask, 'What do they need most? What are the greatest opportunities? How could we bring specialised expertise to this sector?'

Alternatively, consider all the emerging sectors. Which could have an application for you? Are there benefits you can offer which will appeal to that sort of person? In researching potential new markets you would try to find out, in respect of end-consumers or end-user industry, their likely growth, as well as their fears and goals. Then wrap a brand identity round what you find. Rather than offer a generic product, or even worse an 'all things to all people' personality, mirror the personality of your chosen customer base.

So whether creating new markets or creating brands for existing markets the principle is: The highest degree of brand effectiveness takes place when you align specialised product or service with specialised markets. The crux of it is the alignment of seller/buyer personalities. That means rapport, and rapport means business.

The branding process for new products

There are plenty of potential pitfalls in the process of branding new products and it may be advisable to consult a reputable branding consultant. Just remember this is an important investment, and make comparisons with the kind of external help you automatically call on for major strategic investments, let alone shorter-term advertising and product promotion. Here are the steps involved, whether you are carrying out the process internally or externally. If internally, the consultant will be the project manager or brand manager charged with the implementation process.

1. *Project briefing*
   This is the 'getting to know you' stage. The consultant will ask scores of questions because the main job at this stage is to gain product information, to learn about your market segments and assess the competition. An internal manager will finish up with a lot more knowledge about the product and market than he started with. A good outsider may finish up with having a better knowledge of the product than anyone inside the company.
2. *Name plan.*
   This is the basic plan you will follow over the weeks ahead to establish objectives and branding strategies. An essential part of this process should address your corporate personality and the whole branding process should be aligned with this.
3. *Name development*
   To implement the name plan the consultant will call on other resources such as target market creative groups, computer name generators, linguistics experts, freelance or in-house creative specialists and the firm's own rich database of name ideas. Once again the personality test will be applied.
4. *Interim reporting and meeting*
   From possibly hundreds of name ideas the consultant will present a shortlist for discussion.
5. *Name candidate screenings*
   When the list has been modified, prioritised and approved the candidate screening process proper begins. The proposed brands are checked for language and cultural conflicts. A search is undertaken to eliminate legal problems. The likely brands are tested for consumer response and there will be a further test as to whether the brand is aligned with

the company's personality identity. If necessary further creative work will be carried out.

6. *Action plan*
   Once the prospective brands have been given a clean bill of health the final presentation is made to the client company along with the consultant's recommendations and rationale.

The process may take about four months depending on the company's ability or willingness to free up its people to carry out its end of the work and the time that searches and unforeseen hurdles take up. This is not an enormous time bearing in mind that a brand asset can last for years or even decades and generate big profits, while generating a marketable capital value of its own.

Branding and non-branding — case studies
As well as a multitude of examples of successful branding over the years, there are also good examples of the branding process. One such example is PRODIGY(R), an on-line computer service. A branding consultant was called in by IBM for Trintex, a consortium of technical types representing IBM and Sears. Trintex had developed an on-line computer capability that it hoped to market to 'main street' computer users — families, individual investors and students. It planned to call the service 'Trintex' after the corporate name it had already created.

With the expert guidance of a branding professional Trintex changed direction completely and developed instead a user-friendly, familiar human brand name that implied both intelligence and vast amounts of knowledge through the service, but which constantly reminded the users that real people were involved. In its first few months PRODIGY(R) sold more units than its suppliers ever imagined, and became so successful that the company itself was later renamed Prodigy Services Company.

On the other hand an example of an unsuccessful branding is Merril Lynch's introduction of the Money Market Account in the late 1970s. The concept, a catch-all account that earns interest and permits cheque writing on cash it gathers from other accounts in the Merril Lynch family, was innovative at the time. It also positioned Merril Lynch to compete head-on with banks, also an opportunistic approach at the time. Merril Lynch did not brand its new product, nor did it seek a trademark or other protection. As soon as deregulation came in the 1980s, bank after bank copied the concept and the innovative breakthrough was lost forever to Merril Lynch. We can only imagine how the fortunes of Merril Lynch might have been different if their winning product had been properly branded. *Any* name would have offered protection, and a good name might have gone down in brand history, perhaps, like the Walkman and Hoover, taking its place in the English language.

Brands and personality

Some of the world's leading companies have used personality so skilfully in their product marketing over the years that they have almost become real personalities in their own right, and are as well known in all societies and cultures as are film heroes, cartoon characters, sports stars or great leaders.

In Europe, Asia and around the world Coca Cola, Rolls Royce, Nestlé, Batman, Sony, and Mercedes are equally well known. They all have an impact on our lives, and just as crowds of people will go to see an international star's latest film, so they will flock to try the latest brand offering. This was the case when McDonald's opened their first restaurant in Moscow and when Microsoft launched Windows 95. The attraction of a strong personality is irresistible, and people relate to brand personalities in the same way as they do to human personalities. A charismatic or larger-than-life personality is especially attractive, and the same applies to products and companies.

Breathing life into products

You can breathe new life into a product by projecting a strong personality. To establish a successful product brand companies must have products at least as good as those of the competition. Really powerful brands have all the other attributes of other products, but in addition they introduce the elements of personality.

A good example of this is Milo, the nutritional drink made by Nestlé, the biggest food processing company in the world. Although not well known in the UK, it is a household name in many parts of the world. Intended for growing children and targeted at families, Milo is a quality product and several million cups are tested every year. But other companies could, without too much difficulty, match the ingredients, the quality, packaging and so on. What is so difficult for them to match or copy, however, are the personality characteristics and values that Nestlé have constantly projected through Milo since 1934 — good taste, healthiness and energy, and 'winning moments'.

Personification of the Milo brand comes in the advertising material with young healthy children scoring goals, swimming, running and winning races just as top professional sports people do. The children are seen enjoying the drink and full of energy. The advertisements of twenty years ago are basically the same as those today, including brand colours and logo, except, of course, that they feature contemporary sportswear and sports facilities. But the Milo personality shines through with rational, emotional, physical and aspirational appeal. This is a good example of consistency in personality management.

Marlboro is another much-quoted world-class example of power brand building using personality characteristics. It uses the same successful formula:

- choose your personality characteristics that will appeal to your target customers
- project and personify those characteristics consistently over time

Everything follows from the two main personality characteristics of Marlboro, which appear to be 'strength' and 'independence'. Brand managers never do anything that might be interpreted as being out of character with the brand personality.

Strength	Independence
Tough Marlboro cowboy	The self-responsible cowboy
Strong red and white packaging	The wide-open Marlboro countryside
Strong flavour/blend	American West imagery
Strong horses	
Tough activities	

To further promote and personify the personality, the Marlboro product brand only endorses and sponsors masculine sports activities where those characteristics are prevalent, such as Formula 1 Grand Prix motor and motorcycle racing.

Just as with people, product and corporate personalities spell life, imagination and intrinsic value. And, as any sports or entertainment manager will agree, personalities can be reinforced and projected. We all know that some people are hard to remember, and others are hard to forget. The same applies to corporate and product personalities and a world-class strategy means having to be unforgettable.

Brand personality characteristics

Successful branding will depend on the brand characteristics and how appropriately and creatively these are communicated to the customer. An interesting classification of Brand Personality characteristics and their measurement, called the Brand Personality Scale (BPS) produced five major personality factors (the Big Five):

- Sincerity
- Excitement
- Competence
- Sophistication
- Ruggedness

According to the research, as quoted by David Aaker in his book *Building Strong Brands*, these five characteristics account for 93 per cent of the observed differences between the brands measured.

The research concludes that most brand personalities have some or all of these five characteristics to a greater or lesser degree. More complex personalities more often have all five evident. Each of these characteristics breaks down into sub-characteristics:

Sincerity

• Down-to-earth	family-oriented, small-town, conventional, blue collar, all-American
• Honest	sincere, real, ethical, thoughtful, caring
• Wholesome	original, genuine, ageless, classic, old-fashioned
• Cheerful	sentimental, friendly, warm, happy

Excitement

• Daring	trendy, exciting, off-beat, flashy, provocative
• Spirited	cool, young, lively, outgoing, adventurous
• Imaginative	unique, humorous, surprising, artistic, fun
• Up-to-date	independent, contemporary, innovative, aggressive

Competence
- Reliable   hardworking, secure, efficient, trustworthy, careful
- Intelligent   technical, corporate, serious
- Successful   leader, confident, influential

Sophistication
- Upper Class   glamorous, good-looking, pretentious, sophisticated
- Charming   feminine, smooth, sexy, gentle

Ruggedness
- Outdoorsy   masculine, Western, active, athletic
- Tough   rugged, strong, no-nonsense

All of these, of course, can be applied just as much to corporate as to product personality. Again, we must stress that whatever personality characteristics are used it's not just consistency that is important when projecting those to the public. Appropriateness is just as important.

Consider the following examples taken from the above characteristics:

Imaginative and up-to-date
If these aspects of the 'Excitement' category are chosen it might well be appropriate for a technology-based company that wants to be seen as state-of-the-art, innovative, progressive and fantastic, such as Apple, or Nintendo. It would not be particularly appropriate for companies offering more traditional or more serious products or services.

Daring and spirited
If these aspects of 'Excitement' are chosen they might be more appropriate for a fashion goods company targeting young people looking to be individualistic and trendy, rather than an aircraft manufacturer.

Intelligent and reliable ('competence')
These characteristics would be appropriate for some industry leaders such as IBM and the BBC, but not for others such as Revlon and Reebok.

Honest and wholesome ('sincerity')
These would be more appropriate for real estate, foods or life assurance companies, but less so for motorcycles and electronics.

The erosion of brand loyalty

Evidence of how brand loyalty can be eroded presents another strong argument for more work on personality. From a major survey that is likely to give many brand managers a shock, Grey Advertising have published figures that point to the fact that the days of brand loyalty for many companies are numbered.

Using a Brand Loyalty Index focusing on over 100 brands in twenty categories in every region of the world against a perfect score of 1,000, only Campbell's Soup gained a loyalty score of over 500 (533). The average score was only 117 and figures went down to as low as two!

The survey clearly outlined the promiscuity of consumers, and the fact that they look for more than product performance and value for money. The results revealed that they look more to relationships which will earn their loyalty. This tremendous need for trust and confidence in our opinion can only come from the personality relationship. If people cannot relate to personality characteristics, because they are absent or poorly projected, there is nothing really to retain their custom.

Global marketing strategies

A well-devised corporate personality is also the key to global success in branding. The possibilities for a global presence are exemplified by the household names brands we are so familiar with around the world.

Firstly, companies that are developing global strategies

often do so in order to achieve the benefits associated with economies of scale and consistency. Global branding can gain economies of scale in advertising, public relations, promotions, packaging and other activities if they have a consistent image to portray.

Secondly, a recognisable global presence can be created by rationalising design features and presenting a consistent corporate face. The Nike 'swoosh', the Shell logo, IBM's lettering and McDonald's Golden Arches provide instant associations in the minds of consumers with clear concise design. Companies can also reap the benefits of having 'home country' associations, even though they might adapt some market communications to take into account local cultural factors or issues. Coca Cola unquestionably personifies its USA heritage but is sensitive in its campaigns around the world to cultural and national values.

Power brands — the rewards

Power brands combine personality and positioning to take seemingly ordinary products and services to world-class proportions. The financial rewards can be spectacular, because they give:

- competitive differentiation
- premium prices
- higher sales volumes
- economics of scale
- greater security of demand
- wider customer base

All of these elements transfer to the bottom line of the company providing higher sustainable year-on-year profits and increased asset value. Power brands are so valuable that they command astonishing prices when sold. The most often quoted example of this is when Nestlé bought the Rowntree company and its brands, reportedly paying over five times the net asset value of the company. Big brands make big money, but big brands need to have strong personalities as part of their identity if they are to succeed.

Summary

1. A brand is more than just a logo, trademark or product. It is all of these plus the inherent intangible values the customer sees as attractive.
2. What the company decides a brand is to be becomes the brand's identity. What the customer sees is its image. If the two don't match there is cause for concern.
3. People like to buy brands because they offer:

   - a means of choice
   - a guarantee of quality
   - a means of risk avoidance
   - a means of simple understanding
   - a means of self-expression

4. Companies can have corporate, product, or house branding.
5. Many companies seek to extend their brands and enter into co-operative arrangements, but this is only successful when the new lines or brand relationships are in keeping with the core brand identity.
6. It is important to know who gets the credit when brands are so mixed in the market place.
7. In building brands, you will have to appeal both to the rational and emotional parts of potential customers' minds.
8. It is personality that, when added, breathes life into the brand. Personality humanises the product and makes it attractive to customers.
9. The erosion of brand loyalty and global competition means that companies who build brands without personality are less likely to be successful.
10. Brands with a strong personality reap tremendous financial rewards.

CHAPTER NINE

CHOOSING
CUSTOMERS
THROUGH
SEGMENTATION

We have seen how a company can create or change its personality, how it positions itself in the mind of the customer and how brands can help to project the desired image. Perceptions happen, of course, at an individual customer level. They belong to real people rather than just the 'market'. But marketing means attracting and keeping enough customers to make a profit. So it is necessary to identify and attract a big enough group, or market *segment*, otherwise even the most charismatic corporate personality strategy will not succeed. Your personality strategy must be part of a coherent marketing plan, and be in harmony with what is termed the marketing concept — which includes making a profit.

The personality segmentation process started a long time ago. The Greek philosopher Galen recognised that people tended to pursue identity through being introvert, extrovert, competitive or careful in their behaviour. Combinations of these produced four basic personality types: performer, ruler, follower and thinker. Since those early days segmentation has become a science but personality has never lost its significance as a segment differentiator. Companies are just beginning to realise how important is the match between corporate and customer personality.

Knowing your customer means knowing them as human beings, either in a one-to-one way as with true relationship marketing, or modally — through a modal personality that closely simulates your total market. To date, geodemographic data has been the usual basis for market segmentation. Introducing personality adds a further dimension to segmentation. In order to reflect the characteristics of your customers in your personality, you need to segment the market in terms of personality or perhaps more qualitative lifestyle characteristics.

Segmentation is becoming more important every year as mass marketing becomes obsolete and market fragmentation becomes more evident. Traditionally the process used by researchers in segmenting a market involved three steps:

1. Identifying segments by the behavioural and psychological characteristics of the consumers in them
2. Investigating what differences exist between the segments
3. Evaluating the relative attractiveness of each segment in terms of volume and profit

Alternatively, a company can ask some basic questions:

- How is the market segmented?
- Which segments are most attractive?
- Which segment coverage best fits our personality characteristics?
- How vulnerable will we be to attack?

The case for market segmentation

The following are some of the arguments in favour of market segmentation. In each case the argument can apply to psychographic or lifestyle characteristics as well as to geographic, demographic, or other more traditional forms of segmentation.

1. The natural forces at work in world markets are moving in

favour of market fragmentation, with more and more individual segments wanting special attention. This means that to ignore the fact that segments exist is both unrealistic and foolish.

2. Groups of consumers having unfulfilled needs provide companies with a marketing opportunity. Identifying such opportunities might well result from the segmentation process which will give you a better understanding of your customer. New lifestyle segmentation can give special insights into the way your customers think, including their aspirations.

3. Segments provide companies with focus and direction, which means that marketing programmes can be better directed. Companies can focus on growth segments, for instance, rather than ones that are in a stage of maturity or decline.

4. If companies focus on particular segments, it is easier for them to measure themselves, in terms of strengths and weaknesses, against the competition. This enables them to target markets which match both their competencies and personality.

5. Segmentation allows you to set clearer objectives for profitable marketing. Many companies calculate the profitability of products and services, but relatively few calculate this for specific markets, let alone individual customer type. Clearly defined segments can provide valuable information about which are more profitable.

6. For those companies, particularly smaller ones, that are already involved in 'niche' marketing, segmentation provides the opportunity to find and defend niche markets.

7. Segmentation in one form or another is vital to market planning. It gives focus and direction because a company can clearly see how fast certain segments are growing and how potentially profitable they are.

8. Because the dynamics of markets are fast changing, segmentation enables a company to set marketing objectives. Existing segments may limit opportunities for existing products as needs and habits change. By identifying new or

more appropriate segments, companies can either develop strategies to extend their existing product sales, or develop entirely new products to meet new markets.

Segmentation makes marketing sense of a global, impersonal market place. It helps you to identify and communicate with real customers. It enables you to choose your customers, and, having positioned yourself accordingly, it enables certain groups of customer to choose you.

The criteria for successful segmentation

There are three criteria for success in segmenting markets:

Different. Segments must be clearly differentiated from each other in terms of market behaviour and customer perception. It would be no use having a category of 'yuppies' if they thought and acted in the same way as 'grumpies'. It would be inefficient to give the same marketing message to both risk-takers and more cautious, conservative people.

Viable. Each segment should be of sufficient size and potential to make pursuing it worthwhile. The 'yuppies' segment in China is reported to be 75 million people. Most customer type segments are confined to just a few characteristics yet potentially comprise millions of individuals.

Accessible. Each segment must be reachable in terms of your ability to communicate with and serve that market.

Some ways of segmenting markets

Some of the bases of segmenting markets are as follows:

Geographic
Splitting a market by region, city or town size, area, density, climatic differences, etc. This was where segmentation started, as small manufacturers wished to limit their investment, or had limited distribution channels.

Demographic
Age, sex, marital status, income level, occupation and educational level are some of the indicators used here. Although easier to obtain, these data are not necessarily the best predictors of customer behaviour.

Geodemographic
The above two categories can also provide combined variables. You can determine, for example, how many people aged twenty-five to thirty-two, married with two children, with a combined income of X, live in Y part of the city.

Sociocultural
Culture, religion, race, social class, and stages of the family life cycle are often used to differentiate market segments.

User behaviour
When and why people buy and use a product, and how loyal they are to the company or brand, are measures which can be used to target customers more precisely. This approach suggests so-called volume segmentation. It is well known that in most product categories 80 per cent of consumption is attributed to perhaps only 20 to 30 per cent of customers. Repeat purchase and the reasons for purchase decisions can also be studied and some companies segment markets according to degrees of loyalty that consumers exhibit towards them or their products. So, for instance, segments such as 'passively loyal' and 'fence sitters' indicate consumers who buy out of habit rather than rationality, and those who are indifferent between two or more companies or products, respectively. There are other such categories, and the objective of this sort of segmentation is to improve and identify ways in which

communications and other programmes can induce customers to become more loyal to the company.

Benefit
Segmenting markets by the benefits customers derive from a company, product or service can be a powerful method of segmentation. This mirrors the emphasis on benefits over features in product advertising and selling techniques.

Psychographic
This is concerned with how customers think, their attitude, opinions and the more private aspects of their lifestyle. It is a qualitative rather than quantitative basis for identifying customer categories. It is gaining in popularity and is specially significant in reflecting the lifestyle characteristics of customers in your corporate personality.

These are broad bases which should be used with some caution. Take, for example, user behaviour. While two customers may fall into the same high consumption category (on the 80/20 rule) they are not necessarily of the same value. For example, heavy coffee drinkers can be divided into those who drink chain-store brands and those who drink premium brands. Chain-store customers think, in effect, that all coffee is the same so they go for a less expensive brand. Premium brand buyers, on the other hand, are ready to pay a few pence extra for their individual taste and favourite brand. Although both part of the 'heavy buying' group, each of these two types is of very different value to a brand, having different loyalties, and will respond differently to advertising messages. Knowing these crucial customer distinctions will enable more powerful brand messages to be communicated to the right people.

In the sociocultural area there are some classifications such as the Warner Index of Status Characteristics which labels and describes people belonging to a particular social 'class' and their consumption habits, but this is again a little general in nature. The Family Life Cycle approach is another classification that groups people together, combining age, marital status, children's ages and general family stages. This has been used quite successfully in some industries, such as financial services, because it links financial circumstances to consumer purchasing characteristics. But for other applications it is of limited value unless supplemented by further research.

In the case of benefit segmentation, similar caveats apply. It is the total configuration of the benefits sought that differentiates one segment from another, rather than the fact that one segment is seeking one particular benefit and another quite a different benefit. Individual benefits are likely to apply over several segments. Research shows, not surprisingly, that most people would like to have as many benefits as possible. However, the relative importance customers attach to each benefit — or their benefit pecking order — can vary dramatically. Only when isolated in this way can benefits be used as a reliable basis for segmentation.

Benefit segmentation and 'hot buttons'

Campbell Soup made a study of segmentation, classifying which particular benefits appealed to different buyers. They called the classifications 'hot buttons', and this led to some interesting developments in the world of food marketing. They included:

Flavour
People were interested in taste — strong tastes, light tastes or ethnic tastes. Food products responding to this benefit use more spices, wines and flavourings.

Freshness/natural tastes
The more health-conscious prefer salads and natural tasting foods, hence the growth of salad bars in supermarkets and restaurants.

Healthiness
The very health-conscious buyers want less additives, MSG, salt, sugar, and cholesterol. In response there is

a wide range of foods that are 'low in sodium', 'low fat' or 'cholesterol free'.

Variety
For some people food is an experience, an adventure. Exotic and gourmet foods are the response.

Convenience
Customers seeking this benefit can buy foods ready to cook, requiring little or no preparation.

Portion size
Single servings and meals for two have arisen in response to this need.

Campbell Soup also take into account demographics in their product offerings, modifying recipes to suit different regions of the country. So, for example, Texas and California get more spices than other areas of the USA to cater for varied cultural tastes.

Psychographic segmentation

Segmentation is all about breaking down massive numbers into manageable groups. But the increasing importance of psychographic in contrast to demographic information may mean that you have to rethink your categorisation. Dell Computer used to define the segments of the personal computer business by where PCs were sited: in homes, small businesses, large offices, and so on. But this approach misses so much about the customer, and the sort of information you can learn from the segmentation criteria set out above. So Dell now looks at five segments based on the type of user, as opposed to where the computer is used:

- *Techno-boomers*, or neophyte users with a priority on ease-of-use features
- *Techno-to-go users*, with little patience for sales pitches, who

just want a computer in a box
- *Techno-teamers*, who work as part of a network and need both the right hardware and software
- *Techno-critical* users, whose work is in demanding environments where the best available equipment is a priority
- *Techno-wizards*, who are leading-edge users always focused on the newest features

By reframing its market segment definitions, Dell can line up new products to fit particular segments, find product line gaps and develop promotional messages to fit its users. As well as more focused advertising, the company expects a richer array of products to emerge.

In making a segmentation study from a personality rather than demographic perspective, each company will come up with its own categories of customer. Any generalised approach, say by an industry, would miss the whole point. It is not just the reality of different customer images or perceptions, but the marketing power of such an identity — or USP, unique selling *personality*. Some private studies, however, have come up with more standard categories and one such is useful as an example:

- The *status seeker* who is very concerned with the prestige of the brand purchased
- The *swinger*, who tries to be modern and up to date, including in brand selection
- The *conservative* who prefers to stay with large companies and popular brands
- The *rational* person who is after benefits such as economy, value, durability, and so on
- The *inner-directed* person who is especially concerned with self-image, probably considering him- or herself to be independent, honest and having a good sense of humour
- The *hedonist* who is concerned primarily with sensory benefits.

To some extent these sorts of categories will turn up wherever a large product range is offered. And any number of different categories can be readily identified. So although perceptions vary a good deal, in practice there will be segments that respond to just about any corporate personality or product line.

Provided they are big enough to be workable, the closer these psychographic segments can be identified to match your personality (in effect, the more there are), the better will be customer rapport and brand loyalty. But to whatever degree, customer-type segmentation is important to personality positioning and management.

The very process of psychographic segmentation will help you to gain fresh insight into markets. The only limit is in the imagination you bring to bear first in defining customer categories, then in using the information the segmentation provides to better serve your customers.

These ways of segmenting the market may appear like rational analysis. But in practice segmentation can be more intuitive, as were the insights that produced the Mustang car and the first 100-millimetre cigarette. As we shall see in the following chapter, intuition and creativity play a bigger part in psychographic research, where there is little standardisation of terms or factors. Marketing history is strewn with products that 'could not fail'. Whether based on logic or intuition, segmentation has traditionally been descriptive rather than predictive. For this reason we predict that psychographic segmentation, which includes customers' aspirations as well as present behaviour, will become increasingly important in the next century.

International/global segmentation

Some of the big companies are saying that, for strategic marketing purposes, certain segments are indeed global. Companies like Mercedes Benz and American Express target what appears to be an élite type of consumer who desires prestige, status and very high quality. The 'yuppy' segment is another category of consumer pursued by large branded goods companies around the world. BSB Worldwide, Inc. —

a global advertising agency — extends this to lifestyle segmentation, finding international segments that it terms Strivers, Achievers, Pressured, Traditional and Adapters.

Where this can be done, global segmentation can provide companies with opportunities to gain economies of scale in advertising and promotional expenditure, although care has to be taken to make sure that the language used is equally universal. This is where the psycholinguistics profession comes into its own.

Care must also be taken to make sure that the corporate personality is acceptable to the target audiences of different countries with different cultural characteristics. The general personality characteristics of Latin American countries are different to those of people in the Middle East, for instance, but linking personality to lifestyle can overcome many apparent cultural obstacles, as it has done for companies such as Coke and Levi Strauss.

Segmentation and corporate personality

Most of the world's top companies use segmentation as a fundamental part of their marketing strategy. For those concerned with projecting a strong corporate image through corporate personality, understanding and choosing target markets is even more fundamental to business success. Segmentation can help the personality process by:

- stressing or emphasising certain personality characteristics or values to those groups of people that might be attracted to them;
- building personalities to match the requirements, attitudes and lifestyles of certain customer groups;
- understanding how to reach different market segments by broadcasting corporate personality via the media of their choice.

Most segmentation research comprises dry statistics. In order to bring the segmentation types to life some companies try to picture the segment as a 'labelled' person, often through the use of cartoon imagery. As we have seen, sometimes they put names to them, such as 'status-seekers', 'techno-boomers' and 'swingers'. This helps employees to buy into the segmentation process, helping them to understand that each segment does contain real people out there in the marketplace. It also can be used in training sales staff to recognise different segment types, and as a unifying personality theme when briefing advertising agents and consultants. Segments can thus illuminate personality, and personality can give added meaning to market segments by better reflecting the real customers.

Summary

1. Market segmentation is a key requirement for successful business development, especially as the world moves towards greater market fragmentation.
2. Identifying distinct market segments provides focus and direction, helps companies set clearer objectives for marketing, and identifies more closely the needs of specific customer groups.
3. There are many different ways of segmenting markets but for companies wishing to align their corporate personality to certain types of customer, those methods that gain an insight into how consumers think and what makes them behave in certain ways are more effective. This invariably leads towards psychographic and lifestyle methods of segmentation.
4. There are four fundamental questions to ask when considering segmentation strategies:

   * how is the market segmented?
   * which segments are most attractive?
   * which segment coverage best fits our personality characteristics?

- how vulnerable will we be to attack? — how can we defend our segment choice?

5. Market segmentation is not an easy process, and needs careful research. If done well, however, it can transform the way in which you look for and get more business.

CHAPTER TEN

UNDERSTANDING CUSTOMERS THROUGH MARKET RESEARCH

Creating a corporate personality is not just a unilateral process, but one that requires you to identify and simulate the personality characteristics of your customers. This not only involves getting into the minds of your customers, but also identifying and communicating with a viable market segment or segments. But first you must know what information you need to find, as well as the principles and techniques of obtaining, analysing and using it. That is where market research becomes important. And, as is the case for market segmentation, a personality strategy makes effective research even more important than traditionally it has been. This is particularly the case as new kinds of information, more qualitative than quantitative perhaps, are required when the personality perspective is introduced. In some cases the historical dominance of geodemographic data may be reversed as a psychographic approach takes on more significance in your quest to understand the customer.

'Market research' is an umbrella term. A whole industry has evolved serving the marketing function and the type and quality of the data it produces varies enormously. Even more variable, perhaps, is how this data is interpreted and analysed into meaningful information and actually used by marketeers. Here we are more concerned with getting at the sort of information you will need to execute an effective corporate personality strategy. This may include simply asking your customer informally what he or she thinks in the course of normal business. It certainly means listening, even though you may not actually solicit information. Or it may mean incorporating detailed customer feedback into every aspect of your operations with not a market research specialist in sight. Personality strategy may mean big changes in what you do as a company and how you communicate with your customers. By whatever definition, however, market research has to meet your need for relevant, timely information.

Basic research questions

Who are our customers?
Specifically, what kind of people are most loyal and profitable to your organisation? Which represent the middle category — profitable to pursue, but not the best? Which are those only marginally profitable? And which are the people you could best do without? You will have to distinguish between customers, or buyers, and the final *consumers* of your product or service, as this may well affect the message you want to get across.

A proprietary baby cream was once sold in such quantities as to just about drown the infant population but it was discovered by puzzled marketeers that the users were far from babies, and were of both sexes. While surprise sales are serendipitous for any company, if you don't know who your consumer is you are likely to waste time and money sending your message to the wrong people. Customer satisfaction should be based on more than luck. Unless you know who your customers are there is little chance of matching personality to end-user.

What's on their minds?
What are their attitudes regarding your products and services? How do they perceive your organisation and its employees? Do they have established brand preferences? Is

their loyalty to a product or to the company? For example, a customer might be crazy about a certain type of branded breakfast cereal but would be quite happy to try a very similar competitive product, having no loyalty beyond the type of product itself, say cornflakes. Another customer will be less choosy about their cereal type, provided it is Kellogg's. Do your customers value what you make and who you are?

This sort of information is far more difficult to obtain and interpret than demographic data, but has obvious value if a long-term relationship is to be formed. Unfortunately the nature of psychographic surveys is that they are not easily compatible with segmentation. There are no standard category definitions of lifestyles or brand perception as is the case with basic demographic data like address, age and sex.

Where and how can they be reached?

To this question can be added *'efficiently'*. Except in specific areas such as direct marketing, it is frustratingly difficult to measure the effectiveness of advertising and promotion. This difficulty is exacerbated as you move from product benefit to corporate image messages, or from short-term sales to longer-term awareness. It is not enough to know which radio station or magazine to choose, but rather what sort of creative message will reach your actual potential customers amidst all the competitive clutter. And that means understanding their personality and reflecting it in your product, service and message.

Why do they buy from you?

Understanding the real reasons why people buy from you rather than somebody else can be many times more valuable than the fact that they buy from you. Many companies, after spending enormous budgets on customer satisfaction programmes, have found to their horror that satisfied customers were just as likely as unsatisfied ones to switch to the competition. For this reason research has moved toward the 3 Rs: **recruiting** new customers, **retaining** existing customers, and **regaining** lost customers. When it comes to the 'why' question, neat demographic segmentation can thus be close to useless. It is descriptive rather than causal. The crux of this dilemma is understanding why people do what they do.

What are they buying?

This has to be answered on two levels. The first is simply a measurement of product sales. This, of course, has to be linked with an understanding of *who* is buying (above) so that your messages can be focused. On the second level you need to know what part of your total product offering, comprising all sorts of intangibles and subjectively perceived benefits, the customers are paying for. If you mistakenly think they are buying certain features rather than certain benefits, sooner or later you will pay for your lack of basic customer knowledge. Alternatively if you think they are buying because of your carefully communicated benefits — however intangible — and their perceptions and buying reasons are different, you don't really know your customer enough to optimise your marketing efforts. Do they want ¼ inch drills or ¼ inch holes? And what do they the need the holes for? To put up a bookshelf or for the world of aspirations and dreams that the books open to them? By understanding the *core* needs and wants of your customers you will not only be able to get the right products and services but you will also relate to them in a special way. Once again, by understanding what makes your customers tick and the basic values and attitudes they hold, you will begin to simulate and communicate a common personality, and to meet their needs and wants.

Questions affecting corporate personality

Research that answers the questions above is fundamental to your marketing effort. More specifically, to manage your corporate personality you will have to ask questions about:

Corporate awareness

• What proportion of our target audiences are aware of the name?

- Which have depth of knowledge about us?
- Which products and services do they think we offer?

The relative importance of personality characteristics

- How important are your personality characteristics to each other in the customer's mind?
- How important are they compared to those of other companies?

Changing perceptions of personality characteristics

- Are these perceptions changing over time? How?
- Do we want to change these perceptions?
- Which do we want to reinforce?

Personality strengths and weaknesses

- What do people like about our corporate personality?
- Which characteristics are weak, or produce negative perceptions?
- Which offer the most attractions?

More basic research questions

There are a few other basic questions to ask when considering a research project.

- What is the research for? What precisely do you need to know (NB not what you would *like* to know) that you don't know already?
- How will you link this to what you already know?
- Is there any other existing data anywhere inside or outside your company that will throw light on the subject, or remove the need for further research ?
- Is the information you want *critical* to your understanding of the consumer ?
- In what way(s) do you expect the research data to be of benefit to:

- the company?
- the consumer?
i.e. what strategically do you expect out of it?
• Will it add anything significant to the company-customer relationship?
• Is it urgent? Why?

If you are not clear on the above questions than you are in danger of giving too broad a brief to the research agency. Most research projects fail because the beginning and end are not right. The research company can do the middle bit (field work) but the beginning and end depend upon the client company.

The myths of market research

A corporate personality strategy will depend on effective market research, not least in monitoring ongoing customer perceptions. Being particularly concerned with values rather than raw demographic data will lend itself more to qualitative as opposed to quantitative research. The personality dimension requires that you discriminate between what is and what is not relevant to your personality strategy. Here we highlight some caveats, some of which are no less than myths about the nature and effectiveness of market research. By demystifying market research in this way, there is a better chance that you will design your own information needs and be more creative in the methods you use to obtain it and analyse it. Knowing what is possible and not possible you will be able to spend your budget more wisely, and make a better decision about carrying out the research internally or through outside agents. Finally, it should also give you some confidence when specifying your needs to professional researchers.

1. **Perception**: Market research is an effective way to determining successful products and services, including tomorrow's winners.
   Reality: Market research simply documents today's

premises and conventional wisdom, none of which may be relevant to tomorrow's realities. When people are unfamiliar with a product or cannot fathom its use or possibilities, market research will reflect no more than that. Sony's Walkman, one of the most successful products of the 1980s, was greeted by scepticism during prototype tests. Who in his right mind (thought the punters) would want to lug around a tape recorder? And presently, who can really imagine (before it happens) what access to 500 television channels will really mean? So in this vital marketing area of innovative products conventional market research may be useless. Sometimes it cannot even ask the right questions. For this reason the only alternative may be to launch real products on real customers as so many brave entrepreneurs have done over the decades. Ted Turner launched CNN despite the fact that contemporary wisdom mocked the idea. Even at its best, market research is no crystal ball.

2. **Perception**: Market research is an efficient, cost-effective management tool.

   Reality: The operational and logistics pitfalls of market research can easily diminish its usefulness. It is expensive, and given its chequered track record, money may well have been better spent on some other form of marketing, training, or product development. Another inbuilt weakness arises from the increasingly shortening product life cycles which render so much data redundant so soon. Furthermore, data is complex and open to all sorts of assumptions before it is acted upon. At the same time, much already available, especially in the case of quantitative research, is aggregate, and therefore of no use to companies pursuing a customised marketing or relationship strategy. And mass markets — which is what market research was developed for and which it serves best — are rapidly becoming a marketing anachronism.

3. **Perception**: Market research is statistically and methodologically a rigorous tool.

   Reality: The statistical and methodological pitfalls of market research diminish its accuracy. This is validated eloquently by market researchers and analysts themselves who are quick to qualify their findings. Even forgetting sampling bias and other inherent weaknesses, there is the simple fact that people tend to say one thing and do another. Garbage in, garbage out. The decision to replace 'old' Coke with New Coke, for example, was based on the most meticulous, professional market research, and a systematic assessment of more than 100,000 respondents. And the results were accurate, as far as they went. The trouble was that people were being asked what to them were hypothetical questions. Not for a moment did they expect their beloved Coke to be actually taken from them.

Leading players in this field have been embarrassingly exposed. The Nielsen and Arbitron ratings, which drive entire television and radio industries, have been accused by independent sources of 'flimsy statistics', 'unreliable or perhaps obsolete technology' and 'inconsistent, inaccurate and unexplainable numbers'. And these sort of comments could well apply to many well known market research firms serving every industry. We are all fallible when it comes to any kind of quantification of customer perception.

4. **Perception**: Market research is a neutral scientific process yielding neutral scientific results.

   Reality: It is often more political than neutral. In the face of increasing fan discontent the US National Football League concluded from their own poll that 'fans love the game the way it is'. As one sports columnist wrote: 'Well, there's nothing like rigging the mechanism to make it work your way'. But you don't even need such obviously built-in bias. The simple rule is if the results do not meet with your expectations you can always commission more research and sooner or later they will. The *status quo* is the biggest industry of the lot.

5. **Perception**: Market research gets people close to the customer.

   Reality: Market research can be a buffer between the supplier and real customers and their needs. Typically an internal staff group or outside agency does the work, absolving everybody (including marketing managers) of actually facing real customers. There is no substitute, of course, for real customer interaction, but sophisticated market research is one of the better excuses.

6. **Perception**: Market research produces breakthrough products and services.

   Reality: Market research reinforces staying in the middle of the pack. While strategy is about uniqueness and differentiation, research is about convention and so-called best practice. Even successful market research means that you are market driven, rather than driving the market, which is what breakthrough marketing is about.

This is not to say that basic scientific market research is not of value, whether quantitative or qualitative. The trick is to steer through what can be a minefield of myths and conflicting opinions and add your own common sense. Specifically, greater subjective judgement and intuition may be required as the newer psychographic techniques are based on individuals, or small groups that do not have statistical validity. In any event, the non-standard, subjective data now being sought and obtained does not lend itself to either simple categories, like age, address and sex, nor reliable aggregation to reflect a large market segment.

Crossing the market research minefield

With such a minefield of myths it is not surprising that marketing executives at companies such as Benetton, Rubbermaid and Seiko eschew market research, relying more on quick customer feedback based on merchandise actually tested in-store.

The lessons are many. It may be better to concentrate on factors like quick flexible design and manufacturing and action pilots rather than analysis. Paradoxically, some of the most useful market research has been *post hoc*, and has formed valuable learning for the future. Not all products at Benetton and Seiko are successful. But the point is that they have managed to reduce the cost of failure while boosting returns on successes.

Another way to get this balance right is to focus on the market rather than market research. It has been observed that a reason why the Japanese took the lead on fax machines is that instead of asking whether there was a market for the machine, they asked whether there was a market for what the machine *did*. Market research needs to be the servant of both the bigger marketing concept and of common sense.

As Tom Peters keeps repeating, there is no substitute for listening to the customer. And that means the whole staff, not just front-line salespeople. Listening does not just mean listening to the answers to *your* questions. It means listening to customers' problems, concerns, hopes and fears. It means getting insights into how their lives might be better and what part you might play in that.

John Sculley, looking back on his career as President of Pepsi-Cola, concluded that he had never seen a good marketing decision that was based on data. 'It's a healthy dose of intuition that leads you to invent something that's a little special — you have to have the guts to try things that are a little bit different,' said Sculley. The comment is the more remarkable in that Pepsi-Cola as a company seems to be driven by the most sophisticated market research.

For our purposes, personality is too important to rely entirely on market research. Corporate personality is not a product you can quickly drop if things go wrong. It is the very life and soul of the company. Direct knowledge of customer perceptions is the raw data of personality management. If as a mass marketeer you don't know who your customers are, you will be at a loss to know what they think. You cannot even ask them. Thus the increasing trend towards relationship and one-to-one marketing sits more comfortably with strategic personality management. As we shall now see, trends in qualitative market research are more likely to fulfil the information needs of the future.

The what and why of customer behaviour

We have already referred to quantitative and qualitative research. Basically, market research sets out to determine two things:

- what is happening (quantitative research)
- why it is happening (qualitative research)

Quantitative research

Quantitative research might be used, for example, to determine the size and make-up of a particular target customer group (market segment), which companies they buy from, where and what they buy from those companies, when and so on. This research is quite structured and involves studying industry data, retail audits, omnibus surveys and other techniques.

Retail audits

Retail audits, for example, provide information on market size and share, inventories, purchases, prices, distribution, advertising, displays and other aspects of retail sales. Many large stores now have scanners, and scanner panel data is now becoming the main source for retail sales measurement, especially in food and drugstore industries.

Omnibus surveys

Omnibus surveys allow companies flexibility as they are consumer surveys that run on a regular basis allowing any clients to 'board the bus' at any time. As well as using standard questions, companies can add their own questions of specific interest to them. Omnibus surveys are used to look at the structure of markets, corporate and product awareness and positioning, purchase and user behaviour, and advertising and effectiveness. They are cost-effective because they allow companies to share survey costs.

These audits and surveys are best carried out by reputable, objective, market research companies.

Qualitative research

Qualitative research, on the other hand, is more concerned with observing what happens and explaining why it happens. It depends on interview techniques (such as in focus groups and relatively unstructured in-depth interviews) which require highly skilled people to administer them. This sort of research is very useful for testing out new positioning ideas and consumer attitudes towards the company and its personality. A lot of qualitative research can be done by companies themselves. It may not even purport to be scientifically valid and will thus not require sampling and other orthodox market research expertise. On the other hand, the specialised skills needed to conduct interviews and focus groups may demand the best independent outside help.

Mass marketing is dying. Mass research, however, is not, because quantifiable data is still valid. But qualitative research is beginning to take precedence over the quantitative approach, mainly because feelings can be accessed and emotions registered. We are beginning to learn what customers think, getting to know their personality, and reflecting it in our own.

Benefits summary
The following is a summary of some of the uses and benefits of qualitative research.

1. Qualitative research is relatively low-cost.
2. It is the best way of finding out how people perceive corporate personality, what it means to them, which bits of it they like and to what degree.
3. You can use qualitative research to discover what associations customers have with your corporate personality. It helps to answer the following questions:

Why do they like it?
What attracts them to it?
What more do they want/expect from it?
What characteristics do they like more than others?
How do they compare your corporate personality with those of other companies?

4. With corporate personality research the main aim is to assess desire — the desire to be with your company. Qualitative research will help explain what different types of customers really *feel* about your company and its products and services. It will reveal their buying and loyalty 'hot buttons'.

Psychographic research: getting into the minds of the consumers

One of the most powerful recent developments in qualitative market research has been the analysis of psychographic data, with detailed studies of the activities, interests, and opinions of consumers, and their lifestyle behaviour. This, combined with geodemographic and family lifecycle data can give companies a vast competitive edge in reaching the customer.

Values and lifestyles

The focus on lifestyles may be far more important than demographics and target markets: this information about perceptions and images, crucial to every buying decision, as well as to long-term brand loyalty, has dimensions that do not apply to demographics. For example, certain customers may not have a particular lifestyle but may *aspire* to that lifestyle. In this case their age or present income may bear no relationship to their aspirations, and what they perceive as product benefits. Hence the success of the 'Can you see yourself ...?', or 'Can you imagine yourself ...?' sort of advertising. Much of this aspiration happens at a subliminal level, of course, and could be missed by conventional research methods. But it is nonetheless a real buying factor, and applies to the whole range of socio-economic levels.

As well as being patently relevant to marketing, the lifestyle and personality characteristics of consumers are important because they are more enduring and deep-rooted. They reflect patterns of behaviour and thinking that have probably existed since childhood. Because they represent the psychological make-up of consumers, they can be used as profiles to match up to the corporate personality being projected, which, as we have stressed, should also be enduring and deep-rooted. Personality characteristics also help companies to focus their advertising, position themselves, and select the most appropriate media.

The following are examples of categories of data which will help you to get into the minds of your customers:

Activities	*Interests*	*Opinions*
Club memberships	Achievements	Business
Entertainment	Home	Economics
Hobbies/holidays	Family	Education
Shopping	Fashion	Products
Sports	Food	Self
Social events	Media	Others
Work	Recreation	Social concerns
		The future
		Politics

This is not an exhaustive list and there are many sub-categories which could be used.

VALS and VALS 2
Over recent years, a lot of attention has been given to classifications that relate people's behaviour to their values. The VALS (values and lifestyles) typology of the Stanford Research Institute has proved to be one of the most popular. Their second version, VALS 2, describes eight types of personality based on two concepts: self-orientation, and a new definition of resources:

Self-orientation

Consumers buy products and services that give substance and character to their identities, or personalities. They are motivated by one of three powerful self-orientations:

* principle
* status
* action

Principle-oriented consumers are guided in their choices by abstract, idealised criteria, rather than by feelings, events or desire for approval and concern for the opinions of others. Status-oriented consumers look for products and services that demonstrate their success to their peers. Action-oriented consumers are guided by a desire for social or physical activity, variety and risk-taking.

Resources

This includes the full range of psychological, physical, demographic and material means and capacities consumers have to draw upon. These include health, education, income, intelligence, energy level, self-confidence, and eagerness to buy. It is a continuum from minimal to abundant. Resources generally increase from adolescence through to middle age but decrease with extreme age, depression, financial reverses, and psychological or physical impairment.

Using these two dimensions, VALS 2 defines segments of adult consumers who have different attitudes and exhibit distinctive buying behaviour. The segments are balanced in size so that each represents a viable marketing segment. Neighbouring types have similar characteristics and can be combined in various ways to suit particular marketing purposes. The overall system is flexible and highly predictive of consumer behaviour.

A summary of these eight VALS 2 segments is as follows:-

Actualisers

- enjoy the finer things in life
- receptive to new products and technologies
- read widely
- light TV viewers, don't trust advertisements

Achievers

- like premium products
- materialistic, oriented to success
- read business, news, self-improvement publications
- average TV viewers

Believers

- buy 'heritage' products — home country association
- do not like to try new things
- read retirement, home and general interest magazines
- watch a lot of TV

Experiencers

- socialising occupies a lot of their time and money
- fashionable and trendy, impulsive buyers
- influenced by advertising
- like rock and popular music

Fulfilleds

- not interested in image and prestige or status
- above-average purchases of home-related products
- read widely and often
- enjoy education and public affairs programmes

Makers

- like to buy things for comfort, value, durability, not luxuries
- buy basic products

- listen to the radio a lot
- read car, DIY and outdoor pursuits magazines

Strivers

- limited disposable income, credit users
- like to buy clothes and personal care products
- conscious about image
- like TV but do not read much

Strugglers

- do a lot of 'sales' shopping
- loyal to the brands they buy
- read daily newspapers and gender-related magazines
- heavy TV-watchers and like advertisements

Visualising the individual consumer

As markets become more fragmented, segments more numerous, and consumers more demanding, companies are showing greater interest in profiling consumers as individuals. They are trying more and more to find out what individuals believe, how they think, how they live their everyday lives, and even what they look like. In other words they are beginning to think about each person rather than segments or groups of people. This is particularly important as relationship marketing and 'share of customer' becomes more popular. But a better understanding of individual customers can also be of great help in understanding the type of customer, or segment, you are selling to.

Customer prototypes

Quantitative and qualitative research is used to collect as much real information as possible about target customers. From this data, 'prototype' individuals are chosen as target market representatives. Audio-visual modelling and even real subjects are used so that marketing and sales staff can observe their behaviour at first hand. This helps them greatly in presenting corporate and product messages to these customer types, and building relationships. Such categories are, of course, somewhat general, and do differ in different parts of the world, and even in different parts of a country. But such research can give companies a substantial insight into values and behaviour, and reveal positive and negative associations or attitudes to various companies, products and services.

This type of research was apparently used in helping to create the Harley Davidson identity, where researchers spent a great deal of time with bikers to understand how they feel about work, about the freedom bikes give them, about how they look forward to weekend biking trips — all the thinking that goes on inside a biker's mind whilst at work or play. Once the thinking was understood it was a relatively short step to creating the unifying personality for promoting the company and its products.

Although customer prototypes are no more than representative, this trend goes beyond psychographics, and seems to reflect the move towards one-to-one and relationship marketing.

Perceptual maps

The outputs of some focused market research can be extremely useful strategically, and perceptual maps are often produced to summarise how consumers think about a company, its personality attributes, its products and services. In the case of products (sometimes called product maps) the map shows how they are perceived on features such as 'reputation', 'price', or 'quality'. Or, for instance in the case of a pain reliever, specific product attributes such as gentle, effective, long-lasting. They show which products compete in a customer's mind and suggest how a producer can be positioned to maximise preference and sales.

They can also be applied to companies to show, in a simple picture, a comparison of values, attributes, behaviours, etc. against those of competitors as seen by the consumer.

Corporate perceptual mapping is thus an important tool in considering your corporate personality and how to project it. Figures 3 and 8 are examples of perceptual mapping. The following are some examples of how companies have used the process. In some cases they are based on specific psychographic research, such as VALS, which we referred to earlier in the chapter. In other cases they are simply brainstorming tools.

- A telecomunications company, to estimate future demand for products and services.
- A pharmaceutical company, to monitor competition in certain drugs.
- An insurance company to maximise penetration of its direct marketing and improve response rates.
- A drinks company to select its market and create an image and positioning strategy to communicate best with its target.
- A large retailer to reposition its personality.
- A shopping centre to select the best mix of retailers.
- A car manufacturer to redesign its sports utility vehicle to meet the preferences of most likely buyers.
- A house builder to identify the values and preferences of potential home buyers and test responses of prototype buyers.

The statistical techniques involved in producing some maps, are quite sophisticated. Complex 3-D maps are not uncommon, building in other dimensions such as what are termed 'multiple market segment perceptions'. By comparing the preferences of different segments against the positioning intended by the company, a great deal can be learned about how one company rates against major competitors. This could be valuable in terms of showing the company how to play its strengths. It may consider re-positioning itself against the competition, or strengthening where it appears to be weak in the minds of the public.

Here are some of the uses and benefits of corporate perceptual maps:

1. They give a much clearer picture of the corporate personality and its characteristics, as opposed to its products and services.
2. They give rise to strategic marketing and positioning opportunities
3. They can explain clear differences between the perceptions of different target audiences (market segments).
4. If produced regularly over a long period of time they can reveal perceptual changes, which are usually slow. People change their minds about things gradually.

Responses can be represented in different graphical ways, such as concentric circles, grids or hierarchies. The technique can also be adapted to a group discussion in which members place tabs representing brands on a 'map' of the attributes under discussion and discuss why. Numerous brands can be sorted quickly, and feedback gained on packaging, or 'personality' attributes, for instance.

Projective research techniques

Anyone who has tried (especially as an amateur) to find out what people think about a company or a product will realise how difficult it is to get people to reveal more than surface or superficial feelings or attitudes. In depth interviews and focus groups are becoming more popular now as companies try harder and harder to get inside the mind of the consumer.

Depth interviews

Depth interviews are usually one-to-one, and researchers try to get the interviewee to talk freely about the particular subject, putting them at ease so they will reveal their true feelings. There is a lot of probing done but in a very non-threatening way, and the interviewers have to be highly skilled. No formal questionnaire is used, but the objective is to find the real reasons why people like a company or

product, what strong feelings they have about it, what motivates them to want to stay with it, and so on. Because it takes
time, is skilled work, and deals with small numbers, it is
expensive to carry out, although relatively a lot cheaper than
a large demographic study. If tightly focused on specific
segments, however, it can provide very revealing information. Part of the skill is in the interpretation of the findings, as
the open-ended nature of the interviewing poses a problem
for objective analysis, and subjective comments are hard to
standardise in the way that demographic data are.

Focus group interviews

Focus group research is becoming a regular feature of corporate life. A group consists usually of between six and ten
people brought together to discuss one subject, and sessions
are often taped or video-recorded. As with depth
interviews, the objective is to get into the mind of the
consumer and explore below-the-surface attitudes and
feelings about a company or product.

Focus groups are often preferred to depth interviews because they deal with larger numbers and yet still give the
researchers a 'feel' for the individual consumer. They can be
carried out fairly quickly and at relatively low cost, and
always seem to give companies some valuable feedback and
ideas. Focus group moderators also have to be skilful and not
dominate the groups, nor allow strong personalities to do so,
and they should have the ability to identify and explore
valuable areas as the discussion proceeds. Normally, they
have a question framework to use as an overall guide for
introducing discussion points.

The changing values of society

Some interesting work has also been done regarding values
held by society and consumer thinking and this could be
important for any company envisaging a corporate personality strategy.

One survey produces psychographic types of consumers and links these to value changes. It appears, from extensive research across many countries, that some societal values are becoming less important, and others more so.

Less Important	More Important
Familism	Environmental concern
Need for security	Self confidence
Fatalism	Creativity
Fear of change	Risk taking
Status and image awareness	Excitement and escapism
Technophobia	Need for information
Parochialism	Internationalism

The values that are becoming more important will be those that make greater demands on companies, their products and services in future years. Companies can therefore begin to shape their personalities to change gradually in line with these changing values. What is more, they can identify which consumer groups hold those values which are close to those of their company and its current personality for target marketing, stressing 'heritage' or whatever. These changes are incremental but the trend has been identified. Smart companies will position themselves and their personalities appropriately, moving with the value trends and matching their personalities with those of particular customer groups they want to appeal to.

Exercises to test out personality perception

Here are some exercises you can try out with staff and customers to check on perceptions and your competitive positioning. Be ready for some marketing insights and ideas for strategic changes.

Obituary
Write an obituary for your company, then do the same in respect of a major competitor. Think about the key emotional elements that attract people to your company, or drive them away.

Pictures/collages
Draw some pictures to represent your company, or a product or service. Draw a picture and get people to complete the story. Cut and paste a combination of pictures to describe your relationship and feelings about the company.

Experiences
Get people to recall their feelings and experiences connected with when they interacted with the company or used its products.

Differences
Ask people to describe differences between two companies or products.

Agree/disagree
Give statements about the company, product, and obtain degrees of agreement by scaled replies.

What ifs
Ask people what the company would be if it were a car, an animal etc., as discussed earlier.

Person description
Get people to describe your company as a person, selecting 'personality' words such as sophisticated, intelligent, friendly, thoughtful, macho, creative.

Photo sorting
Give people pictures of various types of people and ask them to sort them according to their perceptions of

different companies. Which person would relate to which company personality?

Chronography
Observe people in their own environment, interacting with the company products and services.
Get to know their feelings and perceptions at first hand.

Summary

1. Qualitative research is better than quantitative research for purposes of matching corporate personality to target audience personalities.
2. Qualitative research is relatively low cost and is the best way of finding out how people perceive corporate personality, what it means to them, which bits of it they like and to what degree.
3. Market research answers the questions:

   • Who are our customers?
   • What's on their minds?
   • Where and how can they be reached?
   • Why do they buy from us?
   • What are they buying?
   • How do they perceive the personality of the company?

4. With corporate personality research the main aim is to assess desire — the desire to be with your company. Qualitative research will help explain what different types of consumer really feel about your company and its products and services. It will reveal the 'hot buttons'.
5. Despite the relative merits of qualitative and quantitative research, there is no shortage of myths and minefields. Be prepared to trust your common sense.

6. Asking the right questions is important, and interpreting them in the right way is equally vital. Research companies do not usually have the strategic resources to do this, and often nor does the company. In such cases, employing an outside consultant with relevant experience can be a wise move, and save the embarrassment of receiving a lot of data which is of little strategic importance.

7. As well as projective techniques such as in depth interviews and focus groups, perceptual maps can help with psychographic research.

CHAPTER ELEVEN

MARKET DEVELOPMENTS AFFECTING CORPORATE PERSONALITY

There are some important developments in the world of marketing that may affect any consideration of a personality strategy. Some of these have been referred to throughout the book, but because of their likely importance over the next few years we will address them more fully here.

Direct marketing and relationship management

Protagonists of these developments argue that companies and products can be given a new life by building new and better relationships with customers. The key to business growth, they say, is the interface with the customer, and the challenge therefore is to combine employee commitment and customer relationships in an effective way.

Direct marketing has some useful advantages:

- effective targeting of well-defined segments
- relationship building over time

- interactive quality — the consumer can get involved
- easily measurable responses
- easy customisation — with specific messages to specific people

However, all these advantages can be destroyed if the right personality is not projected. The problem is that nearly half of all marketing expenditure can be wasted by the failure of company employees to live up to the promises given to customers. This is where personality becomes so vital, even (and especially) if you never see the customer. It is the experience a customer has with your company and/or its products that makes or breaks the relationship. When staff directly interface with customers their behaviour is critical, as we have already seen. With direct marketing, how do you develop and sustain the relationship? The answer, yet again, is through personality. Even though customers do not 'see' the person, they 'experience' the communication. If all they can experience is a voice, a letter or a flier, then it is even more important that the personality is felt.

With direct telephone marketing, for instance, even a single scripted response can reflect the true, unique personality of the company. Telemarketing staff should be recruited, whenever possible, to closely match the company's personality criteria. All too frequently, the competence and personalities of many employees used in telemarketing are inconsistent, lack personal impact, and leave one with a sense of *impersonality* rather personality. There is much that companies can do here, building personality strategies into policies and practices as affecting customers. Customer contact should never be treated as a routine matter.

Interactive mail should also communicate the personality, by projecting the values or personality characteristics. It should encourage customer involvement and associations by inviting the customer to the next step in the relationship, just as we would when writing to friends, hoping to get to know them better. And it is more than just personalising the letter; the desire for a real relationship has to be communicated.

Companies can do this by inviting customers to participate in a wider range of activities than just the purchase of a product or service. Magazines, catalogues, newsletters, community projects, surveys and mail that calls for a response are all opportunities for the customer to experience the personality.

The next wave of direct marketing innovations involves on-line access, virtual kiosks and stores, and the Internet. It is vital, once again, not just that the customer feels important, but that he or she *experiences* the personality. Customisation of such technology should allow the interface with the customer to express the values and personality characteristics that make it unique. With direct marketing it is even harder to differentiate a company from competitors unless the personality element is clearly visible and consistent.

As we have seen already there are many ways of communicating personality, and it is the total communication that affects the customer. In one-to-one marketing the communication can be sensitive and very effective, producing a unique personality-to-personality relationship that mass marketing cannot achieve.

Marketing for technology companies

Technology is the principal accelerator of change, and the world of high technology business is extremely competitive. The speed of inventions and the shortening lead times from invention on to innovation and then application have put a great deal of pressure on all companies in technology-driven industries. Added to this are ever-shortening product life-cycles. The market for washing machines and refrigerators, for example, took up to thirty years to reach maturity, then around five years for microwave ovens, and about two years for compact disc players. In the case of personal computers, however, whatever the degree of market saturation or maturity, individual models may become technologically obsolete in closer to six months. This is likely to be a trend which continues and some companies are aiming for two or three new products every month. The USP (Unique Selling Proposition) life has similarly declined, and a sustainable competitive advantage is now almost impossible via this route, as competitors easily copy and improve on new products.

Another marketing issue faced by technology companies is that, because of the nature of their products, they tend to emphasise features (such as capacity or processing speed) which in general do not elicit an emotional response from consumers. They also tend to rely more on distribution channels which themselves are the subject of increasing competition.

Being attentive to these concerns, technology companies have not realised that consumers use, like and prefer emotional associations when they buy things. The most likely emotion in the mind of the consumer is likely to be apprehension about using the product or doubts about its performance. From ordinary consumers to large corporate systems buyers, people don't like to risk making a mistake. If emotion is a fact of buying it will pay companies to specifically address the emotional response they want to stimulate — whatever the product or service. This sort of thinking is central to a personality strategy.

Technology companies must therefore look to become more skilled at marketing themselves in an emotional way. They need to balance the rational appeal with the emotional, and developing corporate personality is the best way to accomplish this. Compaq, Intel, Microsoft and other companies have become successful through their product excellence, but would leverage much more business with the human touch. Up-and-coming technology companies should create their personality as early as possible, balance business values with personality characteristics, and meet utility needs with psychological needs.

To sum up, the greater the technology influence on a company's products, the greater the need to create a strong, endearing, consistent personality that consumers can emotionally relate to, have trust and confidence in, and want to buy from. There is a need to develop a relationship and appropriate image, and to always remember that emotion sells.

Marketing to children

Children are now a major source of business for many companies, and 'marketing to kids' (as is the term in the USA) is becoming a skill in its own right. It is vastly different from marketing to other age groups. Just to get an idea of the size of this business consider that in 1993, in the USA alone, parents spent more than US$120 billion on their children, who themselves (including through their influence on parental spending) were responsible for US$150 billion of spending in the economy. Their influence extends to purchases at every level of the market such as stereos, cars, holidays, computers, furniture, where their families eat, what films and television channels they watch, what foods are bought. This is in addition to all the things they consume exclusively themselves, such as clothes, toys, sportswear and confectionery. They are responsible for all sorts of new products and have opened up many new opportunities for companies. Like adults, they are segmented by age, sex, place and lifestyle. But they have their own feelings, aspirations, hopes about the future; they like independence and freedom. They are in every sense of the words 'little people'. They have personality and can relate to personality.

There is no doubt at all that the most successful companies that have either started by aiming at the kids market, or have extended their business into it, have achieved their success through the projection of personality. Levi Strauss, for example, has developed entire campaigns directed at children — creating personalities in their 'World Creature' TV commercials such as SLIMUS PURSUITUS, ZOOMIS SKATIS, HORROFLICKUS ADDICTUS, HOOPIS ALLEY-OOPUS and HIPPUS HOPPUS RAPPIONUS, targeting different groups of children through an expression of their own unique individual personalities, activities and interests.

For more than thirty years now, Barbie dolls from Mattel have been the leading example of matching personalities to personalities. Barbie can be whatever the little girl wants her life to be, and however she wants to project herself for the future — rock singer, horse trainer, corporate executive, film star, or other personalities. The Barbie World Summit special event brought together children from over twenty-seven countries, raised enormous amounts of money for charities and ensured even greater sales success for Mattel.

Blockbuster films bring with them massive ancillary paraphernalia sales which, although baffling and costly to parents, show the power of appealing to the minds of children by entering their inner world.

Nike and Reebok, Gap and other apparel companies have also gained considerable success from this sector. But these and other successes can really be attributed to a thorough understanding of how personality can be projected to children and how companies and products can become 'friends'.

The kids market is huge and growing. Their influence on worldwide spending by families is enormous. The above companies, and others such as Disney, McDonald's and Nintendo, have found that the key to success in the world of kids marketing is personality.

Greater sophistication in business-to-business marketing

Business-to-business marketing has tended to be the poor marketing relation in terms of the attention it has received and the level of innovation it has experienced. Traditionally confined to issues of price, quality and service, it has not engendered the excitement that is characteristic of consumer marketing. This is beginning to change, however, and large corporates interested in marketing their products to other companies and industries are beginning to apply more end-consumer techniques. They are also becoming more aware of the need to establish a good corporate 'image' and put a lot of effort and money into this.

Caterpillar is a good example of this. Its latest worldwide campaign presents the company very much as a contributor to society and community infrastructure, and in doing so increasing the quality of life for people all over the world. Their commercials send messages representing personality characteristics such as:

- dependable
- powerful
- a leader
- a friend, who cares about improving the world we live in

So Caterpillar is not just concerned with image, but also with projecting a strong personality, differentiating itself from its competitors in a clear and motivating way.

Businesses marketing themselves to other businesses can use personality to make themselves attractive. Projecting characteristics such as 'innovative' can attract other companies to buy from you, as they would like to be seen to be 'friends' with someone who is up to date. Personality represents a great opportunity for companies wishing to build a strong character, reputation and image, and break away from low margin business. Business-to-business marketing should be no different to consumer marketing, because companies are made up of *people*. That is where personality counts, and *personality sells*.

Hypercompetition: the crowded marketplace

This is the age of similarity. Over the past few years we have witnessed an ever-increasing standardisation of buying patterns. All around the world people are tending to demand and buy the same kind of generic products and services, from fashion to fast food, from music to meals. Therefore more and more companies are trying to compete in similar markets, which increases the level of competition.

Technology is a key driver here, forcing companies to provide what others do. But there are other factors making life difficult for marketeers.

Deregulation, for example, is occurring in just about every industry in the world from financial services to photosystems, transport to telecommunications. Market boundaries are being broken down, cartels demolished, and, using technology to the full, companies are crossing over into industries they would not previously have considered.

Globalisation is here to stay, and strategic alliances are inevitable if companies are to stay alive. As World Trade Organisation Chief Renato Ruggerio said in 1996:

> 'We are not presented with a choice on globalisation ... It is a high-speed train driven by the development of trade and the advance of technology.
>
> Anyone who believes that globalisation can be stopped has to tell us how he would envisage stopping economic and technological progress; this is tantamount to trying to stop the rotation of the earth.'

And word has it that IBM has around 400 strategic alliances throughout world markets to ensure its competitiveness and global presence (some with competitors!). Strategic alliances and joint ventures are now a fact of life for companies who aspire to be global players. Customers are becoming more sophisticated and demanding, and less loyal. Even though there is standardisation of buying patterns, within this structure there is increasing market fragmentation as customers insist on their own preferences.

Mass customisation

Mass customisation and one-to-one marketing are also an increasing trend. Buying a car in the USA now for instance, presents people with a bewildering choice of around 750 models — almost a version for every personality. Or you can have your jeans customised to your exact measurements by mass customisation production methods.

So what are the chances of survival in the 21st century? In a crowded, technologically-oriented marketplace, just like in a crowded room, a powerful personality stands out. A distinguished person commands attention in the cacophony of a cocktail party, and so it is in the world of business. A unique corporate personality is the most important reason why the public will choose one company rather than another — because they can relate to it. This may be a subconscious, emotional draw rather than a conscious, rational choice. But it is nonetheless powerful, and nonetheless vital for a company to survive and prosper. Personality brings a company or product to life, reveals the true character behind the name, and provides vivid attraction. It invites people to form a long-lasting, loyal, friendly relationship with someone they want to get to know. That someone can be your company.

Summary

1. As major trends, direct marketing and relationship marketing can result in remarkable growth but only if allied to a consistent personality strategy.
2. Technology companies can benefit disproportionately from adopting a more sensitive, emotional, people focused personality, as can business to business marketing generally.
3. Similarly, a distinctive personality can be the key in the massive children's market.
4. Hypercompetition and mass customisation, likely to be major features of 21st Century marketing, demand no less than corporate charisma as the foundation to long term success.

CHAPTER TWELVE

MAKING THE FUTURE: A NOTE TO CEOS

We have already stressed that success depends on commitment from the very top, so this final note is addressed to chief executive officers and the heads of organisations. You are faced now with a unique opportunity to make the future of your organisation. An opportunity that will provide you with the solutions to many of the problems facing you in your business, especially if the questions in your mind are:

- how to motivate your staff and gain their commitment
- how to make your company different from the rest
- how to achieve a sustainable competitive advantage
- how to get and keep more customers
- how to improve corporate communications
- how to generate sustainable increases in profits

The one strategic move that will deliver these benefits is for your company to create its own personality. This book has provided you with the conceptual and practical skills to be able to do this, but you have to provide the leadership and long-term commitment, and manage the enormous change that may be required, in both attitude and behaviour. The whole purpose of creating corporate personality is to secure better relationships with the world outside, and especially your customers. Specifically, it will mean that everything your company does will be as if you are looking through the eyes of your customers. That may require a different attitude and genuine customer-first values. But this is what true marketing is all about and it will revolutionise any business.

Like any worthwhile corporate strategy, creating a corporate personality is not an easy task. It will take time, it will need investment, it will need perseverance, and it will need bold action. It will also need your personal facilitation and constant attention. But the results will be more than worthwhile.

Involve your top executives, involve your employees as much as you can and they will respond. As you go through the process always remember to lead with action, demonstrate your commitment to the values and personality characteristics, and show everyone that living the personality starts at the top.

Finally, here are some summary guidelines for building a strong corporate personality.

Choose a distinctive personality

- one that fits with your values, vision and mission
- one that will appeal to your target customers
- try to get a close match

Create it and manage it with your people

- involve as many as you can, at every level
- make it motivating for them — project your vision and enthusiasm
- get them to 'care' not just be 'aware'; go for *attitude* changes
- develop a strong corporate communications team
- manage the personality inside and outside the company

Adjust your corporate identity

- make it fit in with the personality
- use personality to reinforce your existing identity
- if you are changing your identity, create the personality first

Look at your positioning carefully

- with respect to your target publics (segments)
- to appeal to 'personalities' in these groups
- to reflect and reinforce your unique personality — to make you *different*
- be brave enough to re-position your company if necessary

Change the company culture

- if values need changing
- make sure that behaviour represents personality
- let your target publics experience the personality

Adapt products and services

- to meet the needs of target audiences
- to reflect the personality in packaging, design, new product development and launch

Communicate the personality

- internally — at an awareness (knowing) and operational (doing) level
- externally — with consistent and appropriate marketing communications
- make sure all relevant departments are involved

Monitor the impact of your company personality

- by qualitative means (how people feel about it, relate to it)
- by quantitative means (what impact it has on sales, enquiries, complaints, and other measures)
- track your advertising successes and failures

Be prepared to invest

- treat corporate personality building as a long term investment
- treat it as you would any other major business strategy
- don't judge it on short-term earning increases, even though these might be substantial

Be prepared for mistakes

- allow for human nature and Murphy's law
- expect some tactical and strategic set-backs

Guard the personality jealously

- as you would a member of your family, or a precious item
- as you would a friend, who relies on you
- establish a formal top-level process for this in your company
- never allow any product, customer interaction, communication (however big or small) to step out of character with your corporate personality

It is never easy for a chief executive to decide what to spend his or her time on. Often the urgent fights against the important for attention, and the short term against the long term. A lot has to be delegated, even matters of strategic importance, if you are to do what you have to in the available time. Creating and maintaining the unique personality of your organisation is one strategy for which you cannot delegate responsibility, yet which requires the co-operation of every member of the staff. It demands nothing less than true leadership. But it represents the best investment of your time and energy. It is a strategy that will have the most significant, long-lasting effect on your company's future. You can *create* charisma. You can create a future for your company.

INDEX

Levitt, Theodore
  *The Marketing Imagina-
    tion* 28
Lexus 118, 130
lifestyles 199-203
location, projection of
    personality through
    47
logos 46-7, 85, 139-40
Lotus 1-2-3 46

McDonald's 37, 38, 45, 78,
    128, 133, 149, 164,
    218
magazines 89, 215
magnetism 7
makers 202-3
maps, perceptual (product)
    204-6
Marconi, Joe
  Image Marketing 76
marketing
  budget 101
  business-to-business
    218-19
  differentiation 28-9, 32
  direct *see* direct
    marketing
  global 169-70
  hypercompetition 219-
    20
  niche 175
  objective 100
  one-to-one 220-1
  perception and reality
    28-31
  and personality
    strategy 99-101
  situation analysis 100
  strategy and tactics 100
  technology companies
    215-17
  timescale 100
  to children 217-18
market research 187-211
  basic questions 188-92,
    211
  corporate personality
    190-1, 210
  depth interviews 206-7
  focus groups 206, 207
  myths 192
  perceptual (product)
    maps 204-6

projective techniques
    206-7
  psychographic 199-203
  qualitative 197, 198-9,
    210
  quantitative 197-8, 210
  society's values 207-8
  visualising individual
    consumer 203-4
market segmentation 173-
    85
Marks & Spencer 78, 128-9,
    137, 139, 152
Marlboro 36, 43-4, 47, 69,
    77, 165-6
Mars 78
Mastercard 75, 118
Mattel 68, 217-18
Mazda 46
MBO (management by
    objectives) 58
Mercedes 36, 41, 42, 148,
    152, 164, 182
Mercury 147
mergers 129-30
Merril Lynch 164
message, product 49, 50-2
metaphors 73
Met Life 47, 48, 133
Microsoft 43, 133, 146, 164,
    216
Midland Bank 140
Mikimoto 40
Milo 47
mind functions 33-6
Mini 148-9
mission 5, 32, 67
mission statement 11, 15,
    17-18, 19, 72
mixed messages 49
morale, employee 14, 103
Morita, Akio 149
Motel 6 108
Motorola 17, 25, 133
multiple personalities 73-5
Mustang 182

names 45-6, 139-40
NatWest Bank 121-2
Nestlé 47, 78, 129, 133, 164,
    165, 170
newsletters 89, 215
niche branding 151
niche marketing 175

Nielsen and Arbitron
    ratings 194
Nike 41, 42, 78, 108, 121,
    122, 123, 133, 152,
    153, 218
Nintendo 168
nostalgia 40, 47
numeric brand names 45-6

objectives statement 100
omnibus survey 197-8
one-to-one marketing 220-1
on-line access 215
'out of character' activities
    10

packaging, product 107
partnership, need for 36,
    41-2, 52
past, need for links with 36,
    40, 52
Pepsi-Cola 36, 42, 44-5,
    122, 130, 155, 196
perception
  changing 29-31
  differentiation 28-9
  long-term nature 30
  segmentation 30-1
Perrier 45, 129
personalities, endorsement
    by 43, 154-5
personality 7-8
  brand 11, 164-70
  mind functions 33-6
  unique selling
    personality 181
personality, corporate 7-14
  and advertising 5
  age 36, 47-8, 53
  assessment of charac-
    teristics 77-80
  blurred perception 129
  characteristics *see*
    characteristics,
    personality
  checklist 60-1
  choosing 79-80, 224
  communication 29, 67,
    99-114, 225
  corporate behaviour 84-
    6
  corporate charisma 4
  corporate culture 22,
    82, 89

Waltham Forest Libraries

Please return this item by the las~~~~~~~~~d. The loan may be renewed unless requir~~~~

SGDT '22		

D1586580

Need to renew your books?
http://www.walthamforest.gov.uk/libraries or
Dial 0333 370 4700 for Callpoint – our 24/7 automated telephone renewal line. You will need your library card number and your PIN. If you do **not** know your PIN, contact your local library.

"A delightfully wicked thrill ride that had me on the edge of my seat. *The Last Girl* beckons the shadows and laughs in the face of fear. I didn't want it to end!" — Chelsea Pitcher, bestselling author of *This Lie Will Kill You*

"Perfect for fans of *Pretty Little Liars* and Gretchen McNeil, *The Last Girl* is a heart-pounding thriller that grabs you by the throat and doesn't let go until the very last page. Brilliantly twisted – I loved it!" — Kat Ellis, author of *Harrow Lake* and *Wicked Little Deeds*

"A bright, smooth candy apple with a razor blade inside. Goldy Moldavsky continues her white-hot streak of unmatched brilliance in the world of contemporary YA." — Derek Milman, author of *Scream All Night* and *Swipe Right for Murder*

"This twisty tour de force . . . is at once a gripping teen melodrama, an incisive meditation on fear, and a love letter to horror and the genre's tropes." — *Publishers Weekly*, starred review

"An atmospheric page-turner about loving scary movies, longing to belong, and uncovering the many masks people wear." — Kirkus Reviews

"Moldavsky manages to both pay homage to and poke fun at traditional horror tropes . . . and the final fear test is keenly chilling." — BCCB

LORD
OF THE
FLY FEST

GOLDY MOLDAVSKY

Published in the US in 2022 by Henry Holt and Company,
part of the Macmillan Publishing Group, LLC
120 Broadway, New York, NY 10271

First published in Great Britain in 2022
by Electric Monkey, part of Farshore
An imprint of HarperCollins*Publishers*
1 London Bridge Street, London SE1 9GF

farshore.co.uk

HarperCollins*Publishers*
1st Floor, Watermarque Building, Ringsend Road
Dublin 4, Ireland

Text copyright © 2022 Goldy Moldavsky

The moral rights of the author have been asserted
CIP catalogue record of this title is available from the British Library

ISBN 978 0 7555 0153 3
Printed and bound in the UK using 100% renewable electricity at
CPI Group (UK) Ltd
1

Typeset by Avon DataSet Ltd, Alcester, Warwickshire

1

Rafi Francisco really stepped in it this time.

She was lost and alone in the middle of a Caribbean jungle, wearing an ill-fitting shirt that clung to all her sweat-filled crevices.

There was an incessant bug, big as a bullet, buzzing into her neck, lured there by her ridiculously poor choice of candy-scented body spray.

Her backpack seemed to be getting heavier, and banged into her lower back with every step she took.

She was thirsty and tired and scared, and this colossal mistake of a trip had cost her two thousand dollars—aka her life's savings.

Yes, Rafi Francisco had definitely stepped in it. But like, literally.

She knew the moment she did it, feeling her shoe slide forward on the sticky stuff. Rafi winced as she lifted up her foot to examine the damage. She didn't want to think of the kind of animal that could make such a massive mess. With her luck it was still close by and watching her through the trees, ready to charge. Thirty minutes on this island had already proven soul—and *sole*—crushing. She scraped the bottom of her shoe across the base of the nearest tree trunk until most of the gunk was off.

A few hours ago Rafi had been on an air-conditioned plane, eating her third bag of free chips. Now she was here, regretting her life choices. Instinctively, she took her phone out of her pocket, but then remembered there was no service here. There was something so silly about a phone in a jungle, like holding a bouquet of flowers in a blizzard. Like things that belonged to two different worlds trying to coexist.

And while Rafi had been here only a short while, a lot of things about this place felt *off*. Rafi had flown to the island of Exuma with a plane full of concertgoers, and then they'd all subsequently boarded a ship that had taken them on a half-hour-long journey here. The island was big enough to take days to explore fully, but still small enough that Rafi couldn't find it on a map. She thought she had once, and studied it long and hard before realizing it was a blueberry muffin crumb. But what was really strange was that when they all got off the ship, there was no one to greet them. Not an organizer or owner or even a volunteer. Which was how Rafi had ended up in the jungle, looking for anyone who could tell her where to find her luggage.

Thirty-five minutes in and Rafi had the sinking feeling that she and everyone else here had been duped. But the biggest tell was the island itself. It looked nothing like it had in the promo video.

Fly Fest had gone from rumor, to viral fact, to the hottest ticket in town in a matter of days. But it really came alive in people's minds when the promo video dropped. Sandy beaches, Jet Skis, and supermodels. And, of course, there was the now legendary voice-over that played over the stunning imagery.

> Fly Fest is a question. An answer. An enigma. A messiah. A sandal. It is all and it is nothing. It will push the limits of boundlessness into an endless quest to enlightened fulfillment you didn't even know you desired but also never really longed for. It is air. It is foundation. It is sand, it is SUPERMODELS. It is the way the sun feels slipping through your fingers, and the way water feels blowing out your nostrils. It is standing at the top of Mount Everest and discovering the lost city of El Dorado. It is the Loch Ness Monster. It is the moment right after Mount Vesuvius exploded but right before the people of Pompeii turned to ash. It is the delicious mix of mental ecstasy and physical ecstasy and synthetic ecstasy. It is yachts. And it. Is. Fly.

So yeah, things were definitely not as advertised. Silver linings, though: At least no one had seen Rafi step in poop.

"Hello!" a voice called.

Rafi turned to find someone rushing toward her. Someone about her age, with a pageboy haircut and phone in hand. "Finally! What is the Wi-Fi password here?"

"Excuse me?" Rafi said.

"You work here, right?"

"In . . . the jungle?"

"No . . . the festival."

"Oh," Rafi said. "I don't work for the festival."

"But, your shirt . . ."

Rafi looked down. Her shirt was neon pink with the hashtag #LiveLaughFLY written across the chest in white cursive lettering. When Rafi bought her ticket to Fly Fest, she realized she had no idea what the appropriate attire was for a week-long music festival in the Bahamas. Her wardrobe consisted mostly of comfortable sweatshirts in varying shades of gray and taupe. But she wanted to blend in on this trip. She wasn't sure her choice of shirt had worked, though. The moment Rafi set foot on the island and saw what all the other concertgoers looked like, she felt instantly different from them.

Her black bob with bangs stood out in a sea of flowing blondes and shimmering browns. Even though they were in the tropics, everyone looked so manicured, not a wisp of hair blowing in the island breeze, while Rafi, in a rush to make it to the airport on time, hadn't put any product in her hair. She hadn't even packed any. Everyone also already looked like they'd made a point to get tanned before showing up, which just made Rafi, who spent probably too much time indoors, feel suddenly Casperish. The pink shirt was the brightest, most carefree, and most expensive T-shirt Rafi owned. When she saw it on the Fly Fest website, she figured it'd be perfect. Though, now that she looked at it, she saw it for the generic thing it was, and couldn't be one hundred percent certain that the word STAFF wasn't written across the back.

Looking at her new companion's shirt, she noticed a button pinned on the collar with the words THEY/THEM on it.

"I'm Rafi, by the way. She/her."

Her introduction was met by a skeptical look that started at the top of Rafi's head and swept slowly down to her offending shoe. "Peggy Yim."

"Hi, Peggy. I don't work here, by the way. I've actually been looking for someone who does. It's weird, right? That there isn't anyone in charge?" She waited for a response, but Peggy was preoccupied with their phone, holding it up to the sky in search of reception.

"I tried that already," Rafi said. "It won't work."

"I have a satellite phone. I'll get online," Peggy said. "It's just a matter of time."

"You a tech whiz or something?"

"Yes." They offered nothing else, but Rafi liked the short answer, how assured Peggy was when they said it. They were probably one of those STEM coder people who were going to rule the world and knew it. Rafi needed more of that in her life, the boldness, the confidence. She'd come to Fly Fest to be bold, do important things. She suddenly felt bold enough to share something about herself, unprompted.

"I'm kind of a tech person, too. I have a podcast."

Rafi paused, in case Peggy wanted to ask a follow-up question or maybe murmur their approval. But the only sound that came was the squawk from a toucan flying overhead. Maybe Peggy's silence was their way of telling Rafi to go on.

"It's called Musical Mysteries. It's about mysteries in—"

"Let me guess," Peggy said. "Music."

"Right. I already have one season in the can. Eight episodes. It was pretty successful."

"Never heard of it."

"Well, successful in the independent podcasting world. It got written up on a few blogs. And Michael Panz called it 'promising,' and he's a contributing sound producer for NPR, so. Yeah. I'm proud of it."

Peggy kept checking their phone, and although they were walking away wordlessly, they also weren't changing the subject, which was new for Rafi, since at this point in the conversation about her podcast, most people usually did. "I'm focusing season two on River Stone."

"Isn't he supposed to be here?"

"Yes!" The word came out way too loud, but Rafi was just glad for the engagement. This was officially a two-way dialogue now. Her podcast was a topic of interest not only to her, but to Peggy, who was clearly a smart and interesting person. "Yes, he's supposed to be one of the musical acts. Which is why I'm here."

"Stalker."

"No, no, no," Rafi said, quickening her step to keep up. "No, I'm like a journalist. I'm chasing a story. And if I'm right, it could break a lot of things wide open."

"The girlfriend disappearance thing?"

"Yes," Rafi said. She was pleased that even Peggy seemed to acknowledge how that story seemed implausible and strange. Which made it perfect for the podcast.

"I heard River canceled his trip here."

Rafi stopped walking. "What?"

"All the musicians canceled. The models, too."

Rafi quickened her step to catch up with Peggy, who hadn't stopped walking and pointing their phone to the sky as though beckoning a higher power. "But I'm only here to meet River."

"Bummer." Peggy's tone did not in any way convey that this was, in fact, a bummer. Maybe their arm was finally too tired, but Peggy put down their phone, letting it bounce against their hip as they leveled Rafi with a serious stare. "There is no one affiliated with Fly Fest anywhere on this island. You know what that means, right?"

Rafi shook her head.

"We're stuck here," Peggy said.

It sounded too heavy, too bleak, and to counter that, Rafi's instinct was to chuckle. "We're not stuck here." If the festival really was canceled, then someone would be around to come get them. A boat. Surely. "Help is coming," Rafi said. A second ago she wasn't aware they needed help, but now nothing in the world seemed more true.

And yet, Peggy did not look convinced. "I just hope help gets here before all hell breaks loose."

Another thing that made Rafi laugh, though the sound that came out of her throat was more like a toad choking on a fly. "Come on. *Hell breaking loose*? Everyone here seems pretty cool."

"I take it you haven't been to the seaport yet."

2

WHEN THEY ALL DISEMBARKED FROM THE SHIP EARLIER, it was the seaport that greeted them. It appeared to be the lone human-made structure on the island, the only real sign so far that, before today, other human beings had set foot here. But it was also a sign that someone had abandoned this place, because it didn't look quite finished.

The building, if you could call it that, was only partially enclosed, with three walls and a few columns in front holding up a thatched roof. Its wooden beams were splintered, plaster-swollen, and chipped; the welcome signs warped with age and moisture. It looked like someone had plans to make this island a place for visitors, and they started with the seaport but then ran out of money. Like the building across the street from Rafi's house back home. It'd been under construction since she was eleven years old, and now, seven years later, it was still only partially done, with half the walls covered in insulation and the other half a skeleton of steel. The seaport was a promise that someone had taken back. But right now it could've been a town hall for how crammed it was with angry people.

When Rafi walked in, the first person she encountered was a girl who looked slightly younger than her, sobbing.

"Are you okay?" Rafi asked her.

The girl looked at Rafi, her eyes twin geysers. The sight of her instantly put Rafi in panic mode, and she did a quick surface check to see if there was something physically wrong. "Are you hurt?"

The girl held up her hands, which Rafi examined for blood or scratches. But they were as pristine as a nail-polish model's hands. "Where," the girl began, pausing to take a shaky breath, "is"—*sob*—"my"—*gulp*—"villa?"

Right. Some people had paid thousands to spend the week in luxury villas on the beach. Rafi had opted for the cheapest accommodation, which the Fly Fest website had described simply as "room." But there weren't any rooms that Rafi could see, let alone villas.

She didn't know what to say.

The girl, exasperated, let out another wail and skulked off to someone else who might be able to help her. But it didn't look like anyone in here could. All around the seaport people were crying, yelling, getting into each other's faces, asking their own desperate questions. It was discombobulating, and Rafi felt adrift in a sea of confusion. She sidled back up to Peggy like they were a life raft.

"Someone has to calm everybody down," Rafi said. "Maybe you should say something."

"Me?" Peggy said. "Why?"

"You're the only one in here not freaking out."

Peggy was extraordinarily calm, still looking down at their phone, trying to make it a little less useless. "It's a condition I have where I don't care about things."

Rafi nodded, though she couldn't tell if Peggy was being serious or not. Their monotonous voice made everything sound sarcastic.

"But you should definitely say something," Peggy continued.

"No, I couldn't." On her podcast, Rafi spoke to her listeners with no issue, but that didn't mean she was comfortable speaking in front of a real-life crowd. Especially not one as angry as this one. Without headphones on and a mic in front of her, Rafi couldn't even be sure she had a voice at all.

"THIS GIRL HAS SOMETHING TO SAY!" Peggy shouted. Turned out their voice could stay expressionless at a much higher octave, which surprised Rafi. But what truly horrified her was that Peggy was pointing directly at her.

"No," Rafi said. But it was too late, Peggy had already gotten the entire room's attention, and they leeched on to Rafi, the force of their questions strong enough to make her back away. Unfortunately, she backed right into the check-in desk at the far end of the room, and it seemed that the only way to get some distance from the increasingly angry horde was to climb onto said desk. So that was what she did.

"Where is everything?" someone from the crowd yelled.

"Where is our luggage?" another person asked.

"The website said there'd be on-site massages!"

"I want a piña colada!"

Rafi tried to keep everyone calm, but she couldn't even hear her own voice over the din. And then she thought maybe she *was* the perfect person to talk in front of this crowd because she had just the tool for exactly this situation. She swung her backpack forward and unzipped it, fishing inside for her portable microphone. It wasn't as high-tech as the one in her studio, aka her closet, but it would do. And the great thing about it wasn't just that it could record audio, but it could amplify her voice. She found her portable speaker in her bag too and set it down by her feet, plugging the mic into it with a thick cord.

"Okay, everyone, calm down!" Her voice boomed over the crowd like a heavy blanket over a bonfire, instantly putting out the questions and concerns.

She glanced quickly at Peggy, who kept their eyes down on their phone but still managed to raise a thumbs-up Rafi's way.

"I'd love to answer all of your questions, but I don't work for Fly Fest," Rafi said.

The crowd, still silent, looked collectively confused. "Are you sure?" a voice asked.

"Why does everyone think I work here?"

"You look like someone who has to work for a living," a boy said.

"You're like, what, thirty-two?" a girl said.

"I'm eighteen," Rafi said, appalled. And then she figured it out. *It must be the microphone.* It was authoritative and adult and impressive. *Yes, it was the microphone*, she thought.

"It's your shirt," someone else said.

Rafi looked down at her shirt and wondered for the second time that day what it was about the brightly colored, generically hashtagged, shapeless tee that screamed STAFF. "This shirt is cute and stylish," she tried to explain.

Their confused silence seemed to be gathering strength. Some of them shook their heads to disagree. Rafi pretended not to see those particular people. "Look, I might not work here, but I do know one thing: It doesn't look like anybody on this island works here either."

Heads began turning, looking at each other, as though checking to confirm that no one from Fly Fest was secretly among them. But there were no more bright pink shirts with generic, festival-approved slogans on them.

"Maybe they're coming on a different boat," Rafi continued. "Or maybe they're on another part of the island, and we just haven't seen them yet."

"Does this other part of the island have the villas?" It was the girl who'd been crying to Rafi, tears now drying on her cheeks.

"The other part of the island has all the yachts!" some guy shouted way too confidently.

"The supermodels are there?" someone else asked.

"Can I get my piña colada on the yachts with the supermodels?" another person said.

Rafi recognized the start of a new angry uprising. She spoke into her mic. "I know we were promised yachts with supermodels." Even as she said this she could see how ridiculous it sounded, how unlikely it was for supermodels to want to party on expensive boats with regular people. "But I think we have to prepare ourselves for—"

"My name is Paul!" a guy said out of nowhere. He was as tall as a goal post and looked like the type of guy who played football at Rafi's school. "And I only have one question: Is O-Town still coming?"

"My name is Ryan and I have the same question!" another guy said. "Is O-Town still doing their reunion concert here?" This Ryan person looked almost identical to Paul. Both of them had short, dark hair, square chins, deodorant commercial auras. Rafi felt like she was seeing double, which was disorienting, but not as disorienting as their weird question.

"I don't know what a Hotown is," she said, "but honestly, it sounds kind of sexist?"

"Are you kidding me?" Paul said. "Do you have any idea who my father is?"

"I don't see how that's relev—"

"If O-Town canceled, I want to get off this island," Ryan said. "Get the boat back. I want a refund, and I'm suing your ass."

"Like I said, I don't work here."

"I don't care!" Paul said.

Rafi glanced at Peggy, hoping for some reassurance, but Peggy only held up their hand again, this time in a thumbs-down.

So now not only was she out two thousand bucks and stranded on an island; Rafi also had a lawsuit on her hands. It would've worried her more if she wasn't distracted by something else.

A new group of people was marching toward the seaport from down the beach, a swarm of money and beauty. There was something about them that was different from everyone else. Maybe it was because none of them was currently suing Rafi, but they looked more dignified. Shinier. They were beautiful, and their clothes looked expensive, even if the attire was all wrong for the beach.

The girls plowed the sand with their heels. They wore crocheted halter tops that were both too much for this climate and not enough to provide cover from the unrelenting sun. Some had ropey bikini tops that looked like overly complex bondage situations and a nightmare for tan lines. And there were way too many of the most maddening clothing of all: rompers.

The boys' clothes were simpler, but no less head-scratching in this atmosphere. Designer sneakers and designer oversize sweatshirts and designer pants that got tighter farther down their legs. All of it looked cozy and kind of quilted, and Rafi could only imagine the deluge of sweat streaming underneath all those layers.

There was something special about them, and Rafi watched them like she knew them. It took her a minute, but she finally realized that they looked familiar because they *were* familiar. Rafi recognized them from little stories she'd seen bouncing around the internet, information that she'd come upon largely against her will.

Influencers. It was so clear now, as though she could see

the blue checkmarks or large figures that ended in *K* and *M* floating above their heads.

Rafi recognized the couple who insulted turkey (the cold cut, the animal, and the country).

The boy who adopted seventeen puppies and re-homed sixteen of them.

The girl who came out with a skin-care line that got recalled because it mimicked the effects of snake venom.

The vegan food guru who accidentally poisoned people with his raw mac-and-cheese recipe.

The crystals guy who started a cult.

The fashion designer who started a cult.

The fitness girl who started a cult.

The candle girl who burned down the West Coast.

The guy whose entire life was an elaborate prank.

The girl who broke travel bans to fly to 120 countries in the pandemic.

The person who went to Uzbekistan to do charity work with earthworms.

The guy who started that war using mindfulness techniques.

And sprinkled among the influencers was an even more rarefied group of elites. Rafi recognized them because they occasionally popped up in photos with real celebrities. They were practically celebs themselves. Well, celeb-adjacent. As in, they had the same hairdressers as certain celebs, belonged to the same invitation-only dating apps. They didn't shill anything on their social media platforms because they were already independently wealthy, thanks to their parents. They had no scandals to their names or anything even in the neighborhood of discernable talent, but they always seemed to be smack in the middle of the most glittering lifestyles. Which, Rafi guessed, was what drew them to Fly Fest. They didn't look so sparkling now, though. They kind of sparkled from all the sweat, but that wasn't the same thing.

At the front of the group, leading them, was the biggest influencer of all.

Rafi knew Jack Dewey from his makeup tutorials on YouTube. He was pretty. Not pretty in the typical teen heartthrob kind of way. Pretty in the *Toddlers & Tiaras* way. Like he could've entered a pageant and definitely stolen the crown from a dolled-up three-year-old. He had red hair that swooped over his forehead, and a body as smooth and stick-straight as an eyebrow pencil. He dressed mildly compared to everyone around him (simple tank top and short-shorts), but he didn't need to wear something ostentatious. His face was the real attention-grabber.

Jack was fully made up, with eyebrows painted in high arches, deep cheekbones cut with contouring, and overdrawn lips. It was a talent, what he managed to do with makeup. Rafi had tried following along to his infamous smoky-eye tutorial once, but it only made her look like she worked as a professional chimney sweep.

When he reached the seaport, Jack stopped, and his gang of influencers stopped behind him. He noticed Rafi right away. "Finally," he said. "Someone who works here."

"This shirt was for sale on the Fly Fest website," Rafi

announced into her microphone in her clearest voice. "Right next to the wristbands and the mouse pads." And as she said "mouse pads," it began to dawn on her that—yep—this festival was a scam.

"So who even are you?" Jack asked.

"My name is Rafi Francisco."

"I mean on social. What's your handle?"

"Oh," Rafi said. "Well, you can find me on Twitter under @MusicalMysteries. It's the name of my podcast. I have a podcast."

The silence that fell over the crowd was devastating. You could hear a dragonfly buzz straight from the room out of sheer mortification. The quiet stretched uncomfortably long, punctuated by one of the newly arrived influencers swaying and then finally falling face-first onto the floor.

"Is he okay?" Rafi asked. "He could have heatstroke."

"Pretty sure it's just secondhand embarrassment," Jack said. He stepped over the collapsed boy to get to the check-in desk and join Rafi on top of it. "I'll take it from here," he said, trying to grab Rafi's mic.

But Rafi held on to it tight. "This is actually mine," she said. "I was just telling everyone we should probably check the whole island to see if there's anyone in charge before we jump to conclusions. I've already been in the jungle, so that's covered. Do you want to team up? Head to the other side of the beach?"

Jack's chuckle hit her like a slap across the face. "And go back out in the sun? Absolutely no—"

"I'll do it."

Rafi searched the crowd for the person who had just volunteered. There was an awed parting as people backed away to let none other than musical sensation River Stone through.

The sight of him, so unexpected, made Rafi lose her voice.

Jack was quick to speak for the both of them, though. "The three of us will go, yes!"

3

RAFI, JACK, AND RIVER WALKED ALONG THE EDGE OF the island, first the mile of white sandy beach, which eventually turned into rocky terrain and cliffs on the east side. They stayed away from the center of the island because it was a mountain they weren't too keen to climb: The land was like a bedsheet that someone had pinched in the middle and pulled toward the sky. Rounding that area, they found themselves in a thick forest of jungle. And the whole time, Rafi held back, observing. She did a lot of talking on her podcast, but her most important job as an investigator (and she did consider herself an investigator) was to know when to stay quiet and keep her eyes peeled. And that was what she did now that she had eyes on *the* River Stone.

The one person she was here for.

Rafi zeroed in on every step he took. Even though River wasn't singing, it still felt like a concert experience. The oppressive humidity of the jungle mimicked the stuffiness of a performance hall, with every leaf and creeping vine like elbows and shoulders invading Rafi's personal space. When it came to River, though, the plants grazed and glided over his skin, wicking the sweat off him like adoring fans delicately dabbing his brow after a set. Typical.

Rafi's silence, she had to admit, was a little bit of the stunned variety. She'd spent all her money to come here and meet River, but now that he was only a few paces ahead of her, she was so shocked to be this close to him that she had no idea what to do or say.

Jack knew all too well, though. He walked in stride with River, gushing and asking endless questions.

"There must be a way for you to contact someone," Jack said. "Arrange a pickup? They wouldn't just leave a superstar to die in the wilderness. Does Uber have boats?"

"You know, I actually don't have a phone," River said. "I have people who handle all my social media and emails and all that. I like to be 'off the grid' whenever I can."

"Wow. Incredible," Jack said.

Rafi could not roll back her eyes enough. At River for having "people" to do his bidding, and at the idea of Jack believing that a phone-free life was "incredible."

"Is Hella here with you?" Jack asked.

Hella Badid was River's girlfriend. Dating for two months. She was a supermodel. In fact, she was one of the supermodels who had been prominently featured in all the promo videos for Fly Fest. When people said they wanted to party with supermodels on yachts, they meant they wanted to party with Hella.

"Uh, nah, she missed her flight. Probably for the best, right?"

20

The words poured out of River's mouth smarmy as an oil spill, but that may have just been because he was Australian. Like his answer to Jack's question, River may have seemed simple and innocuous, but Rafi could see right through him. And she saw his smile go crooked. It was something she'd observed about him in her research. River had a tell when he was lying, and that crooked smile was it.

"I only heard that all the other musical acts canceled when I was already on the ship," River said. "I knew something was wrong when I got off the boat and there was no one here to tell me where to go. In my industry, you rely on a team. I may have had the number-one album three weeks in a row, but I wouldn't know how to get dressed in the morning if I didn't have someone to tell me what to wear."

That explained his lack of a shirt.

Jack laughed and agreed about the "industry" as though he belonged to the same one. But Rafi couldn't giggle along with him. She saw right through River's humble-bragging. He slathered on the charm like it was a bottle of cheap cologne, and he stank of it. Did people really fall for his shtick? His arresting smile? His muscley physique? The way his shiny hair kept spilling over his eyes, and every time he brushed it back with his fingers it seemed to volumize with so much body that if little tiny people existed, they would take their teeny surfboards and ride those waves into the sunset?

The answer, of course, was yes. People ate it up. River had exploded onto the music scene two years ago, and he remained one of the most popular pop boys around. And Jack seemed to be falling for him in real time. Rafi noticed he would find any opportunity to casually rest his fingertips on River's forearm. River didn't seem to mind. His forearm had probably felt the touch of a lot of hands. His forearm was a swell covered in sparse, golden-haired foliage, coming to a point at his wrist, which was slender but strong. From it branched his hand, wide with long fingers. Looking at that hand, swinging idly by his hip, Rafi could so easily picture it wrapped around a knife.

Or a crowbar.

Or maybe pulling a thin rope taut until there was nothing but stillness on the other end of it.

"What smells like poop?"

Jack's question shook Rafi out of her reverie, and she noticed that both boys had stopped walking and were looking at her. Jack's nose was tipped up, lip curling as he sniffed.

"It's not me," Rafi said quickly. She dipped her right shoe behind her left, hoping the awkward motion was enough to hide the smell that was apparently emanating from her. "I don't . . . smell like poop."

"I don't smell anything," River said.

"Me neither," Rafi said.

"I have a scary-good sense of smell," Jack said. "I once smelled the glaucoma all over my great-grandfather. He died two days later."

He kept sniffing, and no matter how many steps Rafi took away from him, Jack's nose led him to her. Rafi backed away until she backed right into a tree and there was nowhere else for

22

her to go. Jack bent low and when he straightened, his green eyes narrowed with certainty. "It's your shoe."

Rafi fixed her features until she felt they looked appropriately shocked, then lifted up her shoe so she could pretend to inspect the bottom of it for the first time. "Oh nooo," she whispered, elongating the small word so it sounded, ironically, Australian. "I must've stepped in poop."

Jack shuddered with disgust. "You just stepped in it? Where did it come from? Did someone just *go* out in the open? We haven't even been here three hours and people are already going in the wild? This is madness!"

"It's natural," River said. "Everybody goes. Even me."

The conversation was steering in a weird direction, and though Rafi was glad it was in a direction away from her offending shoe, she felt the need to get it back on track. "Um, I'm pretty sure it was not human poop."

Jack snapped his face in her direction. "What do you mean '*not human poop*'? Then what kind is it?"

River watched Rafi too, both of them waiting for an answer that she thought was pretty obvious.

"Animal?" she said. "Probably a boar." After bingeing the show *Lost* a few years ago, Rafi knew that the only things that lived on deserted islands were boars, polar bears, and smoke monsters. And out of the three, boar was the most likely culprit.

"Are you saying there are wild hogs on this island?" Jack asked. "If I wanted to party with wild hogs, I would've gone to my cousin Lionel's seventh birthday."

There were three tiers of passes to Fly Fest. Rafi had paid

for the kind that got you "room" and "limitless water." Jack must've paid for the kind that came with private villas, infinity pools, and no poop of any kind, human or otherwise.

"I think we need a change of subject," River said. "I mean, look at this place." He gestured toward the crystal water view shimmering through the trees to their right, the lush jungle to their left, the tropical birds cawing at them from above. It was hot, but there was a strong aroma coming from all around, from flowers or fruit, or both. There was nothing but the blue sky, the fresh air, and nature all around them. "There aren't any power lines. No people. No cars. Not a single cell tower," River said.

"It's a shit hole," Jack said.

"It's beautiful," River said at the same time.

"*So* beautiful," Jack agreed.

River seemed suddenly more interested in exploring the newfound beauty of the island than he was in continuing in a straight line down this expedition. He veered deeper into the jungle, following the sounds of birds in the leaves. Rafi kept her eyes on him, intent on following his every move. She couldn't stand to look at him for too long, but she also didn't want to lose sight of him.

But when she made a move toward River, Jack blocked her way.

"I hope I'm not overstepping here," Jack said, "but I thought I might give you a beauty tip, since it's kind of what I'm known for." He unzipped the black leather fanny pack that he wore around his waist and retrieved a tube of shiny lip gloss.

"It breaks my heart when I see a girl who's never heard of makeup before."

"I've heard of—"

"This goes on your mouth," Jack explained slowly, extending the tube to Rafi. "Your lips are so pale I can't be certain you even have a mouth. This gloss is clear so it won't totally fix the problem, but it's something. And you really need"—he looked her over, the expression on his face darkening—"something."

"Thanks," Rafi said, though she wasn't sure that was the right word to use. "My lips probably look like this because there's a ninety-five percent chance I'm dehydrated."

"Oh, I can tell you're thirsty," Jack said. "How many followers do you have?"

Instinctively, Rafi turned around to see if anyone was trailing her, but then realized what Jack meant. "Around five hundred on Twitter."

Jack's eyes narrowed, confused. "Are you, like, a nano-influencer?"

Rafi didn't know what a nano-influencer was, but she was pretty sure she wasn't it. She shook her head.

Her answer seemed only to confuse Jack further. "Nobody our age listens to podcasts, unless they're losers or incels. When do you have time for TikTok?"

"I don't."

"YouTube beauty tutorials?"

"Also not."

"Of course, of course. Your whole look is starting to make

a lot of sense." As he said this, Jack wiped the sweat off his forehead, unwittingly smearing the penciled-in color of his brows over the side of his face.

"You've got a little something," Rafi said, gesturing to her own face as a map for him. But though she'd pointed to her forehead, Jack proceeded to wipe the sweat from his upper lip instead, painting a swath of his chin pink.

Rafi looked, slack-jawed, at his multicolored face. But instead of saying anything, she found herself giving Jack a thumbs-up.

"Hey, guys? I think I found something," River called.

They couldn't see River through the trees but followed his voice until they were standing right beside him. And in front of an enormous shipping container.

"Oh, thank goodness," Jack said. "Our luggage is here."

They'd been informed that their luggage couldn't all fit on the boat that brought them to the island and so would be arriving separately. But Rafi never imagined it would be like this. At least they found it. She could finally change out of her Fly Fest staff shirt.

River took hold of one door and Jack the other. Together, they opened the container.

It was not their luggage.

4

AT FIRST IT LOOKED LIKE A WALL OF WHITE BRICKS, BUT when they got closer to the shipping container, they saw that the bricks were actually Styrofoam boxes. Rafi dug her finger-tips into the skinny crevices between each box until she was able to retrieve one right out of the center. She reflexively winced, expecting some of the surrounding boxes to tumble out too, but they stayed packed in place, cemented like a brick wall after all.

Rafi opened the box. Inside was the last thing she expected.

"A sandwich." Something she'd seen a million times before, but this sandwich was different. She couldn't exactly ascribe a personality to the food, but there was no denying the thing looked defeated, sad, and kind of sweaty. Rafi could relate. She peeled the top layer of sliced white bread back and found a single square of American cheese. No butter, no sauces. A pale lettuce leaf lay miserably wilting on the side of the box like a boxer against the ropes in the third round of a fight.

Jack peeked over Rafi's shoulder. "What is that supposed to be?"

"I think it's our food."

Jack shook his head. "I paid for the VIP gourmet-chef-prepared organic vegan meal plan."

Rafi checked the side of the box to see if it said anything about this being the VIP gourmet-chef-prepared organic vegan meal plan, but the small print she did find said only: DO NOT REFRIGERATE. CONTENTS MAY DISINTEGRATE.

Rafi glanced at the wall of boxes again, all of them identical, all with the same small print across the bottoms of the boxes like the surgeon general's warning. "Well, it's definitely not real cheese, so I'm pretty sure it's vegan."

"This wasn't on the menu I saw online," Jack said. "Where are the twenty-four-karat-gold-flecked, Incomprehensible Chicken Wings?"

Rafi lifted the sandwich out of the box, searching for anything else underneath it, but there wasn't a speck of gold anywhere.

"What about the diamond-infused water?" Jack asked.

"There's . . . lettuce."

"What about the Tahitian ice cream made with Madagascar vanilla bean, Maui mango compote, and Cook Island caviar?"

"You're looking at the same box I am, right?" Rafi asked.

Jack whimpered but River seemed to take the news in stride. "Hey, it's something. And I don't know about you but I'm pretty hungry." He plucked his own box out of the shipping container, grabbed the cheese sandwich, and took a big bite out of it before violently spitting it back out. He coughed, grimaced, wiped his mouth. "No."

"Can we go?" Jack said, stomping his foot and smearing

more makeup with the back of his wrist. "I feel like I'm melting."

He also *looked* like he was melting. Every ounce of his makeup had started to resemble what Rafi imagined that Tahitian ice cream looked like.

"Okay, we need a plan," Rafi said.

"Turn around and never look back?" Jack offered.

River began to nod, but one look at the expression on Rafi's face, and he started to shake his head instead.

Rafi took this new sandwich development as a progression of what she'd started in the seaport. She'd been bold enough to speak publicly, and she'd taken the initiative to come on this exploratory search. Now she had this. Although the food didn't look good, finding it was. It was a new piece to this weird, music-festival puzzle. It was something. And something was better than nothing. "We should take as much of these boxes back to the seaport as we can. We may not have found anyone affiliated with the festival, or our luggage, but at least we have this."

"People will starve before they touch that," Jack said.

"It's food," Rafi said. "They'll be happy."

Jack shrugged. "Lettuce pray."

The sandwich went whizzing past Rafi's head. "I can't. Eat. *Gluten*!" said the girl who'd thrown it. It was the same girl who'd sobbed to Rafi about not having a villa, sobbing now about the gluten. "Or dairy!" she continued. "Or any food that comes in boxes!"

Rafi wasn't sure what to say to her, or to anyone else, because literally everyone was complaining about the sandwiches. Some people set the open boxes down and took pictures of the sandwiches as though they were art exhibits. Others threw the sandwiches against the walls, the bread and lettuce falling limply like confetti (the cheese, however, sticking to every surface like putty).

One of the jocks who Rafi couldn't tell apart—Ryan or Paul; it was anybody's guess who—held up his sandwich to Rafi's face. "Do you want another lawsuit on your hands?"

She looked around for Jack or River, since they helped bring the sandwiches too, but they were suddenly MIA. The other jock showed up with his own sandwich, a look of incredulity clouding his chiseled features. There was no way he was eating this thing, and his reasoning was simple: "Do you have any idea who my father is?"

More sandwiches flew, like a scene from a college frat movie, or maybe a war. Rafi ducked through the crowd to avoid them, but everywhere she turned there were more people with complaints.

"Guys, this is the only food we have!" But her voice was drowned out. "Guys!" she tried again through the flurry of sandwich missiles.

Hardly anyone could hear Rafi, but even the ones who could didn't seem to want to listen. She found Peggy near the back, a mountain of cheese boxes at their feet. They opened a new box, discarding the bread and lettuce, and flung the square of cheese to the thatched ceiling. It did not return. "You're never gonna get through to them," Peggy said.

"We need to preserve the food," Rafi said. "And it's going to be night soon, we need to make shelter." A rising panic was taking shape in her gut, the reality that there was no good food and no one here to help. "We need to do *something*."

"Most of these people already have shelter," Peggy said, tossing another piece of cheese.

"What do you mean?" Rafi asked.

"You know," Peggy said. "Tent City."

"Tent *what*?"

Five minutes later Rafi and Peggy stood before an encampment not far from the seaport. It was made up of rows of domed structures built with plastic frames and waterproof canvas. The kinds of tents you see on the news to help displaced people going through natural disasters. Which, Rafi figured, Fly Fest was.

They weren't the villas people had paid for, but at least they protected from the elements. They were perfectly suitable for one night, and Rafi felt a surge of relief when she saw them. There was even a set of three porta potties off to the side—more signs that someone had at least been working on trying to make this festival actually happen.

Tents and bathrooms. Rafi couldn't believe her luck. She

gripped the straps of her backpack, ready to set it down for the first time that day and take a breather. "Which tents are empty?"

"None," Peggy said.

Rafi turned to Peggy slowly, bemused, not sure she heard them right. "There's a nun?"

Peggy shook their head, took care to enunciate. "*None*. The influencers got them all first thing. That's why they showed up late to the seaport, when you were giving your speech."

It didn't make any sense. There had to be at least fifty tents out there. If people bunked together, there could be room for everyone. But Peggy seemed to read her mind and shook their head.

"These people don't do roommates, unless it's a TikTok incubator in Calabasas."

"You keep using words that don't make any sense," Rafi said.

Peggy put a hand on Rafi's shoulder and tried to make it as clear as possible. "You're sleeping on the beach."

By the time Rafi got to the beach, the sun had set and a smattering of people had already claimed their spots for the night. Some of them were trying unsuccessfully to build fires, others were using driftwood and the spare sweatshirts and coveralls that they'd packed in their carry-ons to build shelter. Most of them were midway between the tree line and the ocean, but that was too close to the water for Rafi. She found a spot by the palms, away from everyone else. She'd done a lot today, spoken to enough people. At this point all she wanted to do was decompress and be alone.

In theory, it should've sounded romantic: sleeping on the beach, a blanket of stars overhead, the low tide acting as a calming, natural noise machine. Instead, she sat cradling her sneaker, using a twig to try and scrape off every last bit of wild boar fecal matter that might have remained. And even though the bottom of her shoe now looked good as new, Rafi couldn't hold back the sense of dread that was building in her chest.

There really was no food. (As not a single person had actually eaten the cheese sandwiches, the jury was still out on whether they qualified as edible.) And that was only the start of it. The realization of just how screwed up this situation was came crashing down on her like a series of waves trying to pull her underwater.

There was no shelter for half the people here.

All of their checked luggage had been lost.

There was no one in charge.

They had no way of reaching anyone in the outside world.

For the first time, Rafi was facing the fact that she was stranded on an island with people whom she was beginning to suspect were total morons.

Worst of all, she'd spent every last penny she had for the privilege of being here.

Coming to Fly Fest had been a splurge, but she'd convinced

herself that it would be worth it. That she'd get her story for her podcast and maybe she'd even get to enjoy herself along the way. She'd let herself daydream of a world that was so foreign to her, one in which she could rub shoulders with rock stars and party like she was a celebrity herself. She had to admit she bought into the luxury and exclusivity that the Fly Fest social media accounts had been touting for months.

But she wasn't glamorous like the other people here. She'd paid for a ticket, and yet she still found a way to stay just outside that tight, exclusive circle of elitism. She couldn't even get a disaster relief tent to sleep in.

Rafi tossed her sneaker aside, giving up on the delusion that it would ever be as good as new. It was just one more ruined thing. She looked around at the denizens of the beach, settling in for the night: the people who weren't lucky enough to score a tent in Tent City. Their mood seemed to match her own. They'd all paid so much for the promise of paradise, but they'd been shipwrecked.

"Excuse me, you threw this at my head?"

Rafi startled at the voice, which was too soft and preternaturally calm for what it'd just said. The girl it belonged to cradled a sneaker in her hand like it was a baby dove with a broken wing.

Rafi scrambled to her feet, spraying sand in every direction like an ostrich taking a dust bath. "That was—I didn't mean to—" She took back the sneaker.

"People always try to get me to wear their products—"

"Oh, I wasn't trying t—"

"As a rule, I don't do that, and I'm sorry but I won't start now."

Rafi only nodded. Explaining why she'd thrown her shoe didn't seem worth it, and anyway, this girl didn't seem all that bothered. She wore a crown of flowers on her delicate head, which was framed by the most beautiful soft, curly hair. It was beachy and carefree, yet not a strand was out of place. And somehow, though the sun had set long ago, her hair pulled every bit of light from the sky, making it look naturally highlighted. The ethereal beauty bore no signs of the outrage that Rafi herself would have displayed had a projectile shoe come at her out of nowhere. She looked expensive and contented, like her life was a fragrance commercial. A gauzy shawl that looked like it was made from golden thread spun by Rumpelstiltskin himself struggled to keep from slipping off shoulders as smooth as chocolate ganache. The only sign that this angel on earth was a real, human person was a single blemish on the nape of her neck, positioned where a hickey might be. A wine-colored birthmark, roughly the shape of a heart and the size of a strawberry. A gold necklace bisected it, coming to a point with a charm that nestled in the dip between her collarbones. It spelled out a single, perfect word in loopy script: *Sierra*.

Rafi felt like a clump of shower drain hair just looking at her. She could tell from the way Sierra held herself (and from the fact that she did not shill products) that she was a cut above the rest of the influencers on this island. At the very least she definitely did not belong on this beach, mere steps from people crying into their sandwich boxes. But strangely, she remained, looking out to sea, fragrance-commercial life in full swing.

"My name is Sierra Madre," Sierra said to the sea, and maybe also to Rafi.

"Wow, like the mountain range?"

"I'm not familiar."

"You've never googled your name before?"

"The first thing that comes up when I google my name is me. Is there another Sierra Madre? Is she pretty?" When Rafi didn't say anything, Sierra turned to her, her eyes imploring. "*Prettier?*"

Rafi was beginning to realize she didn't know how to communicate with these people. They seemed to speak in a language she'd never been taught and didn't have time to learn. But Sierra wasn't going anywhere, and the awkward silence was a buzzing static in Rafi's ears. "No, you're prettier."

Sierra ironed out the furrow in her brow and turned back to the sea.

"So, it sucks that Fly Fest was a scam, huh?" Rafi said.

"I suppose." Sierra sighed. "But don't despair. Everything will be fine."

"How do you know?"

The girl's glistening shoulders rose and settled again just as quickly. "Because it always is."

Definitely a language Rafi didn't understand. She was out two thousand bucks and had nowhere to sleep. They may have been standing on the same patch of sand, but Rafi very much doubted Sierra knew how devastating that was.

36

"I know just the thing to turn your frown upside down," Sierra said.

Did it involve a two-thousand-dollar check? Because Rafi could really use a two-thousand-dollar—

Sierra lifted the flower crown off her own head and placed it atop Rafi's. "There," she said, looking at Rafi like she was a cake she'd just finished frosting. "I don't need this anymore."

The tone of her voice tricked Rafi into thinking that was a compliment, though she was slowly realizing it wasn't. "Thanks."

"And hey, you've always got your . . . little recording hobby."

Rafi's heart, which had felt as limp and deflated as a week-old balloon, began to expand again. "My podcast? You were at the seaport when I talked about my podcast?"

Sierra Madre nodded and finally wrested her gaze from the sea to look at Rafi, her eyes glinting as brightly as her gold necklace. She placed a palm as soft as a soap bubble on Rafi's cheek. "I don't know what a podcast is and I've never listened to one but as soon as I get off this island, I will listen to yours, alright? I promise you that. Just don't ask me to plug it on my social platforms."

"I wasn't goin—"

"Because I've never done that, and I won't start now."

Rafi nodded, once more at a loss for what to say.

"If you need anything from me you can always find me in Tent City, where I will be going now. Bye-bye." And just like that, Sierra Madre walked away and down the beach, like a breeze wisping flakes of snow off a mountain range.

Their shared moment had been a strange one, to say the least. But it had somehow made Rafi feel slightly less like crap. And Sierra was right. Rafi had at least one thing going for her.

She grabbed her backpack and unzipped it, deciding to take inventory. She'd packed all of her clothes in her checked bag, but everything in her carry-on, when used together, made up the one thing she valued over everything else she owned.

Her podcasting kit.

She laid it all out in front of her the way some people on this trip arranged the "flat lays" on their Instagrams. There was her BoomN2 Handy Mic. A cable. A portable speaker. Headphones. A wireless receiver. A charger. And her phone. Put them all together and they made up the most useful tool she had in her arsenal to give her life purpose. Looked at another way, it was the most useless thing you could have when stranded on an island.

But with nothing else to do, Rafi figured she might as well record the first episode of season two of "Musical Mysteries."

She picked up her microphone, cleared her throat, and hit record.

MUSICAL MYSTERIES
Season 2: Episode 1
"The Australian Outback"

What do you have to do to get away with the perfect crime?

It's a heavy question, but one we've all probably asked ourselves at some point in our lives.

Do you have to plan meticulously until "premeditated" isn't just a word to you—it's the code you live by?

Do you have to develop the kind of personality that would make you seem nice and charming and super simpatico all in an attempt to trick people into thinking you're the best thing since sliced bread?

Better yet, do you take advantage of all your newfound attention and goodwill to become a hugely popular entertainer? After all, wouldn't catchy songs and a sparkling smile be the best wool you could pull over people's eyes?

I guess what I'm asking is, can you be one of the nation's biggest pop stars *and* the perpetrator of a heinous crime?

If you're River Stone, the answer just might be yes.

I'm Rafi Francisco, and if you're anything like me,

you've been pretty skeptical about River Stone and his meteoric rise to fame ever since he showed up on the scene with an old guitar and a tragic backstory.

A backstory that includes love, heartbreak, Australia, and a big dollop of mystery. Or should I say . . . murder?

I know there was an investigation. I know there was evidence to support the abandonment story. And even as I say these words I can feel some of you hearing them and getting angry. *What happened to River was horrible and what his girlfriend did to him was unforgivable; can't we leave the poor boy alone?*

Well, dear listener, no, we cannot. Because what if I told you that River wasn't abandoned by his girlfriend in the middle of the wilderness as he claims, and was, in fact, the very person who made her disappear? What if I told you I've uncovered clues—undeniable evidence—that directly contradict River's version of events? What if I told you that River Stone isn't as innocent as you might think?

All of this might sound like outlandish accusations, but I promise you: By the end of this series you *will* have conclusive answers about what really happened that summer night in the Australian Outback. And I'm not talking about the restaurant, folks. I'll even promise you an exclusive interview with River Stone himself, where I ask him the questions that other reporters have been too shy to bring up.

What really happened to Tracy?

That, and more, on this season of . . . "Musical Mysteries"!

This episode of "Musical Mysteries" was brought to you by Nobrand. Ever wish you'd packed a snack because the only food around are cheese sandwiches that might poison you? Why not try Nobrand protein bars? Nobrand makes everything from food to cleaning supplies, and their products definitely won't disintegrate if refrigerated. Go to Nobrand.com and enter code RIVERKILLER for two percent off your next purchase!

Nobrand was Rafi's sponsor for season two. A big get, and also the only company that responded to her inquiries about possible partnerships. They sent her a list of products that she could plug every episode, and said she could write her own copy for it. It made her happy just thinking about it, and recording this first episode had also helped to lift her mood. She'd have to add more in post, edit in some sound effects and musical cues, but for now it was a pretty good intro episode, if she did say so herself. The problem was she was almost out of battery on her phone. She thought she spotted some electrical outlets at the seaport. She'd have to go back tomorrow and see if she could charge up.

But night had fallen, and though she wasn't tired, she longed for sleep. The morning had to bring good news. It couldn't get worse than this.

She bunched up her backpack full of bulky electronics and placed it under her head. As far as pillows went, this definitely was not one. But Rafi couldn't entirely blame it for her inability to get comfortable. The sand was powdery but it didn't yield to her body at all. And there was a weird sound coming from the trees just behind her head.

A rhythmic hacking.

It was a small sound that could've been anything and Rafi could've just ignored it, but the investigator in her wouldn't let it go.

Rafi stood up and made her way through the jungle. The moonlight shone just brightly enough to cast silver outlines of the trees. She was getting close, the noise coming clearer now. She knew that sound. Not because it occurred naturally in nature, but because she'd heard it in movies a lot. It was the distinct sound a knife made when it came violently down on something.

The hacking was both scraping against something hard and hitting something that squelched. It was the kind of sound that made the back of your throat tickle. It was the most sickening thing Rafi had ever heard in real life, and she suddenly wished she had her mic with her so she could record it. Something bad was happening. The stench of it filled the jungle air.

And then she saw the outline of a man. He was crouched on the ground, bent over something, his arm coming up and down violently, hacking away. The knife was clear now, wrapped in his fingers and glinting in the moonlight, and every time he held it up, it came back more liquidy than before.

Rafi only stood there, stunned. She tried not to make a noise but she must've not been quiet enough, because the guy turned around. And when he did, Rafi could see River, his bare chest covered in moonlit blood and guts.

5

"Rafi."

Her first thought, ridiculously, was surprise that he'd remembered her name.

But that thought was quickly wiped from her mind as she tried to process what she was looking at. River standing (shirtless), covered in guts, holding a knife, and getting closer.

Rafi took a step backward, and she must've looked as scared as she felt because a questioning crease formed between River's eyebrows. Usually when girls looked at him it was with heart eyes and lust. But to Rafi, his whole deal was super predatory. The moment stretched out longer, with Rafi wide-eyed and backing away and River trying to seem docile and nice while *holding a knife*. Then he seemed to remember his weapon and the splattered bare chest.

"Oh, this?" When he pointed at his chest it was with the tip of his knife, which didn't do much to mitigate the situation. "I'm sorry you had to see me like this."

Rafi looked past him, her eyes darting all over the jungle ground in search of a corpse. But all she saw was a fish, long as her arm and dead on a bed of banana leaf.

"I know, it must be weird, you've probably seen me in magazines in designer clothes and now I'm a total mess." There was a chuckle in his voice. "*Ick*."

A fish. Not a dead body. Rafi breathed deep, but not too deep. Yes, she'd jumped to conclusions, but this could also just be a warm-up for him. He did seem really comfortable holding that knife. Which begged the question.

"Where'd you get a knife?"

River looked at the weapon in his hand like he'd forgotten it was there. "This? Someone must've smuggled it on the plane. Anyway, I asked around if anyone had one and lucky me, somebody did."

"You asked around for a knife?"

"Yeah, I needed something to sharpen my spear with."

"Wait, there's a spear now?" How many weapons did this guy have? They'd only been here a day, and he already had an arsenal.

"To go spearfishing with. Of course, my spear was a little more rudimentary than a speargun, but under the circumstances it was all I had."

There were too many guns, spears, and knives in this conversation, and Rafi really, really wished she had her mic with her so she could record it all.

"So anyway," River continued, "went spearfishing, caught that big guy behind me, and then I used this knife to clean the scales and gut him. Which you found me doing."

"That is . . . not how you gut a fish."

The quirk in River's smile was slow and deliberate, like

he'd been caught in a lie even though, to his credit, there really was a dead fish behind him. "It is in Australia."

Rafi knew very little about Australia and would have to take his word for it. "Okay, but why are you hiding in the jungle?"

For some reason, this part of River's explanation warranted a toss of his hair, a twinkle in his eye, and a slowly spreading grin. "Because it's a messy job. And trust me, nobody wants to see their favorite musician covered in fish guts."

"Presumptuous," Rafi muttered.

"That people wouldn't want to see me covered in fish guts?"

"That you're anybody's favorite musician."

River stared at her, mouth slightly open, and Rafi realized she'd gone too far. The only reason she'd come to Fly Fest was to meet River and get him to confess to his crime, and this was not the way to go about it. She was letting her true feelings for him show, and she needed to keep that under wraps. She needed him to believe she was just another fan.

Rafi was about to put on a smile, drum up a giggle, say she was only joking, when River beat her to the punch. He began to laugh. A deep, carefree thing. *Of course he was somebody's favorite musician!*

"I'm gonna go get cleaned up," River said. "Do you want fish?"

Rafi hated how much she was enjoying this fish. She didn't know what kind it was, but she didn't care; River had served her a plump white filet on a broad leaf dish, and she gobbled most of it up in no time. She also hated that not only was River famous, and a talented musician, and a good spearfisher—turned out he could cook, too. Or maybe she was just hungry.

She hated a lot about him, but she had to pretend not to in order to get her scoop. Tonight, she'd be River Stone's biggest fan.

"This fish is so amazing! You're so good at everything!" Rafi was putting it on too thick, and she coughed, embarrassed. But River took it in stride. He was used to this level of adoration.

"I know there are sandwiches but I heard some gnarly rumors about them. Apparently they're growing."

Rafi swallowed. "What?"

"Someone took a ruler to them. The sandwiches are half an inch bigger in diameter. Allegedly."

"They're sandwiches. . . . They can't grow."

River only shrugged like it was the damnedest thing. He took a bite of fish and gave Rafi a closed-mouth smile, and the strange topic of the growing cheese sandwiches was willfully forgotten.

Since returning to the beach, River had managed to take a quick dip in the ocean to wash up, build a fire, cook the fish, and construct two simple tents side by side out of sticks and random bits of clothing he had in his possession. Rafi didn't even realize the second tent was for her until it was done, and though she didn't yet know how she felt about being River Stone's neighbor (Pro: She'd have eyes on him; Con: He might

47

kill her while she slept), she had to admit it was nice having shelter.

The whole time he worked, River rambled on about the great weather, and how gorgeous the beach was, and how the concertgoers were dope people. Rafi realized it was another talent of his: filling the air with pointless noise—empty and cunningly distracting—without revealing anything of substance about himself. PR-approved interview-speak. Earlier, Rafi had secretly turned on her mic to record him. Now she made a mental note to delete all of his useless chitchat.

The only reason Rafi had come to Fly Fest in the first place was for a chance to talk to River, and now she was getting it. They were alone, together, in private, and she didn't want to talk about the weather. This may have been her only chance to interview a primary source for her story. And suddenly, the fiasco of Fly Fest didn't seem so bad. Because everyone else had come here for a totally lit week of music and yachts and rich people wet dreams, but all she'd ever wanted was a moment alone with River Stone. And now she had it.

Asking about his first girlfriend might come off too weird, out of left field, intrusive. But this might be Rafi's only shot. She had to tread lightly.

River went to crouch next to the small fire he'd made, poking it with a stick until embers crackled and disappeared into the night. He looked over at Rafi and a smile played on his lips. It made him look roguish, charming, laid-back. If she hadn't known the truth about him, Rafi might have considered him attractive. Because River's smile was arguably the most beautiful thing about him. Full lower lip, delicate Cupid's bow. Lips lush and pink like they'd spent the whole day kissing. It was a smile that radiated happiness. Security. Safety. Rafi wondered if it was the last thing his first girlfriend saw before she "disappeared."

"Tracy," Rafi blurted.

The smile skidded off River's face like it'd slipped on ice. "What?"

As far as treading lightly went, this was the opposite. This was a sonic boom.

"I'm so sorry. I don't know why . . . I guess I was just thinking about your album. And that got me thinking about who all the songs were about . . . and then I thought about Tracy and how she . . . disappeared."

As River watched Rafi, she realized her mistake. She couldn't just launch into her investigation of his first love. She was scaring River off. She needed time to wade into those waters. No, water metaphors were bad—she would not be wading into any waters, real or metaphorical. But the fact remained: She needed time to gain River's trust before striking.

"I shouldn't have brought it up," Rafi said. "I'm just nervous . . . about this festival and how it's nonexistent. We're all alone on an island with no cell service and no way to call for help."

Rafi looked in River's eyes to see if she could see a glimmer of glee at that prospect. But River only smacked his hands together, dusting off any remnants of the fish or the fire or his decision to ever sit down to talk to her.

"No worries."

Rafi thought he'd been stoking the fire this whole time, but now she realized he was trying to put it out. Soon there was nothing but ash and sand, and River stood, stamping out any flickers that remained.

"Better get some shut-eye," he said abruptly. And he smiled at her. Crookedly.

It was nothing like his natural smile, the one that made him seem safe and cute. This one was performative. There was no reason for him to even be smiling! But he couldn't help himself. Whether he intended to smile crookedly or not, Rafi knew it was what happened whenever he felt pinned. And he was doing it now.

"And hey, don't worry about being stuck on the island. A boat will probably be here bright and early to take us all home."

He gave her the same short wave he gave to fans whenever he was returning a pen they'd given him to sign a magazine cover with, and then he was off, leaving Rafi alone in front of the ghost of a fire.

If a boat really was going to come tomorrow to rescue them all from this disaster of a music festival, then why was Rafi suddenly filled with worry?

The answer came to her instantly. She'd just had a one-on-one private conversation with her ultimate interview subject, and she'd blown it. She didn't get any good sound bites. In fact, she'd effectively scared him off. What she needed was more time. This island, closed off from the rest of the world, was the perfect incubator for the story she needed to tell. On the island, River had nowhere to go. And no duties to keep him busy now that the festival was a bust. The problem was getting him to stay.

And if Rafi wanted River to stay, she'd need everyone on the island to stay, too.

6

ON THE BEACH, CONCERTGOERS WERE WAKING FROM their open-aired slumber to bright daylight. Even this early in the morning the sun was already scorching, beating down on all of them. It was a reminder to get up, that as bad as things seemed yesterday, today was a brand-new day. The sun was like that. It made everything seem shiny and new. Things were looking up.

Well, not Rafi, who literally couldn't look up. Turned out sleeping on a bed of sand was supremely uncomfortable, and she winced and sucked in a deep breath the moment she tried facing the sun. Nope, she couldn't bend her neck back, but that was okay. Yesterday had been bad. Possibly the most disappointing day of Rafi's life. But one of the things Rafi liked most about herself was her ability to look on the bright side. To problem-solve. What didn't work out yesterday would definitely work out today. And in the twinkling hours before she'd finally succumbed to sleep, a plan had taken shape in Rafi's mind, one that got her heart pumping from adrenaline and made her forget that her pillow was a bag of bulky recording equipment.

There was a boat scheduled to pick them all up in one week.

That was one week to get an interview with River and turn her podcast into one of the best true crime stories on record. But if word got out that Fly Fest was a fiasco, then a boat might come back any minute to rescue them. Rafi couldn't stop a boat from coming, but she could convince people to not get on it.

Because if people stayed, then there was a good chance River would stay, too. After all, he was the only musical act to have come this far, despite the early rumors of the festival's shortcomings. If Rafi wanted River to stay on this island, then she'd have to keep the idea of Fly Fest alive. Of course, she couldn't put on an entire music festival by herself, but people had come here for more than a concert. They'd come for the promise of paradise. And that was already here. Sure, there was the ramshackle seaport, and the wasteland on which the disaster relief tents were set up, and the dense, sweaty jungle full of buzzing insects and wild boars, and the cliffs that were too rocky and steep to be scaled; and there weren't any yachts or villas or cabanas or mai tais with little colorful umbrellas sticking out of them, but there was a small patch of actual, white-sand beach with turquoise water.

As Rafi pulled back the muslin sarong that made up the doorway of her makeshift tent, she looked out at that sea view and breathed in the delicious saltwater air. The promise of paradise was right in front of her. Now she just had to convince everyone here of that promise, too. It wouldn't be that hard. She spoke to her podcast listeners all the time. Presented the facts and evidence and convinced them of the truth that was right in front of them. Rafi could do the same with the people here.

Yes, today would be a good day. Rafi's plan was simple: charge her phone, and get everyone on the island to believe there was something here worth staying for.

The second part of her mission would not be easy; on her walk to the seaport she'd heard multiple rumblings of disgruntled concertgoers claiming this place was "hella bad" or that they needed to get "the hell out of here" or just plain "We're in hell." People were really set on the whole "hell" aspect of this nightmare. Or maybe they were talking about Hella Badid—Rafi couldn't be sure. Everything she heard came in hissy, scattershot whispers.

She had no idea how she'd convince the people here to stay, but at least she could take care of the first part of her mission and juice her phone. Even though she couldn't use it to reach anyone, she could still record on it, and that was her lifeline right now. Unmoored as they were on this forgotten island, recording was the only thing that could keep Rafi tethered to a sense of normalcy.

At the seaport, Rafi found those square-jawed guys, Paul and Ryan, sitting on the raised platform that led to the main entrance. Her stomach dropped when she saw that they were on their phones.

"You have service?" she asked them, in lieu of a hello.

"No, are you offering?" one of them asked.

"Dude, maid service!" the other one said. "Finally."

"Don't you need a room first?" Rafi asked.

Paul and Ryan stared at her, like yes, they would need a room first, and why was she just standing there and not getting one for them. Wait. "I'm not a maid," Rafi said, coming to her senses.

"You sure?" Ryan (she was pretty sure it was Ryan) asked. "You look exactly like my maid after she woke up from her coma."

Convincing people to stay on this island, Rafi realized, would be impossible. Mostly because she could not stand talking to them.

"I'm gonna go," Rafi said. She tried sidestepping them to get inside but Paul got in her way.

"I'd like to file a formal complaint."

"For the last time, I don't work here."

"This place isn't very money," he said, pretending he didn't hear her. "O-Town isn't here. And when I tell my father what's going on here, there's going to be hell to pay."

Rafi could've just kept walking, but if she was ever going to convince the people on the island to stay, she might as well start with these guys. Also, if she gave them something else to focus on, maybe they'd leave her alone.

"You know, you don't have to be bored," Rafi began. "There's a lot to do here on the island."

"Name one thing," Ryan said.

"Yeah," Paul said. "Name one."

For some reason, Rafi could not, for the life of her, name a single thing. "Just . . . there's opportunity here, you know? People are struggling. What if you could, I don't know, help them out? Imagine going back home in a week and telling everybody how you actually did something useful with your time here. You guys could be featured in an article or something."

Ryan and Paul stared at each other. "Article?" they whispered.

It was impossible to know whether they were imagining themselves in *People* magazine or if they didn't know the meaning of the word, but rather than stick around long enough to find out, Rafi made a beeline for the entrance.

The seaport was about half as full as it was yesterday, with the people who hadn't gotten a tent at Tent City, or didn't want to spend the night at the beach, glued to the rows of vinyl waiting chairs. Rafi searched for an outlet, but most of the outlets were either already charging phones or blocked by someone sleeping in front of them. Rafi did spot an open one, though. She went to plug in her charger, when someone careened into the spot and cut her off.

"Excuse me?" Rafi turned to see the person who was suddenly beside her, stealing her power.

"You're excused," they said.

Rafi couldn't see their face because it was completely obscured underneath a wide brim hat and shrouded in a black lacy cloth like a mourner's veil. But Rafi did recognize the voice. "Jack?"

Jack's shoulders tensed, and he froze, knuckles turning white around the iPhone in his fist. "You can see through the veil?"

"Not really but—"

"Don't look at me," Jack said, splaying his free hand in front of his face, adding an extra shield.

"Why? What's wrong?"

"Something horrible has happened."

Rafi loved hearing horrible things. Not because she was a horrible person but because horrible things made for great stories. She leaned in just a little bit closer. "What is it?"

"I don't have my luggage."

Not so horrible. "None of us have our luggage."

"But I had all my makeup in my luggage!" Jack's voice had risen high enough to wake the dead, but after a quick cursory check, his veil swinging from side to side, he was sure no one else was listening in. "I don't have any makeup on right now. Which would be bad enough, but I don't have any of my daytime or nighttime beauty regimen essentials, which means I couldn't do my morning cleansing and moisturizing and mystifying routine, which means my skin is a *complete* disaster."

Rafi tried to come up with something sympathetic to say, she really did, but her beauty routine this morning had involved splashing her face with ocean water. And if she was being honest, she would replace *splashing* with *dabbing* and *her face* with *her hands*.

"Oh."

"It gets worse," Jack said. "I don't have any sunscreen."

"That's not so bad, right? You'll get a tan."

Jack's veil was too opaque to see through, and yet Rafi could feel a seething shocked rage emanating from within it. The next time Jack spoke, it was slow and deliberate.

"My skin is as delicate as butterfly wings. TeenVogue.com once theorized that I must bathe in organic, unpasteurized goat milk every morning and night. A Japanese beauty company named one of their gel masks after me. It's a bestseller. I have my own line of face serums that's so advanced it's coming out five years from now with formulas that scientists haven't even invented yet. And the day I met my dermatologist, she took one look at me and died. Do you have any idea what that means?"

Rafi shook her head.

"It means I wasn't wearing sunscreen all day yesterday, and now I'm a deformed monster! My nose is chapped, Rafi. *Chapped*. Lips get chapped and that's only if you're gross and poor. Who ever heard of noses getting chapped?" He took a breath to let out a ragged sob. "*Why* do all the bad things in life always happen to *me*?"

"Can I see?"

"No!"

"I promise not to laugh or recoil or say anything," Rafi said.

Jack sighed, and after a moment his veil bounced sluggishly up and down. Carefully, Rafi pinched the edge of it and lifted, bracing for the worst.

Jack Dewey's cheeks were tinged slightly red. and there was a bit of peeling skin on the bridge of his nose.

"It's really not that bad," Rafi said.

Jack pulled back until the veil slipped from Rafi's fingers. "Call me anything you want, but don't patronize me."

"I'm not," Rafi said. "You honestly look fine. You just need to chill out. You know, sun is actually good for you."

"What nonsense are you talking about?"

"Vitamin D, it comes from the sun and makes you healthy and stuff." Rafi knew very little about vitamins and how they worked, but as she spoke, and as Jack listened carefully, she realized this was the moment she was waiting for. Jack was one of the biggest influencers here. If she could convince him that this island wasn't a complete hellhole and a little more time here might be good for him (and his skin), then there was a good chance he could spread the message.

Rafi smiled at him. "I know just what'll make you feel better."

7

"So I tell you the sun has a personal vendetta against me and you decide to lead me directly to it," Jack said. "Quite the flex."

Rafi and Jack stood ankle-deep in the Caribbean waters, she looking as out of place as a coatrack in the ocean, and Jack, face still shrouded, looking beekeeper-in-mourning chic. If they'd been on one of the Fly Fest Instagram ads, looking like they did now, absolutely no one would have been tempted to come. But none of that mattered when there was this view.

How could Jack not feel a sense of hope or joy or relief, standing on a beach like this? "I know things look pretty bleak right now," Rafi began.

"You said you wouldn't comment on my skin."

"I meant the fact that we're all out thousands of dollars and we're pretty much stranded on a deserted island and there's no food and no way to make contact with the outside world and we don't have any beds to sleep in—"

"You don't have a bed?" Jack snapped his neck in Rafi's direction so sharply that even his veil seemed to react, creasing in confused droopy frowns.

Rafi was equally as confused. "You have a bed?"

"All the tents have beds."

"What?" The crick in Rafi's neck flared up in pain.

"Don't get me started," Jack said. "They're stiff as boards and covered in plastic. The worst."

"I'm sleeping on sand," Rafi said in a quiet voice. "I woke up with sand under my eyelid."

"You don't have pillows either?"

Rafi tried to say the word "pillow," but it came out like a cloud of hot dust from her dry lips, soundless and evaporating into the air.

"Sleeping on sand is probably good for your skin," Jack said. "Exfoliating."

"Right." Rafi's jaw felt suddenly stiff. "Only slightly less good than sleeping on a silk pillowcase."

"Exactly. Anyway, what were you saying?"

Rafi took a deep breath and squinted out at the sparkling horizon. It would take more than just a view to sell this paradise to Jack. "I was just going to say that I get what it's like to feel insecure sometimes."

"About the fact that you have a podcast?"

Rafi paused. "I'm not insecure about my podcast."

"Why not?"

Rafi would've said something but she wasn't even sure how to respond. Jack started talking again anyway. "You know, I've been on this island for over a day and you still haven't invited me to be a guest."

"It's not that kind of podcast," Rafi said.

"Well, I would've turned you down anyway."

"Okay, I think we're getting away from the point here. I was going to say that I get insecure about my looks, too."

"Oh, I can tell," Jack said. "Bangs *and* dry skin? It's like, girl, pick a struggle."

It was seriously taking everything for Rafi not to tackle Jack to the ground—or ocean, as it were—but she had to remind herself that she was on a mission here. If she could make Jack feel better about being stranded here—well, convince him that they *weren't* stranded but in fact lucky to be on this untouched gem of nature—then she could convince anyone. It would be kind of like what she did on her podcast. When she knew someone was listening to her, when she truly had their ear, was the only time she felt she had any purpose at all.

"I'm sorry," Jack said. "My sass is a legendary force of habit. Keep going. You were talking about being ugly."

"I'm not *ugly*," Rafi said sternly.

"I could give you a makeover," Jack said.

"I don't need a makeover."

"You sure?"

Rafi looked down at herself. The T-shirt had obviously been a poor fashion choice, and bangs were always a bit controversial, but Rafi felt good about her looks. Sure, she was lanky and built like a pile of wire hangers, but she wasn't really aware of her posture and awkward elbows and knees unless she saw herself in pictures. She was tall, which she liked. And while her skin may have been a little dry, it was also clear. Rafi was pretty happy with what she was working with.

Sometimes—especially in a place like this, where everyone

seemed to walk out of their Instagrams with their Facetunes and filters intact—Rafi felt less than. And this conversation wasn't helping any. But she also knew that insecurity was just a state of mind. That she could change how she felt by changing her outlook. And she could help Jack realize that.

"Just because things are especially bad right now doesn't mean we can't look on the bright side," Rafi said. "If you don't like your reality, then . . . make a new reality."

"Make a new reality," Jack repeated.

"Yeah. I truly believe there's beauty in everything. You just have to look for it."

Jack did look. It was through a veil, but he looked all around him at the picturesque postcard he was currently occupying. For Jack, it may have been his first time looking out, rather than in. "Looking, looking, looking for beauty," he said.

"Do I hear you guys talking about me?"

Jack and Rafi turned at the sound of that jaunty Australian accent. River waved to them from the shore.

"Literally no one was talking about you," Rafi muttered under her breath.

Without waiting to be invited, or even asking what they were doing out in the shallow waters, River splashed in to meet them. He still hadn't found a T-shirt apparently, but that suited him fine for swimming. "So, what are we doing?" he asked.

"I was telling Jack that he should try seeing the beauty all around him and stop worrying about what he looks like."

"Oh," River said. "'Cause I was going to say I like the new

look. But it'll be hard to swim in that thing. Why don't you take it off?"

Rafi scoffed. Who did River think he was? Just because he asked someone to take off an article of clothing didn't mean—

Jack pulled back his veil and tossed it to Rafi. "Hold this too." Jack pressed his phone into Rafi's hands.

"You coming?" River asked Rafi.

She looked down at her feet, still crystal clear in the see-through ocean. Water was fine, so long as it didn't go past her ankles. "This is as far as I go."

River shrugged and dipped into the sea, Jack was already out there. River splashed him first, and then Jack splashed back, and pretty soon Jack actually began to laugh. Rafi couldn't believe how easy it was for River to loosen Jack up. But then, it just showed how good he was at manipulating people. Because that was all Rafi saw: a guy who was desperate to please, who would say anything, just to get you to like him. And Jack was definitely liking him at the moment. They splashed around together like little kids in a water park.

It'd only taken River a minute to get Jack to feel good about himself, and Rafi resented him for it. And if she was honest with herself, she resented Jack too, for having the kind of fun in the water that she couldn't. Still, their playfulness was contagious. Rafi clicked Jack's phone on and took a picture of the two of them. She figured Jack might want to remember this moment.

But a picture was a powerful thing, and if Rafi had known how this one pic would affect the course of their time on the island, she never would have taken it at all.

8

WORD OF JACK'S AND RIVER'S BEACHY ADVENTURES spread like a viral tweet, and soon it was a full-blown party. With no other means of entertaining themselves, people were all too happy to jump into the water and relieve the tensions of the failed festival. There was hooting and hollering and dunking and people propped up on each other's shoulders, drowning each other in good fun.

Rafi watched it all from shore. The only other person on the beach who hadn't joined the impromptu water romp was Peggy. They sat under their tent, which was nothing more than sticks, shoelaces, and the clothes they'd packed in their carry-on.

Rafi stood before them. "I can't stand him."

"Who?"

"River." She plopped down next to Peggy. "I was on the beach with Jack first, you know? And then River swoops in and lures everyone into the ocean like the pied piper of muscle beach—and they're all falling for his smarmy, faux humble, nice guy act, which is so manipulative."

Rafi detested him, even though she had to admit that this party he'd inadvertently started was a good thing, as far as her mission went. Everyone was too busy splashing around with a celebrity to remember that they'd been swindled. Rafi watched as River chatted with Sierra Madre, showing her his fishing spear. Every time he lifted it above his head, Rafi involuntarily flinched, expecting a stabbing, but none came. Sierra seemed impressed. She did not see a dangerous man with a weapon, only a pop star and his big stick.

"I mean, is he conventionally good-looking?" Rafi asked Peggy as she watched River readjust the waistband of his shorts. "There's no denying that. Is his face perfectly symmetrical? Without question. Is he the sexiest man alive? *People* magazine seems to think so. Does he smell freshly laundered even though he hardly wears clothes? Of course he does. The point is, River Stone is a liar. He's using his looks and status to deceive everyone, and it's working."

"How do you know he's a liar?" Peggy asked.

"His smile." It sounded like a flimsy theory, but she had the proof to back it up. "It goes crooked when he's lying. I first noticed it when I watched clips of him playing a charity poker game. Any time he bluffed, out came that smile. I've seen those clips a million times. And then I started noticing it in interviews and stuff, as a way to deflect from questions he was uncomfortable answering. I have spent the better part of a year studying that smile."

"So, you like him."

"*Like* him?" Rafi wrenched her eyes from River so she could level Peggy with her most incredulous stare. What she would say next was serious, and definitely controversial, and not something you drop lightly into pleasant conversation. But it needed to be said to disabuse Peggy of the notion that her feelings for River resided even close to the neighborhood of "like." Rafi took a deep breath and assumed her most serious air. "Peggy, I'm here to prove that River Stone is a *murderer*."

She let the words hang in the thick island humidity, allowing for their impact to wash fully over Peggy. And for once, Peggy stopped fiddling with their phone long enough to stare at Rafi.

"You can like someone *and* think they're a murderer," Peggy said. "The two aren't mutually exclusive."

She would have to work on her delivery when she disclosed this fact about River on her podcast, because it clearly didn't meet expectations. "What makes you think I like him?"

"Literally everything you just said."

The idea of Rafi liking River was ridiculous. Beyond ridiculous. Inconceivable! "I don't like him, I'm just . . . really invested in this podcast."

"Why?"

"Why?" Rafi repeated.

"Yeah. Are you doing this out of some sense of vigilantism? Are you just nosy? Obsessive? Or is this just a popularity thing for you? Target the most famous pop boy in the world so you could get a share of that attention?"

"No," Rafi said. Definitely not that. Okay, maybe a little of that.

Rafi's podcast was a stepping-stone to a much bigger dream of having an even *bigger* podcast. "Musical Mysteries" was small-time, independently run by her without any producers or technicians or any of the fancy stuff more popular podcasts had at their disposal. But if it became popular, then it might get picked up by a podcasting network, and if it got picked up by a network, then she could truly say she was a success.

She'd actually reached out to a few different podcasting companies, but none of them had responded except for one. SteerCat said they'd give her a shot if she could turn in a compelling second season of "Musical Mysteries." They wanted to see growth, finesse, and whether Rafi could maintain the musical mysteries theme for multiple seasons.

This was Rafi's shot to prove she had what it took to make a blockbuster podcast. She couldn't fail.

And as far as Rafi was concerned, River Stone was the perfect subject. Beloved by the world but hiding an awful secret. He'd used a girl to get ahead, but society just accepted that as the norm and let him do it. He'd concocted this image of himself as the poor victim of an evil girl who'd broken his heart, and now he was using her life as material for his stupid songs. If it were a female artist doing all of that, she'd never hear the end of it. But since it was a cute boy, it was par for the course. River was the archetype of a successful guy and all the double standards that came with it.

All Rafi knew was that when people saw River, they saw a rainbow. But she was the only one willing to follow the rainbow until she found the pot of gold. In this case, the pot of gold was the truth.

"I believe that something bad happened to Tracy Mooney,"

Rafi said. "I believe that River did something bad to her, or at least knows what really happened to her. And I can't just let the world let him off the hook for it."

"So you're doing this for Tracy?" Peggy asked.

"Yeah. She deserves justice. And if lifting Tracy up brings River down, then so be it." She watched River in the water. "I mean, look at how he's holding that spear. Why is he so good at stabbing fish? Has anybody bothered to ask that? He is too good at stabbing and gutting things. River Stone is obviously a crazy, manipulative killer who's completely unhinged."

Rafi said all this even as she watched River delicately help pick seaweed out of Sierra's hair.

"You sure he's the one who's unhinged?" Peggy asked.

Okay, Rafi had to admit she did sound like she was going off the deep end, and she couldn't fault Peggy for thinking her crazy. Peggy didn't know what River did. All the more reason for her to plow on with her podcast. "Are you any closer to getting your satellite phone to work?"

"No," Peggy said, and Rafi couldn't tell by their inflection whether they were devastated by the lack of progress or not. "But I'll get there."

A sense of unease settled over Rafi, hearing that they might have a lifeline to the mainland soon. But she was full of unease, and it wasn't just that. Rafi felt it as she watched River and Sierra Madre walk down the beach together. She couldn't let the feeling go as she watched them disappear into the thicket of trees at the base of the mountain.

MUSICAL MYSTERIES
Season 2: Episode 2
"The Case"

Before we start this episode there is something
I want to get out of the way. It has come to my
attention that my careful, meticulous research on
River Stone might be misconstrued as obsession.
Some (really misguided) people out there may even
be listening to this series and come away from it
thinking that I *like* him.

Listener, let me be clear. I do not like River
Stone. I have never liked River Stone. And after
everything I've uncovered for this story, I can assure
you I will *never* like him.

The idea is just ridiculous. Personally, it boggles
my mind how anyone can like River after learning
about the case.

I first heard about it before I'd even heard any
of River's music. The story is so out-there that it
was all anyone ever wanted to talk about in those
early days. On the *Today* show, when he performed
in-studio for the first time, they followed the
segment with a sit-down interview. That interview
was so heart-wrenching it got River the cover of
People magazine the next week, and that *People*
magazine got him *Rolling Stone*. River's rise to
music stardom is intricately intertwined with

a quote-unquote "tragic" backstory: what his girlfriend did to him.

Tracy Mooney was a seventeen-year-old blond spitfire with dazzling blue eyes and an unconventional sense of style. If you look up old pictures of her, you'll see her wearing jeans that she used to draw on all the time. Little doodles in Sharpie and pen of her favorite flowers and cartoon characters.

Enter River Stone. Seventeen at the time. A mediocre-looking boy with an even more mediocre talent for songwriting. At parties he would be the one to put a damper on the mood by bringing out his guitar and asking for song requests. We know that Tracy must have had a generous spirit, because she took pity on River by deciding to date him.

According to lore, the two teens fell in love quickly, in the pure way that people compare to puppies and sunny days and stuff. River doesn't like to talk about this time in his life. Says it's too hard to revisit those memories, but the few times he has reminisced about his time with Tracy, it sounded like a dream. Trips to their favorite ice-cream shop, chaste kisses on front porches, love notes between classes.

Are you rolling your eyes yet? You should be, because this is just another boring young love story. And it would've ended that way too, as boringly as it began, with Tracy going off to university somewhere while River moved to the big city to go sing in coffee houses or something, if it wasn't for the fateful night the couple decided to go camping in, as the Aussies say, the bush. That night would be the last time River ever saw his girlfriend, and it would go on to change River's life forever.

It was meant to be a romantic trip. In fact, River told the world that he was going to propose to Tracy that night. Anyway, you probably know the rest. While River was taking a quote-unquote "short nap" at around nine P.M.—one hour before he planned to propose, by the way—Tracy vanished. He says that when he woke up, he found his car gone and a note next to his sleeping bag. It went like this:

River, you are the most wondrous guy I know. Unfortunately, I secretly hate you and we can no longer be together. I am leaving you immediately. AND don't try to find me because I am running away and changing my name and you will never hear from me again. Good evening. Best of luck with the music. I really love your songs—especially the ones you wrote about me—and I know you will do great moving forward in your career. You are a very talented fellow with a lot of promise and any record labels will be lucky to have you.
Bye.

And that's where Tracy Mooney's story ends. A vibrant girl who loved her boyfriend, had a kitty named Tiger, and liked to draw on clothes, was never seen again. The girl she purportedly ran away to become? No one knows her name. Or where she lives. Or what's become of her life.

River, by the way, hiked to the nearest town, where he found his car—much like him—abandoned.

I'm sure you will agree that Tracy's note to River will go down in history as one of the strangest goodbye notes known to man. No? You're not thinking that? Well, you're in good company because the cops never seemed to wonder about that either. But hey, maybe that's just how people in Australia say goodbye when leaving the loves of their lives in the middle of nowhere.

Maybe your first thought upon hearing a story like this is how heartbreaking it is. A boy abandoned in the middle of the wilderness on a night that was supposed to be one of the most special of his life. But all I see when I hear this story is how many holes it has. And I can't help but wonder how River allegedly wrote the entirety of *Songs for Tracy* in one single week after she left. How the album was ready to go out into the world so quickly. And how it was the perfect story to get just the kind of attention he'd been craving for so long.

That's next time, on "Musical Mysteries."

And before it's all over, I give you my word, dear listeners—I will ask River Stone the one question that no reporter has dared ask him.

Did he kill his girlfriend, Tracy Mooney, and make it look like she left him?

This episode of "Musical Mysteries" was brought to you by Nobrand. Ever been stuck in the sun for hours on end like an ant under a magnifying glass? Well, Nobrand has just the thing for that. Try their sunscreen! It's probably chemical-free. Go to Nobrand.com and enter code RIVERKILLER for ten percent off your next purchase.

Until next time, Mysterinos!

9

The party in the water eventually died down. By the time she emerged from her tent, Rafi could see only a few people still in the ocean: stragglers who would rather go pruney and pink before letting the festivities end. But someone darkened her doorstep, blocking her sea view.

"You took a picture on my phone," Jack said.

Was he upset she'd used his phone without his permission? "Just thought you'd want to have a memory of something nice."

Jack made a snorty, spitty sound. "As if anyone remembers memories."

Though he didn't sound too pleased, she definitely detected a smile in his voice. He held out his phone for Rafi to see. On the screen was the picture she'd taken of him and River in the surf. She had to admit it was a beautiful shot.

The two of them were waist-deep in the water. River was frozen in the middle of splashing Jack, the water a perfect crystal arch sprouting from his fingers. And Jack stood with his back toward the camera but still glancing over his shoulder, eyes closed but mouth open in the biggest expression of glee. It was as though the two were old friends who'd known each other all their lives and just happened to be caught in a candid moment on one of the most beautiful places on earth.

But there was something a little too beautiful about the photo that made it look almost unnatural. The edges were too sharp while the faces were too soft. The colors too bright. The composition too square.

Rafi's spine cracked, she straightened so quickly. She saw the geo tag. Jack's handle. The caption, little emojis (sandy beach, star, eggplant). Rafi gasped out loud, a jolt as fierce as an electrical shock running through her. "This is Instagram!"

Jack grinned, so many of his teeth on display it was like he was smuggling a blister pack of gum in his mouth. He nodded.

"You got on the internet!" Panic rose in Rafi like bile. "Did you call for help?"

"I only had a connection for a few minutes," Jack said. "I had to use my time wisely."

Rafi stared at him, not entirely sure Jack answered her question. "So you didn—"

"No, duh, I only had time to post this pic," Jack explained. "Do you see how many likes it got? Worth it."

The page was frozen, and no matter how many times Jack thumbed the screen, nothing moved or blinked on or off.

"How did you get on the internet?" Rafi asked.

Jack took back his phone and admired the picture like it was a newborn baby. "Somebody named Peggy."

Rafi did not like to run, especially not in sand, and definitely not in the world's most poorly made, not-quite-staff, chafey T-shirt, but she did so anyway to get to the other end of the beach as quickly as she could.

She found Peggy sitting under their flimsy clothesline tent, exactly where she'd left them this morning. Only now they were preoccupied with a small object balancing between their thumb and index finger. When Rafi got close enough, she realized it was a fidget spinner. It spun and spun and the randomness of it, along with its spinning, was almost hypnotic. But Rafi snapped out of it, remembering why she'd come here in the first place.

"The internet!" Rafi said. "You got it to work!"

"Yep."

"Were you able to contact anyone?"

"Connection was spotty." Peggy spun the spinner once more. "I'll get it working perfectly, though. It'll just take a bit more time."

All the breath Rafi had been holding came out in one go, but the relief she felt was replaced almost instantly with dread so that now it felt like her breath had been vacuumed out of her. She had to tread carefully with what she said next. "You can't let anyone have it!"

Peggy's spinner stopped spinning, and they cast their lazy eyes on Rafi's frazzled ones. "Why?"

Rafi hadn't thought this far ahead. She had no good reason why they shouldn't try hard to make contact with the outside world. She had only the truth, which included her own selfish desires. But Peggy was practically a friend. If Rafi was going to reveal anything about her ulterior motives for staying on this island, it would be to a friend. A sounding board. Some-one with a clearer head who could potentially talk Rafi out of it if her idea was too outrageous.

"Because if everyone leaves the island, then River will leave the island, and if River leaves the island, then I won't get my interview with him, and if I don't get my interview with him, my podcast will be a failure."

The fidget spinner slipped off the axis of Peggy's index fin-ger. "You really are off the rails, aren't you?"

Guess maybe it was more outrageous than Rafi realized. "Please," she said. "I just need a little bit more time. This isn't just about my podcast. This is about exposing a killer and holding him accountable. It's about"—she didn't want to sound too dramatic but—"justice."

"Relax." Peggy tossed the spinner to the side, where it crash-landed on the sand. They stood and dusted off the back of their shorts. "I understand full well what it means to have internet on this island. And even though your plan is deranged—"

"I don't know if 'deranged' is the right word."

"It is without question full-on deranged," Peggy contin-ued. "I will help you."

"You will?"

"Sure," Peggy said. "I'm not exactly in a rush to get back home. And I like when things get a little deranged."

"Oh." Rafi's insides finally stopped feeling like they were being sucked out of her.

"I'm not just going to give the internet to anybody who asks for it," Peggy said. "Not without a price."

Rafi nodded, even though that wasn't exactly what she was hoping to hear. But she didn't worry too much. No, she didn't like the sound of the word "price," but it wasn't like anybody here had anything of value to trade with. For now, Rafi was sure, her plan was safe.

A slow smile spread over Peggy's lips. "Now let's see how deranged things get."

10

THOUGH PEGGY HAD REASSURED HER ABOUT THE INTERnet being kept under wraps, Rafi was still too nervous about word getting out. Jack, for one, already knew, and he was a wild card. If he told even one other person, then it would be impossible to contain the spread. The more Rafi dwelled on the whole situation, the more worried she got. This wasn't just a wrench in her plans; this had the potential to ruin everything she'd worked so hard for. She was already down a couple grand, already sleeping on sand, going hungry, wearing the worst shirt possible—Rafi was sacrificing a lot for her story. But she was willing to do it all if it meant exposing who River truly was.

No, Rafi couldn't just stand idly by while her entire world unraveled around her. She needed to get ahead of this.

She needed to make a speech.

Rafi had borne witness to the seaport torn asunder by panic, and she'd tiptoed through it in the sleepy morning hours, but she'd never seen it quite like this. There were still plenty of people filling all the chairs, but for some reason there was no shouting or frenzy. Actually, there was a semblance of organization. The chairs had been moved so that they all faced the check-in desk, behind which Paul and Ryan sat, like co-heads of a fraternity going over the rules of the Greek system. Piled on the desk in front of them were stacks of untouched Styrofoam sandwich containers.

Rafi had come here on a mission, but the mood in the seaport demanded attention and quiet, so she found an empty seat in the back and sat.

"Let's focus," Paul or Ryan said, tapping something on the desk that was meant to be a gavel but was actually a conch shell. "If we eat the quote-unquote 'cheese sandwiches,' we will, in effect, be setting a precedent for the type of food we are willing to accept from catering." His voice came out strong and clear, filled every corner of the room. "If we abstain from eating the sandwiches, we send a clear message that we expect better. We paid for better. And we will not be denied."

A boy in the crowd stood to speak. "I vote to request Monte Cristo sandwiches. They're part French toast, part grilled cheese, and meaty. They'd appeal to a wide range of people; plus, they're my favorite."

Another person stood with a counterpoint. "Lobster rolls, though."

A boy with Jesus hair stood next. "I would settle for a Wagyu ribeye and foie gras cheesesteak."

A girl shot up from her seat. "Wait, wait, if we're going to get Wagyu, I want it to be breaded."

"It already *comes* in bread," Jesus Hair said.

"It's not the same thing!" the girl said.

"We are in a desperate situation!" Jesus Hair said, his voice rising. "We are in no position to be picky."

Things were getting heated, and a chorus of murmurs and groans broke over the crowd. Ryan (or Paul) picked up the conch and slammed it down on the desk to get everyone to quiet down. "The dude with the long hair is right!" he said. "When I was nine years old and my sailing instructor fell through our dumbwaiter, I begged my parents for the world's next best sailing instructor, but they told me I couldn't be picky," Ryan (definitely Ryan, Rafi now knew) said. "So too, we cannot be picky now. I say we stick to cheeses."

"In that case, I vote for Gruyère," Paul said.

"Did he say Greer?" the girl next to Rafi whispered. It was the girl who cried hard and often, though she wasn't crying right now. "*My* name is Greer."

"Swiss cheese!" Jesus Hair demanded.

"Plebeian!" Ryan spat.

Paul banged the conch on the desk once more, and it was a wonder it hadn't shattered by now. "Screw it! No cheeses! I say we gather up all the sandwiches into a pile and light them on fire. That'll show the organizers how serious we are about our demands. All in favor?"

Hands shot into the air.

The synapses of Rafi's brain were refusing to spark and connect. It was like she'd taken a megadose of some strong drug because she was totally dazed by the goings-on of this very strange sandwich meeting. It wasn't what she was expecting the festival-goers to be discussing, but it was still an opportunity for Rafi to insert herself. This was her shot to have her voice heard. This was her chance to, possibly, influence the influencers.

"Um, excuse me?" She stood so abruptly that she must've accidentally swiped Greer on the side, because now the girl *was* crying, and Rafi felt bad about that. But she'd have to apologize later. "No one is going to make us Gruyère or Swiss or Wagyu sandwiches." It was probably the wrong way to try to convince them to stay, judging by the crowd's reaction. They regarded Rafi as they so often did: with wary confusion, as though she were an alien, or a DVD player. And then Paul spoke.

"What the ever-loving hell are you talking about?"

Rafi gingerly stepped over the knees of the people in her row until she was at the check-in desk. She fixed Paul and Ryan with an incredulous glare. "When I said you guys should do something useful with your time here, this was not at all what I meant."

"Well, you should've been more clear," Paul said.

"We're just trying to keep the people fed," Ryan said.

"You want to focus on food? Great, but this is not the way to do it," Rafi said. Frustrated, she climbed on top of the desk, despite the sandwiches and Paul and Ryan's monosyllabic protestations. A couple of Styrofoam boxes crumpled under her sneakers while a few others sputtered to the floor, but no one seemed too heartbroken about that. Rafi took her speaker out of her bag, set it gingerly atop a stack of boxes, hooked her mic up to it, and positioned it in front of her lips. "We. Cannot. Burn. The sandwiches."

Her amplified voice gave her words their desired gravitas. Greer stood from her chair, vibrating with fresh tears. "I am not eating those sandwiches."

Jesus Hair raised his hand but did not wait to be called on to speak. "I heard that if you get the sandwiches wet after midnight they multiply."

There was a scream stuck deep inside of Rafi's body that detonated suddenly, but she kept her jaw clenched tight and so no sound came out. After a moment to compose herself, Rafi spoke again. "They're just sandwiches, people."

"They're sandwich people?" someone said, and new murmurs began to froth in the crowd.

"They're regular sandwiches!" Rafi said.

"They can't possibly be regular sandwiches," Paul said behind her.

"I assure you—they are," Rafi said.

"Eat one, then," Ryan said.

Rafi looked at Ryan, and their mutual stare became a confrontation. He did not back down, his chin jutting toward the few remaining sandwiches left on the desk. "If you're so sure the sandwiches are food, eat one of them."

Rafi looked down at the Styrofoam boxes at her feet.

Sure, she would eat one.

Just not right now.

"Look," Rafi said into her mic, "we need to preserve the sandwiches because we might be here a while."

The sounds of grumbling spread out from the crowd, and Rafi could feel that it was just the start of a rising angry tide.

"I know there are a lot of things we were promised that aren't here," she said.

"A gourmet chef," someone in the crowd said.

"The villas."

"The models."

"O-Town," said an ornery Ryan or Paul.

"Yes, all of those things," Rafi said. "But those are just tiny, tiny details. The important thing is the place itself. Look around! We're on a beautiful island."

"It's kind of an ugly island," someone muttered.

"A *beautiful island*!" Rafi repeated, louder this time, trying to drown out the dissenter. "You were all at the beach party earlier—wasn't that fun and beautiful? River Stone was there. You got to party with a rock star!"

Though the beach party had occurred only a few hours earlier, it was as though the coming of the night had erased the concertgoers' memories, because a fog of confusion settled over all of them. A fog so thick, Rafi was beginning to doubt she could cut through it.

It was just at that moment that Jack Dewey appeared beside Rafi. She hadn't even noticed him climb onto the check-in desk. In his hand he held his phone, and she could see the still-frozen post from his Instagram. The picture of him frolicking in the surf with River.

"Oh no," Rafi whispered to herself.

"She may have no sense of style, but what this girl says is

true," Jack said. "Despite every odd being against us, we did actually party with a rock star this afternoon. I have the proof!"

"Oh no," Rafi said again. The irony of the moment hit her like a rogue baseball to the face, and she understood instantly that getting up in front of this crowd had been the wrong approach. She understood that Jack was obviously uncomfortable when someone else was the center of attention, that getting up on the desk had summoned him up here too, and he would now put a pin in her ploy.

She could see Jack start to hold up his phone, but short of slapping it out of his hand, there was nothing Rafi could do. She couldn't think quickly enough, couldn't come up with any good reason to explain away the internet that he'd gotten access to.

Maybe he wouldn't mention it.

"Today I got on the internet!"

A collective gasp rippled through the crowd; all eyes that had been on Rafi, and then on Jack, now swung to his phone, which, to them, loomed as large as an IMAX screen.

"I posted this picture in the afternoon," Jack continued. "It has already reached one point three million likes!"

A million? When Rafi had seen the picture, it'd been only at a thousand-something likes. She had so many questions, but the crowd had more, erupting in a cacophony of voices, sounding surprised, excited, baffled. Rafi could be louder than them, though. Rafi had her microphone.

"Wait, everybody, listen!" Her mic did the trick, and for

once an analog device was enough to distract from something as intangible as the internet. "Okay, so there might be Wi-Fi—fine! But what happens if you get on the internet and show the world what a failure Fly Fest is? The world will see a bunch of privileged morons who got scammed out of a lot of money. They'll laugh at you! They'll think you're all losers!"

More murmurs from the crowd, but this time Paul or Ryan banged their conch-gavel on the desk. "Let her speak! She obviously knows about this topic."

But the conch didn't get anyone to stop and listen, and Rafi could feel herself losing them, like sand sifting through her fingers. And she couldn't lose them. She needed her plan to work. She *needed* to stay on the island, to get her River bombshell—to get her podcast on SteerCat Media.

And to get justice for Tracy, of course.

Rafi looked at Ryan and Paul, trying to settle everyone down; she eyed Jack and his phone; she even searched the crowd, desperate for a spark of inspiration, a final straw to grasp—something that would put her message over the edge. One lone sentence carried over from the masses.

"This is hella random."

"Hella," Rafi said. At first, only Jack heard her, and he let his phone drop to the side, waiting for her to elaborate. Rafi brought the mic to her lips. "Hella is here," she announced.

The crowd quieted down.

"Hella Badid is here?" someone asked.

Of course Hella Badid wasn't here. Hella Badid was too smart to fall for the Fly Fest scam, but Rafi swallowed—her nerves, the truth—and nodded emphatically. "Hella Badid is here!" she said.

"What do you mean, Hella Badid is here?" Jack asked.

"I mean I'm pretty sure I saw her," Rafi said.

"Where?" Jack asked.

"By the mountain."

"*By* the mountain?"

"Like, next to it," Rafi said. The lie seemed to fall apart almost as soon as it left her mouth, but it was picked up by her microphone, amplified and emboldened, and capturing everyone's attention like a magnet. Where once the seaport was filled with loud complainers, they had now transformed into Rafi's captive, quiet audience.

And then something strange happened. Something Rafi could not explain, but it was like someone up there had heard the points she was trying to make and put it upon themselves to add some special effects.

A strange *whoosh*ing sound broke out outside. Like dinosaurs were climbing to the top of the mountain, or like a huge angel with a scythe was thwacking its way through the jungle to kill them all. No one in the seaport could see what was going on, but they all heard it, turning to each other and looking out over the open spaces for the source of the noise.

Rafi took the noise and used it. "That's them, setting the party up!"

And somehow, her lone voice was enough to pull their collective attention away from the sound and back to her. The noise, as it were, went away almost as soon as it came, leaving a stunned silence and all eyes back on Rafi.

"Hella's here," she went on, "and that obviously means that Fly Fest is still happening." The lie did not make Rafi feel bad; instead it filled her with hope, and she could sense the same feeling in her audience. "The festival organizers are obviously in a part of the island we haven't checked yet. Like, the top of the mountain."

"They're still setting up?" came a boy's voice.

"Yes!" Rafi said. "So why don't we wait? Let's wait 'til Hella and the crew are ready to accept us. Because if we show the world the real circumstances here—that we're without proper food and shelter and safety—I promise you, you will never live it down. But if the festival is still happening, then don't you want to be here for that moment? You saw what happened on Jack's Instagram when he posted a pic of him partying with a rock star. A million likes."

"It was one-point-three, actually," Jack said.

"One-point-three! We could all get one-point-three," Rafi said. "Just, please. Don't try to go on the internet just yet. Let's wait."

She liked the way it sounded. Like a political campaign phrase. Something hopeful, a promise of excitement. And as she watched the crowd with bated breath, she felt as though she maybe, just possibly, won an election.

And then, all at once, the crowd ran for the exit in a mass stampede, demanding the internet.

11

THE NIGHT BLED INTO DAY, THOUGH RAFI COULDN'T BE sure how much sleep she'd gotten in that time. After her little speech at the seaport (capped by the big stampede through the exit and then the great migration to the internet), Rafi had skulked back to her poor excuse for a tent, dejected. Everyone on the island now knew there was a way to contact the outside world, and though Peggy had promised to keep the internet to themselves, there was no way they didn't cave under the pressure of a horde of angry, starving, influencers.

No, by now the concertgoers would have alerted the world of the festival's failures, probably filed a few lawsuits, and definitely summoned boats and private planes to come and collect them. It was what Rafi expected to see when she pulled back the flap of her tent in the morning. But what she actually saw was two girls, their bikini-bottomed backsides lazily swaying too close to her face.

They were either dancing or having seizures—there was no way to tell which, and all Rafi could do, dumbfounded and tired as she was, was sit back and try to understand what she was witnessing. The girls' movements went from slow to frantic, each motion synchronized. Rafi was able to discern a series of steps, repeated over and over: locked elbows rounding over their heads; two quick hip locks before dissolving into the aforementioned swaying; a little shoulder shimmy; feet stomps; and finally, a full body roll. In the middle of this dance the girls turned and faced Rafi, smiling so widely at her that in that moment Rafi understood why some people were terrified of twins. But these girls weren't twins, and also they weren't exactly smiling at Rafi. Their smiles were directed just above her head.

And then the dance started again.

Rafi stood, wiping the sleep from her eyes, trying to determine if this was a dream. She stumbled into the space between the two girls, and they finally, mercifully, stopped dancing.

"Do you mind getting back inside?" the girl in the leopard-print bikini asked. "We're recording." She pointed at Rafi's tent, or specifically at the phone perched on one of the sticks holding up Rafi's tent.

"Seriously," the girl in the zebra-print bikini said. "You're in our shot."

"Why are you using my tent?" Rafi asked. "Why are you filming here? Why are you filming at all?"

"Because we don't have a tripod and the top of your tent is the perfect height for the angle we want?" Leopard Print said as though it were obvious.

"So can you move?" Zebra Print asked. "TikTok doesn't allow uglies or poors in their videos."

"Ugly?" Rafi had just spoken to Jack about this yesterday, given him a whole speech about feeling confident in one's own skin, but it was a different thing hearing it come out of these girls' mouths. And as it happened, the word elicited a physical reaction in Rafi. It made her stomach drop and her mouth go dry. Who decided what was ugly, anyway? Or was it happening, right here and now? Was it these girls, in stylish animal fabrics, that were the truth tellers, holding up a mirror and forcing Rafi to look into it? She self-consciously patted down her hair.

"We don't make the rules," Zebra said. "It's practically in TikTok's user agreement."

"Ugly" Rafi took objection to, but "poor" was definitely more accurate. And it unnerved Rafi that these two girls could see that word all over her, as if it was written on her forehead. Could they smell it on her? Did her shoe still stink?

"Why do you think I'm poor?" Rafi asked. They were stranded on an island, and people were literally sleeping on sand without any changes of clothes. How could these two girls possibly sniff out Rafi's lack of funds?

The girls looked at each other for a beat, then back at Rafi. Finally, Leopard Print said, "Well . . . your shirt."

Rafi went over to her tent, grabbed the phone placed precariously on the frame, and threw it as far down the beach as she could. It wasn't very far, and all three of them watched it bounce across the sand until it came to a full stop.

"You're crazy!" Leopard Print shrieked. Neither she, nor Zebra, waited for a defense, running off to collect their most prized possession.

Maybe Rafi *was* crazy. Maybe her hair was an ugly mess

sticking up on all sides in perpetual bedheadedness, held aloft by sand and indignation. Maybe her shirt was tacky and her shoe stank. And maybe she was sleep-deprived and looked and felt about a million years old, telling these kids to get off her lawn. But she didn't care. She now knew she wasn't dreaming. No, she'd awakened to a nightmare.

Rafi walked down the beach, heading for Peggy's tent, but when she got there, it was nothing more than a pile of sticks. She looked around for signs of where Peggy may have gone, but all she saw was a girl close by—that forever crying girl, Greer—smiling into her phone's camera.

"Hey," Rafi said, "do you know Peggy?"

"Of course I know Peggy," Greer said. "They're practically saving us."

"By calling for rescue?"

Greer snorted. "By giving us internet. I'm pretty sure I'd be dead if I couldn't go on the internet."

Confirmation that Peggy hadn't been able to keep the horde at bay. "Do you know where I can find them?"

"Tent City. But if you want Wi-Fi, you better bring them a gift."

Rafi took a few steps closer to Greer until she was blocking the girl's sun. Greer looked away from her phone to frown up at Rafi. "You're in my light," she said.

But Rafi didn't budge. "What do you mean, bring a gift?"

"Peggy will only give you the Wi-Fi code if you trade with them. They're very strict about that."

It wasn't hard finding Peggy's new digs. The path to it was littered with people on their phones. Rafi followed their trail like she was observing mice coming and going from a hole in a kitchen wall. Only in this instance the hole was actually the grandest structure in Tent City. It was made up of three individual tents, split at the seams and sewn back together to form one giant hovel. In fact, it was still under construction, and Rafi spied a boy crouched by the eastern wing, crudely sewing one part of canvas to another using yarn and what looked like the underwire from a bra. There was also a boy standing at the front, broad enough to block the entrance.

"Password?" he said to Rafi.

She stared at him. "Uh, Peggy's a friend of mine."

"Peggy has no friends. They have admirers."

It felt like a second ago that Peggy was the most antisocial person on this island. Now they had a boy acting as a human door. The weirdness that started off the day was snowballing, and Rafi needed answers, *now*. "Peggy!" Rafi shouted over the bouncer's shoulder. "It's me, Rafi!"

She waited a moment for a response, she and the bouncer in a staring standoff.

"*Whomst*?" came Peggy's voice from within.

The bouncer smirked and Rafi bit her lip. "We met in the jungle the first hour we were here."

"Can you be more specific?" Peggy asked.

"I'm the one wearing the pink Fly Fest T-shirt?" Rafi pressed on.

"The what?"

"The staff shirt," Rafi admitted reluctantly. "I look like I work here."

"It's a hideous shirt, boss," the bouncer said.

"Rafi Rafi Rafi . . . ," came Peggy's voice again, taking on a singsong lilt as they sounded out the name. "Let her in!"

The bouncer stepped aside without objection and Rafi entered.

The weirdness snowball was officially the size of a boulder now, and threatening to crush Rafi under its weight. Rafi wasn't sure what she'd been expecting to see when she walked in here—maybe simple, curved walls and a single, plastic-covered bed. But she felt like she'd stepped into an *Architectural Digest* house tour. The three combined tents made for a huge living space, and no part of it was left unadorned. Tapestries draped the walls—everything from sarongs to silk wraps to airplane blankets. Peggy didn't have just one bed; they had three, all piled on top of each other like something out of *The Princess and the Pea*. Next to the bed were crates being used as side tables, and on top of them were solar-powered lamps. There were even artworks, or what Rafi was pretty sure was art. Two sculptural pieces were propped on either side of the main door, bundles of branches tied together with twine. Depending on how you felt about wood sculptures, they were either beautiful and introspective, or some kind of shrine to the Blair Witch.

There were people too, lounging on the floor atop throw pillows, heads hunched over phones. And sitting on an inflatable hot pink armchair was Peggy, peering into their own phone. And even though Rafi was standing right in front of them and they knew she was there, it took Peggy a full minute to look up. "Oh, Rafi. Hello."

"*Hey*," Rafi said, her voice heavy with meaning as she gestured all around her. "Where did all this stuff come from?"

"Right, this stuff," Peggy said, as though noticing it for the first time. "Remember when I told you I wouldn't give up the internet without a price? Well, turns out people are willing to pay up."

Peggy looked different, and it wasn't just because they were smiling. They had new duds, too. A fancy, Memphis-style Bonobos dress shirt; pristine, if oversized, Air Jordans; and a cherry Ring Pop on their right index finger, licked halfway to the nub. "I give people the Wi-Fi password, but the genius part is that I'll change the password every day, which means they'll have to keep paying."

"But I thought you were on my side about this," Rafi said. "We were going to try to keep everyone on the island so that I could get my interview with River, remember?"

"Remember?" Peggy laughed. "A harebrained scheme like that is hard to forget. But I don't know if you noticed that even though everyone's got the internet now, no one's actually called for help."

Rafi took a cursory glance around the room, looking at the people lounging on the floor, happily on their phones. She recalled Greer taking selfies on the beach, the animal-print girls dancing in front of her tent. A day ago everyone was desperate to get off this island, and now it was like the Wi-Fi was a pacifier stuck in their pursed lips.

"Why has nobody called for help?"

"They seem to believe Hella Badid and the Fly Fest organizers are still here, getting the party ready."

Rafi let Peggy's words sink in, absorbing them so deep that they pulled her jaw down with them. Because yes, it had been a harebrained scheme—one that, deep down, Rafi didn't think would ever work. But her little lie about Hella Badid still being here had done the trick. People wanted to stay. *River* would stay.

"Nobody's posting about how terrible this island is?" Rafi asked, skepticism seeping through her awe. "No pictures of the cheese sandwiches?"

"Not that I've seen," Peggy said. "They don't want anyone back home to think they're losers."

A zap of glee shot through Rafi's whole body, and she was so giddy she actually jumped in place. People had actually listened to her. They'd heard her, and she was able to convince them of something. Her voice mattered. She'd influenced the influencers.

"Congratulations," Peggy said. "Everyone wants to stay

and I get a bunch of presents. It's a win-win for everybody. But mostly me."

Rafi practically skipped back to her tent. She'd woken up feeling the lowest she had since she'd gotten here, but her mood had done a complete one-eighty. She may have had no bed, and she was starving and itchy in a terrible shirt, but she was happy. Things were finally looking up.

Of course, the moment couldn't last long.

When she got to the beach, Rafi heard a strained cry and saw a crowd gathering around someone. Rafi ran toward the commotion until she saw Greer, the girl who cried a lot. But this was different. She was on her knees and seemed in deep emotional pain. "What is it?" Rafi asked her, not for the first time raking her eyes over the girl to see if she was hurt.

In all her wailing, Greer had only enough breath to say one chilling sentence. "*Sierra Madre is missing!*"

12

"WHAT DO YOU MEAN SIERRA MADRE IS MISSING?"

"I mean she isn't anywhere!" Greer was exasperated, out of breath, and disheveled. Most of her was covered in a thin film of wetness, and it was unclear whether it was snot, sweat, or tears. Probably a combination of all three. Rafi placed gentle but firm hands on the girl's bare shoulders and tried to catch her frenzied gaze.

"Tell me everything," Rafi said.

"I went to her tent this morning to see if she needed anything," Greer said through wheezing hiccups. "I go every morning, because she's amazing and I can't believe I get to be this close to her. I mean, we have a connection, you know? When I met her here, the first day, she gave me one of her rings, which is like, hello? Are you kidding me? I've been following her since forever, and I leave her a comment on everything she ever posts, like I'm pretty sure she looks forward to my emojis? A heart, a teardrop, and the dancing twins. It's kind of my signature comment, so that she knows it's me. She's just so pretty. I'm sorry, but she's just the prettiest person on the planet and that's, like, the *tea*."

Rafi nodded vigorously even though she understood very

little about what Greer was saying. She was still stuck on the fact that Greer went to her tent every morning, considering they'd only been on the island for two days. "Please get to the point now."

Greer took a deep, rattling breath. "I went to her tent and she wasn't there."

Rafi had to admit that when she heard Greer shrieking about Sierra being missing, it was like she'd struck a match and Rafi was the flint. Immediately her investigative reporter instincts got to tingling. But now, hearing Greer explain herself, the morbid thrill slowly seeped out of Rafi's body. And she found herself trying to calm a girl whose defining characteristic seemed to be that she overreacted to things. "Greer, did you ever consider that maybe Sierra just went for a walk?"

Greer shook her head. Though the tears no longer poured out of her eyes, they still clogged her voice. "I looked everywhere. I checked every tent in Tent City. I checked the seaport, I even came here, to the beach, where the dirty people are. Sierra isn't anywhere."

"Dirty people?" Rafi said. "The people on the beach aren't dirty."

"They're sunburnt and sweaty and there's sandflies and they're sleeping on the sand."

"*I'm* sleeping on the sand."

"Oh, well I didn't mean *you* were dirty," Greer said, but she still took a step back until Rafi's hands slipped off her shoulders. "It's been hours and Sierra hasn't shown up *anywhere*. You work here, right? You have to find her."

Once again, Rafi was tasked with explaining that she did not, in fact, work here, but instead of doing that she held off. Maybe Sierra Madre had gone for a walk. Or maybe, as Greer said, she really was missing. And as someone who was pretty good at solving mysteries, Rafi owed it to Sierra and Greer to at least look into this case.

"I will," Rafi said. "I will find Sierra Madre."

The first step to solving a mystery was to ask questions. Rafi stopped everyone she could, asking if they'd seen Sierra Madre anywhere, but it took some time to get through to people. Most of them were busy playing around with their new Wi-Fi access, finding a way to be very online even though they were stuck on an island.

There was so much a person could do on their phone, she realized, that was easier and more fun than telling the truth. Because everyone was pretending that the festival was still on, that this was a once-in-a-lifetime experience, that they were having a good time on this island.

Everyone on the beach was taking pictures: a girl doing yoga poses; a group of boys posturing like a boy band; a girl pretending not to be disgusted by a horseshoe crab, squealing and gingerly dragging it back to her side whenever it tried to scamper away. One girl was livestreaming herself sunbathing.

Rafi accidentally photobombed more than a few selfies and interrupted some livestreams, but she still managed to ask everyone the only question she had: Had they seen Sierra Madre today? The answer from every single person was consistent. No.

She went to the seaport next, where non-twin jocks Paul and Ryan held court. If Sierra Madre was on anyone's radar, it would be theirs. When she got there, she found Ryan and Paul outside, lounging on chairs they'd dragged out and gazing at the jungle with their hands linked behind their heads.

"Hey, guys, can I ask you a question?"

"Rafi!" Ryan (or perhaps Paul) said. The boys jumped to their feet, looking way too happy to see Rafi. "We've been giving a lot of thought to what you said," Paul (or maybe Ryan) said. "About how there was nothing we could do to fix the sandwich situation."

"*And* about finding the untapped potential all over this disgusting island. So, as my skeet-shooting instructor always says, we decided to murder a bunch of birds with one gun."

The terminology was off but Rafi got the gist of what Ryan (definitely Ryan) was trying to say. Still, her eyes furtively skittered over the ground, searching for a discarded gun and dead birds. What she spotted, though, was much stranger. "What's happening in the trees?" she asked.

The landscape here was pretty sparse compared to the lush jungle at the center of the island, but there were some pretty big banana plants next to the seaport. The bunches of yellowing fruits must've been twenty to twenty-five feet high, and the plants they grew on didn't look all that sturdy, but

Rafi spied about six different people, barefoot and panting, clawing their way up the trunks like they were climbing a fire-station pole.

"We thought about getting the bananas ourselves," Paul said.

"But then we were like, does that *really* help anybody?" Ryan said. "So instead, we taught those people how to climb."

"And now they're collecting the bananas for everyone."

"And by everyone we mean mostly us."

"Wait." Rafi had come here to investigate a missing person, but suddenly she had a whole other line of unrelated questioning running through her head. "What is happening?"

Paul and Ryan looked like they'd been waiting their whole lives for this question and were about to give the best, most thought-out answer. They smirked and nodded at each other, and Rafi could tell this was the more refined version of their own chest bump. The boys turned to her with their pecs flexed and their fists on their hips and looked at Rafi like she was a shark. Specifically, one of those TV sharks who judged whether or not something was a good business idea and then invested a lot of money in it.

"When you signed up for Fly Fest you expected the world's finest organic gourmet food, didn't you?" Ryan asked.

"Actually, I opted for the 'water' option—"

"And then you got here and all there was to eat were gross cheese sandwiches," Paul said. "Hey, Ryan, did you hear that most of those sandwiches contain gluten?"

Ryan's chin bobbed, concerned. "I heard some of them even contain asbestos."

"They don't contain asbestos," Rafi said, but she didn't know if that was accurate. The boys were uninterested in her comments, anyway.

"What if I told you Paul and I have the answers to all of your food insecurities?"

"That's not the correct use of *'food insecurity'*—"

"We have for you a non-GMO, zero-waste, zero–carbon footprint, zero-carbs, zero-calorie, zero-sum game, nature's candy."

Paul continued the pitch. "This organic, vegan, kosher, locally sourced delicacy is picked by dedicated and specially trained interns, and even comes wrapped in an unbelievable outer layer that is all natural and completely compostable, whatever the heck that means."

"We present for you—"

"Don't say a banana," Rafi said.

"A banana!" the boys said in unison. Paul's left hand and Ryan's right palm came together to gently cradle a banana like it was their precious baby. Rafi stared at it. Though Ryan and Paul had spent far too much time and words explaining it, Rafi had never felt so confused by a piece of fruit before. The questions she had earlier only multiplied.

"Why?" she said.

Paul chuckled first, then Ryan. Their laugher was so befuddled and nervous, it came out like barks. "Why?" Paul repeated.

"Rafi, *you* were the one who told us to find a way to disrupt the food industry."

"I legitimately never said that."

"Well, at the very least you must admit that this idea is very money," Ryan said.

"So money," Paul agreed.

"We're charging the interns eight bananas for every ten bananas they collect."

"For the honor of teaching them how to climb."

"They were just a bunch of lazy dickwads before we came along." As he said this, Ryan plopped down onto his chair and kicked his feet out, draping one over the other. "Anyway, we're good people."

"I feel like I'm doing community service but not because I failed a drug test and crashed my Range Rover into the Salvation Army this time," Paul said. "Like, I'm doing the *community* a *service* out of the *goodness of my heart.*"

"And we're gonna make a bunch of money doing it," Ryan said.

"Bunches of money out of bunches of bananas!" Paul said.

They loved this particular turn of phrase and clapped their hands so powerfully that Rafi was almost sure they'd leave bruises.

In the plants, one of the lucky community-service recipients lost his footing and let out a guttural yelp as he *thwacked* through every leaf on his way down. The only sound louder than his screams was the one his back made as it hit the ground.

"My dad would be proud of me," Paul said to Rafi. "You'd understand how huge that is if you had any idea who my father is."

Every time she encountered Ryan and Paul, Rafi understood the world a little less. But she didn't even try to speak their language. She let them have their banana pipe dream. She was here on more important matters.

"Do you guys know who Sierra Madre is?"

Paul and Ryan looked at each other, then back at Rafi. "She's only, like, the most famous influencer in the world."

"Right. Have either of you seen her today?"

Ryan and Paul shook their heads. "We've been busy with our—"

"Bananas, I know," Rafi said. "Find me if she turns up."

She'd covered the beach, the seaport, and the areas in between. The only place left for Rafi to ask questions was the one place she should've started her search.

Compared to the rest of the island, Tent City felt like a luxury retreat. Yes, there were the clay-hard dusty grounds, and the dry bramble backdrop, so prickly compared to the lush green jungle, and the fact that these were clearly tents meant for people displaced by horrible disasters, but something about all the white domes—their uniformity, their pristine cleanliness—made Tent City feel like a wellness resort. Like just around the corner there might be someone in a beige tunic waiting with a tray of heated towels, and tongs with which to give them to you.

Rafi took to the tents like a door-to-door salesman, and the residents of Tent City shut their door flaps in her face accordingly. Of all people, Jack Dewey was the most willing to talk.

He greeted Rafi with a beach towel wrapped around his head so that only his mouth and eyes were visible.

"Still protecting yourself from the sun?"

"I have had public disputes with a lot of people, Rafi. My lying fifth-grade bully, my own mother, the president of the United States. But my biggest enemy to date is the sun. That bitch tries to take me down every chance she gets, and still, like dough, I rise."

If he was trying to quote the famous Maya Angelou poem, he was doing it wrong, but Rafi didn't think correcting Jack Dewey would get her anywhere with him. "Good one."

"It's a Jack Dewey original. I can't stop you if you want to quote me, just make sure to tag me."

"Actually—"

"You know what? Don't tag me. I don't want anyone to think we know each other. If you claim that we do, I'll have to deny it, and if you persist, I'll be forced to have my lawyers send you a cease and desist. You understand, don't you?"

"Sure, Jack. Look, I just have one question and then I'll get out of your hair."

"You're in my hair?" Jack whipped the towel off his head and massaged his fingertips into his red-tinged scalp. "What the hell does that even mean?"

"What? Jack, I'm not, like, a *flea*."

Jack shuddered. "I've heard about you beach people. You're dirty."

Rafi rolled her eyes, regretting ever setting foot in Jack's tent. "Have you seen Sierra Madre today?"

The name seemed to pique Jack's interest. His meticulously plucked right eyebrow cocked. "Sierra Madre? No. Has she asked about me?"

"No. I'm looking for her. She seems to be missing."

Now Jack's left eyebrow joined his right one, and they both hovered close to his hairline. "Sierra Madre is missing? Do you think this has anything to do with Hella being here?"

Rafi had almost forgotten about the lie she'd told about Hella last night. It seemed irrelevant at the moment, but she realized that to Jack—and, in fact, to everyone else on the island—Hella being here was the one thing keeping them all from diving into the ocean and swimming home.

Jack took a step closer to Rafi, seeming to forget momentarily that she was a dirty beach dweller. "You weren't lying about Hella being here, were you? Because Hella being here has made a lot of people very happy."

Now it was Rafi who was taking a step back, suddenly interested in every spot of the tent that Jack wasn't currently occupying. Rafi's lie about Hella wasn't hurting anyone. And if morale really was up, as Jack claimed, then she had nothing to be sorry about. She didn't like to lie, but in this case, its harmlessness made it easy. "I'm not a liar," she said.

The grin that sprang onto Jack's face was spellbinding. For one bright, shining moment, Rafi understood how Jack had managed to get millions of followers online. "I knew it," he said. "You wouldn't lie. You have, like . . . morals."

Rafi swallowed, nodded. "So have you seen Sierra, or not?"

"Nope. But you should check her tent. It's right next door."

Rafi had no trouble getting into Sierra's tent, since no one was there to stop her.

After asking everyone on the island if they'd seen Sierra, and hearing nos across the board, a part of Rafi wondered if Sierra had magically booked it, if she'd somehow found a way, through all of her money and influence, to leave without anyone being the wiser. But being in her tent painted a different story.

All of Sierra's luggage was still there. One carry-on, on the floor. When Rafi opened it she found clothes, all made from delicate, expensive fabrics that felt like butter between her fingers. If Sierra had found a way off this island, she wouldn't have left all of this here. And the fact of that left Rafi with a feeling of dread. An avocado pit sinking in her gut.

Maybe Greer hadn't been overreacting.

Where was Sierra?

Asking about her had left Rafi without answers. Now it was about retracing Sierra's last steps. Rafi tried to think of the last place she'd seen her.

Her breath caught in her throat when she remembered.

13

RAFI DIDN'T HAVE TO LOOK HARD TO FIND RIVER; HE was at his tent, and like the sketchy, probable killer he was, he was in the middle of suspiciously fiddling with something in his guitar case that was definitely not his guitar. Rafi poked her head in his open doorway. "Hiya, River."

River started, and when he saw that Rafi was there, quickly palmed whatever it was he was fiddling with and stuffed it in the front pocket of his soft guitar case, zipping it closed in one swift motion. "Rafi! G'day, mate!"

Suspicious, suspicious Australian. Whatever he was hiding was too small to be the knife. Perhaps a handgun? Like the ones they made that were small enough to fit into women's purses? No, a gun would make the case pooch; this had to be even smaller than that. A corkscrew, perhaps? River could do a lot of damage with a corkscrew.

"Uh, Rafi? You okay?"

Her eyes darted up to his. "Yes. Why?"

"You have the same look on your face that I did when Jimmy Fallon asked me what my favorite body of water was, and I just could *not* come up with an answer."

Rafi remembered the segment. She'd watched the clip

about a million times because it showed the perfect example of River being caught off guard and confused and like he was thinking really hard. She dreamt about interviewing him with her hard-hitting questions and drawing that look out of him. "Jimmy probably thought you'd say a river. Because of your name."

It was like the sun was rising behind River's eyes. "Crikey. You're a genius."

Yes, Rafi thought, but she shrugged, faux-modest-like. She stepped gingerly into his tent, feeling bold enough not to ask for an invitation, but she also wanted to make herself seem like a confidante. If she presented herself as the kind of person who came in for a random chat and made herself comfortable in his space, then maybe River would start to believe that they were something close to friends. It was a risk, though, and as Rafi sat cross-legged under the muted green shade of the muslin roof fabric, she waited to see if River would throw her out.

But he just went on talking.

"People always try to make jokes when your name is an actual verb."

Noun.

"Been happening to me my whole life."

"That a fact?"

River nodded. "What's Rafi short for? Raffle?"

She could feel the features of her face morph back into that confused state from a few moments ago, but she had to remind herself she was talking to a celebrity here. They weren't like regular people. "Um. No. Rafaela."

"Wow, what a beautiful name," River said, his smile wide enough to nearly crack his face in half. He really did have a gorgeous smile, and when he coupled it with a compliment and threw around the word "beautiful," it was easy to see how he'd gotten the world to fall into his charm vortex. Rafi could feel the pull right now. Her guts, always on high alert when it came to River, now swooned inside of her like she'd taken a swig of something bubbly and eighty proof.

"*Rafaela*," River sang. He actually sang it, and the melody, along with the loop de loops the vowels made on his accented tongue, elicited a giggle out of Rafi. It shocked her, and she coughed to try to cover it up.

"The name thing always used to happen to Hella, too," River said. "Like, if there was a jewelry brand who wanted her to hawk their products, she'd be in the commercial saying something like, 'This necklace is hella gold,' or whatever."

"Used to?"

"Hmm?"

"You said 'used to.' Past tense. Does it still not happen to her?"

River had to think about it, even though it should've been an easy question. "Yeah, I guess so. Hey, can I ask you something? Do you know why everyone suddenly thinks Hella's here?"

Of course she knew why. "No idea."

"Weird, isn't it?"

"So weird," Rafi agreed. "So, you weren't at the seaport meeting last night?"

"Rafi, I've been on the cover of *Rolling Stone*, *Vogue*, and *Australian Wines* all in the same week. I don't do meetings."

She had no idea what that meant, but now that they were on the subject of questions, she had one of her own. "Have you seen Sierra Madre today?"

"Who?"

A red flag if ever there was one. Everyone knew who Sierra Madre was. "She's tall, stunning, extremely famous?"

A crease appeared between River's eyes. "What is she famous for?"

The question stumped Rafi. Sierra wasn't exactly famous for anything, she just was. She posted pictures of herself, and that seemed to be the extent of what she did with her life. It wasn't the same level of celebrity that River had, but it was definitely a level above the rest of the influencers here, most of whose posts were ads for tea or antacids or vacuum cleaners.

"She just posts stuff."

River shrugged. "Wouldn't know her. I don't go on the internet much."

"Yeah, but you met her," Rafi said. "On the beach yesterday, I saw you two talking."

The crease between his brows deepened, and he had that Jimmy Fallon look on his face, like a mannequin contemplating the meaning of his existence from inside a store window display. "No, I'm not sure I did."

"You pulled some seaweed out of her hair," Rafi said. *And you walked off into the jungle together.*

"You must be mistaken, mate."

River said all this with a smile on his face, but it was a crooked smile. He was lying.

"Are you sure she isn't in the jungle somewhere, doing boar yoga or something?" he asked.

"You mean goat yoga?"

"No, I don't. Or maybe she's meditating. Being at one with nature—isn't she into that sort of thing?"

"I thought you didn't know anything about her."

The crease deepened, his smile growing only more crooked. River's whole demeanor had changed, and where once he was totally open and willing to say just about anything, now he was suddenly closed off. He shifted his eyes away from Rafi, fiddled once more with the guitar case at his knees. He swung the strap over his shoulder, stood, and crouched through the tent flap, and Rafi followed him until they were both standing outside.

"She's probably definitely meditating somewhere," River said. "This island is a wondrous place. She probably just wants to be alone and at one with nature." He was already backtracking—literally walking backward and away from Rafi. "Good luck finding her."

Red flags rose like goose bumps all over Rafi's skin.

Like the mystery item in his guitar case, River Stone was hiding something.

MUSICAL MYSTERIES
Season 2: Episode 3
"A River Runs Through (Bullsh)It"

Richard Evans was born in Melbourne on an
unseasonably cold day in December, the only child
of Melanie and Stu Evans. He was a colicky baby,
who never gave his parents a moment's rest. As a
toddler he talked nonstop, scribbled on every wall
of his house, and threw his toys at strangers' heads.
Both of Richard's parents have described this period
as, quote, "terrible." The boy was an even bigger
disaster when he reached school age, unable to trace
his letters neatly, making truly hideous macaroni
art, and quote-unquote *"accidentally"* killing his pet
goldfish.

It wasn't until Richard picked up a guitar, at
age thirteen, that he showed any real aptitude for
anything. Turned out he could play four chords,
could even sing. He even had a talent for writing
songs. But although the name "Richard Evans" was
perfectly fine, it wouldn't do if he wanted to break
into the music biz. No, "River Stone" had a much
better ring to it.

He picked "Stone" because that's what "Evan"
means in Hebrew. But "River," he claims, is a nickname
from childhood. Says people always called him that
because he enjoyed "jumping into rivers like a little

rascal." Paints a lovely picture, doesn't it? Of a carefree child in an idyllic youth where there were rivers around to jump in and be rascalish. Except, there isn't any record of anyone from River's childhood actually calling him River anywhere. No mention of it in any yearbooks or social media posts. And not a single river anywhere near his house.

The name is just the start of Richard's—sorry, *River's*—duplicitous nature. There's no telling how many lies he's told in his lifetime. How many times did he tell a girl she had a beautiful name when he didn't really mean it? Has he ever lied about not having any STIs? Who knows, but between you and me: probably. The point is, River Stone is a lying liar who lies. Now, there isn't anything wrong with a few white lies here and there. But when your girlfriend disappears in the middle of a camping trip and everything you tell the detectives about the case is a lie—well, that's a different story.

On the surface, the mystery of River's disappearing first love, Tracy Mooney, is scandalous, to be sure. But let's do something that even the case's detectives failed to do: scratch the surface.

Why was River napping at nine P.M.? I mean, who does that? Especially if he planned to propose to Tracy just one hour later?

And the goodbye note. Tracy uses a pretty unusual word to describe River: "wondrous." In all

117

my time researching River and Tracy's story, I was unable to find a single instance in which Tracy used that word. Not in any of her social media posts, not in any of her videos. River, on the other hand? I've found instances of him saying it at least thirty-seven times.

Not to mention the fact that the handwriting on the note itself looks a lot closer to River's than to Tracy's.

Still skeptical? Okay, then let's take a look at his heroic trek back to civilization. After Tracy took River's car, River had to make it back to the nearest town on foot. But judging from the spot where River and Tracy were camping, and the distance to town, a journey that should've taken eleven hours River was able to complete in two.

So he has superhuman speed, you might say. But then explain the river!

Yes, ironically enough, River would've had to cross a river in order to get back to town in the quickest way possible. By car, you can drive around the river relatively quickly. But walking around the river would've added hours to River's journey. Ugh, say "river" one more time—I know, I know. The point is, in order to get to town, in two hours, River would've had to wade into choppy waters. And yet, when he got to the general store where he famously called the police, pictures show that he was totally dry. His boots weren't even wet.

Maybe he dried off in the sun, you say. But may I remind you that it was the *middle of the night*?

You still don't believe me. Well, what if I told you that there are only tire tracks back to town?

No footprints anywhere on the miraculously shortened trail that River supposedly took to salvation.

I mean, *come on*! The evidence against River's story is overwhelming!

My theory? River went on that trip with Tracy and killed her. He wasn't getting anywhere with his music career. And just being another cute guy on YouTube with a guitar wasn't garnering him enough attention. He needed a *story*, a hook. He needed fodder for his song-writing. He needed . . . a dead girl on his hands.

That's next time on "Musical Mysteries."

This episode of "Musical Mysteries" was brought to you by Nobrand. Ever wish you had some toilet paper because you've been using sandwich bread in a way in which it was not intended? Try Nobrand. They've got you covered. And if you use the code RIVERKILLER, you'll get fourteen percent off your purchase.

Until next time, Mysterinos!

14

RAFI'S MIND WAS RACING WITH POSSIBILITIES, MOTIVES, disappearances, and mysteries, and there was only one way she knew how to work through them all. It was a personal project that took her half the day to complete, and when she was done, there was only one person she could think to show it to, and she *did* need to show it. That was part of the process—to talk it out with someone with fresh eyes who could tell her if her hunches seemed sound, if she was on the right track.

It'd been hard to pull Peggy out of their ever-growing tent mansion, but she finally convinced them to come into the jungle. And when Peggy saw Rafi's project, hanging between two trees like a banner, they were glad they came.

"You made a murder board?" Peggy was wide-eyed and slack-jawed, but not disinterested.

It was a cliché, but there was a reason murder boards were so ubiquitous with investigators. It was the best way for Rafi to work out her hypothesis, with the central mystery, the suspects, the motives, and everything else laid out in front of her.

Peggy approached the board slowly, and reached out their

fingers but stopped just short of touching it, like it was a price-less artwork hanging in a museum. Rafi had to admit, she was pretty proud of herself. For someone who had little else than the clothes on her back, she'd managed to make a pretty good board.

"You managed to find cardboard on the island?" Peggy asked.

"It's the bread from the cheese sandwiches, pasted together side by side. Same consistency as cardboard."

"What did you paste it together with?"

"The cheese, what else?" Rafi could've spent hours explaining how she'd achieved such a gorgeous spectacle (the threads linking the different theories were stripped ropes of ivy; the drawings were made in sand art using beach sand and clear lip gloss), but she didn't want to stray too far from the point, which was what the murder board was about.

Peggy still had more questions about the construction, though.

"How did you get so many pictures of River?"

This one was easy enough to answer. "I've been research-ing this case for a year. I printed out every article I could find about him."

"So let me get this straight," Peggy said. "You're telling me that instead of packing literally any other spare shirt into your carry-on, you decided instead to take to a music festival dozens of pictures of River Stone."

Why was this so hard for them to understand? "I'm an *investigator*."

"Okay, but why are there so many *shirtless* pictures?"

Rafi took one long step until she was standing between Peggy and the board. At this point it was starting to feel like more of a distraction than an infographic. "It's not my fault that River is shirtless in nearly every picture ever taken of him; can we get back to the point? He's a killer. And I think he's killed again."

"Like, on this island?"

Rafi nodded. "Sierra Madre is missing. No one's seen her since the beach party. And I saw her disappear into the jungle with River."

"Lots of girls throw themselves at River."

"But he lied about it," Rafi said. "I asked him point-blank about whether he'd met Sierra, and he claimed he hadn't. I think he did something to her."

Peggy considered this. Or, at least, they didn't seem as preoccupied with the murder board anymore, because they focused on a rock on the ground, kicking it around lazily. "What's the use of looking into this?"

Not what Rafi was expecting them to ask, and it was, in fact, kind of insulting. After all the work she'd done on the murder board? "There could be a killer among us," Rafi said, trying to infuse the proper amount of gravitas in her voice. "And he could kill again."

"But what's the use in that line of thinking?"

Rafi stared blankly, and Peggy sighed and tried to put it in terms that she would understand. "You're better off thinking that River's not a killer. Because if he is, that means he's been let loose on an island, free to kill anyone. It'd be like shooting fish in a barrel. Or dumping a cat into a box full of mice. Or a snake in—"

"I get it."

"He'd be free to keep killing with no one to stop him," Peggy went on. "And, if you think about it, it's all 'cause of that big lie you told."

"Little lie."

"Massive lie," Peggy said. "Face it, Rafi, you managed to keep River on the island. But are you prepared for what that means?"

Rafi let Peggy's words sink in, deeper and deeper until she felt like she was six feet underground.

"I meant him killing a bunch of people," Peggy said.

"I know what you meant," Rafi snapped.

River had his guitar out. The denizens of the beach had left their designated spots in order to sit cross-legged and contented at his feet, their phones held aloft, recording the impromptu twilight concert. They'd come to Fly Fest for the music—well, probably for the bragging rights—but they were finally getting music, anyway. An acoustic set by River Stone. And this song was his most popular one. Rafi listened to the lyrics as he sang.

And that was the last night I saw her / ring in
   my pocket
I was a boat / she really knew how to rock it
Oh Tracy
My heart was big / it was not small
You had a phone / Why didn't you call?

Wordsmith. Lyricist of our times. Rafi wanted to gag. But here was the kicker. The coda. The part of the song everyone always howled in unison:

I call your name in anguish but I'm the victim
   here OH!

Rafi had listened to "Victim" a million times, trying to decode the lyrics, see if there was some subtext that would betray River's lies. As he sang, River managed to make his shirtlessness a vulnerability, the slick strands of hair springing into his face with every key change somehow making him look earnest. He was dazzling them all with his body and his stupid songs.

He was so good at looking like an honest, nice guy. But then, so was Ted Bundy.

Rafi hadn't been able to stop thinking about what Peggy had said. About River being free to kill—and about Rafi's own part in that. If Rafi hadn't told everyone that Hella was here somewhere, still planning to party with them, would Sierra be missing?

Was Peggy right? Was all of this Rafi's fault?

The question gnawed away at her. So much so that Rafi wanted to take it all back—the lie, her part in it. She envisioned herself running up to River, in front of all those people, and ripping the guitar out of his hands so she could get their attention. She'd tell them all the truth, say she hadn't seen Hella, that they needed to get back home, that this place wasn't safe.

Rafi took a few steps forward, ready to make her way to the "stage" when something in the distance caught her eye. A rustling in the trees that blanketed the base of the mountain. Leaves dipped and swayed, like an invisible wind swept through them. Or, more likely, a wild animal. It was coming down fast, barreling through, and Rafi was pretty sure she was the only one who saw it. Her whole body tensed, waiting for whatever monster was coming her way to make itself known. Finally, it reached the bottom and broke through the trees.

It was not a monster. It was a girl. Not just any girl—it was Greer. Crying. Again.

"Not another missing person," Rafi muttered under her breath, hating herself for being more annoyed at Greer's crying than at the prospect of a growing body count.

The crying girl locked eyes with the only person who noticed her and rushed right toward Rafi. Greer had a look in her eyes like she was possessed. Maybe she was, because the few words that came out of her mouth made a chill run down Rafi's hot spine.

"Hell is here."

"What?" Rafi asked. But Greer did not elaborate, choosing instead to run through the concert crowd, kicking up sand, and breaking up the relaxed vibe like an out-of-control pinball. "HELL IS HERE!"

On a trip to New York once when she was a kid, Rafi saw a man in Times Square wearing a big sign over his body with print too small to read, but he kept shouting about the devil. Rafi's mother pulled her by the hand until they were far enough away that Rafi could only hear him in the distance, her attention eventually stolen by the M&M's store. This was kind of like that, except no one was there to pull Rafi by the hand. It was her own intuition, her investigative edge, that pulled her forward, after the girl.

Greer continued zigzagging through the crowd, screaming louder and louder until River was forced to end the song before it could reach its tragic coda. He put his guitar down carefully and stood, placing a comforting hand on Greer's shoulder. "What's wrong, hon?"

"Hell is here!" she said again. "I witnessed it. She revealed herself to me." Greer swallowed and smiled through her tears. "Hella Badid is here!"

15

"EVERYONE, CALM DOWN." RIVER SPOKE WITH THE charismatic confidence expected of a teen idol, but it wasn't enough to tamp down the sudden fervor for more information. People continued to talk over themselves, bouncing on the balls of their feet with excitement—the kind of excitement you'd expect if you'd just heard that the coast guard had spotted you after days stranded on an island. Except it wasn't the coast guard, it was a supermodel.

River wasn't convinced, though. "These rumors are just that—rumors. Hella isn't here," he said. "Believe me, I would know."

"But I heard her," said Greer.

"What did you hear, exactly?" River asked.

"I was walking up the mountain when I heard her. We all know her voice—I wouldn't mistake Hella Badid's voice for anyone else's."

Hella did have a truly distinctive cadence. It was deep but still managed to sound flighty with its Valley Girl accent. She also had the world's foremost vocal fry, all of her sentences ending with a staticky whine akin to the sound a monster might make as it tried to climb out of your TV set. The deep Valley, vocal fry monster voice was occasionally topped off with a small exclamation that sounded almost exactly like a sheep's bleat. Lots of girls tried to emulate it. Few succeeded.

"Wait, you went up the mountain by yourself?" Rafi asked. Her curiosity had led her to the front of the pack, standing right beside River. The mountain was uncharted territory. All paths up its steep incline seemed needlessly treacherous, and not even River, Jack, or Rafi had crossed it when they'd made their exploratory trek. Naturally, Rafi had more questions. "What were you doing on the mountain?"

The features on Greer's face tensed up and turned red. "I don't have to answer that." She looked to River. "I don't have to answer that, right?"

Rafi took a step closer to Greer, and a part of her, subconsciously, was trying to get to the bottom of this—whatever this was—through intimidation. "Why are you being so shifty?" Rafi asked.

"What I do when I am alone with my body is my own business," Greer said, eyes welling up anew, voice cracking.

"Look, we don't care what you were doing up there," River interjected. "Is it possible that you only *think* you heard Hella's voice? Sometimes, when I'm alone, lying in a hammock in my Hamptons estate, musing for inspiration, I think I hear an angel singing, but then I realize it's just me, coming up with new melodies. Could it be that you got excited and thought you heard a voice when really it was the breeze rustling the trees or something?"

"Is that what you think Hella sounds like?" Rafi asked. "A breeze rustling the trees? Have you heard her speak?"

"I've been going out with her for two months, I think I know—"

"It wasn't the breeze," Greer said. "It was her. I've never been more sure of anything in my entire life."

This shut everybody up, including Rafi. It couldn't be. Hella being here was just a lie. A lie that Rafi made up. But Greer seemed convinced. And River seemed tense.

"What did Hella say?" Rafi asked.

Greer sniffed and blinked, clearing away her tears. "She welcomed me to the island. And then she said that things were about to get . . . lit."

It was just what everybody wanted to hear, because the crowd, listening to every word, let out a collective squeal of delight. The bouncing started again, the excitement got louder among them. There was something electric in the air, a buzz, like someone had just turned the music on at a party.

But it was a song that Rafi didn't quite know. And River, whose face was set in a scowl for the first time since they got to the island, didn't seem to hear the music at all.

Rafi had made up the rumor. But was it possible? Could Hella Badid really be somewhere on this island?

"Hella Badid is definitely somewhere on this island!" Jack announced to an explosion of cheers.

He was standing in the same spot where River had been performing just an hour ago, the audience now double in size. And while night had fully fallen, Jack nevertheless wore sunglasses in an attempt to obscure as much of his makeup-free face as possible. Though, they probably also helped to shield him from the glare of the burning torches held up by two of his—fans? Followers? Disciples? Greer was one of them. The flames seemed to make her eyes water.

Rafi wasn't sure what she was watching, but she hovered at the back of the pack, paying close attention. It was fascinating to see who influenced the influencers, and now Rafi had her answer: It was the boy makeup artist. She didn't know why Jack held so much sway over them. Maybe it was the way he spoke—the confidence he had to take up any topic and imbue it with more knowledge than he could possibly possess (stating, for instance, that Hella was on this island, without a single shred of evidence).

It must've had something to do with his skill at courting drama. Online, Rafi had regularly heard more about Jack than she'd ever wanted to know, simply by virtue of all the constant fights he was involved in. There was the time he fought very publicly with a rival MUA over credit for the short-lived slug lips trend; or the time he put out a cover of "Ave Maria" that was so scandalous that the pope denounced him; or the time he started a fight with his grandma because of overdue bar mitzvah money and he made her get TikTok so that people could see both sides of the story, and then she accidentally posted one hundred videos of herself sleeping, and Jack disowned her out of sheer humiliation.

The drama had followed him to Fly Fest, too. He didn't have a grandma to fight with, but Jack picked fights with anyone who was around. He accused a fashion influencer of trying to steal his Burberry fanny pack, a wellness influencer of spying on him while he meditated, and Rafi was pretty sure he was currently in a fight with *her* now, though she didn't know why. It was just that any time she made eye contact with him, his eyebrows arched fiercely, like two expertly plucked question marks that only wanted to know one thing: *How dare you?*

Still, Rafi didn't look away. Despite how ridiculous all of this was, Rafi wanted to hear what Jack had to say. This Hella rumor was the biggest thing to happen to Fly Fest since the implosion of Fly Fest. She herself had started it. And thanks to Jack, it seemed, it was only going to become a bigger deal.

"I know it looks like this festival was a bust. A scam. A lie," Jack told the crowd. "I was ready to believe that, too. But people have heard Hella Badid's voice."

"One person," Rafi muttered to herself. "One emotionally fragile person."

Jack couldn't have possibly heard her, but the way he immediately zeroed in on Rafi with one of his patented narrowed stares—even through the shades!—unnerved her.

"And it wasn't just one person who heard her!" Jack proceeded to look over his followers. "More people have come forward to me privately to say they've heard her, too. We know Hella Badid's publicist has confirmed to all media outlets that Hella has come on this trip. And we also know that Hella hasn't been posting anything on social media, so she's obviously in hiding. My friends, my followers—Hella Badid is *here*. Up on that mountain behind me. I'm not making that up—those are the facts."

Jack paced and his torch-wielders followed his every move, making for a compelling sort of stage show. "I've got another fact for you. Sierra Madre is missing."

No one gasped or seemed at all surprised, but that was probably because Rafi had asked everyone here if they knew of Sierra's whereabouts. But she, like everyone else, waited for Jack to make his connection between Sierra and Hella.

"I've got a theory," Jack said finally. "Sierra was, arguably, the best among us. I mean, I'm up there myself but, as some of you may know, I have sadly lost all of my makeup in this horrific ordeal. I know it is probably physically painful for all of you to have to look at my face, it being as bare and disgusting as the day's first snow. The point is! I think Sierra's been invited."

A subtle wave broke through the influencers as they collectively leaned forward with interest. Rafi couldn't help it. She leaned forward, too.

"We know Hella's here, up on the mountain somewhere. We know she's probably helping to make Fly Fest happen. But what if it's already happening? What if the only ones who are invited are the ones who are *worthy* of being invited?"

"Worthy?" Rafi repeated.

"We know Sierra is worthy. Sierra is perfect." Here Jack paused. Rafi could learn a thing or two from him when it came to public speaking. He had the right cadence, the right starts and stops. He had everyone in the audience wrapped around his finger. And he yanked. "What if this is a test? What if Hella is waiting for us to get it together so we can finally experience the real Fly Fest? Because we all came here expecting a party and we got served a big pile of nothing. It just doesn't make sense."

"Make it make sense!" said a lone voice in the crowd. Jack, emboldened by the audience engagement, nodded.

"Hella is here," Jack said. It was not a question. "Which means the party must be here, too. What if the organizers are watching us, from up on their mountain, and making decisions about who they'll let in? They let Sierra in. Do you want to be on that guest list? I know I do."

Rafi listened, but her mind kept responding with skepticism. *What if there was another level of hoops to jump through just to be granted access to a stupid musical festival?* More like, *What if we all got scammed out of our money, but we're clearly susceptible to scams, and so here's another one to suit your fancy?*

But as Rafi looked around, she didn't see anyone shaking their head or walking away. She saw eyes widening and heads nodding and the kind of devotional tearing up you saw in documentaries about dangerously fanatical cults.

"What if we're one step closer to meeting Hella?" The tone

of Jack's voice rose along with his excitement. "What if Hella and the others—"

The others? This was getting ominous.

"—want us to *prove* we're worthy of going to the festival? We must be perfect to go to the world's most perfect party!"

It was a rallying cry, and it was met with just the cheers Jack wanted. For Rafi, all she was left with were questions. How could these people—with their expensive clothes and faces made smooth by diligent skin-care regimens—get any more perfect? And what did Jack have in mind?

Jack bowed, signaling his speech was over, and the crowd closed in on him, eager to be near. Rafi wasn't sure what to make of Jack's speech, or if it would truly change things on the island. All she knew was that a girl was missing—possibly dead. And now everyone thought she'd been let into a bogus festival on a mountaintop.

Meanwhile, River still roamed free.

Things were starting to unravel, and Rafi didn't have the first clue how to get it all back under control.

And now there was a rustling on the mountain. It was the same type of rustling Rafi witnessed when Greer came rushing down that same pathway to warn everyone about Hella.

But it wasn't Greer who broke through the trees this time.

It was River, calmly dusting off his hands on the back of his shorts and checking to see if anyone was watching.

What had he been doing up there?

16

SHE DIDN'T HAVE MUCH OF A PLAN. AND IT OCCURRED to her that it might be too mentally exhausting to try to be sneaky about this, so it all hinged on River saying yes. She hoped he was just vain and delusional enough to do it.

Rafi stood outside River's tent and knocked. Or, tapped on the fabric, as it were, until it swayed back and forth enough to get his attention. He poked his head out almost instantly and lobbed a smile her way. "G'day, Raf!"

It was fully nighttime, and could this guy be any more Australian? But Rafi served River a tentative smile. She needed to be out with it. "Can I interview you?"

River's eyebrows quirked—not skeptically, just genuinely curious, if a bit confused. "Like, about how I manage to make such good art and stay so fit even though those two concepts are diametrically opposed?"

Um. "Among other things. It would be for my podcast." Rafi held up her phone and mic, her most prized possessions. If he said no, then she'd just blown her one opportunity to get the interview of a lifetime when she probably could've just recorded him without his knowledge. But she needed to do this right, and with the way things were going on this trip, it was time to cut out the games.

River stepped fully out of his tent, standing akimbo. "It would be my pleasure."

Rafi matched his smile. Just because she'd asked nicely didn't mean she would give him easy questions. It was time to get to the truth. It was show time.

They sat in front of their tents, a small campfire that River had built making the night come alive, ablaze and crackling. The atmosphere was akin to two neighbors enjoying a beer on their porches after a long day. Except instead of booze there was the impossible-to-ignore microphone in Rafi's hand. She hadn't even started her interview, but River kept looking at it. It was almost like he hadn't been interviewed thousands of times before.

Rafi stuck the mic in the sand, its soft foam cover sticking straight up like a zombie hand protruding from a fresh grave. She hoped that keeping it out of River's sight line would be enough to make him forget about it. She needed to get him comfortable so that he would talk. She needed him to talk. After all, there was a girl missing who still hadn't turned up.

"So, what's your podcast about?"

"It's called 'Musical Mysteries.' It's about the biggest mysteries. In music." She had to find a better tagline.

"Ah. I think I know what you're going to ask me. . . . You,

like everyone else in the world, want to know when the new album is finally coming out."

No. Definitely not at all. Though, Rafi *was* a bit curious. While most of his fans thought he was just a perfectionist trying to get his album in tip-top shape before releasing it into the world, Rafi had a theory that River was dealing with writer's block. It was only natural, given that his sole inspiration for his first and only album was about the tragedy of his missing girlfriend. Without that tragedy, what did he have to sing about anymore?

"The truth is, for the last year, since I sat down to write the thing, I've been majorly blocked."

She knew it.

"And then, last week," River went on, "poof! It was like a dam broke inside my head and all these songs came gushing out. A whole album's worth."

"Wow. That's lucky," Rafi said.

"Nah, I wouldn't call it luck."

She definitely wouldn't call it luck either. "What happened last week?"

"Hmm?"

"Something must have happened last week to get your creative juices flowing. Something big. Did it have anything to do with Hella?"

River got a funny look on his face, but he avoided looking at Rafi's eyes. He focused his attention on the fire instead, stoking it with a stick. "Don't think so?" he said.

It was the most unsure River had ever sounded. Rafi latched

onto this River—the one who couldn't look her in the eye and ended sentences with question marks. This River was the one who would inadvertently lead Rafi to the truth. And the truth was possibly where Sierra lay. Dead.

"It's weird, isn't it," Rafi said, "that everyone suddenly thinks Hella is on this island." Rafi made no mention of the fact that she was technically the one who'd started the rumor, but that was irrelevant. "Is it possible that she *is* here somewhere?"

"What?" River said, befuddled. "No way. Hella canceled on the gig."

"I thought you told Jack she missed her flight at the last minute." Rafi distinctly remembered him saying that when they all went on their trek together the first day.

"Yeah, she missed it." More stoking of the fire, more avoiding Rafi's gaze. "That's what I meant."

To say River was acting shifty was an understatement. The corner of his mouth pulled itself to the side, like a fisherman's hook tugging the life out of him. His tell. He was lying. Rafi felt suddenly bad for Sierra, that she would trust and walk off with someone so shady. Tracy, too.

"Can I ask you about your relationship with Tracy?" Rafi was walking on eggshells now, trying to get to this portion of her interview as carefully as possible. It was imperative that she didn't spook him. From all her research, Rafi knew that River didn't like to talk about Tracy. The topic was pretty unavoidable when he had to promote his album, but he usually sidestepped it by saying the whole thing was still too recent and hard for him to talk about. It worked in his favor and went a long way in garnering him fans who thought he was *soo* sensitive.

"It's been a long time since anyone's asked me about Tracy."

Rafi breathed, waited for him to say the wound was still too fresh.

"You remind me a lot of her."

It was such a left turn from his usual answer that it took Rafi a moment to process what he'd said, and when she finally did, her cheeks went red. Tracy was a blonde with hair that didn't frizz up at the tiniest exposure to the outside and a constant smile holding up her apple cheeks and a row of straight teeth that were small enough to still look like baby teeth even though they obviously weren't. Point was, Tracy had been beautiful, something Rafi never felt she was. Especially not on this island.

"You mean our personalities?" Rafi reasoned.

"Blimey, no—Tracy was a lot of fun."

"Oh."

"I mean she always used to ask me a million questions, trying to get to the core of what I was feeling and thinking and *hiding*, even. But I wasn't ever hiding anything." River shook his head and laughed to himself, recalling a memory. "One time she grilled me for days—*days*—about how she knew I was lying to her. She said she could tell from my smile or something."

Rafi felt an instant kinship with Tracy then. This small thing that seemed to elude all of his fans was something that she and Tracy both saw. Something that bound them together.

"We could be doing something so mundane, like sharing a bag of chippies, and she'd turn to me out of nowhere and say, '*I know there's something you're not telling me.*' That was the thing about Tracy—she knew me better than anyone. And she was right. There was something I'd been hiding from her."

Rafi didn't move except to lean subtly closer, waiting—ready for something that sounded like a confession. River, for his part, leaned in, too. This close, Rafi could see the patchy stubble starting to sprout on his chin and cheeks. He was usually so neat and clean-shaven all the time, which Rafi always saw as a calculated ploy to stay looking boyish and innocent. Now the dark scruff defined his features more than usual, cut his cheeks, made his jaw sharp as a flat blade. His eyes, both dark pools sparkling with the reflection of the campfire, locked onto Rafi, and she couldn't help but drown in them. This close she could breathe him in, practically. He smelled flowery, fresh. Like jasmine. She inhaled. Why did he always smell so good?

Rafi's lips must've been dry because she licked them. "What were you hiding from her?"

River's own lips, plump and properly hydrated, curved into a naughty smile. "A porcupine."

A porcupine.

River rocked back with a laugh that rivaled the cracking of the fire. "It was a silly birthday present. But she was always talking about wanting pets. The thing is, she was majorly allergic to any kind of fur. Cat fur, dog fur, possum fur."

"Possums?" Did people in Australia keep possums as pets? Were tarantulas next?

"Tarantula fur," River went on. "Bird feathers, too. Once we went to an emu farm, and she was sneezing up a storm all over the place."

"You lost me at emu farm."

"I thought a porcupine would do, you know? Nothing fuzzy that you could pet. Well, you could pet her quills, but who would want to? She was called Porky. I picked the name."

"Original."

River stoked the fire, but when he laughed again there was a sniff tagged on to the end of it. "Tracy loved Porky," River said through a sad smile. "I kept her after . . . afterwards. I tried so hard to keep the bloody thing alive and healthy. I even fed her chocolate bars every day. And then she up and escaped. I think my mum let her out of the house one day. I miss her."

"She sounds like a nice pet."

"She was. But I wasn't talking about her."

He kept his gaze on the fire, but looking at him, Rafi could see how glassy River's eyes had become. It was subtle, but he was emotional. She'd never seen him overcome like this. Not even in the hours of concert footage she'd combed for any hints to this kind of outpouring. She could see it plain as day, how much he loved Tracy.

"I'm sorry."

River sniffed and shook his head back in the way he did when he wanted to get his hair out of his eyes. "Thank you for asking about Tracy. It's been so long since I talked about her."

Rafi nodded but she didn't know what to think. She didn't anticipate River reacting like this at the mention of his long-missing first love. She thought he'd be cagey, suspicious, sly. But he was just a boy like any other, talking about a girl he'd loved and lost. Rafi actually felt a pang of guilt for her ulterior motives in bringing her up.

And she was more confused than ever, because of all the Rivers she'd seen, this one had her the most convinced that he wasn't capable of hurting anyone.

Rafi couldn't sleep. It'd been hours since her interview with River, and she still couldn't reconcile the sweet, vulnerable boy she'd seen tonight with the one in her head—the one with a trail of missing girls behind him.

She needed to know, one way or another, who he really was. Everyone on this island was lying about something. Some were lying about what they really looked like outside of Facetune and filters. Some were lying about what an amazing, beautiful experience this was. River had to be lying about something, too.

And maybe Rafi was crazy for what she was about to do, but it was the only way to calm her mind. If she found nothing, she'd give up the game and admit that she didn't have enough to go on to nail River. But if she found something, then she knew her instincts had been right about him all along.

Rafi knew he wasn't in his tent. Not being able to sleep, she'd seen his shadow outside her own tent, moving away until he was gone. And she waited. She waited long enough that she figured the coast was clear.

She was in his tent now, and she had her sights set on only one thing: his guitar case. Specifically, the front pocket. The same one she saw him hiding something inside.

She knew she was violating something here. His trust, his boundaries, his privacy. But a part of her also felt that she had Tracy on her side. Tracy, who also sensed when River was hiding something, was very possibly cheering Rafi on. At least, Rafi told herself that as she crawled to the back of River's tent, clawing sand through her fingers until her hands were on the pocket's zipper. She pinched it and pulled. And when she saw what was inside, all the breath left her body.

She held it up in front of her eyes to get as close a look as possible. Its shininess glinted in the starlight.

It was a necklace with a rose-gold charm with a name spelled out in cursive. *Sierra*.

17

"WHAT'S YOUR NAME AGAIN?"

"Rafi."

The bouncer at Peggy's door looked skeptical, like he didn't believe that Rafi's name was actually Rafi—like anyone's name could actually be Rafi. He took a bite of a hardboiled egg as he looked her up and down, another already peeled egg waiting in a Ziploc bag in his hand.

"Where'd you get eggs?" Rafi asked. "Are there chickens on the island?"

"I'm the one asking questions here," the bouncer said. "And if you want to see Peggy there's a wait time. And a color-coded sticker system. And a line."

Rafi looked back over her shoulder. The day was barely into its twinkling daylight hours, and there was already an ant's trail of people about thirty deep waiting to get into Peggy's tent. They clutched their phones in white-knuckled sunburnt hands, nearly vibrating with anticipation for their next Wi-Fi fix. Rafi couldn't wait in line. What she had to say to Peggy was too important.

She resorted to the same gimmick she'd employed the last time she'd been desperate to enter Peggy's tent.

"PEGGY!" Rafi yelled at the top of her lungs, so loud past the bouncer's ear the sound made him recoil. Not enough to keep him from blocking the door, though.

"Ambrosius?" came Peggy's voice from their cavernous white dwelling. "Who goes there?"

"Somebody named Razzie," the bouncer responded. "I think she works here."

"It's me, Rafi!"

"*Who?*" Peggy's voice said.

Rafi took a deep breath to try to center herself. "We met on day one. We're friends. I showed you my murder board."

"You showed them your *what*?" the bouncer asked, munching on his second egg.

"Of course, of course," came Peggy's voice. "Come in."

The place looked even bigger than the last time Rafi had seen it, and it seemed to still be expanding. There was someone in the left wing, standing on a stack of crates and cutting a hole into the ceiling. For a sunroom or a second floor, Rafi couldn't be sure, and though it was more than adequate shelter, Rafi couldn't say she was jealous of the accommodations. The place was crammed. All sorts of things were littered everywhere, things Peggy couldn't possibly need, like hand sanitizer or endless amounts of airport headphones, or a Rube Goldberg machine made of Styrofoam sandwich containers that appeared to do nothing more than toss bananas limply on the floor. And there were so many people there, too. It was as though someone from an episode of *Hoarders* was also addicted to hosting parties. Boring parties. All the people

145

were too busy with their noses in their phones, frozen in deep concentration. In fact, except for overworked thumb knuckles and the occasional flying banana, Peggy's tent-mansion was stuffed with inanimate objects.

When Rafi got to Peggy's quarters, she found them eating a chunk of milky white coconut, which was being fed to them by a servant standing to the side of the inflatable hot-pink Fly Fest promotional chair on which Peggy sat. The chair matched the color of Rafi's shirt, and she felt repelled by it, though she wasn't sure if that had to do with the Fly Fest logo or of what had become of the person sitting on it.

"Rafi," Peggy said, licking the last bit of coconut milk off their servant's finger. "What brings you here?"

Rafi held up her hand. Sierra's necklace dangled from between her fingers. "I found this in River's things."

Peggy squinted, and lest their poor eyesight get in the way of this revelation, Rafi stepped closer, until the charm practically grazed Peggy's nose.

"So he wears jewelry." Peggy shrugged. "This is much less alarming than you going through his stuff."

Rafi chose to ignore that last part. "This is Sierra's necklace! Don't you see? It proves River was lying to me when I asked him if he knew her."

"And Sierra's the girl who's missing, right?"

Rafi's jaw came unhinged as she struggled to find words. Honestly, she'd made a whole murder board about this to illustrate her point, but clearly she hadn't done a good enough job at it. "Yes. This proves he knows more than he's letting on."

"And that he probably killed her," Peggy said.

Rafi nodded vehemently. Finally, they were catching on. "And I'm starting to think there may be something to the Hella rumor."

"That you started."

"Yes. I mean, I was lying when I said she was here, but what if she really is here?"

"Lemme guess," Peggy cut in, "you think River killed her."

"I know you think this is a joke, but I'm serious. Look—" Rafi turned to the nearest person, a girl lying on the floor not too far away. "You, could you look up Hella Badid's Instagram for me?"

The girl seemed bothered to be interrupted but also like the type of person who'd check on Hella Badid's socials anyway. And she did. "She hasn't posted anything in days."

"See?" Rafi said, spinning back around to Peggy with renewed vigor. "Hella posts every day, sometimes multiple times a day. Why is she suddenly silent?"

"I guess because her boyfriend chopped her up like he did his last girlfriend."

"Okay, I can't tell if you're being sarcastic, but yes, precisely." Fired up, Rafi turned to the girl with the phone again. "Can you look up Sierra Madre's Instagram, too?"

"Do you, like, not have your own phone?" the girl responded.

"Do it!"

The girl was aghast, but she also followed the command. "Nothing from Sierra either."

Rafi shot Peggy a wide-eyed, self-satisfied look. "These people *live* on social media, Peggy. If they're not posting, do they even really exist?"

This was major stuff. Hella not posting was a huge indicator that something was off. A scandal, celebrities, disappearances—anyone would be intrigued. But Peggy couldn't look more bored. Rafi knew what they were thinking. That she was crazy. That she was once again on a bender of her own conspiracy theories. But this necklace wasn't a conspiracy. It was proof. And Rafi owed it to Sierra—and maybe even to Hella—to get to the bottom of this.

Peggy finally spoke. "So, playing dumb devil's advocate here, let's say River Stone is a kidnapper-slash-murderer. What do you want to do about it?"

"Well, that's why I'm here. I need to get on the internet. We need to tell the police—we need to get River away from all these unsuspecting people." Rafi took a breath. "Plus, stuff's getting weird around here."

"How do you mean?"

"Well, for one thing, Peggy, you're wearing a bear-hide rug as a hat."

The head of the bear was mostly intact, its jaw open and menacing over Peggy's bangs. The rest of the hide draped over their back, like a cloak. And that was only the crowning touch of Peggy's outfit. They also wore at least a dozen necklaces, a pair of orange lace gloves, leather pants, and, for good measure, a satin cummerbund. "Aren't you hot in all that?"

"That's why I have my fan," Peggy said. They gestured toward the boy at their side. Not the one with the coconut, the one fanning them with a paperback spy novel. "Can you believe somebody packed this in their carry-on?"

"People read books."

"I meant this." Peggy pointed to the bear on their head.

"Oh, that," Rafi said. After all the absurd things she'd seen on this island? "Yes."

"Well, I won't apologize for it. It's badass."

"It's not just you—it's everybody. I saw a girl on the beach doing a reaction video with a turtle."

"Like, reacting to the turtle?"

"Like, asking the turtle to react to things."

Peggy chuckled appreciatively and motioned for their servant to bend closer to them. "Get me that turtle," they instructed. The servant was off, and Peggy's attention was back on Rafi. "So you realize your lover boy is a killer, and suddenly you want off the island."

"He is *not* my *lover boy*, and yes, I want off the island. You were right. I said Hella was here, and now everyone's staying on this island because of my lie, and it's making it a lot easier for River to potentially kill people. I don't want to be anywhere near a probable serial killer. Do you?"

"Do you see this?" Peggy held up a jar half-full with a greenish liquid. "Somebody gave me this for five minutes of internet this morning. I'm not sure if I'm meant to drink it or apply it, but it's supposed to make my hair shiny, and I'll be damned if I don't try it. People are just *giving* me this stuff, Rafi."

Again, Rafi was confused at the core concept. Was Peggy complaining here, or bragging? Probably bragging, she realized. It was apparent from the state of Peggy's surroundings that they considered every single thing that people traded with them a kind of treasure, even if it was a liquid of questionable origins.

Well, if Peggy required a trade, then that was what they'd get. Unfortunately, Rafi had nothing of value on her. Except . . .

"Would you take the necklace for five minutes of internet?"

"A dead girl's jewelry and your only piece of evidence?"

"I'm sure Sierra won't miss it," Rafi said.

Peggy examined the necklace more closely, even caressing it with their fingertips, until finally, curtly, shaking their head. "Not interested."

"You're wearing candy jewelry. This is real jewelry."

But Peggy only shrugged. "I'm sorry, Rafi, but I can't let you have the internet."

"What?"

"I'm not ready to get off the island yet. And with all the lying everyone's doing about how great it is here, there's a good chance we could all be staying indefinitely. Everyone in the real world believes that everyone here is living in paradise."

"But it's all a lie. It's a lie utopia!"

Peggy shrugged. "People would rather live in a lie utopia than in a true dystopia. Which is what this island is, let's be real."

"But everyone in the real world must know that Fly Fest is canceled."

"Au contraire. Apparently, the people at Fly Fest have realized all the lawsuits they'd be under if the truth came to light. It's in their best interest to play along with the charade."

"But how are they explaining any of this? No bands. No pics of the accommodations. No video of any concerts!"

"They're playing on the whole secrecy thing. Exclusivity. Don't you get it? The mystery adds to the mystique. It's a win-win."

If everyone was winning, then why did Rafi feel like such a loser? She must've looked like a loser too, because for once Peggy seemed sympathetic. But not sympathetic enough to share the Wi-Fi password.

"I'm sorry, I can't help you," they said. "Now, unless you come back here with something I truly can't pass up, River's just gonna have to keep killing girls with impunity."

MUSICAL MYSTERIES
Season 2: Episode 4
"River Stone and His Girls"

This episode was going to be about Tracy Mooney:
who she was, her relationship with River, the legacy
she leaves behind. But there have been some
developments here at Fly Fest that I have to address.

Sierra Madre is missing.

I'm sorry to have to announce something so
alarming and—seemingly—random, but it's true.
One of the most followed influencers in the world
has disappeared without a trace. A feat, when she
was on an island from which no one has come or
gone for the last few days.

Sierra's disappearance is a major news event, but
you're probably asking yourself why I'm mentioning
it here, on a podcast about River Stone. I'll tell you
why: because our boy River was the last person to
see Sierra alive.

I know. I know. Typical River, amiright?

As for River's current girlfriend, Hella, I'm not
sure what to think. Apparently, she's gone radio
silent on her socials, which is unusual, to say the
least. She was supposed to be a featured guest at Fly
Fest, but she is nowhere to be found. And yet, there
is a rumor (how it got started is not important) that
she is here somewhere on this island. Now, I don't

typically put too much stock in rumors—I'm a hard evidence kind of girl. But this rumor has now come from multiple sources. It's picked up so much speed that Hella has almost become more of an idea than an actual person around here. And the idea of Hella has achieved mythic proportions. She is neither here nor there, yet she is everywhere.

No one here can say for sure where Hella is. Well, no one except, probably, River. But any time Hella is brought up, River changes the subject or the story and acts generally shifty. I'm not sure what to make out of all of this. I guess I'm trying to talk it out here, with all of you, my listeners. Right now, it's all a jumbled ball of yarn I can't untangle. But there is one connecting thread that ties all these girls together.

River Stone.

Tracy. Sierra. Hella. Three beautiful girls who knew River. They knew him well enough to have a conversation, were close enough to touch him, intimate enough to be alone with him. Beautiful girls who are now—in one way or another—missing. They followed him into the Australian bushland, a music festival, a jungle. And possibly to the ends of their lives. They were taken in by love, adoration. Manipulated by good looks and mediocre music. But I won't be manipulated. No matter how nice he is to me, or how infuriatingly magnetic the twinkle in his eye is, I won't be swayed by River Stone. I won't follow blindly.

I haven't figured out this case yet, but I believe, now more than ever, that River Stone is a stone-cold killer.

This episode of "Musical Mysteries" was brought to you by Nobrand. Ever have a hankering to wash your clothes because you only have one shirt and didn't anticipate being stranded on an island without a change of clothes? Well, Nobrand has a detergent for that. Go to Nobrand.com and enter code RIVERKILLER for three percent off your next purchase.

Until next time, Mysterinos!

18

RAFI NEARLY CHOKED ON A SCREAM AS SHE STEPPED OUT of her tent. River was standing right there.

"Sorry!" he said quickly, hands up in a gesture of apology. "Didn't mean to startle you."

"What are you doing here?" Rafi asked.

"Just chilling."

This was the downside of Rafi's tent being right next to River's. Yes, she had access to him, but he also had access to her, and she wondered how long he'd been standing outside her flimsy fabric door, and just how much he'd heard of her recording.

River answered the question before she could ask it. "I heard you talking to yourself."

She could feel her cheeks reddening but coughed to try to disperse the color. She gauged River's face for any telltale signs that he'd heard what she'd said about him. But he only looked at her with that doofy smile of his. Maybe he'd only heard indistinct mumbling.

"I was recording an episode of my podcast." Rafi held her breath, waiting for him to say something, confront her, but he did none of that. "What did you hear, exactly?"

"Something about detergent?" he said.

Rafi let out a sigh through her nose, relieved he hadn't heard the meatier parts of the episode. "Yeah. Just wishing I could wash my clothes."

River nodded, which was a perfectly normal response to what Rafi had just said, but there was something uncanny about his expression. In the short time she'd gotten to know him, Rafi had become accustomed to River's way of speaking, which was to say he liked doing it. Liked to chitchat, liked to make little jokes to smooth out the harder edges of any conversation. But he remained silent now, the doofy smile slipping subtly from his face. Being this close to him, under his gaze, reminded Rafi of what she really thought of him.

River was dangerous.

"You want to go somewhere?" he asked.

The question was so unexpected, it took a minute for Rafi to respond. "Where?"

"Just this place I know." He shrugged his bare shoulders. "A secret place."

All Rafi wanted was alone time with River so she could get to the bottom of her case. But was she willing to risk her life, going to a "secret" place with a killer? A possible *serial* killer?

"Lead the way."

Okay, technically Rafi said she wouldn't blindly follow him, but all investigators had to make some sacrifices to crack their cases. She practically had an obligation to do this. An obligation to her listeners, to Tracy and Sierra and Hella, and to the truth. Rafi was brave. She was in awe of herself, really. And that was why her heart was beating so fast. Not because she was afraid. And not because she was out of shape and the uphill journey was leaving her kind of winded. It was the adrenaline. With every new step she felt closer to the truth. She would ask him her burning question. She would corner him, confront him, *bear* down until he *broke* down. It wasn't her who should be afraid for not knowing what lay ahead—it was him.

Unlike the other times she'd hung out with River, when there was always the constant hum of human life in the distance, it was as they walked through the lush jungle trees now that Rafi realized they were truly alone for the first time. The rest of the beach, the people, the island, fell away, and all Rafi could hear was the crisp sound of twigs snapping under their feet and fat leaves whacking their arms.

They were thick in the middle of the island, but they'd taken a detour from climbing up the jagged slope of the mountain, going around it instead. And River was evasive. Any time Rafi asked where they were going, River would give her a vague, "You'll see soon enough."

And then he'd do something infuriating, like turn to her and smile, and the beat of her heart would stumble over itself. And no, it wasn't because he was cute. It was *never* because he was cute.

None of him was cute. She would not be distracted by his

deep brown eyes, or the crinkle they got around the corners, or the way all his teeth lined up perfectly and gleaming, or the way his lone dimple popped.

Well, she couldn't deny he was fit. She watched the way his back moved as he walked, his shoulder blades sharp as wings about to break through skin. The elegant indentation of his spine. And his thighs. It was pretty obvious that River did not skip leg day at the gym. His thighs were thicker than she expected, and only sparsely hairy. "Wait." She stopped. "Why are your pants off?"

"Because we're here."

"I feel like that doesn't adequately answer the question . . ." But her comment died on her lips as she took in her surroundings. A pond. Right in the middle of the jungle. Beautiful and clear for at least a yard beneath the surface, burbling at the far end with a waterfall splashing off the side of the mountain. Sunlight bounced off the crystal liquid surface, casting a shimmering rainbow on the waterfall's spray of mist. Even the birds seemed astounded by the unbelievable sight, chirping a soundtrack to welcome Rafi and River.

This was the most amazing place Rafi had ever been.

And to her left was River, whose pants had gone the way of his girlfriends and disappeared. He was left in nothing but boxers, and though Rafi was fully dressed, she felt equally as exposed with the deep flush crawling up her cheeks.

She told herself it was because of the humidity.

"I brought you here because of what I heard you saying in your tent."

Rafi's mouth went dry instantly. She had a talent for assessing situations quickly, and she now saw the scene before her for exactly what it was. River had heard her recording her podcast—probably the whole episode. He'd brought her here, to a place no one on the island knew about, so no one could find them. Just as she'd suspected. And he'd taken off his clothes so as not to dirty them with all of the blood he would surely be spilling.

"You said something about wishing you had detergent," River said.

"Oh."

"And I know you don't have a change of clothing because if you did, you would have definitely changed out of that shirt by now. Not that it's not a nice shirt, but it's also not a great shirt, you know? But what do I know about fashion? I have stylists who tell me what to wear. Sorry, it's a nice shirt, and it definitely doesn't hurt my eyes with how pink it is. Anyway, I figured this was the next best thing." He gestured toward the pond. "Freshwater. It sure beats bathing in the salty ocean."

River didn't want to kill her. He wanted her to take a bath.

And he was apparently part of the long list of people who hated her shirt.

Bringing her to a bath was the equivalent of offering someone a breath mint. There was no way to take that other than as a clear sign that you stink. She tried surreptitiously to sniff her armpit, but not surreptitiously enough, because River chuckled. "I'm not trying to say you smell bad," he said quickly. "I just thought you might appreciate this place."

"I do appreciate it." Usually when speaking to River, every word out of her mouth was disingenuous, but she wasn't lying this time. This place was beautiful. And yet. "I can't go in there." The pond was stunning, but it was deep, and she couldn't.

"Because of your fear of water?"

Rafi turned to River, his words so surprising that they were enough to steal her attention away from the awesome landscape. "How did you know?"

"Rafi, there's a reason why *Australian Lasses* picked me as their favorite artist last year, and it isn't my looks."

"What?"

"It's my empathy. It's what makes me such a good musician. I'm perceptive. I understand people. And your water phobia was immediately obvious to me. Tell me about it."

Rafi stared at him, not sure what to think, but she wasn't going to just start opening up to him about one of the most terrifying moments of her life. She wasn't here to reveal something about herself, she was here to make him reveal something about *himself*. But River watched her with a look so piercing and patient that the rest of her surroundings fell away. Maybe *Australian Lasses* knew what they were talking about.

"I almost drowned," Rafi said. "When I was eight. Family vacation. We were at the beach, and I was in the water alone for some reason. I went out too far. There was a wave so big—at least as tall as my father—and it just went right over my head. It took me under. I couldn't figure out which way was up."

"That must've been scary."

Rafi shrugged and shook her head, mostly to try to shirk the memory away. She didn't like dwelling on it too much. "I survived."

"You're very brave," River said.

"For not drowning?"

"For being here. You willingly chose to come to this island, a place surrounded by nothing but miles of ocean. There must've been a real good reason for you to do that."

Rafi took in what River said. There was a good reason she came here. And while Fly Fest may have been a bust for everyone else, this place was tailor-made for just what she needed. And he was standing right here beside her. She liked the idea of them both being in the water. There wasn't anywhere for River to go when she'd eventually ask him what she needed to ask him.

She would jump into this, no fear.

And that was just what she did.

19

RAFI POPPED HER HEAD OUT OF THE WATER, GASPING and shivering. Not since she was eight years old had she been so perfectly encased in the thing she feared the most. She was frozen with it, and she had to remember what it entailed to stay afloat. She kicked her feet and tried to pull herself up with her arms, but there was nothing to hold on to, of course. She wanted to scream, but her gasp had turned into hyperventilation, plus there was the pesky problem of all the water pouring into her mouth.

This was how it would all end, she realized. She'd survived her secret detour with a possible serial killer only to die by a little bit of water.

Said possible serial killer bobbed his head right out of that water as rosy-tinged and carefree as a cranberry in a bog. When he saw Rafi, however, the smile on his face slid a bit. "Uh, you know how to swim, right?"

She tried to tell him she'd known how to swim since she was four years old, but through all her splashing and flailing it was hard to get a word out. River seemed to get the message, though, and his patented smile was back, secure as ever.

"May I?" he asked. He placed his hands on Rafi's hips and held her gaze just as strongly as he held her up.

She could see his feet kicking below, but like a duck he was totally composed above the surface. He nodded, prompting her, and she began to mimic him, kicking her own feet, breathing again. She didn't think it'd be possible, submerged in all this water, but her nerves settled down. The fact that she was in this pond was amazing and shocking, but suddenly secondary to the fact that River was touching her.

Knowing what she knew about him, she should have recoiled. But she did not want to.

"Don't let go," Rafi said. Her voice sounded ragged, and she realized just how much water she'd inadvertently swallowed.

"I'm barely holding on."

Rafi looked down. It was just his fingertips on her. How was he possibly holding her up with only his fingertips? "You're so strong," she said without an ounce of irony.

"Yes, I am," River said, without irony either. "But you're also floating on your own."

"I am?"

River let go completely, and Rafi did not sink, even though he looked at her with eyes that could make anyone forget how to breathe. "See? You're a pro."

River did not hold her again, but as they swam in the pond they remained in each other's orbit, as though tethered together below the surface. Rafi didn't know what she expected to happen when she jumped in, but she realized it wasn't so scary here after all. The water felt incredible. Almost as warm as a bath and silky on her skin. It made the turquoise-blue ocean seem harsh to the touch and abrasively salty in comparison. Being here with River was kind of fun, too. He swam like a sea lion released from captivity, but with the muscle memory for performing in front of large crowds. He dove and twirled and splashed, and when he popped back up through the surface of the water, he did that thing that boys with a certain length of hair did, where they whip it so that strands stick sideways and wet to their foreheads.

Like on stage, River loved to perform. He made a big show of climbing up the rocks on the side of the waterfall, then jumping off in a massive cannonball. He invited Rafi to do the same, but there was no way. If she attempted to climb on slippery rocks, she would probably fall and crack open her skull. And she wasn't about to become inspo for River's next album.

It was as she thought of this that Rafi remembered why she was here. Now that she'd conquered her fear, she was ready to conquer the truth.

Rafi watched River swim back toward the spot where they'd left their things. The muscles in his back flexed as he planted his arms on the flat rock and hoisted himself out of the water. He went for the pocket of his pants and rummaged for something inside. The loudness of the waterfall filled Rafi's ears as she watched and helplessly treaded water. What was he getting? A knife? A gun? A candlestick? But why a weapon, when all he had to do was dunk her if he'd wanted to? Taken his big hands, pressed them into her head and shoulders, held her down until—

Her thoughts all vanished when she saw him holding a rectangular white object, small enough to fit in his palm but substantial enough to cause blunt force trauma. Except, it wasn't a stone or a brick or a weapon at all. Rafi gasped.

"Is that soap?"

"Yep!" He dove back in and Rafi winced at the splash. But when she opened her eyes again, River was just a couple of feet away from her, lathering up his shoulders.

"Where did you get that?" Rafi didn't bother to hide the awe coloring her tone.

"Some girl gave it to me. Girls give me a lot of things."

Rafi was aware of the skeevy business of girls fawning over rock stars and gifting them things, and how ethically dubious it was for River to accept gifts, especially since this was a small island and he was likely to see that girl again, and she might expect something from him, or worse, he might expect even more from her. But all those thoughts flitted away to make room for the scent of freshness emanating from the most beautiful rectangular block Rafi had ever laid eyes on. Somehow, her palm was opening up like a lotus flower, and the sudsy, slippery bar was landing on it. "Keep it," River said. "Someone will give me another one."

Rafi finally understood what was behind River's easygoing,

sunny disposition. He never had to worry about anything, because everything in his life always worked itself out. He didn't worry about being stranded on an island, because as a celebrity he knew that eventually he would have to be saved. He didn't worry about staying clean, because someone would always give him soap. And he didn't have to worry about getting away with murder, since he already had.

It was an eloquent thought, if Rafi did say so herself, the kind she might jot down to use later in her podcast. But it was canceled out by how inelegantly she was scrubbing a bar of soap under her arm but over her shirt. She scrubbed everywhere: her hair, her mouth, her jean shorts. She must've looked like an alien who'd been told about soap but who'd never seen it used in practice. And River chuckled as he watched her have at it. But Rafi didn't care if she looked ridiculous. She'd never felt so clean.

When they were done swimming and washing and rinsing off, they dried off by lying out in the sun on the big rock slab at the edge of the pond. River was a lounging marble statue. Water droplets dotted his skin in some parts and casually rolled off in others, like summer rain on a slick leaf.

Rafi, on the other hand, was a soaked, year-old newspaper you find in your gutter and fling unceremoniously onto the street, where it turns into soggy mulch. She glanced over at River and wished she could look so relaxed. Or at the very least presentable. But all she could think to do was bend her knee. Was this relaxed? Did this look sexy? Why was she worried about looking sexy?

River opened his eyes, catching Rafi staring at him, and she immediately darted her gaze up to the sky. She propped herself on her elbow and tilted her head back and tried to whip her hair away from her face, but she almost broke her neck doing so. She dropped the elbow. Closed her eyes. Definitely not sexy.

But who cared? Rafi didn't ever care about looking sexy, not for anybody and definitely not for a serial killer.

Which reminded her. It was time to get on with it. When River serenely faced the sun and closed his eyes again, Rafi slipped her hand into her backpack and felt for her microphone. She always had her mic within reach. It made her brave, gave her a voice. And if she was able to record River's confession without him knowing, then—even if he killed her like he did all the other girls in his life—at least the truth would come out when they eventually found her body. If anyone found her body.

She clasped the mic and she hit record. Time for the interview of her life.

"So, that's pretty nice weather we're having, huh?"

River did nothing for a long moment, then he turned his gaze toward Rafi. He caught her eyes like he had a net, and she found herself unable to break free of it. "You don't really want to talk about the weather."

It wasn't a question, and the way he'd said it unnerved

Rafi. Maybe it was because he'd read her mind. This wasn't what she wanted to talk about at all. She'd been gearing herself up to have The Talk with him. The one about how he was a murderer, etc. It was like he was giving her an invitation to do so without even knowing it. But his net-eyes caught her tongue too, and Rafi didn't know what to say.

So he helped her along. "I'm glad you came out here with me. I wanted to talk to you about something, too."

"Oh?"

"About the thing I heard you say in your tent," River said.

"About the detergent?"

"About me being a killer."

Rafi went so still she wasn't even sure she was breathing. The waterfall roared in the distance, the pond burbled, and birds tweeted. They were the kind of sounds that people selected on noise machines to help them drift off to sleep. But to Rafi it all sounded like alarm bells. Like the musical cues in a horror movie when the villain is about to strike.

"What?" Her mouth was suddenly dry.

"You think I killed Tracy. I heard you say it."

The damning words did not match his even-keeled disposition. Rafi hated that he was so calm while she felt so off-kilter. She was the one who wanted to have this conversation, and somehow he was the one steering the ship.

"If you think I'm a killer, then why follow me into the jungle? Alone? Where no one knows where we are?"

"What are you saying?"

"I'm saying that no one would be able to hear you scream."

168

There was none of that cinnamon-roll, pop-star charm gleaming off him. Not even the hint of a smile. Just an unwavering stare-down. Rafi had to fight not to wither beneath it. Maybe if she said it out loud, she could convince him, and herself, that she could meet this moment.

"I came because I'm not afraid of you." Rafi's elbow dug painfully into the rock as she tried to remain still and composed. "And yes. I do think you're a killer."

River sat up, the movement catching Rafi off guard. But he didn't stop moving. He leaned over her and she froze, unsure what to do but knowing this was the moment. This was the moment River buried this story.

If Rafi was a mouse, then River was the snake, slithering seamlessly toward her, about to swallow her whole. But even as a mouse Rafi was awkward and strange because she didn't try to scamper away. It was almost as if a part of her wanted this.

River was fully on top of her, his dry, smooth body over her still damp one. All Rafi could do was let her elbow fall, and she lay back, looking up at him. Her rough shirt exacerbated the friction between them. When she was in the pond with him, she liked the idea that he had nowhere to hide. Now his face was only inches from hers. She saw the pores around his nose and a scar she'd never noticed on his chin. The tip of one of his incisors was whiter than the rest of the tooth. This close, he had nowhere to hide.

"Tracy didn't just disappear," Rafi said. Her voice was steady as she said the most important thing she would ever say. Maybe the last thing she would ever say. "And she didn't run away. She's dead, isn't she?"

Every second passed achingly slowly as River did nothing but look at her. His glance darted first to her lips, then one eye, and the other. Until, finally, he nodded.

He was reaching his hand out.

It was coming for Rafi's neck.

He was going to kill her.

20

ANDY THEN HIS HAND PASSED HER NECK. IT PASSED HER face. It went for the backpack she'd left next to her head. He reached inside and took out her mic.

"If you want the truth, it needs to be off the record." River clicked the off button, and Rafi felt like it was her heart that had stopped. But she was alive. River tossed her the mic and she sat up, catching it.

Wait, what just happened? She was sure River had almost killed her. Or wanted to kill her. Why hadn't he killed her?

River sat cross-legged, shoulders slumped and kind of sad. "Tracy didn't abandon me in the middle of the bush like I claimed. She died out there. But I didn't kill her, I *swear*."

Rafi couldn't believe what she was hearing. And she couldn't *believe* that her mic was turned off. But more important, she just wanted the truth. And River was ready to spill it. "So, what happened?"

River let go of such a big breath it almost looked like he got physically smaller. "We went to the bush on a romantic trip. We wanted to sleep under the stars. I mean, we didn't even pack a tent, that's how much we were roughing it. We got there late, and by the time we were done settling in, it was already dark. Tracy spotted these purple wildflowers, and she wanted to collect them. She said they'd be perfect for a photo she wanted to post. I told her to just wait 'til tomorrow, but she wanted them that instant. And then—"

The whole time he talked he'd been looking at his hands, tearing at tiny threads of skin on his cuticles. But now he stopped and looked at Rafi like he'd just remembered that she was there. "This next part is not going to sound real."

Rafi was impatient. She didn't want him to stop and editorialize or even acknowledge her. She just wanted him to let it all out without interruption. She wished she was in a sound booth, a small windowless room, dim and intimate without distractions. But the wilderness would have to do. In her mind, the burbling waterfall and tweeting tropical birds were white noise, providing an ambient cocoon of privacy in which she hoped River could speak freely. "Unless you tell me that aliens showed up to abduct her, I will believe you."

River seemed to think about this, a horrified, faraway look in his eyes as he contemplated extraterrestrials. Rafi was worried she was losing him. "River, focus. What happened?"

River looked at his fingers once more. He tore away his skin until a tiny bead of blood bloomed on the corner of his thumbnail. "A pack of dingoes showed up."

If there had been a desk in front of her, Rafi would have dropped her head onto it. She may have even acted out the motion without realizing it, because River said, "See, I knew you'd think it was ridiculous."

Because it *was* ridiculous. *Dingoes?* Rafi didn't know what to say. All she knew about dingoes was that they were basically dogs with stupid names and a punchline to a joke.

"I'm serious," River said. "The leader of the pack bit Tracy on the forearm and dragged her behind this rocky, hill-formation thing, and she was already pretty far from camp when it happened, but I ran. I ran as fast as I could to help her. But when I went behind the hill she—the dingoes . . . They were all gone."

Rafi sat with this information. She said she'd believe him, but now she had serious doubts. River looked contrite. The boy was practically on the verge of tears. But . . . *dingoes*?

"If this is all true, then why didn't you just tell everyone that from the beginning?"

"Because who would believe it?" River said. "No one believed that real-life story with the lady who said the dingo took her baby, and then it became a Meryl Streep movie, and then they remade the movie with Ashley Woodstone, and it came out *literally* a week before Tracy died, and it was just the worst possible timing, and it's just . . . I went on that trip with my girlfriend. If I left alone and told everyone that a dingo had eaten her, I would've been arrested on the spot. Or laughed at."

"Arrested or laughed at." Rafi snorted. "Which is worse?"

"I'm serious, Rafi. If I told the truth, that would've been it for me. My music career? Over before it even began. I couldn't do that to myself. I had already started writing my album. Imagine what the world would look like today if nobody ever got to hear it."

Sometimes, talking to River felt like an out-of-body experience. Rafi was at once in the moment, having a serious conversation with a boy about his dead girlfriend, and simultaneously coming to terms with the fact that River's autobiography may as well have been a book of Mad Libs.

**Shirtless** pop star _**in the middle of the jungle**_
   adjective   location

explains how _**dingoes ate**_ his girlfriend.
                  noun   verb

"A world without your music?" Rafi responded, continuing the conversation instead of walking out of the jungle and directly into the ocean. "Perish the thought."

"I know!"

"So you made up the story of Tracy running away."

River nodded.

"And you wrote fake diary entries for her where you made her look like an awful person who was always planning on leaving you stranded in the middle of the bush."

He nodded, again.

"So, you were never going to propose?"

"Crikey, _no_. I was seventeen! I just put that in there to make the story more heartbreaking. And it worked! It worked so well, Raf."

He was getting emotional again, and Rafi was almost embarrassed for him. It was the only way she knew how to classify what she was feeling. It certainly wasn't pity. And she didn't have the energy to spare anger for something this idiotic.

"I feel so guilty," River said. "And the only way I know how to deal with it is—"

"Through your music?"

"No. I donate all my money to the Australian Dingo Conservation Society even though that feels totally wrong and not the right charity to give to, but I don't know what is, Rafi. I don't know what is. They buy chew toys for the dingoes, so at least that's training them to chew toys and not humans, right?"

There was a desperate hope in his voice that Rafi, frankly, did not know how to assuage. "*Right?*" River asked again, his eyes turning into pools large enough to rival the one behind them.

"Australia is like a different planet, River. I don't know how things work there."

River sighed, his chin perpendicular to his chest. "My whole life is so stupid."

Rafi nodded until she realized what she was doing and stopped. She hated to admit it, but for the first time ever, she believed River. As he'd spoken, Rafi examined his mouth for any twitch or crookedness, any indication that he might be lying. But there was none. He was giving it to her straight. Literally— his mouth was straight. So she had to believe his words were, too. His story was too ridiculous to be false. And it meant that she'd been right all along. Well, not about River killing Tracy, but she'd been the only one to see that he'd been lying about the whole story and he'd falsified documents to cover it all up. That, at least, gave Rafi some validation.

But validation was not the same as being satisfied, and though she'd gotten to the bottom of this case, Rafi felt a pang. An emptiness. She needed something else—something more.

"What about Sierra?" Rafi asked. "I know you lied to me about her. I found her necklace in your things."

River's lips tightened around a groan he was trying not to let out. There was just so much to explain, and none of it made him look like the good guy he was desperate to present himself as. "People give me things all the time! And then she goes and disappears. I lied because I can't be known as the guy who girls disappear around all the time."

"So you don't know where she is."

"No clue."

"And Hella?"

"I have no idea why people think she's here. But she's not."

River rapped his knuckles on the rock he was sitting on with increasing frustration. "Please swear you'll never tell anyone any of this. I know my music is, like, really good, but deep down I wonder if people only like me because of my sob story."

"Wouldn't you want to know for sure?" Rafi asked.

River's shoulder rose by barely a centimeter. "I just want people to like me."

All this time, in the hierarchy of influencers on this island, Rafi thought River was above it all. He wasn't trying to shill anything like everyone here was. He wasn't obsessed with his phone and his brand and putting out a certain image. But now she knew he cared about that stuff maybe more than anyone else here. At the core, River was just like everybody else. He was selling a story, desperately hoping you looked anywhere but at the real him.

"So you believe me?"

Rafi considered herself a good judge of character, someone who could always tell if a person was lying. And every bone in her body told her that River was telling her the truth about Tracy. It was funny—the truth was all Rafi ever wanted, so why did it feel like socks on Christmas morning? A gift she didn't particularly want and could hardly muster up the appreciation for? The truth of River's case was boring, and worse, off the record. She couldn't talk about it on her podcast, and if she did, he'd never confirm it. Ironically enough, Rafi couldn't tell the real story for the exact same reason River concealed the truth too: No one would believe the absurdity of a pack of dingoes killing a girl.

Rafi saw her podcast, her pending deal with SteerCat Media, her dream of becoming a famous investigative reporter—all disappearing into thin air. *Poof*. She couldn't let all her dreams go that easy, not without a fight. The only way she saw out of this mess was to hold on to some versions of River's truth and not the others. She could choose to believe that River was telling the truth about Tracy's disappearance, but not Sierra's. Her story was still too much of a mystery, and happening in real time, with Rafi right in the thick of it. A new case for Rafi to pursue.

"I believe you," Rafi said. What she didn't say was that she still didn't have enough information to believe him in regards to Sierra's disappearance. Which meant he was still a suspect.

And just like that, Rafi had a new mission: Find Sierra.

21

RAFI STOOD BEFORE HER MURDER BOARD ONCE MORE. Even though there was a new mystery afoot, River was still her primary suspect, since he'd been the last one to see Sierra, so the board remained covered in gorgeous images of him. And since Rafi had no pictures of Sierra, she'd had to use the influencer's wilted flower crown in her place. It turned out to be an apt representation of the girl, once thriving and beautiful, now all but forgotten and probably dead.

The longer Rafi stared at her board, the more amped she was to solve this puzzle, but no matter how many hours she spent focusing, she was coming up with blanks on what to do next.

She needed a snack.

Thankfully, there were plenty of banana plants around. But when she went to shake one, nothing fell out. Rafi looked up. There were no bananas to be found, not even unripe green ones. Rafi moved to the next plant and kicked it, but nothing fell out of that one either. She moved onto the next plant. She kicked hard—really giving it her all, even body-slamming it a few times, panting, sweating, hair in her face. All of her frustrations came out on that plant until the stalk cracked in half at the base and keeled over with a slow, yawning crack. No fruit.

In fact, as she looked up at all the plants in the vicinity, she noticed they were newly bare.

All of the fruit, as far as she could see, had been picked clean.

"Paul and Ryan," Rafi hissed, their names curses on her lips.

Rafi didn't stop moving until she was at the seaport. It was fine—she'd get to the bottom of this fruit situation and interview them as witnesses-slash-possible suspects in the Sierra disappearance at the same time.

Paul and Ryan sat just outside the entrance, a huge pile of bananas, coconuts, and mangoes mounded beside them like a sideshow curiosity. Seemed like they'd expanded their business.

"What fresh hell is this?" Rafi muttered upon seeing the monstrosity.

Ryan and Paul were on their feet immediately, arms spread as wide as their smiles. "Look at this," Paul said. "When you told us to disrupt the food industry, I can't lie—we were a little apprehensive."

"It was a big risk. But as my skiing shaman always says, 'Big risk, painless death.'"

"We weren't sure it was going to work."

"But after a few low points, which included minutes of virtual therapy—"

"And high points, which included three different angel investors—"

"We're happy to report that business. Is. Booming!"

"All we need now is a snappy company name."

"At first we were thinking of going with 'It's Bananas!' "

"Simple, cheeky, great SEO."

"But with the addition of mangoes and coconuts to our line, it just doesn't fully capture what we're about, you know?"

"So then we decided to go with 'ManGoes (Coco)Nuts for Bananas.' "

"But the feedback we were getting from our focus group was that it makes it seem like we only have four bananas."

"And as you can see, we have roughly three hundred times that."

"So we're still trying to come up with the right name, but other than that, *wow*, right?"

"You're big impressed, yes?"

Was there cocaine on this island? It was the only thing that could explain what Rafi had just borne witness to.

But she chose to ignore every nonsensical word that had just come out of Ryan's and Paul's mouths and focus on first things first: getting some food. Rafi approached the pile like it was a stack of Jenga bricks, looking for the loosest fruit to pluck, lest she accidentally cause a fruitslide that crushed every life-form on this island.

The roundness of the coconuts made them too unstable; she wasn't going to touch those. She found a banana that was barely holding on, and grabbed it. The mound stayed intact. "Thanks."

"That'll be fifteen dollars," Paul said.

"What?" Rafi asked. "Fifteen *dollars*?"

"Don't balk at the price, Rafi," Ryan said.

"Balk!" Paul said. "Big impressed with our word usage?"

"Fifteen dollars is a reasonable price—"

"For a single banana!?" Rafi said.

"I don't know if you noticed, but bananas are scarce," Ryan said.

"*Very* scarce."

"We're being generous here."

"Bananas are scarce because you picked them all!" Rafi said.

"You can Venmo us."

Rafi could've chipped her teeth with how hard she was clenching her jaw. "I can't Venmo you, I don't have internet access."

To their credit, both Ryan and Paul looked sorry for Rafi. Paul even frowned as he gently pried the banana out of her fingers, remaining patient when she would not let go. He got it eventually, though. It was mushy now, and the peel had split in a few places, but he got it.

"You can't spare one banana?" Rafi asked. "Just one?"

"I can't just start giving product away," Paul said, as if the concept of charity was untenable. "What would people think of me? What will that do to my reputation? Do you have any idea who my father is?"

The edges of Rafi's vision began to get hazy, and a thin, crackling noise filled her ears, but she could not blame this on the blazing hot sun or even her acute hunger. No, the absurdity of this hellhole, nonexistent music festival was finally starting to get to her. She could feel herself physically deteriorating. Paul and Ryan must've seen it too, because they looked at her funny, though they mistook her weakness for anger.

"I don't get why you're so upset about this," Ryan said. "We're just trying to make some cash. Everyone on this island is basically doing the same thing."

"What are you talking about?"

"We heard there's someone livestreaming from the beach, charging people to have the honor of vicariously vacationing through him."

"And there's this one girl who's just started mindset coaching from her tent. So enterprising."

"*So* inspirational," Paul said.

The noise in Rafi's ears took on the high-pitched squeal of a cat in an alley fight. People had figured out how to make money here? They were getting richer while she couldn't even afford a mushy banana? "They're just influencers."

"Don't knock influencers, Rafi," Ryan said. "They have real jobs. They get products and tell us if they're good or not."

"That is not a real job," Rafi said. "I too buy products and determine for myself whether they are good or not."

"Yeah, but are you making six figures doing that?"

It was funny how quickly Rafi's urge to laugh had turned into the need to sob so hard that her tears could propagate a new growth of fruit all over the island. But Rafi could not let this madness overwhelm her. If she started to think about the big picture too much, she'd be paralyzed by it. She needed to think of the issue at hand, and that was that a banana had just been taken out of hers. "You do realize what you're doing, don't you?" she told the boys. "You've taken something that was free and commodified it. You have a monopoly on the fruit. You've created a *literal* Banana Republic!"

Paul and Ryan looked at each other briefly, then directed their blank stares back at Rafi. "I think you just found our company name!"

"There already is a company called Banana Republic!" Rafi never thought she'd be screaming about a clothing retailer on a deserted island in the middle of nowhere, but here she was.

"I'll get my lawyer on it. By the time Herman's done with them, this so-called Banana Republic will be so tied up in legal fees, they'll have to file for bankruptcy."

"I don't think that's how lawsuits work!"

"Rafi, I've been in and out of litigation ever since I set my pet tiger loose on my nanny," Ryan said. "Please. Leave the rich people shit to the rich shit." He shook his head, having misspoken. "Rich shit*s*."

Rafi left before she was subjected to any more of this conversation. In her rush to get out of there, she forgot to ask the non-twins about Sierra.

183

22

Rafi stood before Greer, who sat in the shade of a palm tree. The girl was talking, though Rafi was not sure if the conversation was meant for her or the invisible audience in Greer's phone, its front-facing camera never too far from her face.

Whatever Greer was talking about, Rafi wasn't paying attention and cut her off midsentence. "Don't you care anymore that Sierra Madre is still missing?" Rafi asked. "You came to me crying about that."

Greer's gaze momentarily slipped from her phone's magnetic pull to land on Rafi. "Are you kidding? Sierra is obviously at Fly Fest partying with Hella. She's so lucky."

If it hadn't been painfully obvious before that Rafi would not get any help looking for Sierra, it was now. Rafi needed to get back to the reason she was here, talking to Greer.

"I like your necklace," Rafi said. "Is that copper?"

Greer looked down at the space between her collarbones, where a pair of round rings encircled her neck. The necklaces were accented with a few beads, spread equally apart. "Oh, yeah," she said. "They're energy rings. They give you amazing energy and fill your life with good vibes, and in difficult times like these they're great as a gift for yourself or your loved ones, hashtag ad."

Rafi forced herself to smile.

Rafi held the copper-energy-ring necklace up for Peggy. "Each bead represents one of life's essential elements. And as an added bonus, people swear that it's supposed to grant you all your deepest desires. It's handcrafted by at least a hundred different Andean artisans all born after December 1990 but before January 1991. But I'm sure you've already seen it featured in *Vogue* and on Amazon dot com."

Greer hadn't said any of that about the necklace, but it was probably true. And Rafi felt her hopes rise as Peggy touched it, carefully caressing the beads. Until they let their hand drop, leaving Rafi holding the necklace limply. "No."

Rafi wordlessly, desperately, pointed at the hideous branch sculptures in the room, but Peggy didn't see, already back to their phone once again. "Please," Rafi said, trying once more. This was as far as her plan went—making a trade so that Peggy would let her have the internet. Two seconds with Paul and Ryan, and Rafi was beginning to realize she wouldn't get anywhere with the people here. She'd already surveyed most everyone to see what they knew about Sierra's whereabouts, and she wasn't sure she could withstand more conversation. Her street work, as far as Rafi was concerned, was done. Now it was about research. Plus the whole getting-rescued thing, which was also up there on her priorities list, just not before she solved this new tiny little case.

"I need more help if I'm ever going to find out what happened to Sierra. I was going to start doing interviews again, but the people I just talked to tried to charge me an obscene amount of money for a banana."

"Those jock guys?" Peggy asked. "How do you tell them apart?"

"Ryan grew up in a soap opera, and I'm pretty sure Paul has no idea who his father is."

"They sound fascinating," Peggy said, though their attention was almost entirely consumed by the newly minted, internet sensation pet turtle on their lap. They stroked the animal's shell with a gentle hand.

"Is the necklace a new trophy from another girl River killed?"

Rafi had to think about her answer for a second, then laughed nonchalantly. "No. But I actually don't think he killed Tracy anymore."

"You don't say."

"But the jury's still out on Sierra. River may be the—"

"Serial killer of your dreams?" Peggy leaned forward, the turtle sliding forward on their knees like a precariously piled dish full of food. "You have no leads for this Sierra disappearance, so you're pinning it all on River because a part of you can't accept the fact that you're in love with someone who is nothing more than a beautiful, dumb Australian. Face it, Rafi—you're only interested in River if he's a killer."

Rafi was offended by the accusation. Sure, she had her own biases against River, but she also had mounting evidence against him, plus her own finely honed instincts. The Sierra case was important to her, and to the future of her podcast. It wasn't Rafi's fault that River kept bumbling into the role of lead suspect.

"For the last time, I am not in love with River." Rafi took a deep, composing breath. "And I will find out what happened to Sierra. Now, can you please help me by letting me on the internet?"

"No. Can't." Peggy used a leaf to gingerly tickle the turtle's nose. It snapped its mouth back and bit it. "I know what you're going through. I too was once unimportant and desperate. But now that I'm not, I've kind of forgotten what that feels like and can't really help you out."

It wasn't just Peggy and their internet hoarding or Paul and Ryan and their banana scheme. Random moments of bizarreness were cropping up all over the island, distracting Rafi from her case. But none was more bizarre than the presentation she stumbled onto on the beach.

Jack had made his name on YouTube with his wildly popular tutorials that taught people the finer points of shellacking on a coat of makeup. He'd decided to pick up the habit again, but without his pro camera or studio lighting or any makeup to speak of, he had to innovate. Instead of editing and posting a video, he was doing live, in-person tutorials, and instead of a studio, he had a studio audience. Rows of people sat on the beach and watched Jack's every move like he was Bob Ross and his face was his canvas. Though the whole idea of a live makeup tutorial while stranded and scammed on an island seemed like the last thing anybody needed, this was actually well attended, and Rafi could sort of understand why.

The island was starting to wear on people. The relentlessly scorching sun, the precious little supply of sunscreen, and the fact that there were plenty of facial cleansers but not a single sink anywhere on the island was doing a number on people's skin. That was where Jack came in.

And though all Rafi wanted to do right now was sulk in her tent until the sand gathered over her, swallowing her fully into the beach, she instead sat in the back row of Jack's audience. This was where her feelings of frustration and hopelessness had ultimately led. She wondered if this was how cult leaders got their disciples: Find people at their most desperate and then distract them with a show. Rafi was never going to fall for whatever Jack was selling, but she really was curious to see what he would use for makeup when his precious kit had been lost to airport purgatory since day one.

"Let's be honest, we all look like pigs," Jack began from his makeshift stage (a platform of bedside crates collected from Tent City.) "We may not have makeup, but that's no excuse to not be fierce. And if you really think about it, what if the only reason we're not being allowed into the real Fly Fest yet is because we're tragically letting our appearances fall by the wayside? Fly Fest doesn't want uggos clogging their Insta—it wants glamour! And we can be glamorous. We just have to beat our faces."

He'd fashioned a little table out of a trunk suitcase and gestured toward the beauty essentials he'd placed atop it. Rafi craned her neck to see over the rows of heads before her. She wasn't sure what she was looking at, but it seemed like Jack would be fashioning makeup essentials from things found in nature.

"Now, I've showed you some of these already," Jack continued, "but I've been doing research, and you guys are going to go clinically insane when you see my new line of products."

He picked up a jagged thing that fit in the palm of his hand but didn't look like it belonged in anyone's makeup bag. "THIS is tree bark!" Jack took a lighter to it and lit the edge on fire, blowing it out almost as quickly. In one skilled motion he carefully swooped the charred edge of wood over the delicate rim of his eyelid. "Now it's eyeliner!"

The crowd, made up almost exclusively of girls, let out a collective "*Oooh*."

Jack held up his next beauty product, a cluster of red berries. "You should def remember this from last time, but just in case you missed the show—were you doing something better, you dickheads?!—watch as I turn this into lipstick."

"They could be poisonous," Rafi muttered under her breath. But it was a weak mutter, and she had no intention of rushing to the stage to knock the berries out of Jack's hands.

To her own horror, Rafi was equally invested in the result being a red lip or Jack's imminent death.

Jack crushed one berry after another against his mouth, smearing them around until the glistening juices stained his lips red. She waited with bated breath to see if he would drop dead. But Jack only licked the excess berry juice off his lips like a lion after a kill and smiled at his audience, very much alive.

From a pouch, he pinched a sprinkling of pinkish dirt. "I scraped this off the clay rocks on the cliffy side of the beach. This will work really well for eyeshadow." He used the pad of a ring finger to dab the rock powder gingerly onto both eyelids, and by this point Rafi was pretty astonished. Not because he was painting dirt over his eyes, but because he was doing it expertly, and Rafi couldn't even put on sunscreen without leaving streaks.

"Lastly, my best makeup hack," Jack announced. "This step is essential, and after trying at least ten other different options, I can assure you that I settled on the best one. Behold: the island's best alternative to bronzer."

Jack took something out of the trunk at his feet. It looked like a typical white sandwich container, but Rafi knew there was no sandwich inside it. What Rafi could not know was how arduous the path to this specific product had been for Jack.

He found it in the jungle. He'd lumbered over there one day to find a private spot to sob. He'd been troubled by the fact that there was no Fly Fest, that his makeup was gone, that he didn't have his YouTube channel and his thousands—no, millions!—of fans telling him how great he was all the time. Basically, he felt something he hadn't felt in quite a long time.

Doubt.

And so he went to the jungle to let off some steam, not exactly asking the heavens for help so much as shouting a list of demands and formal complaints. Where was the festival? Where was Hella? Why had his makeup gone missing? How could he possibly overcome this? First his eyes were blurry with tears, but after a particularly dramatic crying jag they dried and cleared. It was like this, with red, stinging eyes, that he saw the sow. A big round thing, oinking away. Slow too, so he could easily catch it without much effort if he truly cared to. And he *could* catch it. Just because Jack loved makeup didn't mean he didn't consider himself an alpha male who could do regressively gender-normative things like catch and kill a big pig and strap it to his back and drag it across the jungle and spit roast it and belch. Jack could do all that, but every day he made a conscious choice not to. And anyway, it wasn't the size of the pig or how much nourishment it could provide that interested him. It was what the sow was doing that caught Jack's attention. Because a pig was more than just food. It provided other useful things. It provided what Jack carefully collected and placed inside the Styrofoam sandwich box.

Jack presented the box to the crowd now, like a prop a magician held in front of his audience for inspection before using it to dazzle them with disbelief. When Jack popped the little tab on the side of the box, he did it slowly, with flair, and paused as the lid bounced open. Rafi was too far away to really identify what was inside. All she could see was that it was brown, which wasn't shocking. This was meant to be bronzer, after all. No, the shocking thing would come soon enough.

"I spent all day yesterday tracking a pig," Jack said, seemingly apropos of nothing. "When that slobbering, hairy sow finally left this for me, it was like the answer to all of my problems. I knew immediately it was just the thing."

Rafi scrunched her face, her mind coming up with conclusions that it desperately wanted to reject. *It couldn't be*, she thought.

"That's right," Jack continued. "Pig dookie."

The announcement was met with silence, and Jack filled it by laughing like what he'd just said was a joke, but it obviously was most definitely not a joke.

"What?" Rafi said to herself. She was trying to understand. Jack followed a pig all day in the jungle, watched it defecate, and his first thought was *bronzer*?

Yes. That was it. That was as simple as the explanation got, and yet, Rafi still could not comprehend what her own eyes were seeing. Or what her ears were hearing.

Jack continued to giggle. "I know it may sound silly, but manure has been used by so many different cultures throughout the ages for so many fascinating things. Like, did you know that some people use manure, as, like, plant food? Wild, right?"

Not wild, Rafi thought with increasing dread. *That* was

definitely not wild. She then watched as Jack bent to retrieve something else from the trunk. A single slice of the cheese sandwich bread. He folded it in half, and of course it did not split like regular bread would. It did not even crack.

"As you know from our other tutorials, this bread is almost the exact same texture as your average makeup sponge, but even better because it's completely disposable and most likely biodegradable. Now, you could just wash it after every application, if you're cheap, but just know that salt water *will* cause the bread to double in size every time. Heck, leave it in salt water long enough and you'd have yourself a cute little floatation device that you could probably float home in! But we're not here to talk about ways to get off the island."

Jack then proceeded to dip a corner of the white bread into a dollop of literal pig poop, and applied it to his cheekbone like it was something out of a Kylie Jenner cosmetic palate. He smoothed it over both cheeks, making them look sharp, popping them out, blending until he looked perfectly tanned and contoured. The crowd was stunned into silence, with a few bouts of nervous laughter sputtering forth from the girls.

"I know, it might seem pretty *out there* if you've never done this before," Jack continued. "But this is also a cool way to turn off your mind. Trick yourself into thinking this is actually bronzer. If you're willing to do anything to get to Fly Fest, then this is nothing. And remember, none of your followers will know what this actually is. As I famously like to say, *you can't smell Instagram!*"

Too many heads bobbed in agreement.

"And there you have it," Jack said. "Don't I look fabulous?"

The absolute travesty of it all was that he did. That weaselly, skid-marked rascal looked like a million bucks. The whole thing made Rafi's gut fill with a heavy dread, and just like that, the Sierra Madre situation took a backseat to a new, unnamable threat. Rafi couldn't pinpoint exactly why Jack's makeup tutorial felt like the harbinger of something terrible, but she couldn't shake the sensation. Like a coming wave when you're already neck deep.

23

SHE PROBABLY SHOULD'VE LEFT WELL ENOUGH ALONE.
Jack wanted to put poop on his face? Fine. Let him.

But try as she might, Rafi was physically averse to letting
things slide. Where there was an injustice in the world, she
needed to be on the side that would make things right. And
while poop makeup wasn't exactly an injustice, it was most
certainly wrong.

Rafi had seen a lot of weird tutorials on the internet, but
what she'd just witnessed by Jack was beyond the pale. What
made it worse, though, was that other people had witnessed
the same thing she had, but they *believed* in it. They believed
in Jack.

Rafi didn't understand why he had such a big audience. She
knew that online, his fans had put him on a pedestal of mythic
proportions. Rumors swirled that he had a twenty-three-acre
winter estate in Wyoming, that he had a standing ticket on
the first spaceship to the moon, that as a baby he'd taken the
world's first selfie with Nelson Mandela. Jack could kill a
puppy in one of his videos, and Rafi suspected his followers
would praise him and be all, "The bitch deserved it!!!"

But the online dedication Jack garnered had fully breached

the confines of the internet and followed him here, to this strange place where logic and reason seemed to have evaporated under the sun's unrelenting blaze. There was a group of influencers getting ready to go hunting for pig feces right now, and Rafi had to believe it was more than just Jack's flair for dramatics or his outsize personality that made people flock to him.

Most of all, Rafi couldn't understand how the power dynamics on this island had so suddenly shifted. She could admit she never really had power to begin with, but it wasn't so long ago that she stood on the check-in desk with her mic in her hand and people listened to *her*. Sure, she'd told a little lie, but it was a million times better than telling people to put crap on their faces!

Rafi found Jack's tent in Tent City, its door flap pulled back. He was inside, busy fiddling with something in his carry-on. This tent was different than Peggy's. Standard size, with a standard cot and a little square nightstand next to it. But it was still the lap of luxury as far as Rafi was concerned. She knocked on one of the rounded plastic poles that held up the structure. When Jack turned and saw her, his face, surprisingly, lit up.

"Well if it isn't Rafi San Antonio!"

The positive response to his tutorial had clearly put Jack in a good mood. "Francisco," Rafi corrected. "I saw your tutorial."

"Oh yeah? Are you here for a makeover?"

"Of course not. You can't tell people to put feces on their faces, Jack."

The corners of Jack's berry lips slipped downward, and he placed his hands on his hips. "And why not?"

"Because feces have, like . . . diseases. Probably. The boars on this island could be sick. And anyway, makeup is the last thing we should be focusing on right now. We need to find a way home."

Jack sighed and took a step closer to Rafi. With only a few feet of space between them, she could see the details of his face. He was no longer that slightly sunburnt boy with the chapped nose, wallowing ankle-deep in the ocean. He was all made up, looking like a secretary right out of the 1980s about to climb the corporate ladder straight to executive assistant. Rafi had missed the part of the tutorial where Jack explained what he used as foundation, but whatever it was didn't match his skin exactly. His neck was a shade deeper than his face, which was pale and vaguely orange. A melting Creamsicle.

"Correct me if I'm wrong, sweetheart, but wasn't it you who stood on a whole damn desk at the seaport and told every single concertgoer present to stay put? 'The party's still on,' you said. 'Hella is here,' you said."

"I lied."

Jack went so still that the only change in him came from the angry heat coloring his cheekbones. It seemed to make the unpleasant odor of his bronzer waft off his face. Jack was a skilled orator, but Rafi hadn't realized just how captivating he could also be without having to say a thing. His silence was beginning to scare her. She needed to intersperse the quiet with more words.

"I never saw Hella. I just wanted everyone to stay on this island for stupid, selfish reasons. But I realize that was a huge mistake. And now that you know that Hella isn't here and Fly Fest is definitely not happening, maybe you can help me convince everyone that we need to send for help and get off this island, like, as soon as we possibly can."

When Jack took his next breath, it was slow and methodical, his chest rising and falling with the action. "Well, you were either lying then or you're lying now. And I choose to believe you're lying now."

"Jack—"

"It's not just you who's seen Hella. Greer saw her, too. How do you explain that?"

Rafi couldn't, and her silence seemed to validate Jack's point. He smiled and tilted Rafi's chin up with the tip of his index finger. "Now, all this flip-flopping—emphasis on 'flopping'—is really causing premature aging to your already-tragic general facial area. You sure I can't offer you that makeover?"

Rafi shook herself free of his touch and took a step back, shivering in disgust at his suggestion. "Emphatically no. Never," she said. "Why *poop*?"

"That's rich, coming from someone who stepped in poop."

His comeback made the kind of no sense that knocked her out for a few seconds. But she snapped out of it. "Once, Jack. I stepped in poop *once*. By accident. I didn't fall face-first into it and decide it was a *whole look*. Why couldn't you use soil? The island is full of soil!"

"Have you looked around?" Jack shot back. "Most of this island is sand or rock! The soil in the jungle is too dry and crumbly, and it doesn't rain enough for mud."

"There's literally water all arou—"

"THIS—" Jack cut her off and pointed to his cheekbones— "is the perfect consistency for bronzer. Do you even know how hard it is to get this kind of viscosity? Did you see how well it took to the bread sponge? Well, *did you?*"

It was hard to tell, but beneath the makeup, Jack had turned red, and he took a moment to compose himself, pressing his fingertips against his temples. "Rafi," he said, calmer now, "why do you hate beauty?"

Rafi's eyebrows pinched together. "I don't hate beauty."

"Really? Because literally everything about all this"—he gestured to her person—"tells me that you do."

"That's . . . offensive."

"You obviously put no effort into how you look—"

"I bought this shirt especially for—"

"Your hair is a mess."

Rafi sheepishly combed her fingers over her forehead only to discover that her bangs had migrated somewhere over her hairline. She tamped them down as best she could.

"Let's face it," Jack continued, "you look like a functioning heroin addict."

"Why are you saying all of this?"

"Be*cause*." Jack gripped Rafi's wrist the way a concerned

friend who just caught you scarfing down caffeine pills might. "You could really use my tutorial."

"I don't need makeup."

"Full offense, but yes, you do." Jack sighed. "It isn't just about the makeup, Rafi. That's what you don't understand. Did you ever think that maybe what people want right now— more than going home with their tails between their legs—is a little bit of comfort? And that maybe that's something that I alone can provide for them?"

"Comfort?"

"Yes, comfort! The people here want something to take their minds off the fact that they're not hanging out with hot musicians, and the villas aren't here, or that their only choice of food is between a ten-dollar banana and a cheese sandwich that might explode if left out in the sun too long."

"Paul and Ryan are only charging you ten dollars?"

"You still don't get it," Jack said. "I'm putting a little bit of beauty back in people's lives. Before I started my tutorials here, people's complexions looked less human and—thanks to that vengeful demon in the sky you call the sun—more lobster. I'm giving them something easy, something that makes them feel good again. Being beautiful is a morale booster. It's what sets us apart from the animals. It's what's saving our lives, damn it!"

As he said all this, Jack's eyes twinkled with the sort of verve that the island had sucked right out of Rafi. She felt jealous that he could be this optimistic when the situation was this dire. But then, his very attitude was proof that what he was saying was true.

The makeup tutorials were making people happy.

Even if it was also covering them in poop.

"But rescue—"

"Screw rescue!" Jack said with an incredulous burst of laughter. "People can't *touch* rescue. They can't *see* it. You might as well be promising them unicorns."

"And you're promising them Fly Fest."

"Oh, that's real," Jack said. "Hella is somewhere on this island, that's a fact."

It felt to Rafi like she was talking to a brick wall. But she finally understood there was no getting through to Jack. He really believed the creators of Fly Fest were just hiding in the shadows somewhere, their little festival so exclusive, so elite, that this island was just a holding area before they could cherry-pick who got in. And for Jack, the only way to gain access was to look as perfect as possible, using whatever means necessary.

Rafi said her next words carefully, deliberately. "Fly Fest. Doesn't. Exist."

Jack took a step closer to her, his eyes suddenly laser-focused and serious. For a second, Rafi saw his delusions slip away. "I have been telling my followers about this festival for months. I did not pay thousands of dollars for something that does not exist." His words were just as deliberate, if a bit icier. "I am not a loser, languishing and desperate on a beach. I will not have the world out there laughing at me. Uh-uh. Couldn't be me."

Jack stepped back and seemed to compose himself, the YouTube-ready smile back on his face with the flip of an internal switch. "How come you never used the lip gloss I gave you?"

Because she'd spent it all to decorate her useless murder board that she was too embarrassed to talk about. "I lost it."

Jack looked disappointed, but eventually shrugged. "I have just the trick." He reached for Rafi's hand, and she felt a pinprick on her finger. She cried out involuntarily, but Jack held onto her hand. She didn't know what he'd pierced her with, but he definitely had pricked her skin, because there was a bead of blood on the tip of her index finger. She was too stunned to move of her own volition, but Jack guided her finger up to her mouth, and she let him. He slid the blood across her bottom lip.

"There." Jack handed her a compact mirror. "Better already."

He was right. Her lips looked rosy and plump, and she didn't look half-dead. And yet. Rafi would not accept that this was now the way of things. She rejected the new normal. And when she locked eyes with Jack, it was with a clearheadedness she had not experienced for days.

"None of this is real," she said. "This isn't real lipstick and that isn't real bronzer and nothing about this is glamorous, no matter how hard you try to convince people it is."

"Oh, young Rafi." Jack leaned forward so that his cheek was nearly touching hers. "Perception *is* reality."

When Jack pulled back, his smile was radiant. "One day you have to let me do a full makeover on you because, I swear, if Hella isn't letting us into Fly Fest because you insist on looking like—"

"I am *not* a heroin addict."

"I was going to say like someone who stuck her finger in an electrical socket, geez! Anyway, if Hella is holding out because of you, I'm going to be really sad." Jack pushed out his bottom lip in a perfect berry-stained pout. "And by sad, I mean violently pissed off, so do think about it, 'kay?"

24

Rafi made her way back to the beach, taking the slowest, most meandering route possible so she could be alone with her thoughts. How did she get herself into this mess? It was easy to look at the totally bonkers shenanigans and schemes these high-key lunatics were cooking up and say she was not a part of it. But that was a lie. Because everything that was happening on this island was, in one way or another, all her fault. Her brilliant Big Lie to get everyone to stay had worked too well, and like a mad scientist working on fumes and ambition, Rafi had turned this island into a petri dish of disaster. Now she felt like she could do nothing but sit back and watch it fester.

Rafi longed for a boat. And when she got to the beach, she thought maybe she had manifested one, because there was a crowd huddled by the shore, and they were waving wildly. There was only one reason to be that excited.

"A boat?" she whispered. Rafi tapped on shoulders and pushed on others, trying to get past the rows of people to see what they all saw. "What is it? What's everybody talking about?"

Finally, someone—a girl with uncommonly long earrings—heard her questions.

"We're on TV!" Earrings said.

"What?"

"Look!" Earrings pointed deeper into the crowd, but all Rafi could see were people's backs. She broke through another layer until she was closer to the center of the inward-facing horde, and that was when she saw it. Greer, holding up her phone and looking into its front-facing camera.

"I can't believe I'm on the news!" she squealed, happy tears streaming down her face. "My grandparents watch the news!"

"Are you live?" Rafi asked, but of course no one heard her. "Is she LIVE?" she asked, louder this time. It was happening. Someone had managed to make contact. The people of the outside world would now know—about the festival being a scam, about the lack of food and accommodations, the total lack of security. The disappeared influencer. The danger. The nonsense! "We're getting rescued!"

But a boy beside Rafi shushed her. "She's being interviewed by Wolf Blitzer."

"Yep!" Greer said, apparently full-on FaceTiming with Wolf Blitzer. "Everything's great here, Wolf! We're having the time of our lives!"

"No," Rafi said. "No no no—" The ridiculousness had gone on long enough. She had to put a stop to this. Jack may have convinced the world that everything was good here with one

205

single Instagram post, but denying the facts would only cause more trouble, or worse. Rafi was about to lunge for Greer, but before taking a single step Earrings, was suddenly holding on to her wrist. "What are you doing?"

"I'm going to talk to Wolf Blitzer!"

"You can't possibly go on TV looking like that."

Rafi blinked. "What?"

"I'm just trying to spare you a national embarrassment. That look of desperation on your face does nothing for your complexion."

Rafi wrenched her wrist out of the girl's hand.

"*Nothing for your complexion!*" the girl echoed after her, but by now Rafi had gotten away, broken through the layers of people in the circle, and finally reached Greer.

"Greer!" Rafi cried.

"Thanks so much for checking in," Greer said to the phone. "Okayseeyouguyslaterbyeeeee!"

"NOOOO." Rafi yelled it so loud that the force of the sound made her sink to the ground, the coarse white sand biting into her knees. The gathered group dispersed, but Greer hovered over Rafi, wiping the drying tears from her plump cheeks.

"Don't worry," she said to Rafi. "That was only the first interview. Soon we'll get Gayle King, then we'll be on with Hoda Kotb and Jenna Bush Hager, and maybe after that Wayne Brady. But never, *ever* Ellen and her *Game of Games*, because I'm afraid of heights; that lady is a beast with the drop button."

Rafi looked up at Greer, the girl's grinning face blotting out the sun, and all hope. Even so, Rafi had to blink a few times to really see. "I don't understand."

"I paid six thousand dollars to be here," Greer explained. "As Jack says, if anybody asks, we're having the time of our lives."

"But we're not," Rafi said.

"Do you really know that for sure?"

Rafi opened her mouth and closed it again, and for the first time in her life she had the weird sensation of knowing what a fish out of water felt like. Not in the figurative I-don't-fit-in-here way, though that applied, too. But in the literal life-was-slowly-oozing-out-of-her-as-she-lethargically-writhed-on-the-ground-trying-to-breathe way. "Yes," she finally said. "I know that for sure."

Greer leaned down even more. "But do you really?"

Greer did not wait for a rebuttal this time. She wiped her cheeks and skipped away.

Rafi remained on the sand, unable to move. She waited to feel human again.

25

RAFI WANTED OFF. BEFORE FLY FEST THIS PLACE WAS just a crumb on a map, no better or worse than any other uninhabited spit of landmass in the sea. But somehow, without supernatural means; or diabolical, secret mad scientists; or governmental overloads; the people here had managed to turn this place into the stuff of nightmares.

There was no clean water, but all anyone wanted to talk about was a phantom party in the sky. They were all alone, but you'd never know from the pics. Turn over a random rock and Rafi was almost certain you'd find a crab brandishing a selfie stick.

Rafi sat on the sand, using a stick to lazily stoke the small fire she'd made. The strange days on the island started to bleed together to the point that Rafi was beginning to wonder how long she'd actually been here—beginning to doubt phone clocks and calendars. The situation felt, at turns, hopeless, dangerous, and smelly, and the more Rafi dwelled on it, the more the claws of restless anxiety ripped at her insides. Though that may have just been hunger. Rafi couldn't remember the last time she ate. She had an emergency cheese sandwich in her backpack but thought better about reaching for it. She'd heard a rumor that half a sandwich was equal to ten milligrams of LSD, and she needed to keep her mind sharp if she was going to get herself out of this mess. And off this island.

River showed up like a mind reader, though. He found her sitting on a quiet stretch of beach, the tide just threatening to lap up her fire. In his hands were two banana leaf plates with a fish apiece. He held one out. "Hungry?"

Rafi still didn't trust River as far as she could throw him, but she was also starving. "Thank you." She tried not to devour it all in one bite, but it was really delicious. River sat next to her, crossing his ankles in front of him.

"So, what's gotten you down?"

Rafi swallowed the food in her mouth. "I'm not down." Was it that obvious?

"Rafi, there's a reason why I've been nominated for awards and have auditioned for a Spielberg film."

He'd been nominated for four Kids' Choice Awards and had auditioned for an *Elana* Spielberg movie, but Rafi had no idea what that had to do with anything.

"It's because I know about emotions," he explained.

Rafi took another bite of the fish to give herself a moment. He was right, she was down, but she didn't want to sound overly dramatic about it. "I feel like I'm witnessing the fall of human civilization and there's nothing I can do about it."

"Mm-hmm," River said, munching thoughtfully on his own fish. "Yeah, that'll get anybody down."

Being stuck here was bad enough, but Jack's makeup tutorials had only made things worse. People were tracking boars just for their excrement. They were already wearing it on their faces, and some of the boys had even started using it in half-assed attempts to sculpt abs on their torsos. The whole island was starting to stink.

"I just don't get these people," Rafi said. "I'm trying to empathize and think like they do but I just . . . I feel so different from them."

"What makes you feel different?"

"Well, for one thing, I refuse to put poop on my face." It was the obvious, go-to answer. But even before Jack's tutorials, Rafi felt like she didn't belong here. There was a lot that made her different from these people—her values, her interests. But she hated to admit that the thing that ostracized her the most was so surface level. "And I'm not beautiful like they all are."

Rafi had come on this island with a purpose, and she was just trying to get things done and achieve her goals, but at every turn she was reminded that she wasn't beautiful. It was unrelenting, and it was made worse by the fact that it always came out of nowhere, when she was just trying to mind her own business.

Rafi had stopped counting the number of times she'd been called ugly since she got here, but the message had been successfully hammered into her head by now. The only times she usually ever thought about her looks were the few minutes a day she spent glancing in the mirror above the bathroom sink. But here, surrounded by these beautiful people who made their looks their business, the way Rafi looked was starting to weigh on her. The surface of her was all.

"I know I'm so much more than just how I look," Rafi said, "but I never thought I'd have to keep reminding myself of that."

She said all this while focusing on the sand, pinching it, raking her fingers through it like it was her own private Zen island. She was speaking about her feelings, and whenever she spoke about something so vulnerable, she could never do it while looking someone in the eye. But when she dared to cast a glance River's way, she saw a question all over his face, sewing his eyebrows together and tugging his mouth open. "What are you talking about?" he said. "You are beautiful."

Her first instinct was a skeptical one. That this was River lying, saying just the right thing to get her to like him. But that gave way to something akin to understanding. Even if he was lying, it was a kind lie, and it made sense why millions of people hung on every word of his songs. Because when someone like River Stone called you beautiful, you wanted to believe them.

So Rafi chose to believe him, and doing so made her eyes water and her throat tickle. She tucked River's comment away before she let herself get completely overcome by it. "All I care about right now is figuring out what happened to Sierra and getting off this island. But everyone here cares more about their phones or looking good or still getting into Fly Fest, which is ridiculous. So long as Peggy keeps giving them internet and

Jack successfully convinces them to keep smearing poo on their faces, I don't think we're ever getting out of here."

River took another bite of fish and nodded. "I think there's a security-blanket aspect to the whole phone thing."

"Security blanket?"

"Yeah, you know, something that makes you feel good when you're with it. I think it's the same thing with people's phones and posting stuff every day. It's kind of reassuring, isn't it? Safe. Normal. Plus, I think some people—and probably a lot of the people here—are used to posting certain things regularly. A curated list of things to make their lives look better than they actually are. And once you're used to creating a false narrative about yourself, it's hard to break that habit. Not only that—it's really soothing to keep that habit up. Maybe posting about how they wish things would be—and giving off the appearance that everything is perfect and beautiful—feels more reassuring than admitting how crummy things really are."

Rafi watched River as he finished his fish, surprised by how astute he sounded. It actually reminded Rafi of something Jack had said about makeup and comfort. And it made her feel like an idiot for not seeing the same subtext that they were seeing all around them. But still, as nice as words like "comfort" and "soothing" sounded . . . "It's still all lies," Rafi said. "Lies that are hurting us."

"Then it's up to you to tell the truth."

Maybe it was the charm that she swore up and down that

River did not have, but as he looked at her now, with so much earnest belief, Rafi found that she could not look away.

"You have a podcast," River continued. "You reveal the truth to your listeners all the time. Reveal it to them now. And it wouldn't even be off topic—Fly Fest is a musical event. And what's happening here *is* a mystery. Tell the world that it isn't all beautiful and glamorous and that you've been cheated and scammed. Tell the world what it's really like."

His words were like palms on bongos, jolting her, making her nerve endings come alive. River was right. She could talk about the festival on her pod. But as exciting as a shiny new topic to discuss was, her hands were tied.

"I can't get the internet," Rafi said. "I wouldn't be able to upload anything I record until we get back home."

River considered the problem—which Rafi felt was a pretty big one—but like everything else he encountered in life, this insurmountable obstacle didn't seem to be a big deal at all. "Does the timeline really matter?" River asked. "Even if people can't hear it right now, one day they will. And it'll be a true record of what's really happening on this island. You're the only one here who's willing to tell the truth. You have so much power, Rafi, and you don't even know it."

River's words felt as hot and as bright as the fire in front of them. Here was someone who believed in her podcast, believed in *her* and her skills. It touched Rafi, and it ignited something within her. She was starting to feel that spark that she got anytime she had a really good idea. It was a spark that almost instantly blazed into a roaring fire, when all she wanted to do was dive headfirst into a new plan.

"I could talk about Fly Fest being a fiasco—on-the-ground reporting, firsthand accounts. I mean, I've got access that real journalists can't even dream about."

River nodded emphatically, right there with her. He even picked up his guitar and started strumming a tune, an upbeat, yet dramatic ditty that totally matched Rafi's mood.

"And I can talk about Sierra's mysterious disappearance and how nobody here cares because they've all been brainwashed into thinking she found a secret party on an undiscovered part of the island," she said.

River's fingers worked overtime, his song taking on a high-stakes cadence.

"And I can talk about Hella being here."

River's song stopped with an abrupt, discordant note. "What?"

"Everyone thinks she's here," Rafi said. "I mean, again, I have *no* idea how those rumors started, but they are persistent. People keep hearing her around the mountain. And the fact that people believe she's actually here has really changed, like . . . the culture, on this island."

River slowly set his guitar down and leveled Rafi with his most serious look.

"Rafi, please believe me when I tell you that Hella is nowhere on this island."

A crowd was suddenly gathering not too far down the beach, and at the center of it were Paul and Ryan, out of breath. Something was up, and Rafi and River didn't even consult each other when they both decided to see what was going on.

The non-twins had news, and in between gulps of breath they announced it together.

"We saw Hella Badid!"

26

Encountering Hella Badid on this island had become as common as lip fillers on an Insta thot, but this felt different. For one thing, Ryan and Paul didn't usually venture far from their banana business, making this sudden appearance unusual; plus, there was an urgency to what they were saying. But most of all, they'd claimed to see Hella. Until now, people had only heard her voice.

"We were hiking up the mountain," Ryan said, "trying to look for more fruit but mostly also to get some cardio."

"Cardio's gotten a bad rap lately, but it's part of a well-rounded fitness routine," Paul explained to the circle of beachgoers hanging on his every word. "We've been doing push-ups and lifting rocks, which is great for your biceps and triceps and upper-body definition, but it ignores your core."

"As my late personal trainer said as he sank into molten lava, 'You can't ignore the core!'" Ryan said. "Walking up an incline isn't really enough either, though."

"We ran it," Paul said. "We pretended the mountain was a *tour de stade*."

"A *tour de stade* is Chinese for climbing up and down every step of a stadium while being a stud."

"Will you get on with it!" Jack snapped. Rafi didn't realize he was among the gathered crowd, but it made sense: Hella sightings were his bread and butter.

"We saw her, man!" Ryan said. "We saw Hella Badid!"

Rafi sneaked a glance at River. His features had settled into concentrated lines.

"First of all, she called to us with the sweetest, softest angel voice."

Paul nodded vigorously. "Also, boobs: huge."

"Booty: round," Ryan said.

"She looked like a dominatrix supermodel beauty queen," Paul said.

"Body like Jennifer Lopez's."

"She looked like Destiny's Child."

"Yeah, but, with like, Madonna's style."

"With lips like Angelina Jolie's."

"So hot," Paul and Ryan concluded in unison.

At this point Jack had joined them at the center of the circle and turned to the listening crowd, positioning himself between the two jocks like he'd been with them on that mountain the entire time. "You see?" Jack said. "She's here. Hella is among us!"

River tapped Rafi on the shoulder and cocked his chin in the universal silent gesture for *Can I steal you away from these delusional dumbasses?* "They're lying," he hissed to Rafi when they were out of earshot.

"Why do you say that?"

"Because Hella doesn't have the voice of an angel. And

she doesn't look like Destiny's Child or dress like Madonna or have lips like Angelina Jolie. I'm pretty sure Ryan and Paul were just quoting O-Town lyrics."

"For the last time, what the hell is a Ho-Town?" Rafi asked.

"O-Town is an old boy band, and those lyrics are from their song 'Liquid Dreams.'"

Rafi couldn't help making a disgusted face. Why did she always insist on asking questions when the answers were always, inevitably, so grody.

"Don't you see?" River whispered. "They're making the whole thing up."

Rafi had seen Hella only in video clips and magazines, but River was right; she definitely didn't look the way Paul and Ryan described her. And even Rafi knew her voice was no angel's. "But what do they have to gain by lying?"

"I don't know," River said. "But something's up. Either they're deliberately doing it or they saw something and only thought it was her."

"Well, what do we do?"

River took a deep breath and gave a curt, decisive nod. He walked back into the circle, breaking up the whispers and questions being lobbed at Ryan and Paul, and now Jack, too. "I don't know what you think you saw," River told them, "but it wasn't Hella. I'll go up the mountain myself right now and prove it."

The whispers in the crowd were replaced by an awed sort of silence. Maybe because here was a superstar, taking on the responsibility of doing something hard, and at such a late hour.

218

"You'll do no such thing!" Jack said. "I'll go with you."

Rafi stepped up. Like hell she was missing this. "Me too!"

So it was settled. There would be a second expedition with the three of them. This time to find the truth.

Since they left almost immediately, Rafi took with her the only thing she needed: her microphone. If they really did see Hella up there, Rafi would be able to use the mic to record her. Concrete, tangible evidence—the only thing that mattered.

Not that Rafi believed they'd find Hella. Jack was way past delusional, and River was so certain his girlfriend wasn't on this island that there must've been a good reason.

"Who takes a microphone to a luxury music festival on a private island?" Jack asked.

The three of them were already halfway up the mountain, and it'd taken Jack this long to make a comment on Rafi's mic, even though he'd been eyeballing it since the start of their hike.

"Show me a luxury music festival on a private island and we can talk."

"Oh, it's here," Jack said. "Trust me, it's here."

Rafi gripped her mic tight. She didn't want to anthropomorphize it, but she still felt the need to protect and defend it from anyone who scoffed at it. "This mic holds power," Rafi said. "It could save us all."

"I feel like you're about to interview me on a red carpet,"

Jack said. "Or tell me I'm the next contestant on *The Price Is Right*."

The now-perpetual teeth-grinding ache in Rafi's jaw was flaring up again. "It's for my podcast."

"Oh, right, your podcast." Jack quickened his step so he was no longer standing so close to Rafi. "I am so excited to listen to it never."

The thing about mics was that not only could they record sound, but at just the right velocity they made great blunt force objects. Rafi briefly fantasized smacking it against the back of Jack's head. But she was horrified by her own violent reverie; it reminded her of River. Well, the old River. The one from her now-debunked conspiracy theory. Rafi turned around to see him but was instantly blinded by his flashlight beam.

"Where did you get a flashlight?"

"Some girl gave it to me."

Naturally. The sun had gone down fully by now, and darkness creeped through the vines and fronds. The farther they went, the more they needed to use their hands to help guide the way. Jack smacked intrusive leaves out of his face, and Rafi held out her mic, pointing it into the darkness like it could ward off whatever scary thing might be hiding in its shadows. She almost tripped over a tree root, but River's hand was quick and caught her arm before she went down.

When she straightened, Rafi found she was standing too close to him and that his flashlight beam shone only on their feet. River's face was shrouded in dark, his features a muddy, menacing swamp. And though she might not have been able to

220

see him clearly, Rafi could still feel him. The air was warm but he was warmer. The heat exuded out of him with every breath he took, and Rafi felt it landing on her chest.

She probably should've turned away, but she couldn't. Rafi found that she was drawn to the darkness, to the mysterious, humongous hulk of a thing he was. It pulled her in.

"You okay?" River's voice broke the strange spell, and Rafi took a step back, nearly tripping again. "Fine."

"Hey, guys," Jack said, "unless step-and-repeats grow on trees, I think I found something!"

River shined his flashlight up ahead, and the beam of light splashed against a wall. No, not a wall—an eight-foot-tall banner held up by a metal frame that looked like a clothing rack. The banner seemed to be made out of some kind of waterproof canvas, not unlike the tents in Tent City. The words FLY FEST appeared in a pattern all over the banner, and it was the exact shade of neon pink as Rafi's shirt. If she stood in front of it, she'd disappear and look like little more than a hairball on legs. Rafi had seen these kinds of walls before—they were what celebrities posed in front of at award shows or premieres while they got their pictures taken.

Jack saw his moment. He stood before the banner with his phone up, snapping away. But he groaned and muttered, "No flash on my front-facing camera." He tossed his phone to Rafi without warning, but she still managed to catch it one-handed. "Take my pic!" he barked, his angry face switching quickly to a smiling one like he was glitching. Rafi clicked a pic, the flash bursting.

As fascinating as the step-and-repeat banner was, River, who'd seen so many over the last few years, didn't seem to care for it. He was more interested to see what was behind it.

"Uh, Jack, Rafi? We're here."

They'd reached the mountaintop without even knowing it. The place was a razed, flat clearing. Not a small clearing either. The space was half a football field, empty like someone had purposefully mowed down a rain forest worth of trees.

River shone his flashlight on surfaces that glinted and reflected the light back. On the four corners of the mountain peak were huge spotlights, tall as three-story buildings. There was scaffolding all around, a tall platform which was clearly supposed to be a stage. River climbed on top of it, gravitating toward his natural habitat.

"I think that's the stage!" Jack said, way too excited. River and Rafi were taking in the site like it was a cursed ancient archeological find. But Jack was acting like he'd just found buried treasure.

"A performance ground on a mountaintop?" River said. "Doesn't make a whole lot of sense."

"No, it tracks," Rafi said. "This whole festival doesn't make a whole lot of sense."

The metal pipes of the scaffold made it look like a derelict fossil, something that was either just being built or abandoned long ago. It wasn't much, but it was something; a sign that there had been life on this island, at least. That there had been an *attempt* at putting on a festival. It answered the question of whether this fiasco was due to poor planning or if everyone here had just been scammed.

"Don't you people get it?" Jack was practically panting with excitement. "This is proof! This is proof that we're in the right place! That the festival is still on! That we still have a shot to go to it!"

"Uh," Rafi began, "is that what you're getting? 'Cause all I'm getting is *garbage dump*."

"SHHHH!"

Rafi thought Jack was trying to shut her up because he didn't like what she was saying, but then she realized it was because he was trying to hear something else. He whipped his head around, searching for the sound, but Rafi didn't hear anything.

Until, she thought, maybe she did.

A whisper.

Rafi frantically thrust her microphone into the center of the darkness, straining to pick up the sound.

"Do you hear—" she whispered, but this time River was the one to shush her. His dimmed silhouette put an index finger to his lips. He heard it, too.

"Hey, guys."

It was a woman's voice. No inflection. It was impossible to tell if she was excited to see them, or surprised. Whatever she was, she wouldn't come out of hiding. There was no one to connect the voice to, not even the shadow of a person behind the trees. River swung his flashlight fruitlessly. It was a disembodied voice in the dark.

Rafi kept pointing her mic. She tiptoed, following where the voice was coming from.

"I'm so glad you made it," the voice continued. Monotone in its vocal fry. The kind of voice Rafi could easily picture coming out of the lips of a supermodel standing on a white sand beach in a string bikini. "Hella?" Rafi breathed.

"Things are about to get *lit*," the voice said.

Jack, River, and Rafi held their breath. They waited for more, but seconds passed silently on, and the air started to become electric, buzzing with bugs or anticipation.

"HELLA!" Jack squealed, his voice going raspy at the last syllable. The air got louder until it filled with the sound of thunder clapping overhead. Soon the only noise was the fat dollops of rain that began to pound down from the cracked-open sky. "HELLA, WHERE ARE YOU?" Jack yelled.

When no answer came, he spun to face Rafi, whipping around so fiercely that rain flicked off his hair and pelted Rafi in the face. His makeup was decomposing with the rain, all the clay and coal and shit streaming away like a raging sewage drain. "You heard her! She's here!"

Rafi couldn't deny it. She *had* heard. She'd even recorded it. And Jack knew that she had. He swiped the microphone out of her hand and ran.

"HEY!" Rafi yelled after him. "Where are you taking my mic?"

"I have proof!" Jack answered, but his voice was becoming faint as he ran back in the direction from which they had come. "I have proof she's here!"

The rain and dark swallowed Jack up, left no trace of him. Rafi turned to River, who stood immobile, his hair slick and sticking to his cheekbones. Rafi waited for him to say something, because if anyone could explain what they'd just witnessed, it would be him. But for the first time, River Stone had nothing to say.

27

THE RAIN KEPT COMING, BUT IT DID NOT DAMPEN THE party that had spontaneously erupted on the beach. Jack had produced a golden calf: Hella Badid's actual voice, recorded for all to hear. And because she told all who were listening that things were about to get lit, everyone collectively decided that she was right, and made sure her words were made true. Now people from all corners of the island had congregated at the beach, dancing around a fire that grew in defiance of the rain, flames licking the black sky. And Jack, who still had the microphone, played Hella's strange, inimitable voice over and over again. A new favorite song.

It wasn't until Rafi finally caught up to Jack that she was able to wrest the mic out of his hands. But by then the entire beach had already heard the message, and Jack didn't try to take the microphone back. He'd gotten what he wanted, and the party raged on.

Rafi didn't stay, though she couldn't go far, seeing as how she lived mere yards away. So she watched it all from her tent—or, what was once a tent and now mostly resembled an unshapely broken umbrella discarded on a street corner. The fabric she'd used for shelter didn't block out the rain so much as collect it in puddles from where it seeped through like a sieve. Rafi sat strategically in the space that the raindrops sort of missed, knees up and arms wrapped around her legs.

River, on the other hand, was staying pretty dry. His tent was made of much stronger stuff than Rafi's, and as he sat inside it and watched the celebration down the beach, he seemed lost in thought.

Rafi was *all* thought. Thoughts raced through her mind, bouncing off the walls of her skull at such a breakneck pace that she was getting a headache. She stuck her head out just enough to catch River's eye. "You know what this means, don't you?"

River shook his head.

"Jack has evidence now that Hella is here. And look at them, celebrating. He's officially convinced everyone of his delusional idea that the festival is still on. There's no way I'm going to be able to get anyone to send for rescue. Jack won."

"Hella isn't here."

River kept repeating the same thing like a broken record, but it wasn't enough anymore. Not when Jack had proof that said otherwise. Proof that he'd played on a loop.

"You heard her voice. You were there."

"That wasn't her." River shook his head, hearing how silly that sounded. "Okay, it *was* her, but she isn't on the island."

The cryptic way River spoke about Hella had always annoyed Rafi, but now it infuriated her. She'd heard Hella's voice for herself—they both had. Why was he still trying to lie about her? And then Rafi understood. "Because you know exactly where she is."

River said nothing, which was all the confirmation Rafi needed. Her heartbeat ticked up slightly, her old suspicions of a murderous River Stone ramping back up again. "And you're the only one who knows where she is?"

"Yes."

Rafi's heart was hammering in her chest now. With Hella seemingly gone from social media, the entire world thought she was on this island, and yet River Stone was the only one— *the only one*—who knew that she wasn't.

Because you did something to her. The thought cemented its place in Rafi's mind, refusing to budge. "Where is she?"

"I can't tell you."

If she'd had something nearby to throw in aimless frustration, Rafi would have, but for now all she could do was let out an involuntary grunt. The noise caught River off guard, and his eyebrows rose as he looked at her.

"You can stop all of this!" Rafi didn't mean for her voice to come out so harsh, but it did, and she wasn't about to take it back now. "Nothing on this island makes sense. You can make it make sense! You can put an end to this madness, tell everyone the truth and make them see how wrong all of this is."

River shook his head, but Rafi wasn't going to let him go that easy. "You're the only one who can save us," she said.

River looked over at the big bonfire, the people dancing around it. Blissful idiots. "They don't need saving."

"Well, I do!" The loudness of Rafi's voice made River stop

and look at her again, his eyes shadowed with pity. But pity was the last thing Rafi needed.

"You talk so much about truth and all the power it has," she said. "But where's your truth now, River? You have the power to change things, and you're keeping it to yourself. You know where Hella is. You probably know where Sierra is."

Sierra's name jogged something in River. He looked affronted. "You still think I had something to do with her disappearance?"

"Of *course* I do! You're shifty and evasive and you refuse to tell the truth about yourself and Hella, much less anything else. I don't trust you about anything."

The rain had fully infiltrated Rafi's broken tent by now, drenching her and her words. River, relatively dry, looked her over with an unreadable expression. But if Rafi wanted something more from him, she wasn't going to get it tonight. River pulled a flap of his tent closed, effectively shutting Rafi out.

MUSICAL MYSTERIES
Season 2: Episode 5
"Where the Hella Is She?"

River Stone is a liar.

He lies about everything. *Everything.* He says his girlfriend isn't on this island, but he can't tell me where she is—probably because he murdered her. *Ugh.* Okay, no, I don't think River is a murderer anymore. I know—plot twist after plot twist after plot twist! I told you this season would be full of surprises! This Hella stuff is probably confusing, so let me start from the beginning.

Hella Badid was supposed to be at Fly Fest, but she never showed up.

Except news has been circulating that she is actually here, hiding somewhere. The rumor that started it all was false. I know that because I was the one who made it up.

Someone here told me that truth has power, so I'm gonna be honest right now. I said that Hella Badid was here, and I did it for selfish reasons. I wanted to keep everyone on this island so I could have more access to River and get the best interview out of him that I could. And why did I need to keep everyone here? Because when we got to the island, we discovered that Fly Fest was a total sham.

That's right. You may believe otherwise, and I

don't blame you. Everyone here has been posting to their social media as if they're chilling in paradise, but they are *lying*. Nobody here is having the fabulously glamorous time that they claim. There isn't a gourmet organic chef—there are cheese sandwiches that everyone is refusing to eat because of increasingly escalating health concerns that I, frankly, can no longer overlook. There aren't villas— there are disaster relief tents, and that's if you're lucky enough not to sleep under a homemade tent you had to make out of borrowed rags.

We've been fooled. Bamboozled. Hoodwinked and throttled. We are all miserable, and the only reason no one is admitting to that is because they don't want you to know it. They want you to keep thinking they're living their best lives.

But no one has a perfect life, no matter how many filters you put on it.

I saw a girl last night who was trying to comb her hair with a sea urchin!

There was a boy who—I promise this is true— was making out with a coconut! And before you ask, no, it wasn't even a young coconut; it was a full-grown, hard, and hairy one. It was obscene.

And everyone's makeup smells really bad!

Telling the lie that Hella was here and the festival was still on was a stupid thing to do, and now I'm paying the price. The lie has taken on a life of its own. People are claiming that they too saw or heard Hella on this island, up on the mountain, inviting them to a party.

And tonight, I finally heard her voice for myself. Pretty conclusive evidence that she's here, right?

No, because River is adamant that she is not. Which is all well and good, but he refuses to say where she is. He is the only one who knows— the only one with the power to come forward and end the ABSOLUTELY ABSURD MADNESS that has overcome everyone on this island—but he refuses to be honest.

I don't know what to think anymore. I thought River was a bad guy. Then I thought he was good again. And now? Now I don't trust him.

Why?

Because River Stone lies.

He keeps secrets.

And I know his biggest one.

Remember his first love, Tracy? The one who abandoned him in the middle of the Australian bushland? Original subject of this podcast? Yeah, her. She never abandoned River. She died on that trip. Killed by a pack of dingoes.

And River lied to you about it. All to ensure that he'd be your favorite Tragic Hunky Dream Boy.

There you have it, folks. Hella is here somewhere. Fly Fest is a scam. And River Stone is a liar. He might be cute and studly and have muscles that scream "Yeah, I do goat yoga, what of it?" But none of that matters, because when you need him the most, he won't be there for you. I can't trust him. And neither can—*Ouch!*

The heel of Rafi's sneaker skidded over wet rock, and her leg went one way while her butt went another. She'd been recording on the run, traversing the island in the dark rain. She'd crossed all the different terrains of the island, from the beach, through the trees, and finally the rocky-muddy grounds of Tent City, but Rafi was finally in front of Peggy's tent.

Unlike every other time she was there, there was no guard at the door. Actually, there was no one inside except Peggy themself. They lounged on their bed, leafing through an in-flight magazine. It looked like for one night only, everyone preferred living life at the beach than spending another night online.

"You've come empty-handed," Peggy said, looking Rafi up and down. "Optimistic of you."

That was when Rafi noticed Peggy's face. One of their eyes was puffy, leaky, and pink. She stepped up to get a better look, but the closer Rafi got, the more she instinctively wanted to keep back. Whatever it was looked contagious.

"What's with your—" Rafi gestured toward her own eye.

"Oh, this?" Peggy tossed the magazine to the side and brandished their face toward the solar-powered bedside lamp. At the full sight of Peggy's eyes, Rafi instinctively recoiled. "Yeah, people pretty much ran out of things to trade for the internet and a few started offering, shall we say, *romantic* favors. Long story short, I made out with someone wearing *a lot* of bronzer, and now I have pinkeye."

Rafi couldn't get off this island fast enough.

"I'm not going to offer you any favors," Rafi said quickly. "I'm just going to beg. One last time. Please, Peggy." She stepped up to the bed until her knees hit the edge, but stopped short of clasping Peggy's hands. "Please let me have the internet."

"Okay."

Wait. Too easy. "What?"

"There's nothing left for anyone to give me," Peggy said. "And I *definitely* don't want to make out with anyone anymore."

Rafi wasn't convinced that it was *Peggy* who didn't want to make out with anybody, and not that people were adamantly refusing to make out with *them*, but she nodded along anyway. Peggy scooted off the bed. "The internet is pretty spotty with the rain, so work quickly. Wi-Fi password is LordOfTheIdiots."

Rafi couldn't believe it. After all this time, she was finally given the keys to her freedom. She took out her phone and found the only hotspot, then typed in the password, quick but careful. It took a few seconds, but the magic word popped up on her screen.

Connected.

She was free.

There was so much she could've done, so many people and authorities she could've contacted. So many people who could come to her rescue. Here was her chance.

But she just needed to get on Twitter real quick.

Rafi clicked the little writing bubble and typed out a new message.

NEW SEASON OF THE PODCAST BEING UPLOADED TONIGHT. Then she took all the files of the new podcast episodes she'd recorded and uploaded them all to her website.

28

IN THE MORNING, THE ISLAND WAS BACK TO BEING QUIET
and sunbaked, last night's rain having washed it clean. But
Rafi awoke remembering everything that happened. She
sprung out of bed, which was to say, she shook off the sand
that clung to her skin, and pulled herself from her tent.

She trekked down the beach, through the trees, into Tent
City, and didn't stop until she was at Peggy's place. The
guard was gone again, but the place was back to full capacity,
packed with lazy loungers scrolling in silence. Rafi gingerly
stepped over legs and torsos until she reached Peggy's bed.
They lay on their back, a teal-silk sleep mask with curled
oversize eyelashes covering their eyes. Rafi hoped they were
still in the same good mood from last night because she'd
come empty-handed again. Plus, she was about to wake
them up.

She gently nudged their shoulder until they stirred.

Peggy pulled back their mask, revealing not one but two
raging pink eyes. They were so crusted with goo that Rafi had
to clamp her lips shut to keep from screaming right in their
face. Not that Peggy could see her. They could barely open
their eyes.

"Heeeeey buddy," Rafi said carefully. "You look . . . good."

"Don't patronize me," Peggy said. "I'm a monster."

Rafi kept her mouth shut and shook her head from side to side. "You're . . . hot."

If Peggy could've looked skeptical right now, they would have, but all they could really do was twist their eyebrows into something disbelieving. "I am?"

"So hot," Rafi said.

"You're just trying to butter me up so I give you internet again."

Rafi started nodding before she realized what she was doing and quickly shook her head instead. "Not at all. You don't look that bad, honest. And pink is really in right now," she said, pulling at the hem of her shirt.

"Please. If there's anyone who knows what's in right now, it is most definitely not you."

Rafi couldn't really argue with that. No matter, because Peggy pulled their mask back down over their eyes and turned onto their side, away from Rafi. "I didn't change the password today. Go on the internet. Leave me alone."

Rafi grinned and whipped out her phone. Last night, she was only able to post her podcast before the storm kicked her off the internet. But today, she'd finally be able to call for help.

She just needed to check how her podcast was doing first.

She plopped down right where she stood and logged on. The first thing she did was check her Twitter to see how many times her post had been retweeted. But it hadn't been retweeted at all. Actually, it'd gotten only two likes. She checked her website stats next to see how many people had clicked on the audio clips she'd posted.

Five people had listened to the first episode of season two of "Musical Mysteries." Two people had clicked through to the rest of the episodes.

Rafi stared at the number, her whole body going tingly with a numbing cocktail of disbelief and humiliation.

No one had listened to her podcast.

Not the fans she thought she'd garnered over the past year. Not the people on this island who she'd repeatedly told about her work.

Nobody cared.

They were never going to get off this island, and it wasn't because Rafi wasn't trying hard enough; it was because nobody was listening. She wasn't popular in real life, let alone on the internet. She didn't have enough followers, she didn't have a good brand, and after being surrounded by beautiful people here, she knew damn well she wasn't pretty enough to get anyone's attention. She spent so much time talking into the void, hoping someone was paying attention. Well, it didn't work on her podcast, and it didn't work on this island either. It didn't matter if she was doing good work, creating something of substance, diligently researching and compiling. Jack had been right. Without a following, it all meant nothing.

Rafi stared down at her phone. She was frozen except for her chin, which had started to quiver, despite Rafi's best efforts to control it. But just then a beacon of hope popped up on her screen in the form of a new email notification. It was from Nobrand, her lone sponsor. She opened it.

Dear Ms. Francisco. We know we committed to sponsoring your podcast, "The Mystery of Music." Unfortunately, we will not be able to continue on in that capacity as we have gone out of business. Best of luck in your future endeavors.

Rafi threw her phone across the room. A few people looked up from their screens and paused their scrolling to watch the phone bounce off the tent wall and fall to the ground with a depressing thud. Greer was sitting closest to it. She reached out with an arm like a tentacle and suctioned it away, storing it behind one of the folds of her flowy tunic. And just like that, Rafi's phone was gone.

Not that it mattered to her. Nothing mattered anymore.

Rafi's plan for the rest of her life was simple: go to her tent and stay there forever. She would become one with the rags until they inevitably fell with the next rainstorm or slight breeze. Then she and the rags would become one with the sand. And then one day she'd get eaten by a crab.

She didn't want to talk to anybody, and when she got to her tent, River wasn't around to show off one of his fishing weapons or lie to her about his girlfriend, so this was going to be easy. Except Jack popped in, out of nowhere. "Care for a makeover?"

Rafi was not in the mood to talk, which suited Jack just fine because he had plenty to say. "Everyone on this Island is either already made up twenty-four-seven or thoroughly beautiful to begin with, so you're the only one who isn't. You don't want to be the only holdout, do you? Because, as I see it, you alone are the reason that Hella hasn't officially invited us up to Fly Fest yet."

Rafi stared at Jack for a long time. His red berry smile did not waver.

If Rafi had learned anything today, it was that it did not matter what she had to say. Maybe the only thing that mattered was how she looked.

"Okay."

Jack blinked. "Okay!" he repeated.

Rafi sat in Jack's tent, on his bed, while he combed her hair with a plastic fork. "I thought you only did makeup."

"In your case, makeup isn't going to be enough."

Rafi almost screamed out—at both the insult and the pain of the plastic prongs pulling apart her knots—but she couldn't even do that because Jack, as always, had more to say.

"This is *a lot* of mediocrity to handle. There really is so much to cover, but while we're on your hair, I'll give you this tip: Normalize using conditioner."

Rafi snorted. "Conditioner? I don't even have a change of clothes."

"There's that no-can-do attitude you're so famous for."

"People think of me like that?" Rafi asked. "But I've been trying to . . . like . . . do so much."

"Where was all that effort when it came to your looks?" Jack asked, making a disapproving sound with his tongue. "And don't snort. It makes you sound ugly. Truly, Rafi, you are fighting this glow up at every turn."

Rafi decided not to fight anymore. Also, this was her first time sitting on a bed in as long as she could remember, and you couldn't pay her to get up. She glanced at the beauty implements that Jack had laid out to fix her. There was an assortment of tools and products, some of which looked like normal things you'd see in normal society. Other things did not belong. Rafi could smell what did not belong. But she didn't have the heart to look at it.

This wasn't the first time Jack had asked if Rafi wanted a makeover. She'd turned him down every time, but now Rafi understood there was no point in saying no. In fact, saying yes was apparently the only way to go through life. No one online, let alone on this island, took her seriously. Today, that was going to change.

"I don't have your exact skin shade for foundation," Jack said. "But I'll just give you the same one I use."

So she would be orange. Great.

Jack worked on her with the deft hand and concentration of a mortuary cosmetologist. "Your brow is very furrowed," he said. "I'm going to need you to stop."

"Sorry," Rafi said. "I was thinking."

"Never a good thing."

She was thinking about what she was doing here. And the more "makeup" that Jack applied, the less she wanted him to. But every touch-up he did was like a hand on her shoulder keeping her in place. "Don't think I'm going to make this a habit," she said.

"Oh, you'll come back," Jack said. "You're hate-following me."

"I'm whatting you?"

"You hate me but you still follow my every move. And you know what? I'm glad. I don't care if you hate me or not. You still care enough about me to be in this tent right now. A hate-follow is still engagement. And it's all about the engagement."

At the start of this hellish trip Rafi wouldn't have taken advice from anybody here, but now she realized that Jack knew of what he spoke. Because he was right. Hate-following was the only explanation for why she was enduring this makeover. If she thought like Jack, maybe more people would've listened to her podcast. Maybe somebody would've alerted the authorities to their dilemma right now and saved them. Alas.

"Time for the final touch!" Jack picked up a small case. Just because he'd managed to pack it neatly in a pale pink

242

compact did not make it any less awful. It took Rafi everything not to gag.

"Um, maybe we can opt out of the bronzer?"

"Don't be silly. You need it desperately."

"I don't think I do."

But Jack put a hand on her shoulder, preemptively stopping her from rising. "Right now your face is one tone. You want to be two tones. Ideally, you want to be at least nine different tones, but we have limited resources so two will have to do. Like an overnight oat parfait. Don't you want to be delicious like a parfait?"

Rafi looked him in the eye. "It's pig poop."

"Tomayto, tomahto!" Jack chuckled. "You get used to it. Personally, I can't even smell it once it's applied."

Rafi didn't know how to explain to Jack that she could smell him from a mile away. Nonetheless, she stayed. Everyone was doing this. And yes, everyone looked ridiculous with a full face of stage makeup on a deserted island. But wasn't it also true that everyone looked beautiful? Rafi had nothing else to lose.

She could be a parfait.

She tilted her chin up toward Jack's face. The last thing she saw before letting her eyes drift shut was Jack's berry-stained lips curl into a grin.

Rafi pretended not to smell it. Pretended not to feel its warm gooiness on her cheekbones as the bread sponge smudged the stuff into her skin. Jack spread it so thin she could even pretend it wasn't there at all.

"*Voilà,*" Jack said.

Rafi opened her eyes to see Jack taking a step back to survey his handiwork. "There. Now you look like a piggy."

Rafi was more confused than ever until she remembered that this was what Jack called his online following. He began and ended all his YouTube tutorials with a salute to his *dear piggies* and even a catchphrase: "oink oink." It was just another aspect of her own generation that Rafi did not understand.

"Why do you call your fans pigs?"

Now it was Jack's turn to look confused, though whether he was confused by the question or Rafi's ignorance, she couldn't be sure. "It's just a joke," Jack said. "It doesn't mean anything."

But words always meant something. Jack may have used the word in an endearing way, but he wouldn't let you forget its scorpion sting.

"Now Hella has to show herself. Now they *have* to let us into the festival."

Rafi had almost forgotten. As sad as she was currently feeling, it made her even sadder that Jack was keeping up this festival charade. "Jack, come on, you know the festival isn't happening—"

"You're a riot, Rafi Santo Domingo," Jack said, cutting her off immediately. You should start a YouTube channel or something."

"I have a podcast."

"Oh. Right . . . Well, this just got incredibly sad and

awkward." Jack did a little sidestep, followed by a restorative throat-clearing. "Anyway! Get out."

Rafi left Jack's tent with no small amount of trepidation. It wasn't just the pig poop on her face—it was the makeover in general. She could feel the makeup like a second skin, weighing down on her, a constant reminder that she looked different— that there was something to look at, period. Her whole thing until now had been about blending in. As a reporter she never wanted to be the story, never needed to be seen. Being made up made her instantly uncomfortable, and all she wanted to do was take cover. But the farther she got from Jack's tent, the more glances she pulled. People stopped what they were doing in order to look at her. Rafi could hear her name whispered on their lips. She touched her hair self-consciously. Jack must've done some magic, because everyone was looking at her. Everyone was talking about her.

And suddenly, that uncomfortable feeling from just a few moments before began to subside, and Rafi began to feel a rush from deep within. A surge. People were looking at her— finally paying attention—and she could show them anything. She could even, maybe, get them to listen. Rafi began to see that the "glow up," as Jack had called it, didn't just have to be a vanity project. It could be a way for Rafi to bring her worth to the surface. Her new second skin began to blend with the first, as seamlessly as the "bronzer" blended with her cheekbones. There was a power in getting all this attention. And Rafi was starting to like it.

And then she heard Jack scream her name.

Rafi turned around. He was standing with someone, who was whispering something in his ear.

"YOU!" Jack yelled, his char-rimmed eyes expanding to double their size. "You told the world the festival is a SCAM?!"

"What?"

"Your little podcast!" Jack rushed toward her until he was close enough that some spittle from his rage-fueled tirade landed on her face.

But Rafi ignored that to focus on the important stuff. "You heard my podcast?"

"Of course not!" Jack spat. "But other people went against their better judgment and did. You told everyone we're a bunch of pathetic losers sleeping on the beach without food or shelter? You told the world we paid thousands of dollars to basically *go camping*?!"

Rafi found herself nodding, despite every bone in her body telling her not to. And she kept hearing her name, kept seeing the looks. People weren't talking about her because she was beautiful now. They were talking about her because they'd heard her podcast. "Have I gone viral?" she whispered.

"Like an STD!" Jack shrieked. "How could you? You're crazy. You're insane."

"I'm not crazy."

"Oh no? Because only a crazy person would—on top of everything—accuse that sweet cinnamon-roll River Stone of being a serial killer!"

River.

She'd forgotten about that part of her podcast. Even though it was the topic of the entire second season.

Jack kept screaming, and at one point he swooned and was about to faint before Greer rushed over to catch him. But Rafi couldn't hear anything that he was saying anymore. Her mind was with River.

She ran back to the beach, straight to River's tent. She pulled back the flap, but he wasn't there.

He must've heard her podcast, too.

She was surprised by the twist she felt in her chest, in the same spot where her heart should've been.

29

RAFI WENT TO PEGGY'S TENT FIRST. SHE DOUBTED SHE'D
find River there, but she still needed to check everywhere.
Also, she kind of wanted to be in the center of the Wi-Fi bubble, to see if it was true—to confirm that, somehow, people
really had listened to her podcast.

"Oh yeah, it's the talk of the island," Peggy told her. "Most
people here think you're *OMG so nutso* for calling River Stone
a murderer. But I've been telling you that forever."

Peggy sniffed, then looked at Rafi. Or, more appropriately,
looked in her general direction, since the pinkeye had taken
over their ability to see. "Did you step in poop?"

Rafi checked the seaport next. Paul and Ryan were standing
in front of their pile of fruit with the desperate eagerness of
perfume sprayers at a fragrance counter.

"Rafi!" they said.

"Can we interest you in some bananas?"

"We're having a big sale."

"Only nine dollars."

"Yeah, we gotta move product."

"Remember when we said business was booming?"

"Well, it turns out business is now rotting."

"Who could have possibly known that fruit went bad so quickly?"

"Please, Rafi. Buy a banana. You could really use the potassium."

Once the boys stopped talking, they finally took a good look at Rafi.

"Whoa," Ryan and Paul said simultaneously. They stared at her, and it was only when Rafi touched her hair and felt the stiffness of the hair spray that she remembered her makeover.

"You look . . . different."

"You look like the tennis instructor I had when I was thirteen," Ryan said. "She was good, but I never learned anything because she was really . . . distracting." He swallowed. "Also, she was having an affair with my father."

Rafi wasn't really sure why the boys were acting so strange, and the confusion stunted her in place, making her forget what she was even doing there. Paul grazed her arm flirtatiously with the back of his fingers. "Hey," he said, sotto voce, smirking. "Name-dropping isn't really my style, but do you have any idea who my father is?"

Rafi stepped back, snapping out of her weird trance. This makeover couldn't have been *that* good. In fact, it was too much of a distraction. The attention that she savored earlier was the last thing she wanted. Not only was her makeover irrelevant right now, it was getting in the way of what she was here for.

"Have you guys seen River?"

"River?" Ryan asked. "You mean the guy who murdered his first girlfriend and possibly also his current girlfriend?"

"He didn't murder Tracy."

But the boys only looked at each other and snorted. "Are dingoes even a real thing?" Paul asked.

"They sound like dogs who wear clown costumes," Ryan said. "I mean, that's gotta be fake."

"River seemed so chill."

"Same thing happened with my butler," Ryan said. "He was super low-key all the time and then—*kaboom!*—half the staff turns up dead."

"Is that the guy who's doing time?" Paul asked.

"Yep," Ryan said. Then he turned to Rafi to explain further. "Time is the name of my former nanny. He ran away with her to the Cayman Islands."

Rafi squeezed her eyes shut hard enough that she could feel the burnt powder of her eyeliner crumbling between her eyelids. "River isn't a killer," she said again.

"The internet says he's a killer," Paul said. "And I believe everything that's on the internet."

She would never get through to them. And she was wasting time. "Do either of you know where he is?"

"Um, I obviously can't say this about my man Ryan here, but I don't associate with killers," Paul said. "Do you have any idea who my—"

"I gotta go," Rafi said.

"Wait!" Ryan caught up to her and gently squeezed her hand. Paul was next to Ryan in an instant, neither of them exactly blocking her way, but standing shoulder-to-shoulder, the jocky non-twins cut imposing figures.

"Maybe it's because we never got distracted by the O-Town reunion that never happened," Ryan said.

"Or maybe it's because we're not bogged down by a successful produce business anymore," Paul said.

"*Bogged*, nice," Ryan whispered.

"I don't usually go for the nerdy girl," Paul said.

"Neither do I," Ryan added adamantly. "Absolutely never, ever. Would rather die, probably."

"But I feel, like—"

"Enlightened."

"Like, maybe we could—"

Rafi didn't let Paul finish. "What are you guys—"

"We're saying you can't just go," Ryan said. His eyes were wild, desperate, like he was racking his brains to give her a reason to stay. Like this makeover was really *that* good.

"Why not?"

"Because I need you to teach me to read," he said.

Rafi yanked her hand away and left the seaport.

The pond was just as stunning and serene as the last time she'd seen it. It really was the most beautiful place on the island.

Of course she found him there. He sat on the same flat rock, the one he'd told her the truth on. And though he had his back to Rafi, he must've sensed she was there, because he began to speak before even turning around.

"I listened to your podcast."

She nodded, though he couldn't see her. Some girl must've given him her phone. Rafi assumed he was one of the first people to listen to it, since he'd been gone from the start of the day. And the idea that he didn't go into it already angry—that he sought out her podcast to support her—made her stomach feel like it'd been through a garbage disposal. "I didn't mean for you to hear it like this."

"Did you plan on posting it after we'd left the island?" River stayed focused on the water as he spoke. "Were you going to say goodbye and it was great to meet you and smile and then still post it when we weren't beach neighbors anymore? 'Cause that kind of makes it worse."

It was at that point that River finally turned around and saw her. The new Rafi, all dolled up. She didn't know what she expected his reaction to be. She could do nothing but watch as his jaw slackened slightly. For a long moment he didn't move much else, until he finally pulled himself up, and the closer he came to Rafi, the more his eyebrows drew down, his eyes searching for something within her he could recognize. "What did you do to yourself?"

It wasn't the resounding adulation she didn't dare to hope for. And under River's gaze she could almost feel herself wilt.

Everything she wore on her face, and even the way her teased hair floated above her head, made her suddenly feel like an extra in a community theater production of a postapocalyptic dystopia set in the world of *Working Girl*.

She knew it shouldn't matter what he thought. Intrinsically, she knew to be offended that he would even question what she chose to do or not do with her appearance. But all her empowered, self-assured airs fell away, and instead of feeling like the makeup gave her an extra layer of protection, it felt like it took one away. She stood there, flayed.

"I got a makeover."

River didn't respond, only kept examining her, his gaze like sandpaper over her skin. The longer his silence stretched, the more it put her on the offensive. "Don't say this isn't me. You don't know me."

"No, I don't," River agreed. "How could you record all that stuff? How could you *post* it?"

She didn't know how to answer that. She really hadn't thought she'd ever have to answer for the things she said on her podcast, least of all for the subject of it. She was quickly learning the flaw in this thinking.

"I thought when we talked . . ." He stopped, took a breath. "I thought when we talked, you believed me."

"I did believe you—"

"So you're either lying to me or lying to your listeners and telling the world I'm a killer for, like, ratings, is that the right term for it? I don't know how podcasts work."

"It was just a theory." Her voice came out meek. "It was just the first few episodes."

"And then the last episode," River said. "Where you told the world my biggest secret."

This was the moment for Rafi to try to defend herself. But she couldn't. "I'm sorry. I was frustrated and wanted to get the truth about Fly Fest out. I forgot about everything I said in the first few episodes. And then the last episode . . . I was mad. I was going to edit it, I just . . . I wasn't thinking."

River didn't look like he believed her. She couldn't blame him.

"And you were still being shifty," Rafi added quickly.

"About what?"

"About *Hella*," Rafi said. "Every time I ask you about her, you lie."

"I don't lie—"

"You have a tell," Rafi said. "Your smile goes crooked when you're lying. And you do it every time I bring Hella up."

He was doing it now. Yes, his smile was rueful, but it was also twisted sideways. "I think you might know more about me than any of my most diehard fans," River said. He did not say it kindly.

He took a deep breath, looked up at the sky, and seemed to consider something. After a moment, he looked back at Rafi, most of the anger melting away from his glare, leaving only defeat. "I guess it doesn't matter now." He sighed. "Hella's in rehab."

"Rehab?"

"Yes. For exhaustion," he explained, before muttering, "and other stuff."

Of all the places Hella could've been, Rafi never even considered rehab. Though it seemed perfectly reasonable now. The last time she'd heard anything about Hella, it was a week before Fly Fest, when video spread all over the internet of her shrieking drunkenly at another girl outside of a club while being held three feet off the ground by a bouncer. Along with being a successful supermodel, the girl was also a lush.

"Why didn't you just say so?" Rafi asked.

"Because it's none of your business," River said. "So, yeah, I knew for a fact where she was and I couldn't tell you. But she's not on this island. No one from Fly Fest is."

The trees provided shade but Rafi still felt hot, unspeakably hot under all the makeup. She felt like she was melting, but she didn't think it was just from the climate. It was the way River was looking at her.

"It's funny," he said. "You think you're above everyone here because they're all fake and manipulating the truth about who they really are. But you're doing the same thing. You're painting a whole weird, twisted, false image of *me*. And that's so much worse."

There was nothing that Rafi could say. All the humidity in the jungle couldn't stifle her the way River's words just had. He was right; she was the fake one. She felt it all the more now, standing here like a pig wearing lipstick.

"I'm sorry." It was all there was left to say.

"I wish I believed you." River looked at her face, her eyes, her cheekbones. "But you're full of shit."

Rafi watched him go until he disappeared in the jungle foliage.

She couldn't take the heat anymore. She sank to the ground, and melted.

30

THOUGH THEY WORE THEIR SLEEP MASK OVER THEIR eyes, Peggy could still sense someone was near. It was the flowery perfume that alerted them. Mixed with the faint smell of pig dung, of course. They knew that smell all too well by now.

"I'm not making out with anyone anymore," Peggy warned, infusing as much authority in their voice as they could. But the nasty aroma lingered. "Okay, fine, one more makeout sesh but that is *it*. I think this pinkeye is getting to my brain."

The smell persisted. This was starting to get annoying, but also mysterious? Which was kind of turning Peggy on. They lifted their sleep mask over their eyes and put all their effort into prying their lids apart. Through the small slit of an opening, Peggy could see Jack Dewey's face an inch away, staring at them. Peggy was back to being turned off. "Can I help you with something?"

"Yes," Jack said. "You gave Rafi Santa Barbara the internet. Prepare to die."

Peggy scooted back on their bed until they were sitting up against the headboard that two sexy and intrepid concertgoers had made for them out of wood and spider webs. "What?"

"I'm kidding about the die part . . . for now. We're here to take your internet." Five of Jack's influencer followers hovered behind him, four girls and a boy, in full makeup, looking just as angry (and also kind of menacingly hungry?) as him. "You can't be trusted with it anymore."

"What?" Peggy asked. "Why!"

"Because that lunatic Rafi told the world we're dirty losers stranded on an island without running water or roofs over our heads!"

"So, the truth?"

"*Ugh*, you're just as bad as she is." Jack turned to his influencers. "Hayes, Stanton, Jayde-with-a-Y, Jayne-with-a-Y, Mahoney: Find me the internet."

Jack's beautiful goons lurched into their rampage. They grabbed anything within reach and overturned it, smashing it on the hard ground. And there was a lot within reach. Peggy's tent was basically a museum of *stuff*—probably the biggest collection of stuff this side of the Caribbean.

There were at least seven other people in Peggy's tent, lounging on the throw pillows on the ground, leeching off the internet that streamed through their phones, but they were either apathetic to the chaos mounting around them or too sucked into their social media worlds to notice it. With no one rising up to help, Peggy was beginning to panic.

"You can't just take my internet!" It was the source of all of Peggy's power. The reason anyone even talked to them in the first place. "You can have the password, no charge—I'm giving it away!"

"And look how good that turned out," Jack said. "The

internet in irresponsible hands breeds disinformation. It needs to be reigned in."

The influencers smashed the ashtray Peggy never used but sorely loved, made by the gorgeous Gio. They ripped down the psychedelic poster Peggy hated but still needed, provided by the stunning Destiny D'Bavio. And they ransacked the drawers of the nightstand Peggy forgot existed but couldn't live without, given to them by the supremely dexterous Nichard Archimedes Bonzalez III.

Peggy shook their head. "You'll never find it."

"Found it!" one of Jack's disciples said, holding up Peggy's satellite phone and grinning with lipstick between every single one of his teeth.

Jack smiled too and held out his hand, where Lipstick Teeth promptly set the brick of a phone. "From now on, *I* control the branding on this island," Jack said. "Nothing gets out without my approval."

Peggy sighed. They were nothing without the internet, and they knew it. Jack knew it, too.

"Let's party!" he told his followers.

There was some sun left in the sky, burning orange and pink as it made its way over the horizon, but River still used the flashlight to wade through the trees as he made his way up the mountain. When he'd left Rafi by the pond, he wandered around for a while, needing to be alone. It wasn't like he could go back to the beach, anyway. By now everyone had probably already heard the sordid claims in her podcast. Everyone probably thought he was a monster. So he stayed hidden in the comfort of the jungle, letting the sounds of nature inform his next moves.

Soon, River found himself going upward. Before he even realized it himself, his feet were guiding him to the spot that he, Rafi, and Jack had explored the night before, where they'd heard Hella's voice.

River knew it was Hella's voice; there was no denying it. He'd been listening to that voice asking him to fetch a bottle of rosé twice a day every day for the last two months. His girlfriend definitely had a drinking problem, which was precisely why he'd convinced her *not* to come to Fly Fest. A boozed-up musical bonanza on a tropical island was the worst place for her to be. To his surprise Hella had agreed and realized it was the perfect time to go to rehab instead. Well, actually, the rehab was ordered by the judge in her assault case, but the official story Hella's publicist was planning to release if word ever got out was that Hella had made the decision on her own. No one was supposed to know, except River. And the week of the festival was supposed to be the perfect cover. People would be too focused on the event of the season to care where Hella was.

Except the opposite had happened, and now everyone here wondered where she was *all the time*, and River couldn't keep up with the lies. Especially not with someone like Rafi asking questions nonstop.

He'd really screwed this up.

But this—this weird disembodied voice in the mountain—this was screwing with River's head.

He needed to find out the truth behind it.

By the time he reached the top of the mountain, the sun was gone and the beam from River's flashlight shone bright enough to illuminate the gnats buzzing in its path. There was the step-and-repeat that Jack had posed in front of. Vines grew over it like it'd been here for a very long time, even though that was impossible. Everything about this festival was last-minute. So last-minute that it wasn't even complete.

The stage platform was bare bones, and though he'd already stepped on it the night before, he did almost fall through a crack in the wooden planks and break his neck. River did not want to take his life in his hands and do that again. So he went around the stage, to the back, where an intricate maze of scaffolding and wires and plant overgrowth ran the length of the space. River didn't know what it was all connected to, but the thing felt alive, like a pumping humanoid heart. He could feel heat emanating from the jumble as he got closer to it. He was hesitant to touch any of it, but he was also looking for answers. He found a compromise. A stick at his feet. He dragged it along the metal and wires, poking some areas that he couldn't see too well and pulling back leaves that obscured others.

Until he found a monitor. The screen was black but it buzzed, like a TV that was still on, even though the cable was off. He tapped the monitor with the stick and it flickered to life. First there was only a grey glow. Then an image came into focus of a beautiful beach backdrop. And then Hella was on the screen. She wore a string bikini, and her face was fixed in its usual expression: bored hottie. "Hey, you," she said to River.

River's mouth fell open. Maybe it was the strange twilight hour, or the heat coming from this part of the stage, or the fact that his girlfriend was suddenly before him, but the moment felt surreal. It was like Hella was looking through the screen, right at River—really seeing him.

And then she continued speaking.

"Welcome to Fly Fest," Hella said. "Things are about to get *lit*."

The screen went black again. And with the darkness went all the magic River felt for that one brief second. And he understood immediately what this was. When Hella had participated in the viral promo video for Fly Fest, she'd also made these little clips, clearly to be shown throughout the concerts. Before the organizers obviously ran out of money and abandoned the whole endeavor.

It all made sense now.

A fly landed on the corner of the monitor, and it was enough to get it going again, the screen coming back to life and Hella there, demanding things get lit once more.

River dropped the flashlight and stick and grabbed either side of the monitor. He shook it and yanked until the thing came loose and a *shzzmm* buzzed out from the screen. And then he ran.

31

"Is it on?" Jack smiled at the camera. Smokey eyes gleaming with wing-tipped liner; drawn-in bold brows in perfect arches; overlined red lips stretched in a supple, practiced smile; cheeks rouged to hell and back; and, of course, to bring the whole look together, contoured cheekbones sharp enough to cut glass brushed and blended with a "bread" sponge and his patented secret ingredient. The orange flames of the raging bonfire nearby danced across his fully made-up face. Jack Dewey had never been more stunning. "We're live?"

He got a confirmation nod from Greer, holding the camera phone. Show time.

"Hi, piggies! *Oink oink* and all my love!" He shaped his fingers into a complicated salute before settling them into a demure wave. "We're coming to you LIVE from Fly Fest where the party is dead-ass nonstop. Now, I don't know what you may have heard, specifically from a total nonentity named Rafi San Bernardino—if that's even her real name—who's been telling people through her podcast—um, who listens to those?—that Fly Fest is a hoax. First of all, I know Rafi, and if there's one thing I can tell you about her it's that *she's* the hoax. She's a bitter, thirsty, nerd who'd never even *heard* of feathered eyebrows before I set her straight. Not an original or smart thought in her body."

Jack beckoned the lens with a hooked index finger until it was zoomed all the way into his face. He tilted it expertly to get his best angle, and spoke his next words as though he were a twenty-two-year-old Academy Award–winning ingenue starring in her first fragrance commercial. "Rafi San Bernardino is a known nobody. A liar. A dirty loser. Just a very nasty girl. Don't believe a word she says."

He breathed in deep.

"Second of all, does this look like a hoax to you?" The camera zoomed out enough to capture Jack with his arms open wide and his head thrown back. All around him were people dancing barefoot in the sand with a raging bonfire in the background. "This is the party of the millennium. And that little pang you're feeling in your gut? That's you wishing you were here."

He started to skip down the beach, but not before winking over his shoulder for the camera to follow him. Jack stopped in front of a girl with a crown of tropical flowers decorating her hair. "Hey, girl, we're live on my Insta right now; tell us your name."

"I'm Emerson, or, I guess, DreamTwoDreamTravelerOne on Instagram." She waved at the camera phone.

"Emerson, you're gorgeous."

"Thank you!"

"What are you drinking?" Jack bent to sniff the coconut husk in Emerson's hand.

"It's the punch."

"Ooo! The Fly Fest signature punch. *So* exotic."

The camera panned to an Hermès luxury titanium-lined suitcase trunk, open on the sand. People were dipping their own halved coconut husks into it and scooping out a murky-colored cocktail.

"Don't stand too close to the fruit punch or you *will* combust," Jack told the camera. "That special juice is full of the richest, most glamorous, secret ingredients."

"I think it's fruit and rainwater," Emerson said, poking her head into the frame. "And hair spray and Listerine."

"Pure, undiluted mouthwash for those of you with a *nasty* mouth; I'm looking at you, Rafi." Jack walked to his next interviewee, a girl dripping freshly from a stint in the ocean. "Oh, look at you!" Jack said. "Skinny dipping in the moonlight?"

"I think I got bit by a man o' war," the girl said.

"HOT!" Jack did not slow his stride. "Hey, look over there!" He pointed up and the camera followed, spanning the cliffside in the near distance until it settled on two boys. They high-fived each other and then jumped, disappearing into the darkness. "We even have cliff diving!" Jack trilled. "It's the *Midsomer* vibes for me."

Jack kept moving, caressing shoulders, shimmying next to dancers, chatting briefly with those who were sober enough to respond. "Tell my followers how much fun you're having right now!" he shouted into one girl's ear.

"So much fun," she responded.

"Do you want for anything?"

"I want for nothing," she said. "Except maybe, like, clean water?"

"She's kidding!" Jack said to the phone. "Hey, look over there! It's the Chainsmokers!"

The camera swung quickly and stopped on two lanky-haired girls, smoking cigarettes. But before the camera could linger on them too long, Jack grabbed it and pointed it in the direction of a boy holding court behind a homemade drum kit of overturned sandwich containers. He was using something peculiar with which to bang on his drums, and Jack's eyes lit up when he saw them.

"You guys are gonna love this," he said to his viewers. "Yesterday we found bones on the beach!" The boy on the drums nodded and banged the bones together in the air.

"One-two-three-four!"

"BONES!" Jack said.

"See, this festival is incredible. Greer, read me some of the comments."

Greer began to read the stream of comments popping up in real time:

"What happened to those cliff divers? Question
    mark question mark question mark."
"I am deeply concerned for the safety of everyone
    there."
"Is this a party or a string of ways to kill people?"
"Man o' wars are no joke."

"The creators of Fly Fest in no way endorse what
    is currently happening at Fly Fest."
"Is that guy passed out on the sand still breathing?"
"Viscerally unsettling."

Greer zoomed in on the guy passed out on the sand, but Jack
moved the phone until it was back on his face. "Uh, what?"
he asked his followers through the camera. "Guys, no, this is
fun."

He stared into the phone, as though daring it to respond,
but Greer wasn't reading the comments anymore. And though
she didn't appear on-screen, anyone tuning in could guess
what she was doing.

"Greer, why are you crying?" Jack asked. He rolled his
eyes. "Greer, stop crying."

A ruckus broke out behind Jack, and though she still wept,
Greer had the wherewithal to zoom out and get a wide shot
of the beach. Festivalgoers were cheering for River Stone, who
had just broken through the trees of the jungle and run onto
the beach. In his hands he held a thirty-two-inch TV screen.
His facial features were set in a sweaty urgency.

"Everybody listen!" River said, loud enough to make everybody stop and look at him. "Hella isn't here! She isn't coming!
What you all heard was a promo video." River shook the TV
screen. It was a useless relic in his hands, but the mere reality
of its existence clearly meant something to him, and he was
hoping it could mean something to everyone else. "There are

screens set up all over the mountaintop. They were playing promos for Fly Fest on a loop—"

"NO!" Jack yelled. The sudden shrillness of his voice cut through the air like a clap of thunder. "You're lying!"

River began to respond but Jack wouldn't let him. "We don't want to hear it! You're canceled! Hella *is* here!"

River shook his head but Jack didn't see it. He was too busy clutching his ears in desperation, trying not to tear the hair out from his temples. "Enough of these lies! We're just trying to live our best lives!" he cried. "Will you please just let me *live*?!"

"Hella—" River began, but his voice was cut off by Jack's, who shouted at Greer to turn off the livestream.

But while Greer may have thought she turned it off, she actually did not. She merely dropped the phone and ran toward the action, her bare feet in stark focus until they got hazier the farther she got from the camera. And although the grains of beach sand directly in front of the lens were the only thing on screen that weren't completely blurry, the camera still captured what was going on in the background. Anybody watching the livestream could see Jack charging for River, and then a stampede of bare feet stomping the sand, spraying the camera with granules of it as they ran toward the two quarrelling boys. It was hard to make out what anybody was saying because all of them were shouting, until their voices blended into an angry chorus. Jack's hand, poking high out of the center of the gang, gripped a nail file like a butcher knife, and it came down in a forceful, terrifying swish.

The phone tipped forward, belly-flopping onto the sand, the feed finally cutting off.

Rafi, standing in a corner of the seaport, watching the livestream over someone's shoulder, stared at the suddenly blank screen in horror.

32

Rafi ran to the beach as quickly as she could, but the chaos seemed to have ceased just as quickly as it had flared up. By the time she got there the party was over.

Almost like something had killed the mood.

River wasn't anywhere, and neither was Jack. A few stragglers were stumbling around on the sand or slumped in close proximity to the drunk-punch trunk that now sat dry and empty beside the dying bonfire.

Rafi bent over a boy who was lying facedown, and pushed his shoulder until he flopped over. "Hello? Have you seen River?"

The boy responded with a belch. It was both minty fresh and toxic enough to style Rafi's hair. She looked around, but no one seemed coherent enough to answer her questions. So she went looking for Jack. But when she got to Tent City she was stopped by the same guy who used to guard Peggy's tent, now promoted to guard much bigger real estate.

"Yes?" He put his arm out, moving it in front of wherever Rafi moved.

Rafi slapped it away. "Is River here?"

"There is no river here, miss. Only a beach."

"River Stone!"

"Beach seashell!"

Rafi wanted to destroy something, and she would've been angrier, but she really wasn't sure if this guy was messing with her or if he genuinely thought they were playing some sort of word game.

"River Stone. The most famous singer in the world right now!"

"Never heard that name in my life."

She'd had enough. "Let me through."

"Are you one of Jack's followers?"

"Not even if my life depended on it," she spat.

"Then I'm afraid I can't let you in."

Rafi didn't have to take this—she was her own independent woman who could go wherever she wanted, and there were no rules on this island. But as soon as she tried to sidestep the guard, he grabbed her around the shoulders and picked her right off the ground like she was a garbage bag.

"Let go of me!" Rafi shrieked.

The guard put her down. "I'll do it again," he said. "But please don't make me."

Rafi tried weighing her options. She could make a run for it, but this guy was bigger, faster, and stronger than she was. All she could think to do was scream.

"RIVER!"

The guard winced. Rafi didn't care. She'd stand there and scream all night if she had to.

Except, after screaming River's name three more times, her

throat was getting dry. And who was she kidding; she didn't have the willpower to do anything all night long. She turned around and headed back to the beach, but instead of going inside her own tent, she went into River's. It was empty, like she'd feared it would be. His carry on bag was in the corner, his guitar leaning against it.

Rafi was so lost and scared and confused that her mind started running away from her, and she wondered wistfully if maybe there was a secret party somewhere on this island after all. Maybe River had found Sierra and the two of them were there now, having the amazing time that Fly Fest always promised.

But how could River regale the crowd without his guitar?

Rafi sank down and crossed her legs. She'd sit there until River came back.

Because he had to come back.

She stayed in that position for hours, willing her eyes to stay open, until the salty beach air made them feel too dry, and she let them rest.

When she opened her eyes again, the sun was shining flower patterns through the tent's fabric. And River had still not returned.

"Does anyone have any idea what happened to River?" Rafi asked.

She was back at the seaport, asking the same questions she hadn't stopped asking since last night. Most everyone who liked to hang out at the seaport was gone now, defected to Jack's eternal party, apparently. The only people left were Paul and Ryan, who stood on either side of the room, volleying a conch shell the size of a football over Rafi's head. With Rafi having washed all the gunk off her face, Paul and Ryan had gone back to seeing her as little more than a girl who sometimes blocked their peripheral vision.

But there was a new visitor to the seaport. Now that no one was coming to Peggy's tent for the internet anymore, they needed people to talk to, and Paul, Ryan, and Rafi were the only sane people left on this island.

Except for River. Who still had to be here. Somewhere.

"They murdered him, obviously," Peggy said.

Rafi whipped around to face them. "What?" She was usually the one to posit wild theories having to do with River and murder, only for Peggy to call her crazy. Now Rafi and Peggy had switched roles. "Of course he isn't dead, how can you even say that?"

"You saw the same video I saw, right?" Peggy asked. "The one where Jack stabbed River with a nail file and then everyone joined in and then River disappeared into the ocean?"

"No, no, I didn't see any of that," Rafi said. "I mean, I saw the nail file, but that was all. Who knows if Jack even touched him? And River's strong—have you seen his arms? He has strong arms."

"Again with how fit and muscular he is," Peggy said. "Sorry, *was*. You really have it bad for him, don't ya? Sorry, *had*."

"I don't have it bad!" Rafi took a breath and a moment to collect herself. If they were going to find out what happened to River, they'd need clear heads. Paul and Ryan were useless in that department, but Peggy was smart. Peggy was practically a genius. "River is missing. We have to find him."

She was looking for agreement or, really, any sort of reaction. But Paul and Ryan continued their game like they hadn't heard her, tossing the conch over Rafi's head without a break. And Peggy only watched her with mild sadness. "This isn't like one of your podcast mysteries," Peggy said.

"I know. It's more serious."

"No, I mean, there's no mystery about it—pretty sure he got murdered."

Rafi wouldn't let herself believe that River was dead. She didn't come here believing that he was a killer just for him to end up getting killed. That was not how his story ended. And, sure, it was easy for her to believe that anybody could be a killer, but—Jack? The guy could be a little kooky, putting dookie on his face, but he wasn't a murderer. That was ridiculous. The festival—or lack thereof—couldn't have turned him into that big of a megalomaniac.

Could it?

Something shattered, rousing Rafi from her dark thoughts.

Not too far from her feet lay the remains of the conch-shell football. Paul and Ryan looked at the pieces, mouths agape.

"Whoa," Ryan said.

"We've never dropped a football before," Paul sad.

"Not a football," Rafi corrected.

"That's, like, an omen," Ryan said.

"Yeah," Paul agreed. "Like, that bad things are gonna happen."

The two boys turned to Rafi, waiting for confirmation.

"Have you guys heard a word I said?" Rafi asked. "Bad things *have* been happening. River is missing and possibly dead, and Jack may have been the one to kill him. Or capture him. Or *I don't know what*."

"Don't forget there's an influencer missing," Peggy added.

"Right!" Rafi said, exasperated. "Sierra vanished into thin air. This whole festival is a nightmare—are you just now realizing this?"

Ryan and Paul shrugged and faced each other. "We've been having a pretty chill time, actually."

"We have to go to Jack," Rafi said, because it was true, and because she needed to cut off Paul and Ryan from whatever nonsensical digressions about making millions on bananas they were about to launch into. "We have to know what happened."

"And we have to get my internet back," Peggy said.

At this point, Rafi couldn't care less about the internet. It hadn't helped her when she actually got her hands on it. Actually, it'd only made things on this island exponentially worse.

But if it meant that Peggy was on her side and willing to face down a possibly insane murderer, then she'd go with it.

"And we have to know what happened to O-Town," Paul and Ryan said.

"Okay, then," Rafi said, nodding to herself and ignoring the boys. "Let's confront Jack."

33

Rafi found herself standing in front of the guard
of Tent City yet again, but this time she wasn't going to allow
him to throw her around like a rag doll. She had Ryan and
Paul with her, who each were equally as big as the guard, and
there were two of them. Peggy was there too, but apart from a
mean—and literal—stink eye, their skill set was minimal in a
situation like this.

"I'm usually extremely against violence, but if you don't let
us in, these guys will beat you up," Rafi told the guard.

He looked over her head, trading eye contact with both
Paul and Ryan. After a short stare-down, he sighed and gave
in. "River isn't here."

"We're looking for Jack," Rafi said.

"The MUA holds court at the Cliffside."

The MUA? And also, *holds court?* Rafi vigorously
rejected the way any of that sounded, but there was no time
to stand around and ask questions. She turned to her small
group and gave a quick, curt nod. If Jack was at the Cliffside, then that was where they needed to be, too. She led
the way.

The Cliffside was at the far side of the beach, where the sand gave way to something rockier and became the color of bleached coral reef. Until Jack proposed collecting eye shadow from the dusty pink rocks there, nobody ever ventured that far because there didn't seem to be a point to climbing the jagged rocks when there were so many more convenient places to settle. But standing there now, Rafi understood why Jack would choose this place as his new headquarters.

There was a small formation of boulders leading the way to the top of the cliff, and there, with the view of the ocean as a backdrop, was a natural structure that resembled a throne. It had a flat seat, a lopsided but definite back, and uneven armrests, but it was a chair made of stone. And on it sat Jack. There was a person standing on either side of him, one boy waving a palm frond next to Jack's face, and one girl, who seemed to be tasting fruit before dropping the bitten-off chunks directly from her mouth into Jack's. It seemed they'd gone straight from their jobs at Peggy's tent to working for the MUA.

Rafi and her group approached the lip of the shallow rock hill, but Jack pretended he did not see them. He sniffed the air instead, and said, "It stinks. Is Rafi Santa Ana Winds here?"

"For the last time," Rafi stated, her voice steady and authoritative. "My name is Rafi Francisco. And I think what you're smelling is your own face."

Jack finally settled his glare on her. He managed to look

down without tilting his head, or even distorting his perfect posture. It was like he was mid-photoshoot for an ergonomic office-chair ad. But while he usually looked gorgeous, there was something off about his eyes. They were puffy and had a pink tint to them, kind of like Peggy's but to a lesser degree. Now Rafi noticed that the eyes of Jack's grape-feeder and palm-frond flapper were the same shade of nasty. Rafi doubted very much that it was a new makeup trend.

Pinkeye was becoming a pandemic on this island, and it had clearly started to ravage Jack's group. And judging by how it had so thoroughly taken over poor Peggy's face, Rafi figured they had a few hours left before going completely crusty and engorged. She wondered what they'd do about their precious Instagram pics then.

Probably below-the-neck stuff.

"You sure it's my makeup?" Jack asked. "Or is it theirs?" He pointed over Rafi's head, and she turned, unsure what he was referring to. But then Jack's meaning instantly became clear. The Ryan and Paul she thought she knew had been replaced by two big athletic guys with *their faces smeared with poo.*

"What the . . ." Rafi looked up at them, her brain trying to catch up to what was happening. No such luck. *"What is happening??"*

"We thought he'd listen to us if we put on makeup," Paul whispered in response.

"Everyone else is doing it," Ryan said, shrugging.

"Yeah, we didn't want to look like idiots," Paul said.

"Oh, you didn't want to look like idiots, did you?" Rafi said, nodding maniacally, letting her hands fall limply against her thighs. Paul and Ryan hadn't delicately applied and blended. It looked more like they'd just tied for first place in a shit pie-eating contest. "That's not how makeup works," Rafi hissed.

"So we look bad?" Paul asked.

"This isn't, like . . . pretty?" Ryan said.

Rafi did not dignify their questions with answers. She should've realized what they'd been up to by the smell, but she didn't because literally everything on this island smelled bad at this point. Every surface was beginning to attract flies to the point where Jack might get his wish and this could become a Fly Fest after all. *Ugh.*

"Why didn't you stop them?" Rafi asked Peggy.

"And get in the way of this?" Peggy said. "No. That was never going to happen; this is the best thing that I've ever witnessed."

"Your makeup is terrible and borderline offensive," Jack said loudly, in an effort to bring the attention back on himself. "But no worries, I can fix it. Boys, grab them!"

Two boys from Jack's camp materialized from behind the throne and came down to Paul and Ryan, grabbing their arms. Rafi was about to shout out in protest, but Paul and Ryan went willingly. Rafi couldn't even blame them. They really did need their faces fixed. And, to be honest, they were of no use to her right now.

"I guess that just leaves you and Peggy," Jack said to Rafi. "It's only a matter of time before you both see the light and join us here."

"We're not here to join you," Rafi said. "We're here for River. Where is he?"

"Who?" Jack fluttered his eyelids innocently and cupped a hand over his ear.

"Stop playing dumb!" Rafi couldn't help the outburst. She was escalating things far too quickly, but she was done playing. Jack could lead the whole island in a weird cult of makeup and make-believe, but for Rafi this had gone far enough. Plus, she found strength in her loudness. As calm as Jack was pretending to be, her voice was a chaos agent. It was overturning tables. It was a firing squad. It was starting something and ending something right here, right now. Her voice was her most powerful asset. She used it to great effect on her podcast; it was about time she used it in real life, too. "Where are you keeping him?"

Jack giggled and shared a look with his servants, who dutifully also laughed. "I never met River Stone. And that's my official statement."

"Okay, I've heard enough," Peggy said. "I didn't say anything when you stole my satellite phone, and I didn't say anything when you clearly murdered River. And I didn't say anything when you convinced people to start wearing feces on their faces, but I've had it." What Peggy did not say was that, most of all, they couldn't stand the fact that someone other than them had managed to become king on this island. The fun was over now. "We need to go back home, Jack. You know it as well as I do."

"Not until the festival—"

"There is no festival!" Peggy said. "We got suckered into a scam. No amount of poop is going to cover up how bad that stinks. You know, when I first got here, I was upset, too. Then I found a way to make it better. You and I are alike in that way. And it's ironic, because my eyes are nearly swollen shut, but I can finally see something that you so clearly can't. And it's that—hey, what's happening?"

With one flick of his wrist, Jack had commanded two of his people to grab Peggy. They hadn't seen them coming due to the aforementioned eyes-swollen-shut predicament. "Unhand me!" Peggy demanded. But no one was taking orders from them anymore.

"What are you doing to them?" Rafi shouted, watching as the two cronies led Peggy closer and closer to the edge of the cliff.

"We can't go home again," Jack said to both Peggy and Rafi, and no one in particular. "We can never go home again."

As batty as those words sounded, the way Jack spoke them made Rafi finally understand his position. Jack didn't want to go home because home equaled admitting defeat. Admitting the truth. Admitting that there was another reality, an alternate reality to the one he'd made for himself here, where everyone and life itself appeared beautiful.

But Rafi didn't have too much time to dwell on what Jack said, because the words also seemed to be a command for his cronies to push Peggy over the edge.

Like literally over the edge of the cliff. Not being able to see where they were going or what they could grab, Peggy stumbled backward. Their clumsy feet skidded over the gravelly terrain, and their arms pinwheeled, trying to find purchase. The whole thing looked like it was the latest complicated TikTok dance.

"Peggy, watch out!" Rafi yelled. But it was too late. One minute Peggy was trying to hold on to air, the next they were gone.

Rafi ran to the edge of the cliff, stopping just short of the open air. She swung her arms back to try to regain her balance and ended up getting help from the people who'd launched Peggy off the cliff. The influencers caught her wrists, probably to prevent her from unwittingly swinging her fists into their disgusting, beautiful faces. They let her go when she was stable, though, and went back to join Jack's ranks.

Rafi looked down, searching for Peggy's broken and bloody body splayed on the jagged rocks below. But there were no rocks. It turned out this section of land wasn't a cliff so much as a lip that jutted out like a spout. Below, there was deep blue sea. But more specifically, there was—

"A boat." Rafi's breath caught on the word.

The boat bobbed in the sea like a cork, and it was so close—approximately only one story below. And on its bow was Peggy. Not so much broken and bloody, but definitely splayed out and moaning. They sat up, rubbing their back as they looked around. They seemed to have fallen on a pile of debris littering the surface of the boat, a mix of dirty-looking mounds of whites, grays, and yellows. Rafi wasn't sure what she was seeing, but a laugh bubbled up in her unexpectedly. "A BOAT!"

Behind her, Jack was laughing, too. "That's not a boat, sweetie, it's a garbage barge." He tilted his head back to the followers standing around his throne and proceeded to laugh about it with them. "She doesn't know the difference between a boat and a garbage barge."

Rafi was too amazed by the sudden turn of events to worry about the fact that everyone was laughing at her, or to remember just how much she could not stand Jack. "Where did it come from?"

"What do you mean?" Jack asked. "It's been coming every day. The barge stops at different islands collecting garbage. Steve, the captain, stops here for his lunch and dinner breaks."

"*Steve?*"

"He enjoys the shade beneath the promontory you're standing on. If you'd bothered to get to know him, you'd know that."

Just then someone from Jack's group walked over to the ledge with their stem of grapes and threw it over. It landed on Peggy's thigh.

And as Rafi watched all this, she tried to puzzle out the warring thoughts in her head, but there were too many jockeying for her attention. "Wait a minute," she said. "There was a boat coming to this island every day? *Twice* a day?"

"How many times do I have to say it?" Jack said. "It's a *garbage barge*."

"Why didn't anyone get on the boa—the barge?" Rafi asked.

Jack and his tribe looked at Rafi like it was *her* face that was covered in crap. "It's full of garbage," Jack stated, like it was obvious.

The tribe murmured their agreement.

"But we could've been rescued!"

"Me? Get on a boat that transports garbage?" Jack asked, confused. "Honestly, Rafi, you've never lorded over an island full of influencers at the world's most exclusive music festival and it shows."

Rafi rolled her eyes, which was not to Jack's liking.

"If you're so eager to get out of here, go ahead," he said. "Jump on the garbage barge, it's about to leave. And it's clearly where you belong."

Rafi looked down. She looked at Peggy sitting among the muck, at just how much muck there actually was. It really wasn't that long of a fall. With the amount of Styrofoam containers and other bags of cheesy sandwich garbage there, Rafi would probably have a soft cushion on which to land. And she'd finally be off this forsaken island and on her way back to civilization.

The barge was so close, actually, that she could smell it from where she stood. The waves of pungent garbage juice wafted up to her, masking the last of the fresh smells the island had left.

"Jump on the barge!" Jack barked. And he repeated it again, until it was a chant. His followers picked up on it and began chanting, too. "Jump on the barge! JUMP ON THE BARGE!"

The garbage barge. Her salvation. All Rafi wanted to do was follow their direction and jump.

But it really did smell very bad.

And there was so much ocean all around.

The barge began to move slowly, away from the cliff's scree, but Rafi's sneakers stayed glued to the cliff. She didn't move, even as the barge was moving in earnest now, picking up speed and getting farther and farther away.

"You want me to jump onto that?" Rafi said to Jack in a smallish voice. "I could never make it."

Jack shared knowing looks with his followers before turning back to Rafi. "Of course you can't. You don't have that special something that the rest of us do. That *Jenna-say-quack*. You think you're interesting because you have a podcast? *Everybody* has a podcast, Rafi. The sad thing for you is that nobody our age listens to them. Nobody! Also, you're tone-deaf, you have to be the center of attention, and you are far too concerned with your looks."

It was a lot easier for Rafi to take Jack's insults once she realized that everything he said was projection. "And *you* don't look anything like your pics," she said.

The perma-smirk on Jack's face disappeared like a magic trick. Rafi felt like she finally landed a lethal blow. "Excuse me?" he said.

"People only ever saw you with studio lights or behind Facetune or filters or from certain angles. You always controlled the image. But that ubiquitous influencer face? Nobody ever looks like that in real life. The first day here you were sad that you didn't have any of your makeup. But now I realize you were mostly horrified that people would see the real you."

For a moment, everything stopped. None of Jack's follow-ers moved; Steve's barge was frozen on the horizon; even the flies that had been lured by the stink seemed to rest on the rocks. Actually, the only motion came from the nearly imper-ceptible clench of Jack's jaw. Finally, he spoke. "Grab her."

34

RAFI FOUND HERSELF SITTING IN A CAGELIKE STRUCTURE (okay, it wasn't cage*like*; it was a cage, period). It couldn't have been more than four feet tall in any direction, and she was surrounded on six sides by metal bars, much stronger stuff than even the plastic tube frames of the tents in Tent City. She wondered who made this. When? How? Though, as her clammy fingers encircled the bars, she remembered where she'd seen them before. The raw, unfinished scaffolding of the concert stage at the top of the mountain. Where had all these materials and builders been when she needed shelter that wouldn't fall at the flap of a butterfly's wings?

Rafi shook the cage, not so much to demand her freedom but to test the sturdiness of her cell. It was pretty durable, especially considering the fact that it was currently holding her about five feet above the ground. The people who'd set this cage up had put a lot of work into it. They'd found a clearing in the jungle, and a tree with a high enough—strong enough—branch from which to dangle the cage. Like a chandelier from one of their mansions.

But as impressive as the cage was—and, no question, it definitely beat her tent—Rafi was left with only one desire.

I want to go home.

She thought of speaking the words out loud. She had an audience, after all. Every concertgoer on the island was gathered here, in a wide circle below her. Even Paul and Ryan guiltily stood watch, if a bit isolated thanks to the raging stink coming off their faces.

No, Rafi saw no point in saying she wanted to go home. They wouldn't let her anyway. But she realized, as she looked down at the silent, staring crowd, that they were waiting for her to say something. This wasn't exactly the check-in desk at the seaport, and she didn't have her mic with her, and as far as daises went, this one dug into her tailbone. But it was something.

It was time to put an end to the lies and rumors. It was time for the truth. And they needed to hear it directly from her.

"I know some of you have already listened to season two of my podcast, 'Musical Mysteries.'"

"Stop plugging your podcast!" came a voice from down below.

Rafi squeezed her eyes shut, annoyed at the interruption but also at herself. Whoever had said that was right. This wasn't about her or her podcast. She needed to start again.

"When I came to this island, I thought I was better than you."

The faces down below, beneath the clay and crap and crustiness, wrinkled subtly with deep lines of anger, which Rafi knew she deserved. But they still listened, and that was all she asked for.

"I thought I was here to do important work and you were all here to party. And I never cared about what I looked like or how popular I was, but you guys—you all cared about that. It was the *only* thing you cared about."

More angry stares. Rafi was beginning to wonder if their faces were frozen that way now, their makeup casting them like plaster molds.

"But I'm not better than any of you," Rafi continued. "I know now that my need to be a famous investigative podcaster? It's just like you all wanting to be popular influencers. And we *all* care about our looks—it's human nature!"

There were sounds steadily rising from the crowd, a restless grumble, and Rafi could tell she was losing them. It appeared her epiphany was not relevant to their interests. She needed to get to the point.

"I told a lie!" Though she tried to make her voice as clear and loud as possible, the truth still came out shaky and beaten down. But it emerged, nonetheless. "I said Hella Badid was here and that Fly Fest was still on, somewhere in an unseen part of the island. But none of that was true. I made it up so that all of you would want to stay. So that River would stay. So I could get an interview with him. It was wrong, and definitely the worst choice of my life, and you have no idea how much I regret it."

No interruptions, no disgruntled murmurs. It was a good sign, and it spurred Rafi on. "Now that you know that Hella was never here and that there is no festival, don't you want to go home? Don't you want to end the madness and—I don't know—take a hot shower? We've all had our fun. Some more than others, am I right?" Here, Rafi allowed herself to cautiously chuckle and rattle the bars of her cage. "But I think we can all agree that it's time to go."

She knew she wasn't the greatest orator in the world, and she sure as heck wasn't as influential as anybody else here, but she was presenting them with something that was impossible to ignore.

Logic.

The truth was out in the open now from a primary source. There was no more reason to keep up the charade. It was time to wipe off the "beauty" masks.

But Jack—whom Rafi had almost forgotten about—cleared his throat and broke through his circle of followers, strutting into the open circus ring beneath Rafi's cage. He looked up at her. "You really think we're dumb, huh?"

Jack took his time walking the perimeter of the ring, addressing his people. "It's plainly obvious that the organizers of Fly Fest are telling Rafi to say all this. They are trying to test our loyalty. See who the real believers are."

"No," Rafi said.

"Yes," Jack said, batting his eyelashes (or maybe trying to blink away the ooze congealing on his eyelids). He caressed the shawl draped around his neck. It was golden, with thread that looked like it was spun by Rumpelstiltskin himself. Rafi stared at it, sure she'd had this exact thought before, until, finally, it jogged her memory. She gasped out loud.

"YOU!" Rafi pointed with her whole arm through the

metal bars at Jack, who stared up at her innocently. But he wasn't so innocent. Rafi remembered where she'd seen that shawl before. It had once graced the supple décolletage of Sierra Madre!

Instantly all the pieces fell into place, and Rafi couldn't believe she hadn't solved the puzzle earlier. Of course it was Jack. The same person who killed River and threw Peggy over a cliff would've disposed of Sierra, too.

Anytime anyone got in the way of Jack's Fly Fest delusions he had to get rid of them, as proven by the fact that Rafi was currently dangling over the jungle in a manmade cage. Sierra would've been his first victim because she was always too good for this place. She never would've stayed, never would've believed Rafi's lie like everyone else here. If she got her hands on the internet, the first thing she would've done was charter a yacht back home. Jack couldn't have that, so he got rid of her.

Rafi had been so focused on her idea that River was a serial killer that she hadn't even noticed the actual serial killer in her midst.

"YOU KILLED SIERRA MADRE!"

Jack's not-so-innocent eyes flashed in alarm, but it wasn't him who refuted Rafi's accusation. Greer did that for him.

"How dare you!" the girl cried. "Jack wouldn't even hurt a fly!"

"That's right," Jack said. "Now, *kill the pig, cut her throat!*"

"What?" Rafi said. But no one heard her over Jack's rallying cry. There was a frenzy of movement that Rafi couldn't keep track of, with influencers scurrying about and raising their fists into the air and making off-putting ululating sounds with their pointy tongues. But one movement caught Rafi's attention over the others. A rush toward the rope holding her cage aloft. And then there was a *whoosh*—the sound of a roaring flame come to life. There was a torch suddenly, and it was tipping toward the rope at the base of the tree.

"Oh no," Rafi whispered. Below her, the crowd parted in anticipation, like a ripple effect before the pebble ever touched the water. "Oh no no no no n—"

The metal bars broke and crumbled in the crash, but somehow, miraculously, they'd created a skeleton that cocooned Rafi from harm. The top of the cage cracked off like a soda can tab, and Rafi saw her only chance.

She ran.

35

GRAVEL SLIPPED UNDER HER FEET AND SPRAYED AT HER heels, but she was determined not to lose her footing, because if she did, she'd be finished. A scream came out of her that was so primal, it was like a bottle rocket, propelling her forward.

Kill the pig, cut her throat. The words rang through Rafi's ears at the same pace as her racing heartbeat, two thoughts warring in her brain: *Jack has to be kidding*, and *Jack is absolutely going to kill me.*

Just like he did Sierra. And River. And tried to do to Peggy.

Rafi had to stop thinking. Thoughts like these were just weighing her down, and what she needed was speed and distance. And a good hiding spot. There was nowhere to hide on the coastline—her only choice was to get lost in the thickest part of the jungle and hope Jack and his mad pack of followers couldn't find her.

But the roaring sound of them rushing en masse behind her—a crazed stampede of wild and crusty influencers—was impossible to shut out.

Rafi needed to focus. She hoped the mangle of green jungle would provide at least enough cover to give her a bigger head start.

She spotted a thicket of vines and shrubs and ran to it. It was a cavelike structure but only big enough for an animal, like a boar. Perhaps it was a boar's home she was invading. Rafi hoped not. The last thing she needed right now was to upset a wild hog and get herself killed that way when she was trying to avoid getting killed another way. But it was all she had.

The place was hollow and empty. She squished herself through, ignoring the way the bramble scratched at her exposed skin and caught on her clothes. She tried to be as still as she could be, contorting her body to stay uncomfortably hunched over. And then she waited. Maybe Jack's horde wouldn't see her. Maybe they'd run right past, and she could breathe easy and emerge from this prison and come up with a better plan.

"She's in there!"

Greer was the one who'd spotted her. Her pink eyes were runny, but, ironically, this was the one time the girl wasn't crying. A group of people, about a dozen thick, stood behind her. And in Greer's hand—the one that wasn't pointing directly at Rafi—was a torch.

Rafi pretended to be invisible.

"Stop pretending you can't see us seeing you!" Greer said.

Rafi's eyes darted from Greer's face to everyone else's. They all nodded.

"The bush you're hiding in is like a jack-o'-lantern, and your shirt is like the candle you light inside of it," Greer explained. "You really did not pick the right shirt for this trip."

"*Damnit*," Rafi hissed under her breath. This shirt was the single worst mistake she'd ever made in her life, she thought, as she hid in a boar's home from a rabid crowd with torches on a deserted island that she'd spent her life savings to visit. "I'm not getting out of here!" Rafi shouted. "And you can't make me."

Greer approached the bush-cave and bent her waist sideways to look Rafi in the eye. "You sure about that?"

"Yes," Rafi said.

"But are you really sure?" Greer asked.

"I'm serious, Greer!"

"Me also." Greer touched the flames of her torch to the base of the bush Rafi had burrowed into. The dry bramble caught fire immediately.

Rafi did not even attempt to put it out with her shoe before lunging out. "Are you *kidding* me?"

Greer shrugged. Rafi looked around at the others, searching for a compassionate face, someone who might see through the madness and would be willing to help her out. But it was hard to see what any of these people actually looked like behind their makeup masks. All of them—boys and girls alike—were so heavily decorated that Rafi wasn't sure their faces were even faces anymore. They were just mounds of dirt and dung staring back at her. The stuff packed their pores and creases, made mountains out of every bump and blemish, rivers of sweat in the valleys.

Also, the pinkeye epidemic had finally caught up to them, making their faces puffy and grotesque with infection. No amount of berry lip stain and clay shadow and crap bronzer could cover it up.

No, their makeup did not make them beautiful anymore. Rafi knew now that it made them savages.

She ran.

Again.

And they chased her. Again. It seemed like more people than before. It seemed like it was everyone on the island, and everywhere Rafi looked, there they were—torches up, fires *lit*.

Or maybe she was just seeing things. Maybe it wasn't that everyone was holding torches, maybe it was that they'd started setting fire to everything, because she was sweating now, heat fanning her skin from every direction, and her peripheral vision was full-blast hot and orange.

Water. She needed water.

Rafi followed the sound of the ocean waves. It was the only safe place to go.

She touched sand at last, and she stomped so hard that her feet dug in. The faster she ran, the more she seemed to sink into it. But she stopped abruptly when the tips of her sneakers touched the wet part of the shore. This was the end of the road. There was nowhere else to go.

Could Rafi really just walk into the ocean?

She'd gotten over her fear of water, hadn't she? But it was more than that. The water wouldn't stop them. And there came a time when Rafi would have to stop and face the people she was running from.

This was it.

She turned around.

They were all there. Everyone who had come to Fly Fest.

Sweat-soaked kids who were yelling unintelligible things at her. Their makeup nothing more than brown and rosy-hued smears dripping down their faces, leaving angry tracks around their mouths and creases fanning from the corners of their inflamed eyes. They held their sticks and their phones aloft, weapons both.

They were crazed, but they were still cognizant enough to follow orders, and they parted to let Jack through. He walked until he was close enough for Rafi to catch a whiff of his makeup. And though his followers stayed back, a swarm of flies trailed him, surrounding his head like a floating crown. He held up his torch with the grace of Lady Liberty.

Rafi thought about the witches in Salem and wondered if this was what they felt like, watching their executioner approach. She sank to her knees and looked up at Jack.

"Why are you doing this?"

Jack seemed to think about it, his chin tilting upward like the sun was a camera flash. "Okay, yes, maybe this is a little extreme, but can you really blame me? We've been on this island *forever*."

"We've been on this island for *six days*."

"There you go, thinking you're smarter than everyone else!" Jack said. "That's your problem, Rafi. You're a stick-in-the-mud. You're getting in the way of our fun."

"I'm sorry, okay?" The last thing Rafi wanted to do was apologize, but it was a last-ditch tactic to appeal to Jack's humanity.

"Your apology has been declined. Do you have another?"

A tiny whimper left Rafi's lips. "Please. It's just—I was pretty sure you killed—"

"You were never pretty *anything*!" Jack bent low to whisper the next part. "No one will miss you anyway."

"People know I exist. People are waiting for me back home."

"Remind me again how many followers you have?"

Rafi sighed and in a small voice she replied, "About a thousand over three platforms."

A thousand individual people knew about her, believed in what she was doing. Believed in *her*.

"You sad, little Tupperware lid." Jack's flies took turns landing on his sharp cheekbones. They didn't faze him. "Are you really sure you exist?"

Rafi closed her eyes.

Jack lowered his torch, and the heat of the flame was strong enough to force Rafi to lean back. She fell on her butt, her hands clutching the sand behind her. She was practically on her way to doing a crab walk right into the water, guided by Jack. She closed her eyes.

Rafi waited. Minutes passed, and then something strange happened: Jack squawked. Rafi squinted one eye open. Jack wasn't even looking at her anymore. But he did squawk again, a hideous, birdlike sound that emerged from his lips as spontaneously as a burp. But it was not a burp. Jack was looking past Rafi, out to the ocean. His face was openmouthed, frozen with shock, but after a minute it broke into a grin. "Omigawd," he snorted. He bounced on the balls of his feet and squawked again. "OMIGAWD. She came!"

Rafi sat up straight and followed Jack's gaze. At first it looked like a mirage, and Rafi had to squint to make sure she was seeing right.

Butting up against the sand was a small dingy, and coming out of it was none other than—

"Hella Badid!" Jack squealed. He forgot about Rafi and dropped his torch so thoughtlessly it nearly singed her knees before sand eventually snuffed out the flames. "I told you all she'd come!" Jack shouted to his followers. "I told you she'd come for us!"

Hella's feet (bare except for a couple of toe rings and a jangly ankle bracelet) stepped out of the water and onto the sand until they reached all the way to Rafi and Jack. Rafi's eyes roved up Hella's figure, still not quite believing she was real. She wore a short, emerald romper, and her hair was in a topknot. She looked as glamorous and enticing as a bottle of champagne wrapped in crinkly cellophane. Rafi felt bad for the analogy, given Hella's alcoholism, but the girl looked fancy and Rafi was parched. The supermodel towered over Jack, which was fine since he seemed mostly interested in slobbering at her feet.

"Hella." His face was a mess of wet, happy tears. "I've been holding down the fort until you showed up. I've made sure we were all worthy. I would never want you to be disappointed in us."

Hella didn't seem to know what to say. Her normally stoic, dead-behind-the-eyes look, which had graced so many magazine covers, had a little bit more life in it as she stared

300

at Jack. Then she scrunched up her nose and sniffed. "You smell," she said.

The confusion seemed to transfer from Hella's face to Jack's. Hella turned to Rafi and held out her hand, helping her up. "You're Rafi, right?"

Rafi nodded.

"I've heard all about you." Hella looked back to the dinghy bobbing in the water, where River was trying to keep it anchored.

36

It was the real Hella. Not just the mythic idea of her that had filled the minds of the concertgoers. And the sight of her had been so bizarre that Rafi hadn't even noticed River. Or the huge yacht in the distance that had brought them to the island in the first place. But now River was all Rafi could see.

While the rest of the beach fawned over the supermodel, Rafi stood numbly, watching as River pulled the floating raft to shore until it was stationary on the sand. And when River straightened and looked around, it was Rafi who he settled on. She was so happy to see him alive. But she couldn't say if he was happy to see her. His face, with his mouth usually on the cusp of a smile and his eyes sparkling, remained neutral as he regarded her.

It was a stare-off. Their gazes unwavering, focusing only on each other, even as everyone on the beach started running straight toward the ocean.

Eventually, the rush of people hurtling past them was too big a distraction, and Rafi and River turned to see what was going on. Hella was pinching her nose and breathing through her mouth, which must've triggered everyone to realize they were wearing poop on their faces. They were suddenly desperate to wash it all off, Jack chief among them. He splashed his face compulsively and scrubbed the abrasive salt water into his pores.

In the end, he had been right: All it took was Hella finally showing up on the island to save them all.

Rafi turned back to River and the two approached each other, stopping with a few feet of space between them. They both knew that there was a lot to say, and that this wasn't the spot for it.

"I know a place," River said.

They only went farther down the beach, to their tents. The same spot where they'd had so many of their conversations. Only, Rafi's tent barely held together anymore, and River had definitely outgrown his. He looked strange before it, like he'd come back to visit a childhood home that didn't belong to him anymore. Or maybe it was just that he was actually wearing a shirt for once. He looked like a brand-new person.

They sat in the sand, side by side, close enough to the commotion on the shore but far enough away to have a private moment alone.

"I am so glad you're alive," Rafi said.

"Did you really think they killed me?"

"I wouldn't put it past them."

River seemed lost in thought at the terrifying memory. "They jumped me. And I think Jack tried to file my nails.

Anyway, I was able to get away, but they chased me to the cliffs and ended up pushing me off. Good thing I had somewhere to land. Did you know there's a garbage barge that comes to the island every day?"

"Just found out about it."

"Steve's a great guy."

"Oh yeah?"

River nodded, and there was a lull in the conversation. Rafi could've continued talking about Steve the garbage barge captain all day if it meant avoiding the hard stuff that she and River had to talk about. Luckily, River brought something else up.

"Sierra Madre is fine, by the way."

Sierra. In all the madness, Rafi had nearly forgotten how certain she'd been that Jack killed the world's most prominent influencer. "Where was she?"

"She called for a helicopter to come get her. Remember that weird whooshing noise?"

This bit of info was shocking, until Rafi began to think back on that time on the island. Now that she thought about it, the whooshing did sound like it could've been a helicopter's propellers. And there *had* been a lot of talk with the word "hell" in it for a good couple of hours there. Of course, Rafi had just heard that word and assumed that people had been talking about Hella. But she realized that was all conjecture on her part. They easily could've been talking about seeing a *hel*icopter.

As outlandish as it was, this made the most sense. And it also tracked with how Rafi collected and processed rumors and news. Where there were hoofbeats, she thought zebras instead of horses. She chased the conspiracy theory instead of stepping back and assessing all the evidence in a rational way.

She was a bad investigator.

Rafi was wrong. Often. About a lot of things. She looked at River, knowing there was no way to avoid this part of the convo any longer. "I'm sorry about the things I said on my podcast. It was wrong to accuse you of all that stuff. And then to share something you told me in confidence."

She meant it. She really did. Thinking about what she'd done to River made her stomach twist. "I don't expect you to forgive me. What I did was unforgivable."

She deserved all his wrath, and she braced herself for a storm, but River didn't say anything. And he didn't look angry either. Not like he did the last time they'd spoken.

"I've appeared on *Entertainment Tonight* thirty-four times, Rafi. I've heard way stranger conspiracy theories about myself."

Rafi nodded, but River's reaction was almost too kind for her to accept at face value. "I'll take the podcast down. I'll post a retraction."

River shook his head. "I've been thinking about what you revealed about me. And, weirdly, I'm okay with it."

Rafi wondered if she heard him right. She knew a lot had happened since their fight to put her podcast into perspective, but this was the last thing she expected him to say.

"I mean, the first few episodes—your theories about me being a serial killer—that stuff is . . . pretty out there. But the rest of it? It's the truth. You told it without my permission, but now that it's out there . . ." River took a deep breath, and his toned shoulders rounded and fell. It was not his usual always-on, stage-ready posture. But he actually looked kind of comfortable. "I was getting really tired of lying. It's kind of a relief not to have to do it anymore."

Rafi took a deep breath, too. Hearing him say all that made a huge weight lift from her chest. She felt relieved, invigorated, free. Though some of that definitely had to do with the huge boat in the background ready to rescue them finally. The point was, Rafi was happy. River wasn't mad, Jack wasn't currently trying to kill her, and they were all saved.

And then River said something that Rafi really didn't expect. "What if I give you an interview?"

"Really?"

"Yeah," River said. "A real one. I'll be up-front about whatever you want to know. The truth."

This was the only thing that Rafi had ever wanted. The reason she'd come to this wretched music festival, her ticket to a legitimate podcasting network, presented to her on a silver platter. Everything inside of Rafi screamed *Yes!*

"No," she said.

River looked surprised enough for the both of them. "No?"

"I think I need to step back from the investigations for a little while," Rafi said. "I wasn't delivering news, I was creating theories. And it—clearly—got completely out of hand."

"But your podcast. I thought you were really passionate about it."

Rafi nodded. She couldn't deny that. "I'll come back to it. But for now, I think it'll be good for me to step away, enjoy the real world for a bit."

River nodded and smiled. Together, he and Rafi looked out wordlessly at the shimmering ocean, unbothered by the influencers in it frantically washing the muck off their faces.

MUSICAL MYSTERIES
Season 2: Episode 6
"Where Are They Now?"

Hi, Mysterinos. It's been a while, huh? Six months, to be exact. Six months since Fly Fest became the butt of every joke. Six months since I touched this podcast. But it felt like the right time to come back.

By now, there have been countless news stories about what happened on that island in the Caribbean. You don't need me to rehash why the organizers of the festival abandoned it on day one of construction, and we probably don't need to go over the zillions of lawsuits the concertgoers launched as soon as their feet touched American soil. In fact, maybe you're getting a little tired of hearing about Fly Fest completely. You're probably thinking I should move on, time to get over it. But I still think about the week I spent at that music festival with neither music nor festivities. And I think about the people that I met there, and what they're up to now.

Paul and Ryan successfully sued the organizers of Fly Fest, the social media platforms that helped promote it, and the retailer Banana Republic. Though they jointly describe their time on the island as "not very money," they acknowledge that it made them experts in the world of produce and have since started their own line of gourmet bananas. I'm not sure what that means, but as they would say, business is booming. They had a launch party in Malibu and got O-Town to perform.

As it turned out, Peggy wasn't just trading bad tchotchkes for access to the internet—they were also accepting personal information, like phone numbers, email addresses, and Social Security numbers, which they then sold to third-party buyers. It was all kind of illegal, but they collected enough money to buy the island we all stayed on, where there is no extradition. They just finished construction on a mansion that rivals the size of their massive tent, and employs a staff of twenty.

Jack's reputation took a hit once the truth came out about why everyone's bronzer looked so . . . shitty. People were appropriately disgusted by his island makeup methods, companies dropped him as their spokesperson, and he lost a hundred thousand subscribers after the *New York Post* called him "gross." Jack subsequently tried to salvage his brand by releasing a special twenty-four-hour apology video marathon, where he posted a new apology video every fifteen minutes. Jack started his first video with the words, "This is a conversation that needs having. It's time." His last video was just seven minutes straight of him sobbing while perched on the edge of a Sealy Posturepedic. But by then he had lost the rest of his followers.

Hella had no career setbacks despite having actively promoted a sham festival. Anytime she's asked to comment about the mythic role she unwittingly took on in the concertgoers' eyes, it takes her a moment to recall the scandal at all. For Hella, Fly Fest was an hour of work that took up no space in her mind. She's since cut a lot of things out of her life, including alcohol, deals with shady festival people, and River Stone.

River. He came clean about what actually happened to Tracy in a sit-down interview with Oprah. It garnered even more sympathy than his original lie about being abandoned in the bush on the eve of his planned proposal. He's writing a new album about it all, and even his time at Fly Fest. It's called *Deep as a River, Hard as a Stone*. People continue to love him. And I understand why.

As for what I've been up to for the last six months? For a long time I blamed myself for the role I had in making Fly Fest an even worse experience than it would've been all on its own. I never fully realized how much influence my words had on those who listened to them. For six months, I was too afraid to say anything at all. So I stayed away.

But that's no way to go through life. I still have a voice and things to say. I just know now that the truth is everything. You just have to be careful how you wield it.

And River, if you're listening . . . I think I'm ready for that interview now.

THE END

Acknowledgments

Depending on whether you like/hate this book, here is a list of people you and I can thank/blame, for helping me bring this story into the world.

I had a long talk with my agent, asking her whether I should go forth with this story or dump it in favor of something more traditional, more palatable, something that "young adult readers will actually want to read." My agent said absolutely not! That I should write this story like only I could. So, Jenny Bent, thank you/this is all your fault. And to Gemma Cooper, for your valiant wheeling and dealing. Thank you so much for your endless and unwavering support of my stories.

Through no fault of their own, many editors were burdened with whipping this manuscript into shape. The first was Tiff Liao. Truthfully, I was terrified that Tiff would take one look at this book, print it out, and then set it on fire. But to her credit, Tiff did no such thing! She texted me as soon as she'd read it to tell me how much she liked it. She then left for better job opportunities. I can't say my book lead to her departure, but I also can't say it didn't. Tiff, I am eternally grateful for that text, for your thoughtful notes that truly made this book better, and for the time and patience you had for me and my work.

Sarah Levison also had to edit the heck out of this book.

Sarah, I can't imagine what you were thinking when I saddled you with this, but I'm so glad for your guidance through the many iterations of it.

Dana Chidiac, I think you had the most difficult task of all, looking at this almost-finished beast, maybe (probably) wanting a whole rewrite, but with little hope of me changing much. Thank you for coming through on this journey with me, and I can't wait for the next one!

Did you think this book had enough editors? Well, joke's on you because it had even more! Ann Marie Wong, what an absolute surprise and delight it was to have you on board the team! I worried those other editors didn't know what was in store with one of my manuscripts, but you had to have known. And still, you were my cheerleader the whole way! It was such a gift to know I had your support. Here's to Mr. Henry Holt for bringing us together and footing our bills!

Jennifer Abbots, publicist extraordinaire! This wild ride is sweeter with you in it.

Writing a book is a lonely endeavor, but making one is a team effort, and I want to thank everyone at Henry Holt, especially Jean Feiwel; Jess Harold; Rich Deas; Alexei Esikoff; Lelia Mander; Mariel Dawson, Melissa Zar, and their team, especially Leigh Ann Higgins; Brittany Pearlman; Sara Elroubi; Molly Ellis; Mary Van Akin and her team; and Jen Edwards and her team.

Thank you to: Sonia and Irina, for giving me the time and space to write when I needed it. Yasmin, Maayan, Hadas, and Akiva. For Tove, my Silly Billy, and Imri, my Silly Goose. Being silly is the best. It can get you paid!!!

And for Alex. The absolute worst ideas in this book are also the best ideas in this book, and they're usually always yours. You giggle across the table, making jokes about my characters and suggesting they smear [redacted] on their faces and you so innocently think, "She'll never do that. I'm just saying stupid stuff because there's no way she's going to put that in a traditionally published book." And I throw my napkin on the table and I think, "Well, damn." Because the ideas are so stupid, so good, that how can I not put them in a traditionally published book? How can I not. So, thanks/I blame you the most.

When it comes to horror movies
the rules are clear ...

THE
LAST
GIRL

AN EXCLUSIVE CLUB.

A DANGEROUS GAME.

WHAT WOULD YOU
DO TO SURVIVE?

GOLDY MOLDAVSKY

Break them and it's game over